[VIEWS] ON THE MISSISSIPPI

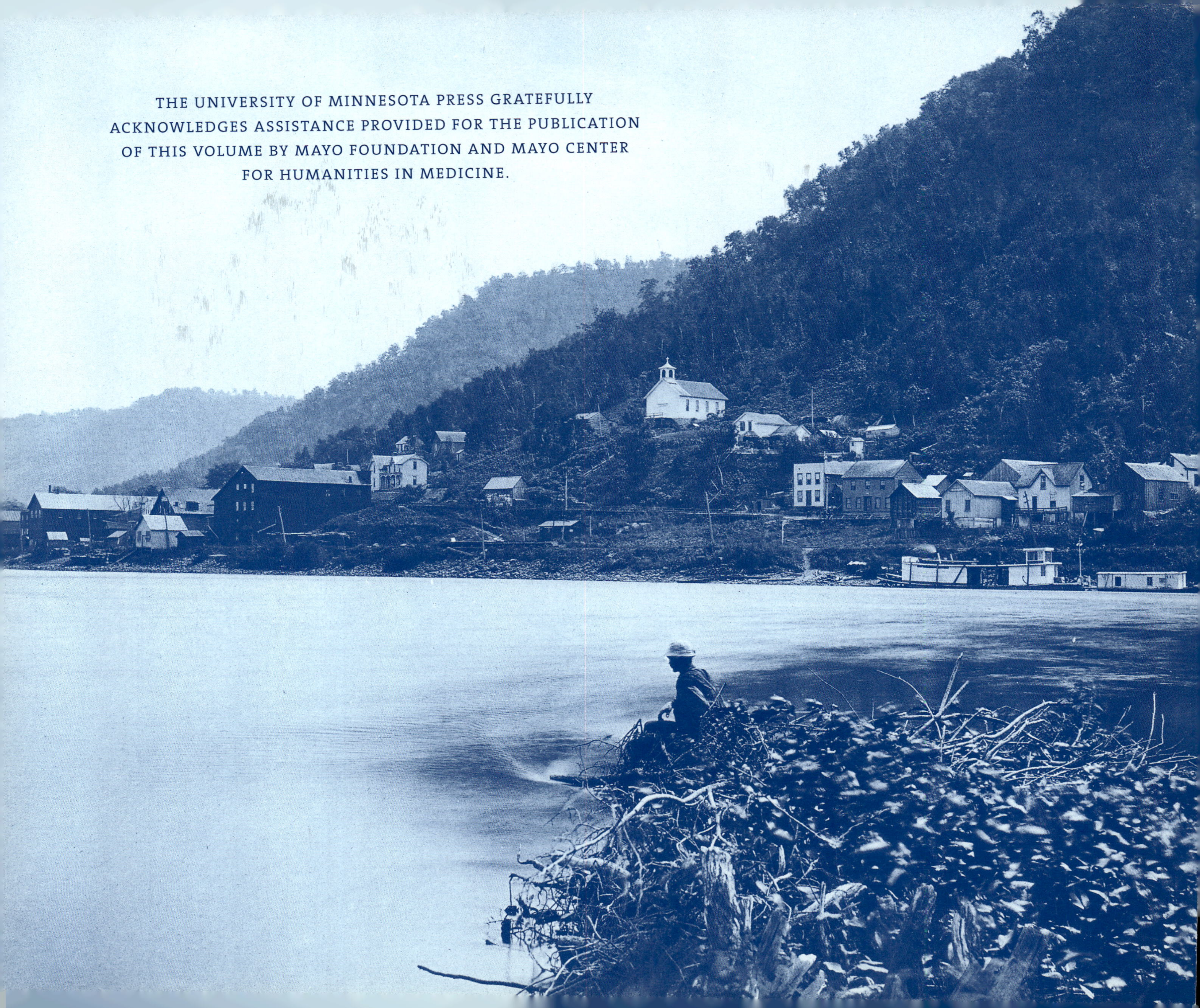

THE UNIVERSITY OF MINNESOTA PRESS GRATEFULLY ACKNOWLEDGES ASSISTANCE PROVIDED FOR THE PUBLICATION OF THIS VOLUME BY MAYO FOUNDATION AND MAYO CENTER FOR HUMANITIES IN MEDICINE.

VIEWS ON THE MISSISSIPPI

The Photographs of Henry Peter Bosse

Mark Neuzil

Foreword by Merry A. Foresta

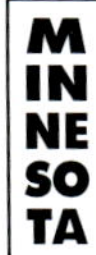

University of Minnesota Press
Minneapolis • London

The University of Minnesota Press gratefully acknowledges permission provided by Mayo Foundation and the Mississippi River Museum at Dubuque, Iowa, to reproduce prints by Henry Bosse from their collections. We also appreciate the assistance of the St. Paul and Rock Island districts of the U.S. Army Corps of Engineers in reproducing prints by Henry Bosse from their collections. The caption for each print notes the collection to which it belongs.

Map of the Mississippi River from the Falls of St. Anthony to the Junction of the Illinois River, by H. Bosse and A. J. Stibolt, is reproduced courtesy of the Borchert Map Library, University of Minnesota.

View South on Riverfront at Biddle Street, Lindell's Stone Quarry and Roy's Mill, by Thomas M. Easterly, is reproduced by permission of the Missouri Historical Society, St. Louis.

Fur Traders Descending the Missouri, by George Caleb Bingham, is reproduced by permission of the Metropolitan Museum of Art, New York.

The photograph on page 3 is reproduced by permission of William F. Quaintance.

Published by the University of Minnesota Press
111 Third Avenue South, Suite 290
Minneapolis, MN 55401-2520
http://www.upress.umn.edu

Book design by Brian Donahue
Printed in China by HK Scanner Arts International Ltd

Library of Congress Cataloging-in-Publication Data
Neuzil, Mark.
Views on the Mississippi : the Photographs of Henry Peter Bosse / Mark Neuzil ;
Foreword by Merry A. Foresta...
p. cm.
ISBN 0-8166-3648-6
1. Photography, Artistic. 2. Mississippi—Pictorial works.
I. Bosse, Henry, 1844–1903 II. Title
TR654 .N448 2000
779' .99762—dc21
00–012570

12 11 10 09 08 07 06 05 04 03 02 10 9 8 7 6 5 4 3 2 1

CONTENTS

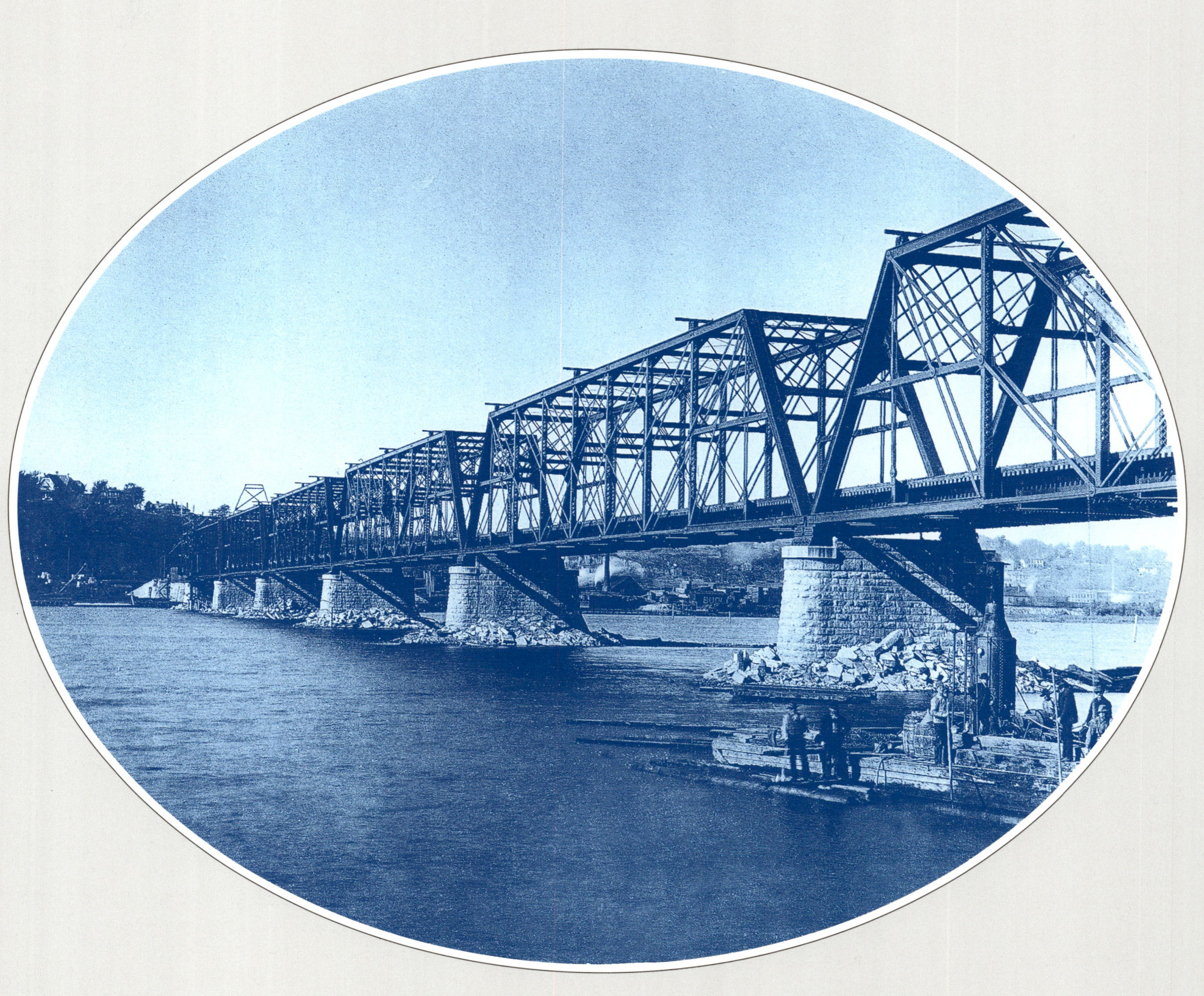

FOREWORD

Merry A. Foresta

Throughout the history of photography, a remarkable number of individuals with little experience in photography or art, and whose use of photography was brief, have succeeded in producing some of the medium's finest images. Henry Bosse is one of them. As a mapmaker in the service of the U.S. Army Corps of Engineers during the late 1870s and 1880s, Bosse made a comprehensive photographic record of engineered improvements on the Upper Mississippi River between Minneapolis and St. Louis. He documented newly constructed dams, locks, and railroad bridges as well as the landscape such state-of-the-art engineering would transform. The photographs, often printed on the same blue paper used by draftsmen, engineers, and architects for their blueprint drawings, are the result of both keen observation and a romantic sensibility.

Recently there has been a great deal of interest in photography in nineteenth-century America. Perhaps the dawning of the computer age with its promise of greater access to ever more information prompted a reflection on earlier moments of visual and technological collaboration. Or we may be looking for new ideas clothed in the certainty promised by pictures, which have already survived the process of history. Whatever the reason, the result has been the discovery of photographers who were previously unheralded and wondrous images that had disappeared into the vast archives of historical records and attic cupboards. Because of these discoveries, we have learned that traditional categories of art are no longer adequate for any useful examination of our large visual culture. We also have learned that photographs represent a much more complicated series of relationships than we had previously suspected.

Since its invention in France and introduction to America in 1839, photography has cut across many lines, attracting diverse practitioners and audiences. In the United States the medium developed through the cross-cultivation of different disciplines, and photography's history is tangled in the histories of technology, commerce, and the popular appreciation of photography as an entertainment. The nation eagerly welcomed a medium that functioned as both an effective witness and a powerful new art. Photography served not only as a reflection of the world around it but also as a validation of what that visual world—"measured by the angle at which man looks at objects," according to Ralph Waldo Emerson—meant to society at the time. In the mid-nineteenth-century context of national expansion and progress, the purpose of the medium was to picture, in the words of photographer James Ryder—whose work for the Franklin and Warren Railroad of Ohio in the mid-1850s is among the earliest photographic survey projects—"the rugged and the picturesque."

By the time Henry Bosse began to work for the Army Corps of Engineers in the 1870s, photography was considered the truest and most efficient agent for listing, knowing, and understanding significant facts. At the end of the Civil War, many photographers who had been employed by the U.S. military continued their relationship with the government and joined surveyors assessing the potential for western expansion. Photographers, who during the war had made photographs of bridges, fortifications, and other marvels of military engineering, were hired by railroads, mining companies, and land developers as part of survey teams to chart the potential of western territories. Some surveys were led by scientists, some by military men, and others by government officials. The expeditionary archive—albums of photographs, sketchbooks of drawings, pages of written text—was a comprehensive attempt to explore, catalog, order, and disseminate the accumulating mass of information about the territory. Surveys were also useful as inspiration for use of the land. Photographic images contained information that was geological and geographical as well as sociological, economic, metaphysical, spiritual, and philosophical.

Photography in the mid-nineteenth century joined a discussion taking place in all the arts. A product of an age of invention, photography coincided with an expansive period in the United States that emphasized to artists and explorers alike the importance of seeing clearly. By 1863 the American Pre-Raphaelite journal, *The New Path*, published by the aesthetically radical Society for the Advancement of Truth in Art, stressed photography and geology as the two chief guidelines for landscape painting. American artists, directed by the early writings of English critic John Ruskin, were encouraged to look thoroughly at the details of nature for inspiration. Detailed compositions painted by realists Frederick Church, Asher B. Durand, Charles Herbert Moore, and others operated like photographs. Their attention to the details of topography was matched only by their beautiful and accurate renderings of native plants and trees. Society member William Stillman eventually gave up painting altogether for photography. With this new medium, based on a new technology that depended completely on the intense scrutiny of the maker *and* the viewer, he could operate as both artist and scientist.

"It is the power of seeing on which will depend the value and importance of any work, whether canvas or negative," wrote Philadelphia landscape photographer John Moran, brother of the landscape painter Thomas Moran, in 1865. And if, as he believed, the most important thing in art is to know what is most beautiful, "We claim for photography the ability to create imagery that calls forth ideas and sentiments of the beautiful." Especially as landscape, photography introduced a singularly awesome beauty in natural forms properly recorded.

Henry Bosse, however, was not a photographer but a mapmaker for most of his career. As Mark Neuzil notes in his essay for this book, Bosse, born in Germany in 1844, was tutored in traditional classical studies, and his education included classes in engineering and art. These courses suggest that he may have attended a state-run specialty school for mechanical and architectural studies. If so, he would have been required to learn the techniques of freehand drawing. He would have mastered the difficult coordination of eye and hand necessary to describe the angle of the fall of light for accurate renderings of buildings or natural topographies. It is tempting to think that student Bosse might also have encountered and been impressed by contemporary

"We claim for PHOTOGRAPHY the ability to create imagery that calls forth ideas and sentiments of the beautiful." —JOHN MORAN

German painting by artists Robert Weir and Oswald Achenbach and other members of a group who called themselves the Nazarenes. Like their American Pre-Raphaelite counterparts, they produced carefully painted landscapes with finished details from foreground to background. If their ideal was the German Renaissance master of the exquisite line, Albrecht Dürer, rather than an American love of utilitarian fact-finding, their dedication to precision had similarly spiritual intentions.

After immigrating to America by 1870, and for a short period working for a book and stationery shop, Bosse went to work for the Army Corps of Engineers. By 1874 he had begun his mapmaking duties on the Upper Mississippi River. He was made chief draftsman in 1878, the same year the Corps was authorized by Congress to begin an enormous project of wing dam construction, dredging, and levee building that would radically reconfigure the river. A few years later he began to use a camera and make photographs.

It is not known exactly what prompted Bosse to begin using photography as part of his mapping work. Perhaps he was asked to add the innovative picture-making technology of photography to the more traditional techniques of drafting and mapmaking. The supervisor of the project, Montgomery Meigs, was a photographer himself, and it is likely that he taught Bosse the rudiments of camera and darkroom. Meigs, the son of an engineer who had used photography to document important projects, must have understood that photography could also be useful for more than reporting the details of topography. Just as the photographs made as part of the western geological surveys were turned into promotional materials to sell the next survey project, photographs of the Mississippi project would give the Corps of Engineers needed picturesque proof of its work. Or perhaps Bosse recognized the creative possibilities of using a method of picturing that simultaneously captured and interpreted the facts of place.

There were precedents in the use of photography for the documentation of techniques and structural projects. Prior to the Civil War, the War Department used its engineering expertise to undertake a variety of important projects across the nation. General Montgomery C. Meigs, father of Montgomery Meigs, was an enthusiastic amateur photographer as well as an ardent patron of the medium, believing "three stereographs of a machine better than the most elaborate model." In the late 1850s he employed photographers to document many of his most important engineering projects, including the extension of the national Capitol building and the construction of the Washington Aqueduct. By the 1850s agencies such as the Topographical Bureau were instrumental in mapping and accurately describing the Great Lakes and the Ohio, Mississippi, and Tennessee rivers. Later, incorporated into the Army Corps of Engineers, it was a participant in many of the early western explorations. Surveys were made for roads, canals, and rail lines. They established national boundaries and fixed the routes of major transportation links. For all its projects it accumulated precise visual information: maps, sketches, drawings, and, most important, since the training of engineers at schools such as West Point increasingly emphasized innovative technological skills, photographs.

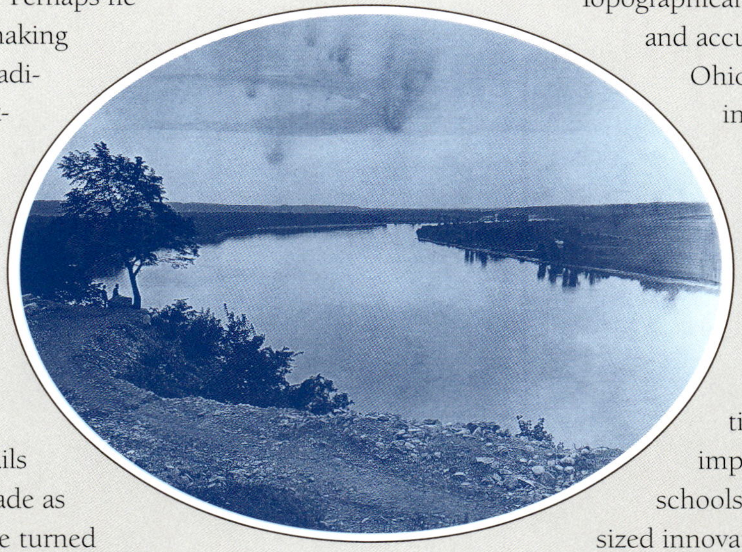

From Dayton's Bluff—St. Paul, Minn. looking down stream, 1885 (Mayo Foundation).

The use of photography for the documentation of scientific and artistic projects of various kinds was not limited to the activities of geological surveys or the hands of engineers. The hundreds of photographs made by William Bell beginning in 1865 for the Army Medical Museum, for example, became a catalog of war wounds and surgical cases used by medical students to understand the effect of newly designed ammunitions on human flesh and bone. His elegant portraits of afflicted soldiers and still lifes of shattered bones and skulls balance scientific inquiry with the spirit of picture making. In some cases the purpose of the expedition was art itself. In search of views on which to base his paintings, the artist William Bradford hired Boston photographers John Dunmore and George Cricherson to accompany his 1869 expedition to the Arctic. The frozen wilderness was captured, in this case, not as territory but as picture. Bradford did not anticipate that the photographs, collected as an album and offered for sale, would be as popular as his paintings. Photographs, it seemed, offered an enticing pictorial element: the tinge of the real that heightened the perception of knowledge and understanding.

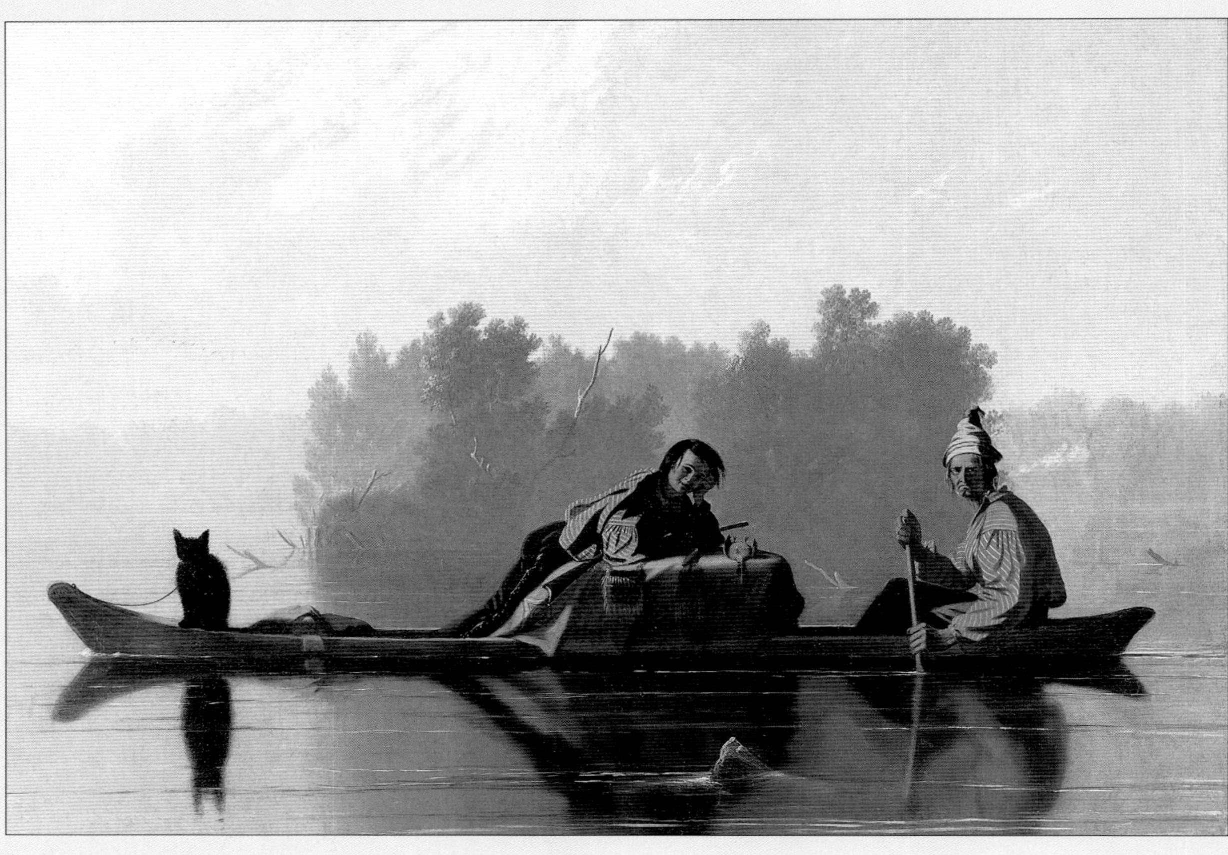

Fur Traders Descending the Missouri, by George Caleb Bingham, 1845. Oil on canvas, 29¼ x 36¼ inches (Metropolitan Museum of Art, Morris K. Jesup Fund, 1933).

Certainly Bosse was not the first to be compelled by the subject of the Mississippi. In the 1840s and early 1850s an artistic search for real American characters and landscapes lured painters to the Midwest's great rivers. George Caleb Bingham found his subjects in the trappers and boatmen who populated the territory of the Missouri and the Mississippi. For him the river—a place where he had grown up and that he knew well—was a subject that both characterized a particular region and offered the larger aspirations of the nation: the progress of work and the harmony of humans with nature. Emphasizing the abundance and peaceable stillness of nature, his river scenes are evocations of the pastoral potential of America. In paintings such as *Fur Traders Descending the Missouri* from 1845, river men enjoy a natural Eden. Other American painters such as Thomas Cole and William Sidney Mount also described human relationship with nature, but it was a formal, more distant environment.

The Mississippi also interested early photographers. Among the first was St. Louis daguerreotypist Thomas M. Easterly. Using a type of photography—extolled as "nature painting itself"—that produced unique images on silver-coated copper plates, he was among the United States' earliest landscape photographers. The 1852 *Missouri Republican* noted that his "collection of illustrative views about the city and its waterfront are a treasure." During the 1850s and early 1860s Easterly compiled a portrait of St. Louis as a rising frontier town. He photographed the construction of significant new buildings, made portraits of its leading citizens, and, most importantly, made views that take us from the dry docks to the heart of the levee. His photographs, detailed in the silvery exactness of the daguerreotype process, are a unique pictorial counterpart to contemporary written reports that repeatedly expressed amazement at the spectacle of St. Louis's waterfront activity.

Easterly also took his camera to more isolated sites along the river, where signs of the once dominant French presence were quickly disappearing. He daguerreotyped many buildings that reflected the original character of the settlement, often with the river as a backdrop, creating a catalog of historical landmarks that would soon disappear in the wake of progress. While Easterly was recording them as romantic artifacts, few people in the city shared his interests. The citizens of St. Louis were occupied with making their city the "star of the West." The promise of a more affluent future was far more compelling than the abandoned remains of an earlier era. The photographer was not the only one to notice, however. On his 1842 stop in St. Louis, Charles Dickens had been charmed by the picturesque character of the Creole section of town near the waterfront, noting that the place seemed to "grimace in astonishment at the American Improvements."

"American Improvements," or the shaping of nature for the ends of progress, were also Bosse's subject. His views of the Mississippi were part of a mapmaking project, but one that had less to do with exploration than with development. In 1878, the year Bosse began working in Rock Island, Illinois, the U.S. Congress began funding a project that would provide at least a four-and-a-half-foot channel of navigable water in the Mississippi River from the Illinois River to St. Paul. Dredging continued and wing dams were constructed, highly visible activities with immediate and long-term effects on river navigation. As the work progressed, the area behind the dams silted in and

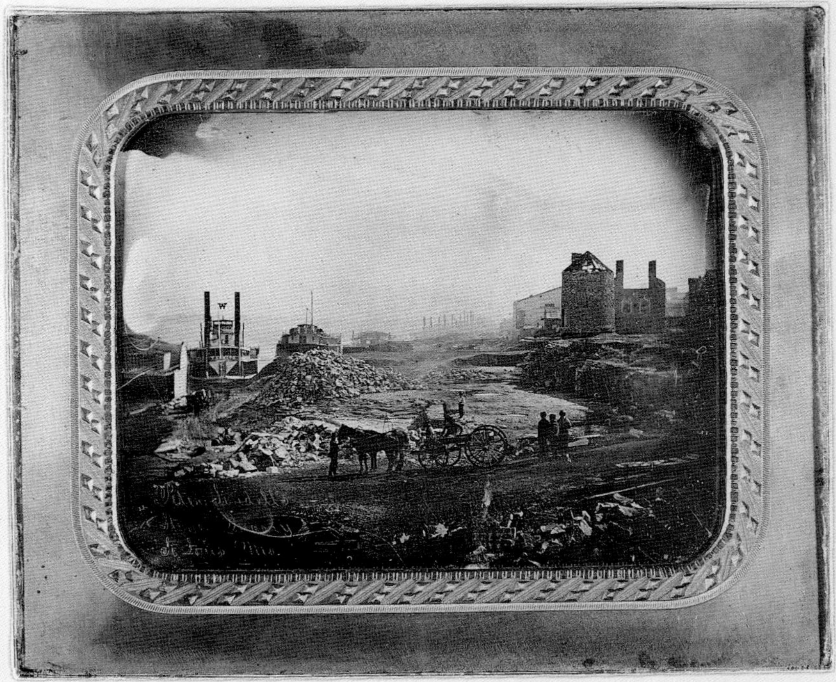

View South on Riverfront at Biddle Street, Lindell's Stone Quarry and Roy's Mill, by Thomas M. Easterly, c. 1852. Half-plate daguerreotype (Missouri Historical Society, St. Louis).

became overgrown with vegetation, further constricting the channel. In the words of Major Alexander Mackenzie, chief of the Rock Island office of the Corps, "The improvement...is a work which can be best carried on gradually as to give the river itself full opportunity to assist." With human prompting, the Mississippi River tamed itself.

Essential to preparing a comprehensive plan for adjusting nearly seven hundred miles of river was the compilation of images. Working documents, they initially were sharply drawn maps and sketches by Bosse and his assistant, A. J. Stibolt. Like diaries, they contained everyday information concerning the civil works in the charge of engineers. Published in 1887, *Map of the Mississippi River from the Falls of St. Anthony to the Junction of the Illinois River* is primarily an update and improvement of the map drawn by Bosse's predecessor as chief draftsman, F. S. Eastman. The individual pages were meant for use, not for contemplation. Drawings, especially the scaled drawings of bridge profiles, were added as insets to the maps. Navigation hazards were noted. The new map provided more named landmarks, depicted improvements, and rendered more topographical and hydrological detail throughout.

The photographs Bosse made during this period of river improvement achieved another level of particularity. Like Bosse's maps, they served as a practical reference for the engineers who used them daily to navigate changes in the river. New photographs of the same subjects could provide comparative information on the condition of completed navigation improvements and on the effects of these changes on bank erosion and bar formation. Often printed on the prepared blueprint paper that the Corps bought in large quantities for its district offices, the photographs were immediately useful references to Bosse and his fellow mapmakers as they tried to capture the essential characteristics of dam alignments, islands and banks, vegetation, fields, and bridges along the upper valley.

Sometimes Bosse's ability to organize space in his photographs generates incidental truths that interest us more than the central object of the picture. The structure of his photographs is open, orderly, spacious, and rhythmic. For instance, in some photographs the sophisticated geometry of a bridge or the outline of a river town is rendered with the precision that the nineteenth century had come to expect of photography, especially the commissioned photography of topographical survey work. A closer examination of Bosse's photographs reveals another narrative. Once we have understood the architecture and its spaces, our attention is drawn to the small, often isolated figures in the landscape. The people of Bosse's photographs who lean against a machine or stand on the banks of the river or sit, back to the camera, and thoughtfully gaze out at the view give both a physical and an emotional scale that are at once specific and metaphoric.

What often distinguishes Bosse's photographs is the subject of OBSERVATION itself.

Although the pictorial antecedents of Bosse's photographs may be found in paintings and photographs of similar subjects earlier in the century, the engineered structure of the landscape has prevented the photographer from creating an Edenic idyll. Though Bosse, like Easterly and Bingham, used the medium of water metaphorically as the agent for both practical and philosophical movement, the river has been transformed. No longer is water seen as a mirror, reflecting together the sky, the land, and human beings; rather, it is a construction to be viewed separately and at a distance.

What often distinguishes Bosse's photographs is the subject of observation itself. Unlike strictly topographic imagery, Bosse's views are as concerned with aesthetics as with information. Often, especially in his long views made from the high bluffs that flank the river's edge, he is less interested in establishing facts than in capturing a sense of place equivalent to the act of looking. These views emphasize the natural textures of foreground objects, a grassy shore in middle distance, the graceful sweep of the long curve of the river through the valley. The dreamy quality of atmospheric space is paramount. The effect is paradoxically prophetic of modern photography, still thirty years in the future. What counts most is intensity of vision accompanied by a certain reverence for the thing seen.

Eventually it was photography that sold the image of the Corps of Engineers to a larger cultural audience. For its presentation at the 1893 World's Columbian Exposition in Chicago, the Corps preferred photographs to sketches and drawings as a means of showing the progress of its work. According to Captain William L. Marshall, the planner of the exposition display, photographs were "instantly comprehended" by a general audience. The installation, which included contributions from all the district offices, featured large transparencies that hung in front of windows and photograph albums placed on tables for individual viewing, including albums from the Rock Island (Illinois) District by Henry Bosse. As narratives, not merely reports from the field, Bosse's photographs function on several levels, simultaneously moving between persuasion and illustration, information and picture.

Although the scope of Bosse's aspirations for his photography is framed by his work as a draftsman and mapmaker, his images survive as works of art as well as history. Today, we may have forgotten the great importance of river transportation to the economic goals of the nineteenth century. We know little about the navigation of side-wheelers or packets, or the tricky backwaters that prompted the demand for navigation improvements on the Upper Mississippi in the second half of the nineteenth century. The river, long ago tamed by itself, seems as though it were always as we see it now. Perhaps that is why the photographs now seem to have more in common with the romantic commentary of Mark Twain than with the atlas of maps Bosse first worked on. By the end of the nineteenth century, the American landscape was already so transformed and settled that artists' views expressed a certain romance and nostalgia for the frontier life that had disappeared almost as soon as it had arrived. We are encouraged to ponder the fragile balance that Bosse's photographs show us between the forces of nature and the human ability—of engineer or photographer—to alter the landscape.

ACKNOWLEDGMENTS

I NEED TO THANK several people for their assistance in the making of this book. First and foremost, John Anfinson, formerly of the U.S. Army Corps of Engineers, went above and beyond the call of duty in offering assistance, materials, and his bibliographic knowledge of the Upper Mississippi River. Ron Deiss of the Rock Island District Office of the Corps was of invaluable help, as were Paul Walker, chief of history, and Martin Gordon, archivist, both in Washington, D.C. • At the University of St. Thomas, where I teach, Bob Craig has probably shaped my thinking about these photographs more than any other individual. Tom Connery, Kris Bunton, Dave Nimmer, Kendra Gale, Stacey Kanihan, David Landry, and Mike O'Donnell also deserve thanks, as do Steve Hoffman and the several French, German, and Spanish professors who helped translate old maps. The hardworking librarians, led by Dan Gjelten, are a credit to the university. • Thanks to Pat Nunnally, Bill Kirchgessner, Rick Hauser, Stacy Kuebelbeck, Peter Fairley, Beth Nodland, and Sara Klomp. • At the Mississippi River Museum at Dubuque, Iowa, Bob Wiederaenders, Tacie Campbell, Denise Vondran, and Jerry Enzler run a beautiful facility the entire region can be proud of. Thanks to Bob Fogt for photographing the Dubuque prints. At Mayo Foundation in Rochester, Minnesota, Carolyn Stickney Beck, Matthew D. Dacy, Cheryl J. Hadaway, and colleagues are worthy of special mention. The foundation was generous in its sharing of its Bosse holdings. • Many, many talented people assisted in the research on the photographs and maps. Among them were Mike Ware, Larry Schaaf, William Becker, Mark Osterman, Nora Hague, Michael Gray, Rolfe Sachsse, Luis Nadeau, Shannon Perich, Jane Ehrenfeldt, and Helena Wright. • For editorial and design reasons, the captions to the photographs do not include footnotes. Among the resources consulted were the following people or their published works: John Anfinson, Ron Deiss, Roald Tweet, Raymond Merritt, William J. Petersen, Walter Havighurst, George Byron Merrick, Timothy Severin, Charles Edward Russell, Mark Twain, Meridel Le Sueur, T. H. Watkins, Giacomo Beltrami, Calvin Fremling, Ron Larson, Frederick Johnson, Mike Ware, Phil Scarpino, Todd Shallat, Lucille Kane, Richard Olsenius, John Barry, Leland Baldwin, J. T. Lloyd, Frederick Way, William Lass, F. E. Dayton, H. S. Drago, G. L. Eskew, E. W. Gould, Louis C. Hunter, Ron Powers, Mike Conner, Martin Reuss, George Catlin, Mildred Hartsough, William Faulkner, Erik F. Haites, James Mak, Gary M. Walton, Edward North, and H. M. Chittenden. The archives of the Corps, chambers of commerce, and state, city, and county historical societies also provided a wealth of information. • Important to me in investigating Henry Bosse's life were John Thompson, Elizabeth Sroka, Brian Thornton, Mark Cioc, Glen Longacre, Cheryl Oakes, and numerous clerks in county, city, and federal offices in several states, Germany, and Canada. • Mike Conner, Merry Foresta, Denise Bethel, and Charles Wehrenberg are all part of the story; my thanks to them for participating in retelling it. Sandra Phillips, Jean Trumbo, Pat Nemo, Mark Cioc, and John Anfinson read early versions of the manuscript and offered helpful suggestions. Todd Orjala of the University of Minnesota Press believed in the project from the first day. • My wife, Amy Kuebelbeck, and our children, Elena, Maria, and especially our beloved Gabriel, have been in my thoughts constantly as I completed this manuscript.

Mark Neuzil
St. Paul, Minnesota
February 2001

[VIEWS] ON THE MISSISSIPPI

THE LIFE AND PHOTOGRAPHS OF HENRY PETER BOSSE

The gray granite memorial sitting heavily on river clay in Oakdale Cemetery in Davenport, Iowa, offers only tiny hints at the mystery and complexity of the person who reposes nearby. The stone reads "Bosse," marking the resting place of one of the nineteenth century's most important photographers. Henry Peter Bosse's headstone sits in a city he did not call home, a few blocks from a river he knew more intimately than any person in his era.

The memorial reveals no hint that Henry Bosse would one day be considered the premier Mississippi River photographer of his time. By the end of the twentieth century, his original prints sold for tens of thousands of dollars, and the nation's finest galleries displayed his work. Experts now consider Bosse's compositions alongside those of renowned frontier photographers like William Henry Jackson, Timothy O'Sullivan, Carleton Watkins, and Jack Hillers, although Bosse's photographs drifted in the backwaters of history for nearly a century.

The government paid these men and many others to document the nation's westward expansion in the years following the Civil War. Their photographs are often filled with images of people at work, machines in motion, and landscapes being forever bent to the whims of industrialism. Bosse's photographs highlighted expansionism, exploitation, and capitalism as the United States finished the job of taming the frontier. His known prints, taken between 1883 and 1893, came a few years later than the bulk of the historically significant photographs taken by Hillers, Watkins, O'Sullivan, and Jackson, who often worked farther west in a wilderness setting. When Bosse learned the art of photography to aid his work as a mapmaker for the Army, the frontier was very nearly closed. But if one looks closely, the end of the frontier is visible in Bosse's photographs as the Mississippi's great wilderness of islands, chutes, rapids, sloughs, coulees, and its immense floodplain was tamed by social forces.

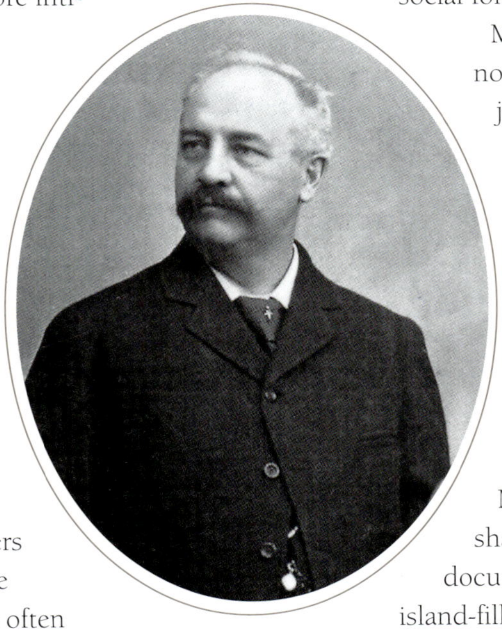

Henry Bosse (William F. Quaintance).

Much of Bosse's life is a mystery. He left no papers, no diary, no notebooks, and no children. He didn't join any of the several German-American associations in his adopted hometown of Rock Island, Illinois, nor was he listed as a member of any of the area's major churches.[1] All we have left are his pictures. All of Bosse's photographs were composed on or near the Mississippi River and were taken while he worked as a draftsman for the Corps of Engineers from Minnesota to Missouri. His work, in the unusual shape and style of large-format cyanotype albums, documents a river being transformed from the braided, island-filled Father of Waters familiar to the native tribes to a dammed, dredged, and channeled industrial waterway. In addition to landscapes, Bosse photographed the bridges and booms, locks and log rafts, wing dams and canals, snag boats and towboats, and cities and quarries that wrestled the river under human control. It was a time of dramatic change on the Mississippi River and in America, and Bosse's photographs became part of the great commercial and military achievements of the late 1800s. His legacy is secured by rare pictures of a river never to be seen again. The photographs leave the modern viewer with a sense of nostalgia, a yearning for the natural river that was lost to the forces of commerce.

Several geographic features were named after government photographers. There is a Jackson Canyon and a Jackson Butte, a Mount Watkins and a Mount Hillers. Such physical places help keep memories of the photographers alive. But Bosse had no bluff, no tributary or chain; a towboat was rechristened in his honor, posthumously, but it was lost in a storm. Without some plain luck, Bosse would have been lost in history, too.

UNCOVERING THE PHOTOGRAPHS

In 1919, Alexander Mackenzie, a seventy-five-year-old retired Army general, purchased a home on Kalorama Road Northwest in Washington, D.C. Mackenzie had more than forty-five years of active service in the Army and wanted a permanent home for his only surviving child, Lucia Mackenzie Hendley.[2] The general collapsed and died in the lobby of the Riggs Bank on February 23, 1921, moments after making the last mortgage payment on the house.

The house became the repository of the general's personal possessions while his daughter and her husband lived there for the next several decades. It also became home to the Hendley School of Music, as Lucia gave lessons to the children of many prominent Washington families and hosted recitals attended by John and Jackie Kennedy, Dwight Eisenhower, and Douglas MacArthur. One of the students in Lucia's music classes, Henry Bond, later went to work for the school as an instructor. When Lucia, who was widowed in 1948, died in 1958, she left the estate to Bond, as the Hendleys were childless.

An antique dealer with a degree in history, Mike Conner, moved into the neighborhood in 1982 and struck up a friendship with Henry Bond. Conner considered Bond to be something of a surrogate grandfather, and he spent many afternoons at Bond's house. One day, Conner came across an album of cyanotype prints stored on a lower bookshelf in the second-floor study. The photographs of the Mississippi River, printed in the now-obscure cyanotype process that is similar to a blueprint, fascinated Conner. The pictures, some more than a hundred years old at the time, were large-format landscapes, printed on fifteen- by eighteen-inch sheets watermarked "JOHANNOT ET C^{le} ANNONAY ALOE'S SATINO," a nineteenth-century manufactured cyanotype paper. All the photographs were printed as ovals, and, as Conner was to discover, all were taken on the river between Minneapolis and St. Louis.

Bond told Conner that museum experts examined the album in the 1970s, but they placed a relatively low value on the book and Bond wasn't interested in selling anyway. By the mid-1980s, Bond's health was fading and the upkeep on a three-story home in an expensive neighborhood was more than he wanted to handle. He sold the home in 1988, moved some possessions to a condominium, and sold or gave away the rest. Among the items he shed was the album of cyanotypes, given to Mike Conner for helping him get resettled.

After Bond died in 1989, Conner began to research the photographs. None of the professionals at the Library of Congress, National Archives, or Army Corps of Engineers in Washington had knowledge of the photographer, Henry P. Bosse. About a year later, Conner took the album to a photography show, and none of the experts there knew of Bosse, either. An unknown photographer didn't stop collectors from bidding on the photographs, however, and Conner received one offer for $20,000.

The album's frontispiece reads "Views on the Mississippi River, from negatives taken and printed under the direction of Major A. Mackenzie, Corps of Engineers, U.S.A. by H. Bosse, Draughtsman,

1883–1891." The album held 169 cyanotypes. Mackenzie, a native of the river region, was chief of the Rock Island office of the Corps from 1878 to 1894, spoke fluent German, and was the principal engineer of the first large-scale channel project on the Upper Mississippi River.[3] Bosse was his friend, business partner, and chief draftsman for much of his career in Rock Island and gave Mackenzie the album as a gift.

While tracking down more information about his discovery, Conner called John Anfinson, a historian with the Army Corps of Engineers St. Paul District, which is in charge of the uppermost section of the river. Anfinson told him the Corps only had black-and-white copies identified as Bosse's work. After talking to Conner, Anfinson fished out the black and whites.[4] Sandwiched between two images was a black-and-white photograph of the cover of an album that read "Presented to U.S. Dredge William A. Thompson by Mrs. William A. Thompson." But where was the intact album? Did it still exist? Digging through his archives, Anfinson learned that Thompson, an engineer, worked for the Corps from 1878 to 1925, spending all his years on the Upper Mississippi River; a dredge was named after him in 1937.

The *Dredge Thompson* was still a working boat on the Mississippi, so Anfinson called the district's head of channel maintenance and asked him if he had ever seen any photographs of the river on board the vessel. To Anfinson's surprise, the supervisor reported that a volume of blue photographs sat in the pilothouse. The district photographer, who had retired, had made copies of the album a few years before, so the black and whites Anfinson possessed were actually copies of the originals. An album soon to be worth tens of thousands of dollars was still on the dredge, which was docked in St. Louis.

Meanwhile, Conner began showing his album to experts. He was concerned about the condition of the prints and his financial ability to keep them in the best shape possible. Among the persons he contacted for preservation advice was Denise Bethel, then at Swann Galleries, a rare book auction house in Manhattan, and later a vice president and head of photography at Sotheby's auction house. Bethel is an expert on the value of historic photographs in the United States. When Conner telephoned Bethel to describe the album, Bethel thought he was one of her friends pulling a prank. When, several months later, she finally got a look at the pictures, she said the reality was far better than anything she could have imagined.[5] Bethel and Conner placed the book's value between $40,000 and $60,000.

On October 16, 1990, Conner sold the album for $66,000 at Sotheby's fall auction. The winning bid for what was called "the breathtaking cyanotype album" came from dealer Simon Lowinsky of New York.[6] Charles Wehrenberg of San Francisco subsequently bought into the photographs, broke up the album, and began to resell and donate pieces from the collection. A single image sold for $20,000 in a private transaction, and Wehrenberg valued the collection at between $650,000 and $1 million.[7]

Since the discovery of the first two sets, three more sets of Bosse's cyanotype photographs have been identified, along with several individual prints. A two-album set is in the archives of the Mississippi River Museum in Dubuque, Iowa; two surviving albums of a three-album set are in the possession of the Rock Island office of the Corps; and a third volume is in private hands at Mayo Foundation in Rochester, Minnesota.

The cyanotype prints in the two-volume set owned by the Mississippi River Museum in Dubuque are not numbered and bordered, and many are not dated in the typical style Bosse favored, nor was the paper of an expensive quality. Some of the prints are sloppy, with the edges blurred because the border moved during processing; in some cases cyanotype solution was spilled on the print. Almost half—as many as eighty prints—are unique to the Dubuque set. In addition, the lettering on the prints is most certainly not in Bosse's handwriting, and it is in black ink rather than his typical cyan.

We could be looking at outtakes from Bosse's studio. Given the dedication on the front page—"M. S. Heagy to A. L. Richards, 1937"—it is probable that the two volumes were lettered and bound (or rebound) after Bosse's death. It is also possible that a few of the unique Dubuque prints were taken by another photographer or photographers—Bosse's assistant, A. J. Stibolt, perhaps, or another Corps employee familiar with a camera, like Montgomery Meigs. One photograph, of a blasting scene in midchannel, has "Wittick" written near the bottom.

Inscriptions indicate that many of the albums—like the one to retiring district engineer A. L. Richards—originally were given as gifts to Corps officials or others. Corps employee Ron Deiss at the Rock Island office also located a handsome presentation album of seventy-two black-and-white images. The Rock Island cyanotypes have a 210-photograph index, which indicates that they may have been a master set used for reference. The Rock Island master set also contained an atlas, now missing, showing the locations near where Bosse took at least some of those 210 photos. The atlas was a copy of a Corps field map from 1878–79, dotted with colorful names like Whiskey Chute, Deadman's Bar, Bad Axe, Queen's Bluff, Bloody Run, Tête du Mort, and Mechanic's Rock.

Including the single prints, about 350 original images are known to exist. Only seven of the original glass plate negatives remain, and they are in the hands of the Corps in Rock Island. The rest were reused, broken, lost, or destroyed. Many, perhaps as many as two hundred negatives, were dropped and crushed in a move at the Rock Island offices several decades ago.[8] In addition to the cyanotypes and black and whites, at least a few albumen prints and one tannin print that may have been made by Bosse still exist. Three prints that exist in multiple copies have different dates on each copy.

The coin of the realm in the art-photography world is the marketplace. Once Bosse's prints were given a high dollar value, his place in the history of photography was all but ensured. The efforts of Conner, Bethel, and Wehrenberg were critical in getting Bosse national acclaim. Conner recognized the value of the photographs and took the steps necessary to get Bosse recognition. If he had kept the album to himself, it is likely that Bosse would have remained in obscurity. Bethel understood the photography market well enough to know that even an unknown photographer could bring top dollar at auction. Because the photography auction market is relatively young, new discoveries can command attention and occasionally large sums, whereas an undiscovered nineteenth-century painter, for example, would be less apt to attract attention because the masters of the field are well established. Wehrenberg primed the market by selling or donating nearly one hundred prints in the first decade he owned the album, creating interest

Bosse experimented with black and white photography, like this image of the *David Bronson*, as well as albumen prints (U.S. Army Corps of Engineers, Rock Island District).

among dealers, collectors, and museums around the country, all the while driving up the price.

WHO WAS HENRY BOSSE?

Inscribed on the gray memorial stone in Davenport are two other names. The first is that of Bosse's maternal grandfather, General Neithardt von Gneisenau, one of the greatest Prussian soldiers, the man credited with devising the strategy to defeat Napoleon at Waterloo; Bosse never met him. The second name is that of Bosse's wife, Hulda Thiele Bosse, a woman thirteen years his junior from a prominent Davenport family whom he married late in life and who accidentally poisoned him to death in 1903 with contaminated canned asparagus.

Henry Peter Bosse was born on November 13, 1844, in Sommerschenburg, Prussia, on or near the estate of his deceased grandfather.[9] Evidence is sketchy, but it appears that Bosse may have been the son of the general's daughter Ottilie, who never married. The identity of the father is uncertain, but Henry's surname points to a village schoolmaster also named Bosse, who was a reserve officer in the Prussian Army, serving under Gneisenau in the campaigns of 1813–14 and 1815 against Napoleon.[10]

It is possible that the photographer's given name was Pieter Heinrich Bosse or Bose, and that he adopted the more American "Henry Peter" upon his arrival in the New World, perhaps in honor of his father. No birth certificate has been found.[11]

The lineage is distinguished. Bosse's grandfather, Count August-Wilhelm Neithardt von Gneisenau, was among the German troops sold to the colonial powers, in his case Great Britain.[12] His unit of mercenaries reached the shores of New England in 1782, when the war was nearly over, and Gneisenau did not see action against George Washington's army. Back in Prussia and promoted to major, Gneisenau became embroiled in the Napoleonic Wars, organizing the revolt against the French from the ashes of defeat. As Field Marshal Gebhard Blücher's chief of staff, Gneisenau rallied an exhausted group of Prussian troops to counterattack at Waterloo while Napoleon and his 130,000 men were attacking the outmanned Duke of Wellington. Gneisenau's men pursued the French through the moonlit night of June 18–19, 1815, and two-thirds of Napoleon's army was destroyed.[13] Before the final victory over the French, King Friedrich Wilhelm III awarded the castle at Sommerschenburg to the career soldier.[14]

Gneisenau's second of four daughters, Ottilie, was born in 1802 and died in 1883. The family records indicate that she never married, and if Bosse listed his birthdate correctly, she gave birth to him when she was forty-two years old. Bosse's possible father, the former soldier, was brought to the village by Gneisenau after the Napoleonic Wars and given a job as schoolmaster. An anecdote told by the Gneisenau family has it that one day the famed warrior visited the school where the elder Bosse was teaching and became upset at the stuffy air in the classroom. "Bosse, how can you stand it?" Gneisenau asked. "It is my duty to teach in these circumstances," Bosse replied. Gneisenau instructed the teacher to have the artisans construct wooden tables and benches in the nearby forest. When the weather permitted, instruction took place outdoors in the fresh forest air.[15]

Young Bosse's early years were spent on the estate; he was tutored in Greek and Latin and completed classical studies at Magdeburg, the provincial capital, where he added courses in engineering and art, both of which influenced his photographs.[16] There was no university at Magdeburg at the time, but Bosse claimed to have a rich educational experience, de rigueur for the son of a Gneisenau heir. In 1865, according to census records, he left Germany, but where he went is unknown.[17] Bosse appears in the 1870 U.S. Census as a resident of Chicago, working as a partner in a bookstore and stationery shop with another Prussian immigrant, Frederick Lang, also his roommate.[18]

Working in a stationery shop would have honed Bosse's skills with a quill, as a stationer produced birthday and other holiday cards, and personalized paper. The Great Chicago Fire roared through the city the following year, but it seems the store was closed by then. Bosse appears in a Chicago directory in 1871 and 1873 as a bookkeeper for a rolling stock and bridge building firm.[19]

Germany reunified in 1871, and much intellectual talent returned to the homeland, but Bosse did not, at least not permanently. In 1874, Bosse received an appointment to the U.S. Army Corps of Engineers by a Monroe County, New York, congressman at the starting salary of $175 per year.[20] His initial appointment dealt with harbor improvement in the Great Lakes,[21] but by the end of the year the Corps assigned him to St. Paul. He began his mapmaking duties with a lithograph of the Upper Mississippi River at a place called Thousand Islands, between St. Cloud and Anoka, Minnesota.[22]

In 1878, the Corps transferred Bosse to its Rock Island headquarters, where he was employed as chief draftsman until his death in 1903. As chief draftsman, mapping the river for the first of the huge navigation projects that would alter it forever, Bosse began to take pictures. He worked with some of the premier engineering talent of the day, including Mackenzie, Montgomery Meigs, and C. W. Durham. All spoke German, and Meigs and Durham held advanced degrees from German universities. It is impossible to know for certain where Bosse learned photography, but Meigs may have been his tutor. Meigs, the son of a skilled Army engineer and photographer, was experienced with a camera and also worked in cyanotypes, producing several that remain in Corps archives.

Mackenzie, Meigs, Durham, and Bosse used the Corps's finest boat, the *General Barnard*, for much of their work on the river over the next two decades. In the floating office that was the *Barnard*, Bosse possibly enjoyed the company of Mark Twain. It is not known for certain whether Bosse met Twain, but he may have been influenced by him. Several of the pen-and-ink drawings left behind by the German artist resemble the original sketches of Huck in the first 1885 edition of *Huckleberry Finn*.[23] Twain wrote a series of articles for *The Atlantic Monthly* in 1875 that became the basis for *Life on the Mississippi* in 1883. Some of the author's river travel in 1882 came via the *Barnard*, constructed in 1878–79 and captained by the 300-pound Davey Tipton, a friend of Twain's. Coincidentally, the *Barnard* was Bosse's most popular riverboat subject and, probably, the home to his portable darkroom. The boat was also something of a social club, with the best food, drink, and tobacco supplied its passengers.[24]

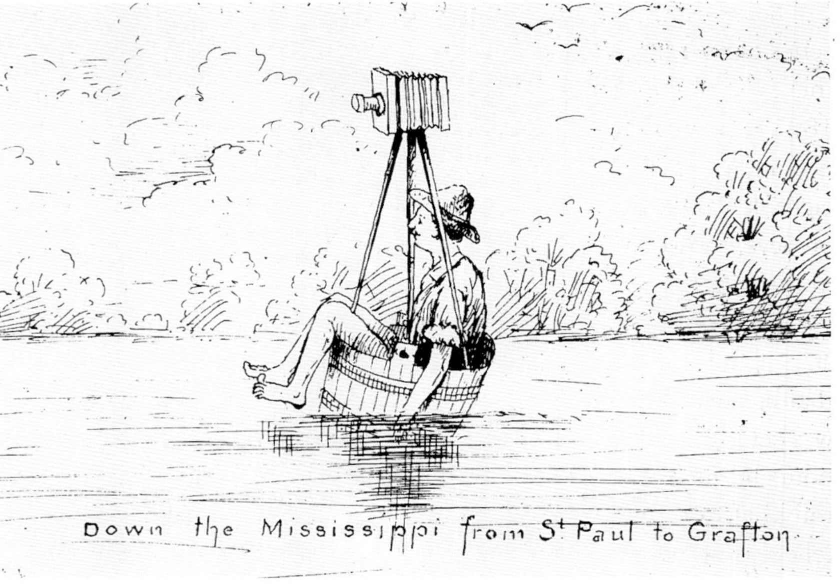

Bosse could be whimsical, as demonstrated by this drawing on a page from his field-size map book that shows himself floating down the river (U.S. Army Corps of Engineers).

Bosse became a U.S. citizen in 1892 in Illinois.[25] After living in a series of boardinghouses, Bosse married Hulda Thiele of Davenport at the home of the bride's stepfather, F. W. Haller, on October 24, 1895.[26] He was fifty-one and in his second marriage (the marriage register indicates that Bosse was married once before); Hulda was thirty-eight. In 1899, Henry and Hulda moved into a large three-story house on Seventh Avenue in Rock Island with a shed and a two-story stable in the rear.[27]

Henry Bosse died in 1903 at the age of fifty-nine. The circumstances surrounding his death were unusual. The newspapers reported that he ate a helping of poisoned asparagus at a Sunday dinner and was sent to nearby St. Anthony's Hospital in Rock Island. After several hours in the hospital, he was feeling better. The following day, another round of stomach pain led doctors to prepare him for surgery to relieve what they diagnosed as an intestinal blockage, but Bosse suffered a heart attack and died before the surgery, on December 14, 1903. His contemporaries and his wife's relatives remembered Bosse as an intelligent, cultured, aristocratic man, with a barrel chest, a thick German accent, and a pronounced military manner.[28] He had saved his money and invested in land, buying property in St. Paul and Duluth, Minnesota, as well as in Rock Island. The St. Paul lots were purchased in partnership with his boss, Mackenzie, in December 1885 when Mackenzie was district engineer in Rock Island. Bosse owned the properties in all three cities until the time of his death.[29]

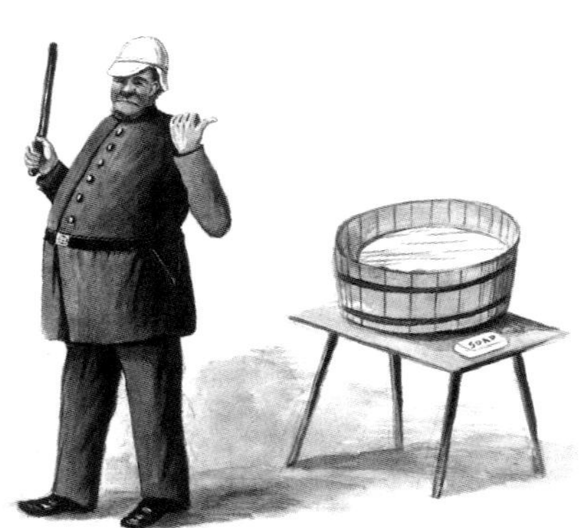

Bosse did not want visitors with dirty hands to touch his prints displayed at the 1893 World's Columbian Exposition, so he sketched this poster for the exhibit (U.S. Army Corps of Engineers, Rock Island District).

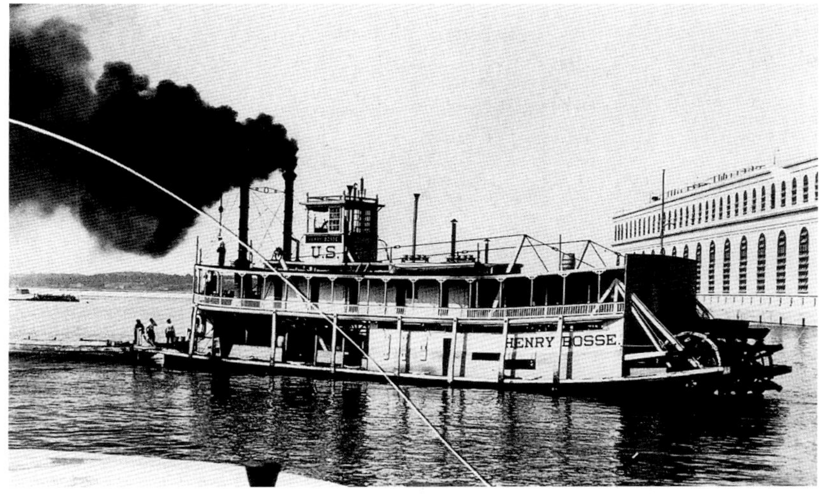

The Corps's boat *Vixen* was renamed *Henry Bosse* in 1908, but it capsized in 1913. The fragility of the glass-plate negative process can be seen in the crack in this print (U.S. Army Corps of Engineers, Rock Island District).

The untimely demise of Henry Bosse may have contributed to the lack of historical record about his life. The man had no warning to get his effects in order. His name was kept alive a bit longer when the Corps, recognizing his accomplishments during a twenty-nine-year career as a draftsman and photographer, renamed a towboat the *Henry Bosse* in 1908. But the ship capsized off Keokuk, Iowa, in a severe storm in 1913, killing six men.[30] Bosse's wife never remarried and was buried beside her husband in 1934.

THE MISSISSIPPI RIVER IN BOSSE'S DAY

The Mississippi River Bosse knew will never be seen again. In his day, the upper stretch from the headwaters at Lake Itasca to the mouth of the Missouri River at St. Louis was an island-braided, free-ranging river with dramatic changes in flow and level, depending on the season. By the 1950s, the river could be more accurately described as a series of turbid, shallow river-lakes, staked out by a system of locks and dams that regulated the river to assist navigation.[31] Construction on the river changed the Mississippi forever, and Bosse's photographs and maps document the before, during, and after phases of a new channel. Bosse's domain was the upper river, which begins at Lake Itasca in northern Minnesota and ends at the mouth of the Ohio River at Cairo, Illinois, south of St. Louis. The river is often split into upper and lower pieces for geographic and political reference, but the division is born in geologic time. The modern upper river is thousands of years old. The lower river is millions of years old. The youngest stretch of the upper river, the 493 miles of headwaters above St. Anthony Falls, near present-day Minneapolis, is perhaps 10,000 years old, which is the date of the last glacial retreat. The 854-mile stretch from Minneapolis to Cairo is about 700,000 years old. The general course of the lower river is as old as the oceans; it dates to the late Paleozoic era, more than 250 million years ago. By the twenty-first century, the river measured 2,301 miles, the third-longest river in the world. The river was at least 142 miles longer in Bosse's day, before channels, closing dams, and canals shortened it.[32]

The Mississippi basin is the fourth-largest drainage in the world, covering 41 percent of the U.S. mainland, extending from the highlands of West Virginia to peaks of the continental divide in western Montana. Its major tributaries include the Missouri, Ohio, Arkansas, and Red rivers. During preglacial times, much of the central lowlands of North America drained north into what is now Canada. When the Nebraskan, Kansan, and Illinoisan glaciers advanced south (to the current position of the Missouri and Ohio rivers), their mass—two miles thick—blocked almost all northward passage, so their meltwater flowed along the path of least resistance to merge with the ancient Lower Mississippi River to the south.[33] The melting of the Wisconsin glacier, beginning about 100,000 years ago, formed the Upper Mississippi Valley. During the last major glacial period in North America, the glacier advanced and retreated in several spurts, each advance slightly shorter than the last. Rapid draining of glacial lakes bracketed the advances and retreats of the glaciers, causing great floods. For example, Glacial Lake Agassiz, which covered parts of central Canada, Minnesota, and the Dakotas, spilled into Glacial River Warren and fed the flow with a huge flood from about 12,700 years ago to 10,000 years ago.[34] The Minnesota River now flows through the valley formed by the River Warren, and it joins the Mississippi in the Twin Cities.

The geology helps explain Bosse's photographs. The geologic features important to the photographer were the steep bluffs, the rapids, and the braided main channel. Where the young, restless river met the least resistance, on sandstone, its valley became broad and wide as the river flattened and swept away everything before it. Where the river met the most resistance, on limestone and dolomites, the valley stayed narrow as the rocks fought erosion and scouring. Below St. Anthony Falls, the Mississippi flows through a deep gorge carved into sedimentary rock; its tributaries are correspondingly deep, so deep that early white explorers thought low ranges of mountains surrounded the river. The steep, 900-foot-high bluffs created the perfect spot for a cameraman to set up a landscape photograph. The valley, more than six miles wide in places, created a panoramic scene. "Those hills and valleys gave rise to some of the most sublime and romantic views I ever saw," wrote the explorer Zebulon Pike after an 1805 trip.[35] Where the river alternately flowed over the tougher, resilient bedrock strata into softer sandstones, waterfalls and rapids were formed. Those sites, which bottled up shipping and gobbled up unwary boats, became the bane of commercial interests and pilots and the object of decades of attention from the government, including its photographers.

The Mississippi was a well-established commercial waterway, one of the oldest highways in North America, by Bosse's time. Transportation on the river began with human settlement. Although the facts are subject to intense archaeological debate, the first human artifacts in North America date to about 10,000 B.C., but *Homo sapiens* may have occupied the area much earlier.[36] Hunter-gatherers' spear points have been found on the river dating from about 9000 B.C. Waterfowl and fish thrived in the bottomlands of the upper river and some of the slower-moving tributaries, while nut trees stood limb to limb in the valleys, making for an abundant food supply. Seasonal Paleo-Indian settlements appeared as early as 7500 B.C. in the Illinois River Valley.[37] In the Ohio Valley, about 1000 B.C., the Adena people may have adopted long-distance trading routes using rivers. At about the same time, settlements rich in copper, located in what is now Wisconsin and Michigan, traded metal with people as far away as present-day Florida and New York.[38] About 400 B.C., the Hopewell culture's exchange system, as evidenced by burial mounds and other artifacts, emerged in the Midwest; its trading spread from the Gulf of Mexico to the Great Lakes to Wyoming. Rivers, navigated with canoes and rafts, helped it find new markets.

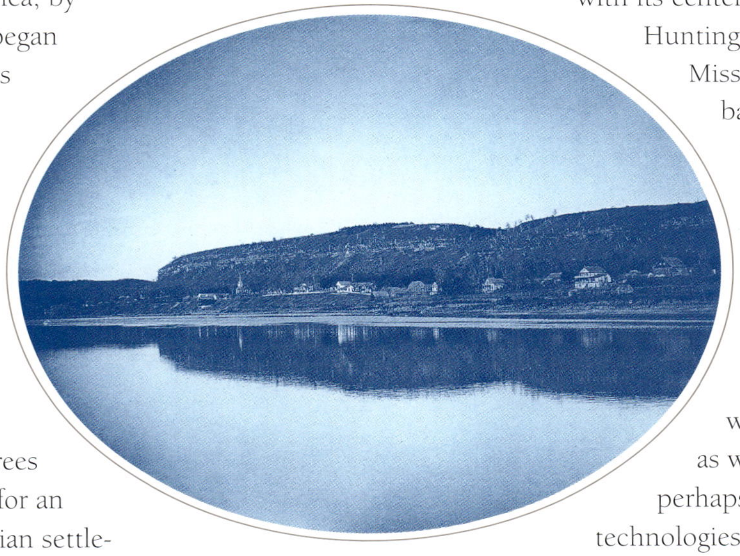

Diamond Bluff, Wis., 1889 (Mayo Foundation). Diamond Bluff is the site of Indian burial mounds. The mound builders used the river for transportation as well as food.

The most populous and organized native societies of North America, the Mississippian cultures, grew up near the river. The locus of a social system first inhabited about A.D. 700, residents set up an agricultural network that supported as many as 40,000 people with its center near present-day Cahokia, Illinois. Hunting and gathering supplemented the Mississippian chiefdoms' agricultural food base, which included corn, squash, tobacco, and knotweed. Planting took place on the arable Mississippi floodplain soil, easily tilled with wooden sticks. Some of the gathering was done in the deciduous forests and plains of Minnesota, which were accessible by hide and birch bark canoes. The tribes ate cattail, waterlily, and Jerusalem artichoke tubers, as well as wild rice, acorns, goosefoot, and perhaps purselane and sumac.[39] Mississippian technologies existed in settlements near present-day Red Wing, Minnesota, as early as A.D. 1000 and at Cambria, Minnesota, on the Minnesota River.[40] Diamond Bluff, near Red Wing, was a favorite spot for Bosse to photograph; it is also the site of Mississippian burial mounds. Oak, willow, birch, poplar, ash, maple, elm, and butternut trees dotted the hillsides, along with some ironwood and hackberry. Farther south, wild grapes, plums, and wild peas provided food.

With the arrival of the Europeans came guns, germs, and steel. The Spanish explorer Hernando de Soto was credited with "discovering" the river in 1539. Diseases, including influenza and smallpox, jumped from tribe to tribe and preceded the Spanish explorers into the North American heartland, weakening the social structure of the Mississippians.[41] When the Spanish appeared with their armaments, horses, and military organization, they faced a culture already in dramatic decline. The native peoples who survived the epidemics were no match for the Spanish muskets. After leaving death and destruction in his wake, de Soto died violently upon the riverbank at what is now Memphis.[42] Water-related diseases remained a problem for hundreds of years. Of the mouth of the Ohio River, Herman Melville wrote, "At Cairo the old firm of Fever & Ague is still setting up its unfinished business."[43]

As the Spanish came and went in the central and southern river valley, French trappers and missionaries appeared in the north. Among the first whites to see the upper river were the Jesuit missionary Jacques Marquette and his guide Louis Joliet, a French Canadian fur trader. With five companions, they portaged and paddled down the Wisconsin River to its mouth on the Mississippi in the spring of 1673. Marquette wanted to name the big stream Rivière de la Conception, but the Algonquian moniker Messipi (Great River) was not to be displaced.[44] Huge catfish and other fish struck their frail craft with such force that it was "about to break the Canoe to pieces."[45] The French Canadians adopted the native way of travel, the birch bark canoe, as their own *canot du nord*. The demand for beaver pelts and the hides of other fur-bearing mammals drew more and more white explorers to the upper river by the late 1700s. Improving on the birch bark canoe, the French trappers designed the pirogue, a longer dugout canoe made from two logs with a plank or two between them for carrying heavier loads.

The trappers and settlers soon developed an array of boats for river travel, and a few were still in use in Bosse's day. Among the first was the keelboat, a French design dating from the 1750s, which had replaced the canoe and pirogue by 1800. A keelboat, the choice of travel for Lewis and Clark, could float up to 30,000 pounds of freight. Steered by bow and stern rudders called sweeps, a keelboat was usually forty to eighty feet long and ten feet wide with a crew of ten. It glided downstream, of course, but also could be poled upstream. Sometimes pilots threw up a sail; occasionally they tossed a rope ashore and the crew hauled the boat from stump to stump, a process called cordelling. Flat-bottomed and sharp-prowed, a full keelboat drafted only twenty to twenty-four inches of water. An experienced crew could make twelve to fifteen miles per day out of St. Louis. Keelboats were the freighters of choice in the 1820s and 1830s, though they all but disappeared by 1845.

Keelboats vanished because they were only a few short years ahead of steam power on the upper river. The *New Orleans* steamed down the Ohio River from Pittsburgh all the way to New Orleans in 1811. The *Virginia* chugged into Fort Anthony (later called Fort Snelling, near present-day St. Paul) in 1823 carrying government supplies from St. Louis; the 700-mile trip took twenty days, about three times as fast as a keelboat.[46] Steamboats were more efficient on the lower river because it was an easier stretch to navigate, but they soon became common in Rock Island, Dubuque, and La Crosse, Wisconsin, as well. The original steamboats were not much more than a boiler and a ramshackle cabin sitting on a raft. It wasn't long before an extra engine was added—there was one on the port and one on the starboard—to create a side-wheeler, which could be maneuvered more easily through sharp river bends, although big stern-wheelers still worked best for pushing log rafts. Soon, some steamboats became more passenger-friendly, and many, mostly on the lower river, began to resemble opulent floating hotels.[47] By the 1840s, hundreds of steamers made the trip from St. Louis to St. Paul each year with loads of manufactured goods and coal. On the return trip, they often hauled lumber and grain. One type of steamer, called a packet or packet boat, made prescribed runs carrying passengers and freight. Their boilers burned wood at the rate of twenty to twenty-five cords every twenty-four hours; boats stopped to pick up wood two or three times a day.

In terms of volume of freight, neither keelboat nor steamboat was the dominant shipper on the upper river in the nineteenth century. By the 1830s, white and red pines drew crews of lumberjacks to Minnesota and Wisconsin. Logs were floated on tributaries to the big river and tied together in huge rafts. Raft boats, called log rafts (raw timber) or lumber rafts (milled timber), floated downstream as two acres of wood steered with oars, carrying materials to build Omaha, Des Moines, Rock Island, and Kansas City from the forests and mills of the north (Plate 48). Some were a quarter mile long and a city block wide. These huge cribs of timber roped together were the most common vessel on the river for much of the midcentury. Flatboats, a version of a log raft, also shipped up to thirty or forty tons of freight sitting on the raft; when the flatboat reached its destination, the entire boat, sometimes with the exception of the cabin, was broken apart and sold.

All boats had to contend with a long list of obstacles on the river and on board. Fire was a constant worry on the wooden crafts, as were collisions and explosions on steamers.[48] "Western steamboats usually blow up, one or two a week, during the season," Charles Dickens wrote in 1842.[49] A fire at St. Louis destroyed twenty-three steamboats in 1849. Snags, rapids, chains (a series of rock outcroppings, ledges, and rapids), and sandbars threatened from below. Steel hulls, which replaced wood by the twentieth century, somewhat reduced the fire hazard, while natural dangers became the focus of efforts to alter the river. The river's erosive powers were greatest during floods, which often threw more trees into the channel to become snags. The floating trees and brush that collected on a snag were called an embarras.

Navigation was impossible over mighty St. Anthony Falls; Minneapolis sprang up above the falls, using the water to power its lumber and flour mills. St. Paul, about ten miles downstream, became the de facto head of navigation on the river. St. Paul was iced in for as long as five months each year, and the appearance of the first boat after the thaw was a major event. "The arrival of the first steamer of the season is a great day for St. Paul," wrote local resident Harriet Bishop in 1853. "Anxiety has long run high; eyes are strained in anxious expectation, and when it finally rounds the bend, hundreds of citizens gathered at the river, send forth a prolonged shout of welcome, and the bluffs echo the general joy."[50]

Ice gorges were a threat up and down the river, but nowhere were they as intimidating as at Lake Pepin, above where the Chippewa River deposited sediment from central Wisconsin into the Mississippi and created a tricky crosshatch of islands and backwaters. A major headache for all boats, Lake Pepin, twenty-two miles long and one to two miles wide, was susceptible to storms and often had a rough wake.[51] "Lake Pepin," wrote the Italian adventurer Giacomo Beltrami in figurative terms in 1823, "is the headquarters for rattlesnakes."[52] A rough Lake Pepin could block travel for days to St. Paul, the St. Croix Valley, the Minnesota Valley, and the northern forests. It was no coincidence that when the four-and-a-half-foot channel project began in the late 1870s, the river south of Lake Pepin, at the mouth of the Chippewa River, was among the first objects of attention.

Major trouble awaited the riverboat pilot at two locations on the Iowa-Illinois border. The Rock Island Rapids were the first, and the Des Moines Rapids near Keokuk, Iowa, the second and more treacherous. The river's channel, or what there was of it, was dotted with boulders and limestone strata at those two locations and, although they were 150 river miles apart, they formed a formidable one-two challenge. At the Des Moines Rapids, the river fell twenty-two feet in twelve miles and there was no definable main channel, called a thalweg. At Rock Island, the fall was twenty-one feet in fifteen miles, and although it did have pieces of a channel, less than three feet of water covered the rapids during low flows.[53] All but the shallowest-drafting boats had difficulty steering through the rapids; much of the time, freight had to be unloaded, placed on a flatboat and shoved through the danger, then reloaded. The rapids were a major impediment to shipping and added substantially to the cost of manufactured goods heading upstream from the major trading center of St. Louis.[54] Another succession of rock bars and ledges, the seven-mile-long Great Chain of Rocks in the Mississippi channel upstream from St. Louis, in no small way contributed to the Missouri town's status as a major port.

The navigable portion of the entire Mississippi River system, including tributaries, in 1890 was 16,090 miles.[55] New Orleans was the second-largest port in the United States, trailing only New York. The Twin Cities of Minneapolis and St. Paul, near the head of the river, and St. Louis, at the beginning of the worst of the geologic pitfalls, were significant voices in the call for navigation improvements on the upper river. The U.S. Army Corps of Engineers carried out those improvements, starting before the Civil War and increasing in intensity after the great national conflict.

THE CORPS OF ENGINEERS AND MANIFEST DESTINY

Henry Bosse was a civilian employee of the U.S. Army, and recognizing the Army's role in the navigation of America's rivers is important to understanding his job. Engineers played a significant part in the new country from the time they built a breastwork on Bunker Hill during the Revolutionary War. The Corps of Engineers was created shortly after the new nation was formed. The civil works branch began modestly, clearing harbors of wrecks. The Corps's more important work was in exploration and mapmaking—and fort building—as part of the Army's taming of the frontier. The Corps attracted the best and brightest graduates from the U.S. Military Academy, men like Robert E. Lee, Joseph Totten, George G. Meade, and Alexander Macomb, and it was not until 1866 that a nonengineer commanded West Point. Statesmen like Henry Clay, Martin Van Buren, and Andrew Jackson sent sons and nephews to the school on the Hudson.

The connection between soldiers, exploration, and trade is an old one. It is sometimes overlooked that Meriwether Lewis and William Clark were soldiers when they embarked up the Missouri River to the Pacific Ocean in 1804. The officers were specifically asked by Thomas Jefferson to explore the Missouri and Columbia rivers to find the most direct water route across the continent "for the purposes of commerce."[56] In 1805, Lieutenant Zebulon Pike set out on a keelboat to find the mouth of the Mississippi, a task in which he failed. The United States, having purchased most of the region from the French in 1803, affirmed its control over the Upper Mississippi Valley territories that became Wisconsin and Minnesota in the Treaty of Ghent in 1814. Major Stephen Long, a member of the Topographical Bureau (later to be combined with the Corps of Engineers), surveyed the upper river for fortification defenses in 1817 as far as St. Anthony Falls in a six-oared skiff. "A beautiful cascade," Long wrote of the falls, "the most interesting and magnificent of any I have ever witnessed."[57] By the 1820s, the upper river was a commercial highway for trappers, soldiers, lead miners, and others. By 1828, the government had established five forts in the region. Three were on the upper river: Fort Anthony, Fort Crawford at the mouth of the Wisconsin River at Prairie du Chien, and Fort Armstrong at the Rock Island Rapids.[58]

One of the things Army officers from all these forts did was to map the land and water. Surveys were an important form of federal involvement in creating a habitable West.[59] For example, Corps lieutenant

Robert E. Lee mapped the dangerous Des Moines and Rock Island rapids in the 1830s with Montgomery Meigs's father, Montgomery C. Meigs, as his assistant. Lee was a talented engineer and the senior Meigs built the Washington Aqueduct, but perhaps the best of the early mapmakers was Joseph Nicollet, a French immigrant scientist who traveled with Lieutenant John C. Fremont of the Topographical Bureau. Working from the steamer *St. Peter's* in 1836, Nicollet left the boat at St. Anthony Falls and went all the way to Lake Itasca, marking latitude and longitude, and measuring altitude using a barometer (a new technique in the States in the 1830s). Nicollet's "Map of the Hydrological Basic of the Upper Mississippi River Basin" was published in 1843, the year of his death. As a mapmaker, Bosse was one in a long, illustrious line who served the government.

Low and high water made for major transportation problems. The timber industry, the most important shipper on the river after the Civil War, needed a constant flow of water to float logs from the northern white pine forests downstream to the sawmills in Wisconsin, Illinois, and Iowa. During low-water periods, some rivers dried to a trickle, and it became impossible to move logs. Low water also meant a loss of power for sawmills and flour milling at St. Anthony Falls. High water affected shipping interests as much as low water, but in different ways. Floods loosened soil on the riverbank and washed trees into the current, where they often lodged and became snags. The increased flow sometimes rerouted the channel, bedeviling pilots and mapmakers. Floods also altered sandbars, sweeping some away and creating new ones in unexpected spots. Sandbars might rise above the surface or lurk a few inches beneath it. Successful pilots became adept, in the words of one of them, George Merrick, at "dodging reefs and hunting the best water."[60] The first of several congressional river and harbor acts, passed in 1824, included $75,000 for clearing sandbars and other obstacles from the Ohio and Mississippi rivers. The Corps, with the blessings of Congress, went to work.[61] Money for blasting a channel through the Des Moines Rapids and rerouting the main channel at St. Louis followed in the 1830s as the Corps became established as the river's engineer, mapmaker, and contractor.

The government reorganized the Topographical Bureau in 1831 and made it a separate branch of the military whose primary duties were to explore and develop the West for immigrants.[62] The government encouraged steamboating by contracting with ship owners to move troops, mail, and military supplies. Packet service to St. Paul began in 1847, and ships were working above St. Anthony Falls in 1849 and on the Minnesota River starting in 1853. Settlement was rapid, and it was helped along by Indian land cessions. Statehood was granted to Illinois in 1818, Missouri in 1821, Iowa in 1846, Wisconsin in 1848, and Minnesota in 1858. In 1849, when Minnesota became a territory, its population was 5,000; nine years later, Minnesota was a state with a population of 150,000. Settlers were drawn by cheap land for farming and jobs in milling, timber, and mining. Major cities, towns, and villages grew along the river as the Corps worked to make it a national highway for freight and people.

Prior to the Civil War, the federal government spent relatively little on navigation improvements on the upper river. The Midwest had little clout in Congress, and the national mood ran against much federal spending on *any* projects, much less reconstructing the largest river system in the country.[63] The government financed some work at St. Anthony Falls, the Rock Island Rapids, and the Des Moines Rapids, the three most imposing natural barriers to shipping on the river. St. Anthony Falls, now part of Minneapolis, was a focus of concern for the Army. The military built a grain mill and a sawmill powered by the fast-moving water. Businesses were prohibited from using the water around the falls for power until 1847, when Franklin Steele started milling timber.[64] Shortly after the falls opened to commercial interests, plans were made to bridge the river. The first suspension bridge across the Mississippi was built in 1854 from Minneapolis to St. Anthony (Plate 1).[65]

The effect of the arrival of railroads on river shipping has long been debated; it wound up doing some good and much bad. Railroads supplied steamboats with immigrants and manufactured goods; but they also competed for freight and caused shippers to make shorter runs between railheads rather than traveling the entire upper river. By 1854, the railroads had reached the river at Rock Island and Alton, Illinois. The Chicago and Rock Island Railroad, in 1856, became the first to bridge the river. Fifteen days after the bridge opened, the side-wheeler *Effie Afton* stopped at Davenport, Iowa, unloaded freight and passengers, and passed upriver through the swing gate on the new bridge. As the captain navigated the Rock Island Rapids, the shaft on the starboard paddlewheel snapped. The disabled ship, caught in the current, spun helplessly back down the river, smacking into the new bridge piling. The *Effie Afton*'s twin smokestacks tumbled over; the wood-burning cookstove in the galley tipped and the boat caught fire. As rescuers in small skiffs and rafts fought their way to the passengers and crew, three hundred oxen on the main deck gave up the ship and leaped into the cold waters of the Mississippi. The fire jumped from boat to bridge, destroying part of the new structure, as the *Effie Afton* burned to the waterline. No lives were lost, either human or oxen, although it took almost a week to corral all of the latter.[66] Lawsuits and salvage operations followed. The victorious attorney for the railroads was Abraham Lincoln; the salvage operator was James B. Eads, later to be internationally famous for his bridge at St. Louis (Plate 84).

Soon wagon bridges and railroad bridges were built up and down the Mississippi, and it became the army's responsibility to regulate the structures because they became major obstructions to river traffic.[67] Much of Bosse's work consists of bridge pictures, including some photographed under construction (Plate 32) and others shortly after they opened. Bosse photographed bridges because the Corps was pressured by steamboat interests and others to limit the number of structures across the river in an era when one out of every four collapsed. Photographs also provided a visual record in the event of an accident, fire, lawsuit, or other dispute.

Once the Civil War ended, Americans pressed westward at an unprecedented pace. While states east of the Mississippi River had been largely settled, those west of it still held millions of unsettled acres. Much of western Iowa, western and northern Minnesota, the Dakotas, Kansas, and Nebraska remained open. (Native Americans, of course, considered the land occupied, though not with cities or agriculture.) The timber and farming industries fueled a growing Midwest economy throughout the nineteenth century, an economy that needed an efficient transportation system. Railroads, for which surveys had been done before the war, were completed on the west bank of the river after the war and allowed commerce to grow where navigable waters did not run. But the monopolistic freight rates charged by the railroads irked farmers and shippers. The pace of the Midwest's settlement and the growing size of its population and agricultural output between 1860 and 1880 created the need for a cheaper, competitive transportation system and gave it the political clout to demand one.

Congress balked at more expensive river improvements because it did not want to use government money for direct support of particular commercial interests. The powerful railroad lobby also fought the navigation interests. In the debate over river funding, four feet became a magic number. A four-foot draft line was painted on many steamboats; pilots like George Merrick wanted their boats loaded to that measure, because "a big packet not loaded below the four-foot line was not laden to the money-making point."[68] Forty-two inches of water was considered "deep," and a strong crew could drag a heavy boat through six inches of sandbar if it had to, or "grasshopper" the paddlewheel across the top. In the first two hundred miles below St. Paul, the river averaged only three feet deep and dropped to a foot or less in many spots during low-water years.[69]

In 1866, when the railroad reached St. Paul from Chicago, Congress appropriated funds for navigation improvements, including $200,000 at the Des Moines Rapids, $100,000 at the Rock Island Rapids, $550,000 for snag boats and dredges for western rivers, and $550,000 for "general improvements" of the Mississippi, Arkansas, Ohio, and Missouri rivers.[70] Among the projects given the go-ahead was a Corps survey of the river between St. Paul and Rock Island for building a four-foot channel, measured at the low-water point in the drought year of 1864. If the river fell as low as it did in 1864, the plan allowed for at least forty-eight inches of water to remain in the channel. It was the first major step in decades of efforts by Congress and the Corps to clear a channel for shipping on the upper river. Corps offices were established at St. Paul and Keokuk (which moved to Rock Island in 1869).[71]

Other than cementing the Corps of Engineers at the center of federal involvement on the river, the 1866 act didn't get much done. The Corps undertook a plan of scraping sandbars and removing snags, overhanging trees, and sunken vessels in hopes of making a clear four-foot channel. Competition from railroads and low-water years in 1868 and 1871 helped scuttle the scraping project short of the four-foot depth, and a call went out for more permanent measures. Merely moving sand, gravel, and stumps would not work. In 1874, the year Bosse was hired, the Rock Island district commander, Colonel J. N. Macomb, was ordered to survey the river from St. Anthony to Grafton, Illinois, to assess the feasibility of a continuous channel of four and a half to six feet at low water.[72] The Corps ordered Montgomery Meigs, the son of Robert E. Lee's assistant, to supervise the job.

In 1878, under pressure from farm groups, merchants, railroad critics, and lumber and milling interests, Congress authorized the Corps to establish and maintain a four-and-a-half-foot channel (measured at low water) from St. Paul to the mouth of the Illinois River at Grafton, a few miles above St. Louis. Ships laden to the four-foot watermark could remain profitable and free floating, and, it was thought, compete with the railroads. The timber industry, represented by the powerful Frederick Weyerhaeuser and his Mississippi River Logging Company, would get a constant flow of water for lumber rafts. This would be the first project to radically change the Upper Mississippi River's physical and ecological character. The days of the free-flowing river were numbered. In the next fifteen years, the Corps built sixty-six miles of dams and seventy miles of shoreline protection from St. Anthony to Grafton.

Bosse was transferred to Rock Island in 1878 to help map the Mississippi as part of the channel project. The work made him intimately familiar with the river. He spent the rest of his life surveying and drawing, sounding the river, measuring elevation, and calculating flow, drainage, and slope between towns. He and his assistant, A. J. Stibolt, completed an eighty-three-page map of the upper river in 1879, although the map was not published until 1887–88 (this map is reproduced at the end of this book). The maps, which detailed every wing dam, closing dam, levee, and island, were updated three times and were in use on the river until the 1930s, when lock and dam systems made them outdated.

As Bosse mapped the river, the four-and-a-half-foot channel began with dredging and wing dam and closing dam construction. The engineers' goal was no less than to change the natural course of the river. Countless streams and rivers flow into the Mississippi, and the floodplain contained thousands of acres of backwaters. In some places, there were multiple channels. Where the river became wide and shallow, wing dams—piles of willow mats called fascines and limestone rock that jut into the river perpendicular to the shore—were built to force the water into a single narrow channel (Plates 41 and 42). The principle is to increase the flow of water by decreasing the space through which it runs. The name and design, first used in America by Major Long on the Ohio River in 1826, had been in and out of favor for decades. Its effect was permanent. Silt eroded from the Mississippi's shores along with the silt of hundreds of tributaries to settle behind and between the wing dams. The Corps succeeded in constricting the river, moving its banks together.[73] The effects can be seen in Bosse's photographs (Plate 17). Brush mats and rock called revetments lined the banks opposite the wing dams, slowing erosion caused by increased current. Closing dams, built from shore to island or from island to island, shut off the braided river and side channels. By 1905, the Corps had built 226 miles of dams and set down 197 miles of revetments, at an estimated cost of about $20,000 per mile.[74] Hundreds of men and a fleet of towboats, dredges, snag boats, steamships, and barges did the work (Plate 13).

Wing dams did not always work well, particularly during periods of low water. Typically in late summer or early fall, a low-water period meant less scouring volume and more breaks in the main channel. And at the two major rapids, wing dams and closing dams would not be enough. At Rock Island, blasting and chiseling through the bedrock continued between 1867 and 1886 until a channel of four feet was created. At the Des Moines Rapids, where the bedrock ran for eleven miles, engineers designed a lateral canal dug between 1867 and 1877 and an intricate system of three locks to move boat traffic.[75] The Corps also built a series of reservoirs between St. Anthony and Leech Lake between 1883 and 1912 to make it possible to increase the river's flow during low water.

Ironically, commercial traffic on the upper river declined even as the Corps continued the multi-million-dollar project; steamboats carrying freight were supplanted by the railroads in the 1880s, leaving timber rafting the only significant traffic on the river by the 1890s. Mark Twain, in *Life on the Mississippi*, commented on the phenomenon: "When there used to be four thousand steamboats and ten thousand acres of coal-barges, and rafts, and trading scows, there wasn't a lantern from St. Paul to New Orleans, and the snags were thicker than the bristles on a hog's back; and now, when there's three dozen steamboats and nary a barge or a raft, government has snatched out all the snags, lit up the shores like Broadway, and a boat's as safe on the river as she'd be in heaven."[76] In 1870, federal inspectors examined 113 steamboats on the upper river and found them to carry 41,810 tons; by 1900, even with a part of the new channel finished, inspectors examined 159 boats, but they carried only 17,301 tons.[77]

Despite competition from railroads, Bosse's river was still a commercial highway of some import in the last half of the nineteenth century. Lumbering remained a significant river-related business. In 1879, 73 mills dotted the river between Lake Pepin and St. Louis. In 1880, one estimate placed the number of sawmills on the Upper Mississippi River and its tributaries at 275. Together they processed 2 billion board feet of lumber for shipping downstream.[78] Bosse had a particular affection for lumber, and his photographs feature acres of rafts visible from the bluffs and muscular towboats churning downstream pushing the remnants of the northern forests. The trend toward urbanization in the north following the Civil War created a great demand for high-quality lumber, and the ideal tree for city building was the white pine. Plentiful in the northern forests of Wisconsin and Minnesota, white pine was lightweight yet strong, it grew straight, and, most important for getting to market, it was buoyant.

The primary by-product of millions of board feet of cut forest was sawdust, most of which was dumped into the Mississippi and its tributaries. In Minneapolis, home to the greatest concentration of sawmills, the Corps estimated that mills produced 1.5 million board feet of sawdust in 1880.[79] Much of it traveled only as far as St. Paul or Hastings, where it found a home on a spit or a sandbar and settled. The four-and-a-half-foot channel project would help scour the river of the sawdust sandbars.[80]

But the four-and-a-half-foot project was never finished. Political pressures on the Corps resulted in a deeper, more expensive and ecologically damaging six-foot channel plan in 1907. It, too, was never completed. Since the river below St. Louis featured a nine-foot channel, the six-foot project was criticized as outmoded almost from the moment it passed Congress. Shipping interests had to break bulk at St. Louis for upstream travel or use smaller barges that drafted less water. The opening of the Panama Canal—also built by the Corps of Engineers—in 1914 and an agricultural panic from July 1920 to March 1922 put financial pressure on farm and navigation interests, as well. A nine-foot channel project that resulted in a system of twenty-nine locks and dams replaced the six-foot plan beginning in the 1920s, helped along by Secretary of Commerce Herbert Hoover. Opposition from the Izaak Walton League and other sportsmen's groups indicated a national awareness of environmental issues, but the project was funded over their objections in 1930. Signed by President Hoover during the depths of the Great Depression, the bill authorized an initial funding of $7.5 million for reconstruction of the river channel. The price would rise into the hundreds of millions of dollars. By the 1950s and 1960s, the river had become a series of river-lakes, or what the engineers called "slack water navigation pools." As one engineer told *Time* magazine in 1951, "We enjoy pushing rivers around."[81] And the river from Baton Rouge to the mouth, as measured by volume of cargo, would become the world's largest port.[82]

By the turn of the century, the environmental effects of settlement, lumbering, milling, and navigation improvements were profound. The timber industry, for example, was its own worst enemy. Forests slow the runoff of snowmelt and rainwater, and when all the trees were felled, runoff flowed too quickly into the rivers and streams. Flood and drought cycles became more pronounced, making navigation troublesome or impossible. Some saw it coming. "The ploughing of the prairie, felling of the forests, erection of the mills, and other causes have already begun to disturb the former state of things. The water is no longer as clear and dark as it used to be, and more sand accumulates in the stream, and a noticeable quantity of saw-dust and chips from the lumber mills of the Mississippi, St. Croix, Chippeway, and Wisconsin is also deposited along the banks," wrote G. K. Warren, a district commander.[83] When Bosse began making maps on the river in 1874, the Mississippi possessed almost all of its natural character. When he printed his last photograph in 1893, after the construction of hundreds of wing dams, closing dams, revetments, locks, and levees, it was a picture of another river.

BOSSE AT WORK

Bosse's first prints, dated 1883, immediately place him in a rich tradition of government photographers and artists. Survey photography in the United States grew from both the art and the documentary traditions. With President Thomas Jefferson's Louisiana Purchase of 1803 and the Lewis and Clark expedition, interest in the western United States grew rapidly. Many expeditions, both public and private, followed. Written descriptions of the wonders and scenery of the region taxed the credulity of readers. To better document the landscape, Major Long was among the first to include an artist on a western expedition. Long went to the Rocky Mountains from 1819 to 1820 and took Samuel Seymour, a painter. Seymour attempted 150 landscapes and finished 60.[84] By the 1850s, artists (painters and illustrators) were an accepted part of any expedition, including government-sponsored trips. Still, the artwork was criticized as unbelievable—the images of geysers and amazing rock formations were beyond people's imaginations.

Landscape photography developed shortly after the unveiling of the daguerreotype in 1839. Two shapes of photographs emerged: the portrait, which was vertical, and the landscape, which was horizontal. Some authors note that portraits allowed photography to gain wide acceptance in society while landscapes won the attention of the elite and allowed photography to be greeted with interest by scholars and scientists.[85] Because exposure times for daguerreotypes were so long, the stillness of landscape made it a practical subject. Two years after the introduction of the daguerreotype, Joseph-Philibert Girault de Prangey made topographical views of the Near East and Egypt.[86] Historian John Wood argues that the daguerreotype aesthetic fit with the romantic aesthetic, which was steeped in a picturesque view of the world but also in the ideals of science, experimental observation and understanding nature.[87] Landscape pictures developed at the same time as the fields of biology, geology, and sociology became established in Western cultures. Coupled with the exploration of new lands in the frontier culture of America, the new medium gave meaning to the landscape, allowing it to be "ordered" visually at the same time the social system needed it to be scaled for settlement.

View is an important term. Another historian, Peter Bacon Hales, suggests that a view is a particular form, "surrounded at its boundaries by the landscape painting, the lithographic 'bird's eye,' the city plat, the map, the scientific survey report, and the government topographer's panorama."[88] Much of that description fits Bosse's work. No matter the specific subject, the view combines art, photography, capitalism, and science—in short, American culture and social change. When Bosse named books of his photographs "Views on the Mississippi," he was but one of many nineteenth-century photographers and essayists to use *view* in the title.[89] The view as a dominant form ended by the early twentieth century as photography became more democratic and pluralistic.

The largest and most comprehensive views of the American West, by Robert N. Vance, S. N. Carvalho, and John Wesley Jones, were lost or destroyed. (Most of Bosse's negatives met the same fate.) Carvalho and Jones risked their lives trying to make daguerreotypes of the frontier, indicating that survey photography was a romantic journey whose purpose was to catch a glimpse, make a record, and create a sense of the place called "the West." Oliver Wendell Holmes, who wrote several essays on photography between 1859 and 1863, said outdoor photography was an agent of modernization, uniting the nation.[90] As the country became known and occupied, there may also have been a sense of nostalgia in landscape photographs.

Isaac Stevens's party, which left St. Paul in the spring of 1853 looking for a northern route for a Pacific railroad, was representative of government-sponsored trips. Stevens, governor of the Washington Territory and a former lieutenant in the Corps of Engineers, reported that the northern route was a good possibility because it had "vast resources of land, for agricultural development, timber, water and minerals."[91] Stevens's group included "two civilian engineers, a professional artist, a geologist, a surgeon-naturalist, and two noted scientists, Dr. George Gibbs and Dr. Thomas Cooper."[92] Daguerreotypist J. M. Stanley also went along. In the four major federal surveys after the Civil War (led by George Wheeler, F. V. Hayden, Clarence King, and John Wesley Powell), photographers were included. The surveys indicate not only the intent to explore, learn, and report, but also the intent to plan and build. Postwar images of the West continued to awe the public, but now they began to mark the expansion of the eastern infrastructure westward to exploit vast potential resources of the Midwest for agriculture, the Upper Mississippi Valley for timber and minerals, and the West for mining and ranching. Through a series of related developments in timber, mining, farming, and transportation, photographs show the progress of American expansionism.

Documentary photography is generally made from a particular point of view that attempts to persuade as well as inform. The aesthetic feelings of beauty and awe elicited by landscape photography may have furthered its persuasive intent. For example, exploration photographs were often included with legislative lobbying materials. William Henry Jackson's photographs were bound in leather and sent to members of Congress in 1872 as part of the campaign that made Yellowstone a national park, though their effect is under debate.[93] Photography became linked with the power of the state. Examples include images of Napoleon and Abraham Lincoln, propaganda photographs in wartime, photographs illustrating national achievements like railroads, and images of society's deviants whom the state controlled by taking their pictures.[94]

During this same time, America was establishing a cultural identity. While American painting tended to be constrained by the European traditions of portrait, historical, and landscape painting, photographs by Carleton Watkins and Eadweard Muybridge won awards for innovative composition and technical expertise in European photographic shows. Thus, while survey photography was documentary and concerned with expansionism, some photographers were concerned with their photographs' aesthetic qualities.[95] Well-known landscape artists such as Albert Bierstadt, S. R. Gifford, and Thomas Moran accompanied surveys on which Muybridge, Jackson, and Timothy O'Sullivan worked as photographers. And photographers learned about art from their interaction with painters.[96] Moran and Jackson explored Yellowstone together in 1871. "Moran became greatly interested in photography, and it was my good fortune to have him at my side during all that season to help me solve many problems of composition. While learning from me, he was constantly putting in far more than he took out," Jackson wrote.[97] As early as the 1860s, critics argued to include landscape photography as fine art.[98]

Bosse, who was an accomplished portrait painter, was not opposed to painting on his photographs, and his retouching had precedents in the work of Muybridge and others. In fact, Muybridge sought the help of the painter Bierstadt in making his images as early as 1875.[99] Muybridge, who thought himself in competition with Watkins, would dress up his landscapes by adding a second negative to a print for more depth to the sky, for example. He would chop down a few trees to get a better view. Bosse did the same thing; fresh stumps are evident in many of his landscapes, including his *Mouth of Chippewa River,* 1885 (Plate 25). Bosse also had workmen move out of the way, sometimes leaving their tools, lunch boxes, and coats behind in the scene (Plate 54). In a few photos, he painted in three birds in flight.

None of this was qualitatively different from O'Sullivan and Alexander Gardner's moving a dead Confederate sharpshooter to four or five places on the Gettysburg battlefield for posed pictures. Bosse also extended horizon lines for aesthetic reasons and painted in clouds where none existed at the moment of the photograph. A few fluffy clouds made the sky less stark and the photograph more sentimental. In his way, Bosse was anticipating the pictorialists championed by Alfred Stieglitz after the turn of the century; they would "make a picture" rather than merely record nature. Of course, the first to do this were the daguerreotypists, who employed engravers to produce copies for sale. The engravers added clouds, carriages, and even people because the insensitive plates could not record them.[100]

Fine art sells, and many government photographers sold their photographic views on the open market, linking their aesthetic properties to profit. Stereoscopic photography was invented in 1857 and quickly became extremely popular and profitable. A stereoscopic camera has two lenses two and a half inches apart on the same horizontal plane, which is the same relation as the average human eyes from center to center. A thin partition divides the left and right portions of the camera. The effect is a double camera and a three-dimensional view when the photograph is placed in a viewer.[101] The same effect could be reproduced without a special camera by moving a single-lens camera a few inches left or right. The market for these pictures was such that photographers on the western surveys did not need to be paid by the government, for they knew that the sale of their photographs would more than compensate them for their time.[102] Photographs of all sizes and types sold at photographic galleries, studios, and exhibits.

Unlike most of his predecessors and contemporaries, Bosse ignored the marketplace even though the Western View Company, a stereocard marketer, was located near his home in Rock Island and the river cities of Dubuque and Keokuk also had stereocard publishers. Bosse did not sell stereoscopic views to the Anthony Company, the leading publisher of the day, or submit any image to the *Philadelphia Photographer* (at least none that it printed). The Army did sell Bosse's unmounted prints for forty cents each to interested parties, and a few showed up on letterheads and in books and articles.[103]

Though people in the Midwest could not buy a Bosse stereocard as they could an O'Sullivan or a Jackson, there were opportunities for the public to view the German immigrant's photographs. The most prominent was the World's Columbian Exposition in Chicago in 1893. Jackson's Denver-based company was there, showing landscape views, as was Muybridge and his firm. The photographs of O'Sullivan and Jack Hillers were put on display by their sponsoring government agencies. The sale of photographs and negatives was tightly controlled on the grounds at the exhibition, which irritated photographers of nature like C. C. Curtis, who wanted to sell his images of giant sequoias.[104] But interest in the exhibit among photographers ran high, and there was competition for display space.[105]

The Corps of Engineers, like many other government departments, produced an impressive exhibit. Located in the Government Building, the Corps preferred photographs to maps and sketches. Captain William Marshall, the man in charge, showcased twenty-four by thirty-inch glass transparencies, a panorama of the Chicago lakefront, twenty-seven framed bromide prints, and seventeen bound volumes, including at least one of Bosse's cyanotype albums.[106] Marshall asked his district engineers for contributions to the exhibit and specifically requested photographs; Bosse asked that his work be included.[107] Unfortunately for Bosse and the exhibit, a shipment of three of Bosse's negatives was dropped during transport and destroyed. The pictures, including two of the Des Moines Rapids guard lock and a snagging scene, were meant to be converted to glass transparencies. "The injury will be in good cause," wrote Major Mackenzie to Marshall. "They are intended for public use and must take their chances."[108] Mackenzie sent two negatives of the locks at the Des Moines Rapids to replace the broken three (Plate 74). Thousands of people viewed the photographs and the Corps won an award for its exhibit. And, in no small coincidence, historian Frederick Jackson Turner read his essay announcing the closing of the frontier at the newly opened Art Institute of Chicago during the exhibition. A few blocks away, Bosse's blueprint photographs inadvertently illustrated Turner's thesis.

Exposure at the Columbian Exposition resulted in a call for copies of Bosse's photos from several quarters, including the U.S. Department of Justice, a professor at Columbia College in New York City, and a hydrologist from Mississippi who was writing a book on the river. Organizers of the Louisiana Purchase Exposition in St. Louis in 1903 asked for materials, and they displayed at the exposition a map made by Bosse.[109] The record is unclear as to whether the St. Louis exhibit also included Bosse's photographs. The U.S. Commission to the Paris Exposition of 1900 asked for Bosse's photographs, and there is some evidence that Meigs loaned photographs from his personal collection, but it is unclear whether those pictures were taken by Meigs or Bosse or someone else.[110]

Although Jackson and some of the other government survey photographers whose work was displayed at the Columbian Exposition occasionally experimented with cyanotypes, none of them stuck to that form as extensively as Bosse did. Critics of the day did not like the intense color of the cyanotype prints: brown or gray was okay, blue was not. The critic Peter Henry Emerson, Ralph Waldo Emerson's brother, said, "No one but a vandal would print a landscape in red, or in cyanotype."[111] An English critic, R. Child Bayley, wrote, "There are certain subjects which the colour is said to suit, and I live in the hope that one day I may see such a subject."[112] Bosse's extensive use of the Prussian blue process was probably attributable to the culture of the Corps of Engineers and its use of cyanotype chemicals and manufactured paper for mapmaking and engineering drawings and sketches. Viewed a century later, it gives his photographs a fresh look.

As the 1880s were a time of great technological change in photography, Bosse used both old and new methods and equipment. Cyanotypes, for example, dated back to 1842, when Sir John Herschel filed for a number of patents on the process. Dry plate photography was introduced in 1880 and Bosse made use of it by 1885.[113]

Bosse's extensive, almost exclusive, use of cyanotypes makes his photographs different from those of other landscape photographers, who only occasionally used the process for making proofs. His use of landscape, rather than portraits of flora and fauna, makes him different from other noted cyanotype practitioners. Herschel's invention held several distinctions: it was the first successful nonsilver photographic printing process; it was used for the first photographically illustrated book; it eventually became cheap, simple, and relatively permanent; and it enjoyed a successful run in commercial drawings that would become known as blueprints.[114] As chemist and cyanotype historian Mike Ware has noted, the cyanotype process is the only pioneering printing technique that survives unchanged to the present.[115]

The inventors of photography, Louis Daguerre and Henry Fox Talbot, used silver as the key element in making photographic prints. Herschel, who was interested in new types of printing processes and photosensitive chemicals, used iron salts instead. Herschel's process called for two chemical compounds, ferric ammonium citrate and potassium ferrocyanide, to be mixed and applied to ordinary paper with a brush or a sponge. The paper is dried in the dark and ready for exposure. The color made from his process was Prussian blue, a pigment discovered in 1704. Botanist Anna Atkins employed the technique to photograph plant life in the 1850s in her series of books titled *British Algae*.[116] But by the time of Herschel's death in 1871, cyanotype printing had fallen into disuse ("lying dormant," his obituary stated).[117]

Commercial operators looking for a cheap and easy way to proof negatives and make drawings reinvigorated the process in the late 1870s and 1880s with the introduction of prepared "ferro-prussiate" paper; the process also enjoyed a brief revival among amateur photographers at about that time. Though many art critics scorned the deep blue prints, the cyanotype did have its defenders. John Tennant, editor of an influential photography magazine, wrote in 1900: "This prejudice against the blue print because of its color is, in itself, curiously interesting. In everyday life we are inclined to be enthusiastic about everything blue, from the deep blue of the sea or the deep depths of blue in a woman's eyes, to the marvelous blue of old Delft ware or the Willow Plates of years ago."[118] As Ware pointed out, blue certainly held a distinguished position among painters, but it occurs in nature infrequently, which may have led critics to dismiss it as unrealistic.[119]

Bosse probably became familiar with cyanotypes in his mapmaking assignments for the Corps; the Army bought prepared paper in large quantities for its district offices.[120] To Bosse and his German-speaking colleagues, its color was *Berliner blau*, named after the home of its discoverer, a Berlin artist named Diesbach. Cyanotypes are extremely vulnerable to light and alkali, which makes the survival of Bosse's prints more remarkable (particularly the album that lived on the dredge for sixty years). Printing times could also be relatively slow; thirty minutes' exposure to an ultraviolet light source was not uncommon. Nonetheless, his large-format pictures are extremely sharp and detailed, indicating that Bosse took great care in making exposures in good light and on still days and was particular about his prints.[121] In some instances, reflections of sunlight on the windows of houses and boats indicate that the photos were taken fairly early in the morning, before the sun was high in the sky. The clarity of the photographs is no doubt due to Bosse's using a fixed-focus lens and making contact prints. The originals have lines so delicate and razor sharp that they look like engravings printed in blue. The painting on some of the prints is done in a carefully matched blue wash, possibly in a solution made of the same substance as the cyanotypes. Others have ornate, Victorian-style borders.

Cyanotype paper was best prepared fresh each day, but that would not have been a problem for Bosse because the chemicals were easily manipulated in the field. Once the paper was prepared and dry (in a room or container away from the rays of the sun), a negative could be placed on the paper and the entire setup exposed to the sun. A weak image would appear and be brought to full strength by washing in water, of which there was no shortage on the Mississippi River. Many of Bosse's pictures have great depth of field (Plate 29). Aperture settings must have been small. A horse and carriage are substantially blurred in one of his pictures of the Rock Island flood of 1888, indicating that the vehicle moved a few steps during exposure (Plate 57). In a photograph of Fort Snelling, the river is blurred to a lake-like smoothness by the length of exposure (Plate 9). In other pictures, trees and bushes in the foreground are moving (Plate 19).

The photographs are carefully composed. Horizon lines are straight and usually fall high in the prints, in keeping with the principle that unequal division of space creates more dynamic pictures. The subjects are seldom photographed straight on. Instead of positioning his camera directly adjacent to the steamboats and bridges on the river, Bosse moved up or downstream to shoot the subject from an oblique perspective. Thus, whether he was shooting from the bank of the river or from a bluff, Bosse created dynamic images in oblique and aerial (two- and three-point) perspectives (Plates 16 and 39).

Some of the photographs have classical compositions, in which the viewer looks off the side of a bluff to the subjects in the middle distance and the background (Plate 12). Many of the photos have more romantic and picturesque compositions, which include foreground in the composition. Often, as in European landscapes, Bosse posed someone (possibly his assistant, A. J. Stibolt, or his boss, Mackenzie) in the foreground (Plate 36). Sometimes these observers point to the river or to projects in the river that the Corps was working on. Other times the observers stand or sit or lie back gazing at the river, and occasionally they sit in boats or even reach into the water. Sometimes the figures point to Corps projects. The arrangement of the line of the river often carries the eye from the foreground to the middle ground, then to the background.

Many of the photographs are taken from vantages on bluffs. This makes the views into dramatic landscapes. The bird's-eye perspective empowers viewers, who are looking down at the river, though the river holds its own visually because of its sheer size and through the objective view, which displays how it dominates the terrain. Since the river is usually the subject of the photos, it is nearly always arranged obliquely. Thus, it is diagonal and usually recedes from bottom left to top right or bottom right to top left.

The albums themselves are distinctly Victorian in design and vary slightly from one another. In the St. Paul set, the pictures are oval. The Rock Island cyanotypes (many of them printed from the same negatives as the St. Paul set) are printed as ovals with decorative borders, some geometric and others stippled. Many of the Dubuque images are rectangles or full frame. In all sets, the calligraphy on the covers is large; its baseline is curvilinear and the largest letters for the title are outline letters with illustrated interiors. The title pages use an interesting mixture of clean modern letterforms in script, roman, and italic styles and a sans serif type. Almost all photographs are clearly and precisely hand-titled and dated in ink (baselines in light pencil are visible on some prints). The prints are always displayed from upriver to downriver, so one can take a photographic journey by turning the pages.

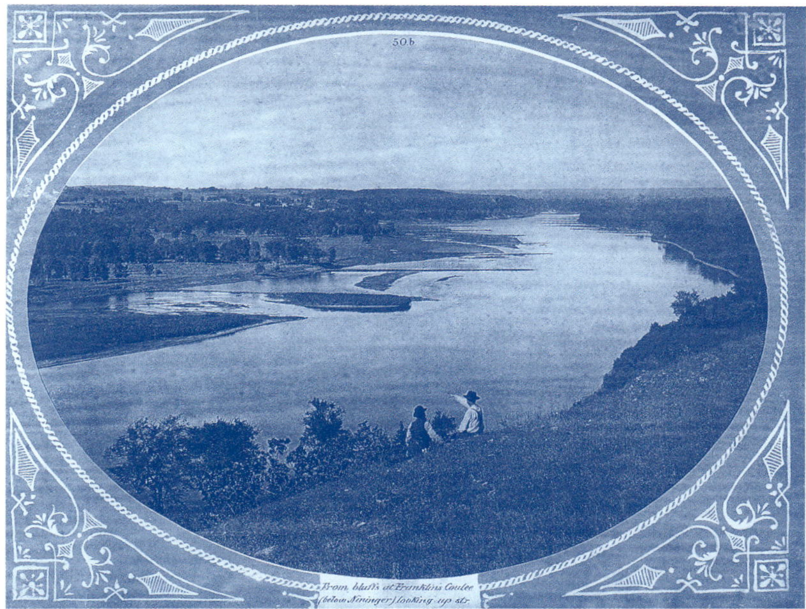

From bluffs at Franklin's Coulee (below Nininger) looking up str., 1891 (U.S. Army Corps of Engineers, Rock Island District). *Franklin's Coulee* is a study in how to compose a landscape photograph as well as a documentary on environmental changes in the Mississippi River.

How did Bosse work? Since none of his notes survived, we can only speculate. He needed a darkroom to prepare the cyanotype paper; a room aboard the *General Barnard* or a surveyor's barge would have sufficed. It seems that Bosse was accompanied by at least one assistant, probably Stibolt, when he did his camera work, for there is usually at least one person in his photographs and toting the bulk of the gear to the top of a bluff would have required another set of hands. Most of the photographs were taken in the spring or fall; one exception is a series of five to eight prints taken in January 1890 in the Twin Cities. The trees are bare, snow covers the riverbank, and there isn't a boat or a person in sight. It was a rare year that Lake Pepin was open and passable in early winter should Bosse have traveled to St. Paul by boat.

Environmental changes are evident in Bosse's landscapes. The view in a photograph taken below the Minnesota town of Nininger can inspire a sense of loss; it is a glimpse of ecological disruption to come. The 1891 picture *From bluffs at Franklin's Coulee (below Nininger) looking up str.* is a typical Bosse photograph. The Mississippi River near Nininger, located twenty-one river miles south of St. Paul, posed characteristic threats to navigation: a slough that flowed into the river, several bends, islands, and a wide area where the water ran shallow. Between Hastings and Nininger, the shallow portion of the river often kept steamboats from reaching St. Paul; during low water a person or a horse could walk across the river. "The steamers have lately been forced to take the narrow channel around the island, and so confined it is, that the banks are literally worn off by the rubbing of the steamer's guards," Meigs wrote in 1875.[122] In the summer of 1891, the river ran so dry at Nininger that it fell below the 1864 low-water mark, the shallow depth at which all navigation construction decisions were based.

The second closing dam built on the river was constructed at Nininger Slough in 1875 to divert water from the slough into the main channel. An obstruction called Nininger Bar had formed near the end of Franklin's Coulee and the lower mouth of Nininger Slough. The wing dams and closing dam channeled the water into the bar (which consisted primarily of sawmill refuse) and had washed it away by the time the photograph was taken in 1891. Between 1875 and 1930, the Corps added dozens more closing dams and wing dams. Bosse's photograph shows that by 1891, several wing dams were built there.

Bosse's 1891 photograph highlights several aspects of wing dam construction. In water hydraulics, the channel tends to fall along the outside of a bend in the river since the water flows faster at that point, scouring the river bottom. The wing dams are placed on the inside of the bend to enhance this effect. In straight stretches of the river, especially at low water, the thalweg meanders, often in small pools, each unconnected to the next. The shifting shallow spaces between the pools of the main channel were problematic for riverboats. By carefully situating the wing dams, the Corps was able to use the Mississippi to scour itself a clear channel, washing away the low spots by the force of the current. Several series of Corps maps, many drawn by Bosse, show how wing dams changed the bottom of the river and its depth, eliminating the shallows. Bosse's photograph shows the constricting of the channel.

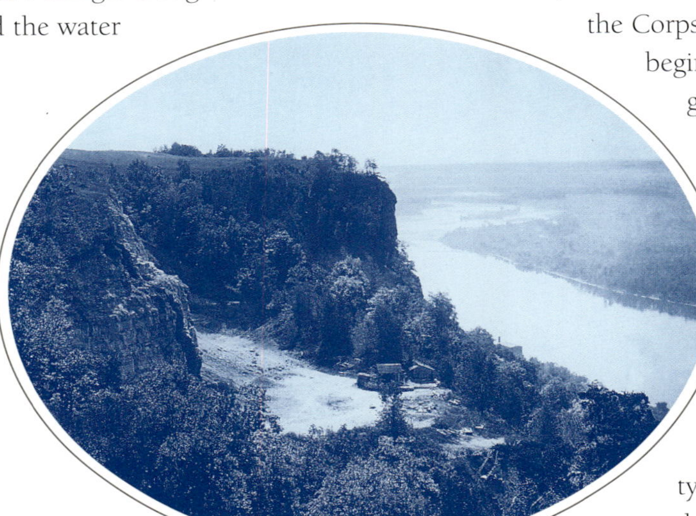

Richtman's Quarry at Fountain City, Wis., 1891 (U.S. Army Corps of Engineers, St. Paul District). Jacob Richtman and his partner, Albert Kirchner, supplied the Corps with limestone for dams from this quarry.

Another effect of the wing dams, sedimentation, is shown in Bosse's photograph. Bosse's work illustrates how the wing dams redirected and then captured sediment, permanently narrowing the river. (Sometimes sediment was dumped behind the dams by the Corps's dredges.) An ecological progression then begins. The sediment becomes riverbank, and grasses and bushes take hold. Willow trees and other early-growth plants move in, and soon the old riverbank is nothing more than a memory. As the right bank of the shoreline in front of the wing dams in Bosse's photograph indicates, the Corps lined the outside bend in the river with revetments to slow erosion from the increased current.

Artistically, *Franklin's Coulee* is also typical. Two observers are posed for scale and to help establish the foreground (along with the bushes at the bottom left). The river creates a dynamic visual line, flowing left to right, bottom to top in the distance. The composition in the picture is geometric, with the camera positioned and the scene framed to form a large triangle on the left and three small ones on the right. The high horizon line creates an unequal division of vertical space, and the jutting wing dams, decreasing in size toward the horizon line, establish an interesting pattern.

The use of photographs to document the construction of wing dams is also significant. There are only a few such photographs, but they show a fairly complex and ingenious process (Plates 40, 41, and 42). Willow saplings were cut and woven into mats called fascines, a German design. The fascines, one hundred feet long, five feet deep, and twenty feet wide, were floated on barges to the dam site and laid in place. Limestone was piled onto the floating fascines. (There are also several photos of quarries that supplied the limestone.) Workers then lowered the rock-covered fascines into place in the water, one layer after another. Men threw rocks on the mats to sink them. The photos show that the Corps built the dams by putting layer after layer of rock-filled fascines in the river. No concrete or stone pilings were needed, although wooden poles sometimes were driven into the muck to help anchor the structure.

A few memoirs from those days survive. A granddaughter of one of the dam contractors, Alberta Kirchner Hill, spent nineteen summers with her family's fleet. "I could even smell the delightfully blended odor of the willows and the creosoted marline twine with which the bundles were held together," she wrote in 1961. "It came to me strongly every time the men hoisted a swishing bundle of brush to their gunny-sack-protected shoulders."[123] Hill's grandfather was a partner of Jacob Richtman in a quarry near Fountain City, Wisconsin; Bosse photographed the quarry in 1891. The government paid its contractors around one dollar per cubic yard of limestone and thirty-nine cents per cubic yard of brush.[124] The stones weighed from five to one hundred pounds each.

Closing dams were the most dangerous to construct. Water would rush through the new channel, uprooting the anchors of the boats and barges doing the work. Occasionally the entire fleet would be swept downstream. The men had to work quickly. "No sooner had a barge of rocks been pulled up to the dam than the symmetry of the load was destroyed as the men began the routine of sinking the mat," Hill

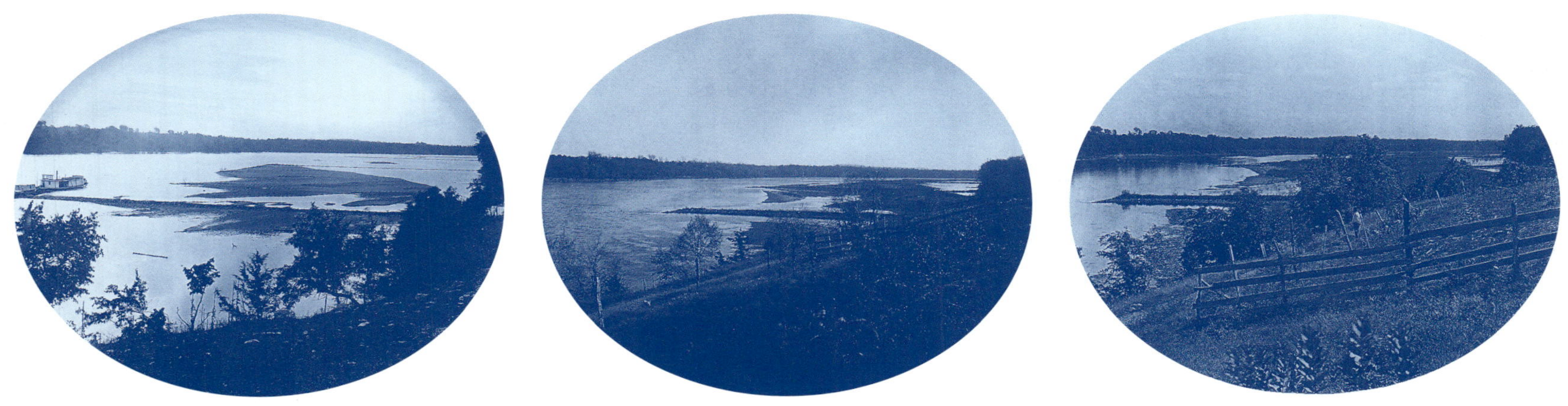

From left: *From bluffs at Merrimac, Minn. looking down stream,* 1885, 1889, and 1891 (Mayo Foundation). Showing environmental change over time is one of the unique qualities of Bosse's photographs. During the six years these photographs were taken, the river downstream is slowly filling in behind a series of dams. Bosse's development as a photographer is also apparent.

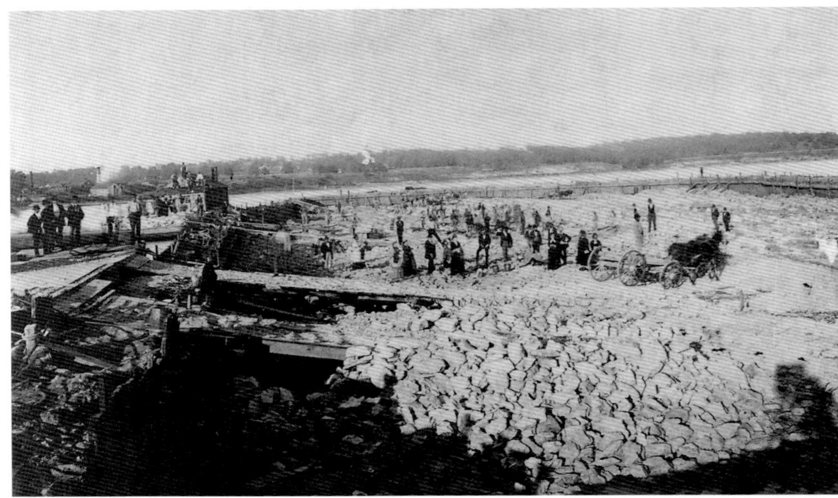

wrote. "From the quarterboats you could hear the big rocks hitting each other, like a rapid-fire rage. . . . As the mat went down under the load . . . a splashing began. The sound grew in intensity as the mat sank lower and lower in the water."[125] Sediment filled in behind the dams, cementing them in place. The process works well on the Mississippi, and most wing dams live useful lives for many decades.

Bosse used photographs as an aid to his drawing and mapmaking. Here he sketched a coffer dam on the Rock Island Rapids with the aid of a photograph (U.S. Army Corps of Engineers, Rock Island District).

The organization of all of the albums is important to interpreting Bosse's work. While they are organized in a north to south geographic presentation, they are not chronological. Instead, the photographs are grouped by location, so views taken two, four, and six years apart are together. Photographic clusters of from two to six photographs allow us to become witnesses, with Bosse, of changes that were occurring in the history of the river. The photos that appear to be landscape river scenes actually document the building and impact of the wing dams and closing dams. The clusters of photographs across a number of years show the dramatic effects the dams had on the river. The 1889 and 1891 photographs were intentionally taken during low water, so the dams and other landmarks could easily be seen. High water made dam construction impossible, so perhaps the lack of pictures in some years may have been due to environmental factors like flooding (although the 1880s were unusually low-water years). Maps, many drawn by Bosse and his assistant, also illustrated environmental changes. It is probable that Bosse used the photographs to help him prepare maps, as photographs were often taken as aids to drawing in the nineteenth century.

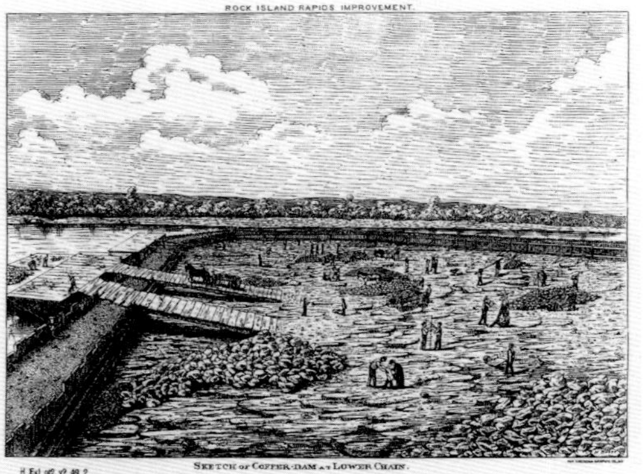

Bosse made prints from photos taken in the years 1883, 1885, and 1888 through 1893. His work in five of those years—1883, 1888, 1890, 1892, and 1893—resulted in fewer than ten prints from each year. It is possible that in some years government funds were available for his photography and in other years money was scarce. Presidents Chester A. Arthur (1881–85) and Grover Cleveland (1886–89, 1893–97), for example, were generally opposed to the river and harbor bills that supplied the Corps with its funding. There are only two prints (of those that are dated) that survive from 1883, two from 1892, and two from 1893. Eight photos taken in 1888 documented the flooding of Davenport and Rock Island. That leaves 1885, 1889, and 1891 as his most productive years. Some of the 1885 shots are relatively simple compositions of steamboats and bridges, although he had begun to experiment with landscapes in that year, including photographs of Minneiska, Minnesota (Plate 29), and Queen's Bluff (Plate 34). By 1889, Bosse was photographing everything from landscapes to steamboats to bridges to cityscapes.

His 1889 photographs provide a glimpse into how the man did his job and the environmental factors that went into the pictures. That year the river was at low water, which was a good time for engineers, surveyors, and mapmakers to do their work: islands, sandbars, chains, and other hazards normally out of sight were often visible. The Corps requested an extra $100 for photographs in October 1889.[126] The low stage of water in the Mississippi River presented a good opportunity for illustrating by photographs certain portions of works of importance, Mackenzie wrote to the chief of engineers, and he had ordered Bosse to begin work with his camera.[127] It was also a contentious year for the Corps: a dam near Read's Landing was blown up by a lumberman in August, and Mackenzie and lumber baron Frederick Weyerhaeuser battled in court over use of a boom near Beef Slough.

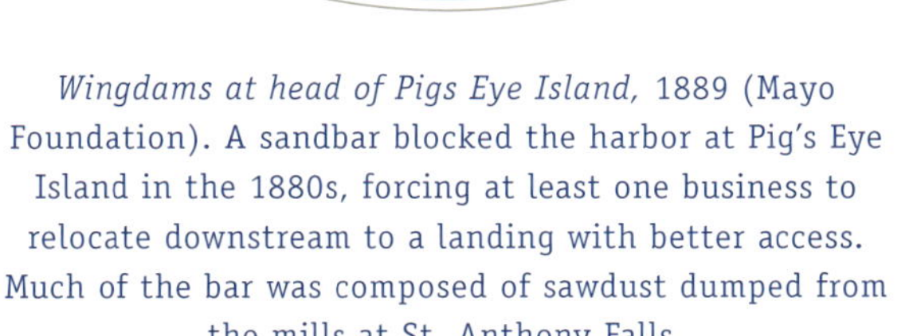

Wingdams at head of Pigs Eye Island, 1889 (Mayo Foundation). A sandbar blocked the harbor at Pig's Eye Island in the 1880s, forcing at least one business to relocate downstream to a landing with better access. Much of the bar was composed of sawdust dumped from the mills at St. Anthony Falls.

The 1889 trip began in late September or early October, possibly aboard the *Barnard*, which was the Corps's best boat on the upper river. Over the next two months, Bosse took at least forty-one photographs. The first two photographs were taken at Keithsburg, Illinois, on October 4, near a beach where nude bathing was allowed after sundown (Plate 62). Twelve days later, Bosse's party was in St. Paul, and he went to work with his camera again. On October 16, he took two photographs of St. Paul, one of the city's Smith Avenue wagon bridge (Plate 11) and another at the site of Dam No. 2. There were environmental reasons for the Corps to be in St. Paul. In 1888, a spring flood year, there was so much refuse from the sawmills in Minneapolis (sawdust, wood chips, and other debris) that businesses along the river were forced to move when boats could not reach their docks. A plant on Pig's Eye Island (near South St. Paul) relocated ten river miles downstream to Merrimac because a sandbar blocked its harbor. On October 17, Bosse took two photographs of the Pig's Eye site; Mackenzie was about to ask Congress for more money to clean up the sawdust sandbars, and Bosse's photographs and maps may have served as visual evidence.[128]

The boat slowly made its way back to headquarters in Rock Island, on to Fort Madison, and back to Rock Island again, with Bosse disembarking every few days to make more exposures. In a few spots, like Merrimac Island and Nininger, he returned to points where he had made pictures in 1885. Going back to the same spot over several years made Bosse's pictures different from those of other government photographers and provides valuable documentation of the environmental changes wrought by the Corps and its channel constriction project. Near Minneiska on November 4 he photographed the steam launch *Elsie* moving a gigantic pile of brush used in wing dam construction (Plate 40) as the workers hurried to complete the task before winter iced them in. Near the Des Moines Rapids, on November 19, he made perhaps his best man-at-work photograph, a striking image at Mechanic's Rock of a figure holding a stadia rod behind the huge boulder named for a steamboat that crashed on its stone and sank (Plate 70).

A few days later, Bosse and his colleagues were at the Des Moines Rapids Canal, where the Corps anchored much of its fleet for the winter. By December 1, with winter closing in, the party was back upriver in Rock Island. Bosse made three more photographs of navigational hazards near the Rock Island Rapids in December before retiring his camera until January.

Bosse's views from the 1890s, including his 1892 photograph of a wagon bridge at Winona (Plate 32), show a craftsman at his best. For unknown reasons, just as his work was getting national attention at places like the 1893 Columbian Exposition, he quit making pictures. Or perhaps he did not quit. The answer could be as simple as that he created negatives up until his death in 1903, and the evidence is lost.

John Wood, in a 1997 essay, described the Prussian blue of cyanotypes as "joyous-ominous."[129] Perhaps this serves to describe the Prussian-American Bosse's career in its obscurity and resurrection. If Bosse quit making negatives in 1893, his reasons are as mysterious as the rest of his biography. There may have been a decline in interest in landscape photography in general and on Bosse's part in particular. Perhaps some of the romance of the river was gone: by the time of Bosse's death, the upper river carried only a handful of passenger packets, and the most difficult work of mapping the river was finished.

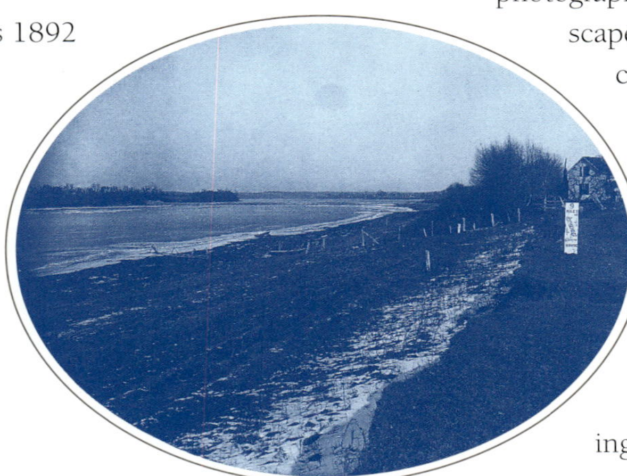

Behind Campbell's Island Rock Island Rapids, 1891 (Mayo Foundation). One of the threats to navigation above the Rock Island Rapids was the tricky current around Campbell's Island. The island is on the far left. The road sign advertises a boardinghouse.

Perhaps the new camera technologies, the negative reaction to cyanotypes among critics, or even something as mundane as the completion of the four-and-a-half-foot channel maps caused Bosse to put down his camera. Certainly the democratization of photography led many others to the craft, including some at the Corps. Meigs said as much in a 1900 letter to his superior: "A good many of the assistants and inspectors own cameras and are taking similar pictures."[130]

Some have suggested that Bosse might be considered a transitional figure in the history of photography, as the subject matter of leading photographers moved from a romantic concern with landscapes to an urbanized, industrialized twentieth-century America. With technical advances in mechanical reproductions, plates, enlargers, hand cameras, and flexible film in the 1880s, Bosse's old-fashioned way of taking documentary photographs was on its way out in favor of the pictorialist and photo-secessionist periods of the late nineteenth and early twentieth centuries.[131] Yet in his extensive use of the cyanotype, coupled with his style of printing, Victorian borders, retouching, use of models, and his eleven-by-fourteen camera, he may be seen as a predecessor to the art photography movement at the turn of the century.

Bosse's pictures leave us feeling nostalgic. We see the river as it will never be seen again, and our sense of loss is heightened by the appearance in the photographs of the environmental changes taking place. The wing dams and closing dams, the men at work, the dredges and snag boats and locks remind us that industrialization was served. The meandering, island-braided river is gone. All we have left are the photographs.

NOTES

The prints in this book draw from four of the five known collections of Bosse's photographs. The majority are from a volume at Mayo Foundation in Rochester, Minnesota, which was photographed by Brady Willette. The St. Paul and Rock Island district offices of the U.S. Army Corps of Engineers and the Mississippi River Museum at Dubuque, Iowa, each own a set of photographs. • If Bosse dated a print, the date is noted in the caption. Some prints include Bosse's own numbering system inked in at the top, indicating the placement of each print within the bound volume from which it was taken. The caption titles are his, in his original spelling. All of the prints are cyanotypes.

1. In the region then known as the Tri-Cities (Rock Island and Moline, Illinois, and Davenport, Iowa), German Americans were an important ethnic group. There were three German-language newspapers, five Turner clubs, and seasonal theatrical performances in German. Turner clubs, or *Turnverein,* were societies that offered social opportunities as well as organized gymnastics training for German immigrants in the United States in the late nineteenth century up until World War I.
2. This section is based on telephone conversations, e-mails, and the published record from a number of sources. Most important are an e-mail from Mike Conner to the author, November 12, 1999, and a telephone conversation, Mike Conner with the author, October 19, 1999.
3. "In Memoriam, Alexander Mackenzie," Annual Report of the Association of the Graduates of the United States Military Academy, June 12, 1921, 1–6.
4. This section is based on numerous conversations between John Anfinson and the author, as well as John Anfinson, "Henry Bosse's Priceless Photographs," *Ramsey County History* 27, no. 4 (Winter 1992–93): 4–9.
5. Denise Bethel, transcript of panel discussion, "Henry P. Bosse Photography Exhibit: Views on the Mississippi . . . Images of a Changing River," St. Paul, Minn., September 24, 1998.
6. Sotheby's Photographs (New York: Sotheby's, April 7–8, 1995).
7. Telephone conversations between Charles Wehrenberg and the author, October 27, 1999, and November 15, 1999.
8. As of 1894, according to Corps correspondence, there were about two hundred negatives in the Rock Island office.
9. Details of Bosse's early life were gathered from his obituaries, which appeared in at least six newspapers in the Tri-Cities. See "Causes His Death," *Rock Island Argus,* December 15, 1903, 7; "Henry P. Bosse," *Rock Island Union,* December 15, 1903, 5; "Henry Bosse Dead," *Rock Island Daily Times,* December 15, 1903, 9; "Prominent Man Passes," *Davenport Republican,* December 15, 1903, 8; "Henry P. Bosse," *Davenport Wochentliche Demokrat,* December 17, 1903, 4; and "Henry P. Bosse," *Rock Island-Moliner Volks-Zeitung,* December 15, 1903, 4. Among the relatives claimed by the Gneisenau family is John Gneisenau Neihardt, 1881–1973, an American poet famous for his writings on American Indians. See Lucile F. Aly, *John G. Neihardt: A Critical Biography* (Amsterdam, Netherlands: Rodolphi N.V., 1977), 12.
10. A Henry Bosse was among those listed in English newspapers as slightly wounded in the Battle of Waterloo, but that man fought in a British brigade. *http://napoleonic-literature.simplenet.com/WE/Casualties-18_June.html.* "List of Officers, Killed, Wounded, and Missing; Battle of the 18th," *London Gazette.*
11. Because Bosse claimed to be raised by the Roman Catholic Gneisenau family, his birth certificate may have been destroyed in 1945 along with other Catholic birth certificates in that section of East Germany at the close of World War II and the time of the Communist takeover. Of course, the lack of a birth certificate also leads to doubt about the identity of his parents, but two world wars, the history-erasing Communists, and uneven recordkeeping in mid-nineteenth-century Europe must be taken into account. Confounding the question is the listing of his birthplace on his tombstone as "Sonneburg, Magdeburg, Prussia." Maps of the day show no such village near Magdeburg. Perhaps his family supplied the headstone carver with information and simply misspelled Sommerschenburg as Sonneburg. Some of his obituaries list his birthplace as Sonnenburg, which isn't near the castle either.
12. Hajo Holborn, *A History of Modern Germany, 1648–1840* (New York: Knopf, 1964), 295.
13. See Christopher Kelly, *A Full and Circumstantial Account of the Memorable Battle of Waterloo* (London: T. Kelly, 1818 [1839 edition]).
14. Gneisenau retired from active duty in 1816, although he returned to lead an expedition against the Polish insurrec-

tion. He contracted cholera in Poland and died in 1831 at age seventy-one. The definitive works on Gneisenau's military career are G. H. Pertz and H. Delbruck, *Das Leben des Feldmarschalls Grafen Neithardt von Gneisenau*, 5 vols. (Berlin: G. Reimer, 1864, 1880).

15. Letter from Professor Emeritus Manfred Beckert, Magdeburg, Germany, to John Anfinson, October 26, 1996. I am grateful to Dr. Anfinson for sharing this letter with me.
16. "Causes His Death," *Rock Island Argus,* December 15, 1903, 4. "Henry P. Bosse," *Rock Island Union,* December 15, 1903, 3.
17. Census records from 1900 in Illinois indicate that Bosse entered the United States in 1865. Bosse is not listed as emigrating through Hamburg between 1850 and 1871 in the Staatsarchiv, Senat der Freien und Hansestadt Hamburg. Letter to the author from Gisela Fabian, June 11, 1999. Unfortunately, if Bosse left through Bremen, most passenger lists from the 1800s are lost. Letter to the author from Carola Berkefeldt, Freie Hansestadt Bremen, June 11, 1999. Bosse is not listed in Hamburg on the arrival lists for America for 1865, but the arrival lists are notorious for their mistakes. E-mail from Elizabeth Sroka, Tourismus-Zentrale Hamburg, June 8, 1999. Canadian records show a Henry Bosse docking in Quebec City in 1869 on the SS *St. Patrick*, a ship that sailed from Liverpool, England, to Dublin, Ireland, before leaving for America. The passenger log listed this Bosse as twenty-one years old, three years younger than the photographer, and his occupation as a miner, so it seems to be someone else. National Archives of Canada, May 23, 1869, passenger manifest, SS *St. Patrick*, Ottawa, Canada, RG 76, C 1 a, microfilm reel C-4524.
18. U.S. Census Office, Tenth Census of the United States, State of Illinois, County of Cook, Sheet 372. It appears that Lang was the shop's primary owner, because he listed the value of his personal estate at $1,000, and Bosse did not list any assets.
19. *Edwards' Fourteenth Annual Directory of the City of Chicago* (Chicago: Richard Edwards, 1871), 137, 987. *Edwards' Sixteenth Annual Directory of the City of Chicago* (Chicago: Richard Edwards, 1873), 195, 234.
20. *Official Register of the United States, Containing a List of the Officers and Employees in the Civil, Military and Naval Service on the First of July, 1895,* vol. 1 (Washington, D.C.: U.S. Government Printing Office, 1895).
21. Letter from Jas. S. Lusk, Major, Corps of Engineers, to Brig. Gen. G. L. Gillespie, chief of engineers, December 15, 1903. RG-77 Records, National Archives, Great Lakes Branch, Chicago, Entry No. 1652, Letterbook No. 13, 476.
22. Edward P. North, "Wingdams in the Mississippi River above the Falls of St. Anthony," *Transactions of the American Society of Civil Engineers*, 1877, 268–76.
23. Michael Conner, "Henry Bosse and Samuel Clemens as Mark Twain—Parallel Lives on the Mighty Mississippi," *Ramsey County History* 33, no. 3 (Fall 1998): 18–25. Conner speculated that Clemens and Bosse did not know each other, but they were probably familiar with each other's work.
24. Ibid., 21–22.
25. U.S. Department of Labor; Immigration and Naturalization Service, Circuit Court, Cook County, Illinois, Cert. No. R-35, 286. Gottlob Reiter was listed as his witness.
26. Iowa, County of Scott, Marriage License Records, 1893–1896, 12:588, Marriage Register, 1889–1898, Entry No. 11472. Also, "Weddings," *Davenport Daily Democrat*, October 25, 1895, 3.
27. The couple employed a live-in domestic, Maggie Linzy, who was from Tennessee. U.S. Census Office, Twelfth Census of the United States, State of Illinois, County of Rock Island, Sheet No. 488. See also William Roba, "Who Was the Mysterious Henry Bosse?" *Ramsey County History* 27, no. 4 (Winter 1992–93): 10–11. The marriage register indicates that Bosse was married once before he married Hulda. There are other hints to Bosse's past on the document. His place of birth is listed as Summersdorf, Prussia, probably a clerk's misspelling of Sommersdorf, a village near Magdeburg. His mother is listed as Julia Gneisenau and his father as Neuhart Bosse. The general's daughters were Agnes (1800–1822), Ottilie (1802–1883), Hedwig (1805–?), and Emilie (1806–1855). Hedwig married Count von Bruhl; Emilie married Count Karl von Hohenthal. Neither Agnes nor Ottilie married. As none of Gneisenau's daughters was named Julia, the mystery of the identity of Bosse's mother and father remains open.
28. John Thompson, "Biographical Notes and Commentary on the Work of Henry Bosse," Rock Island, Ill.: U.S. Army Corps of Engineers report, 1991, 3. See also "Henry P. Bosse," *Rock Island-Moliner Volks-Zeitung,* December 15, 1903, 4.
29. Minnesota, County of Ramsey, Abstract Clerk, Cert. No. P00572. Minnesota, County of St. Louis, Abstract Clerk, Agreements E:44, Deeds 26:575, 202:520. Illinois, County of Rock Island, Circuit Court, Probate Record, File 317, Roll 148. Illinois, County of Rock Island, Recorder of Deeds, Grantee General Index, 19–22.
30. The boat was launched as the *Vixen* in 1881 and renamed for Bosse. See J. V. Swift, "Valuable Upper Mississippi River Photos Discovered," *Waterways Journal* 105, no. 22: 8. In another of Bosse's life's ironies, the German navy launched a corvette named after his grandfather in 1880, the first of four German ships named after Gneisenau. Thus grandfather and grandson had ships named after them in two very different cultures.
31. Ruth Patrick, *Rivers of the United States*, vol. 4, Part A (New York: John Wiley and Sons, 1998), 1, 140.
32. Luna Leopold, *A View of the River* (Cambridge, Mass.: Harvard University Press, 1994).
33. E. C. Pielou, *After the Ice Age: The Return of Life to Glaciated North America* (Chicago: University of Chicago Press, 1991).
34. Thomas F. Waters, *The Streams and Rivers of Minnesota* (Minneapolis: University of Minnesota Press, 1977), 197.
35. E. L. Coues, *The Expeditions of Zebulon Pike to the Headwaters of the Mississippi River, through Louisiana Territory, and in New Spain, During the Years 1805–6–7,* vol. 1 (Minneapolis: Ross and Haines, 1965), 306.
36. Pielou, *After the Ice Age.*
37. Brian M. Fagan, *The Great Journey: The People of Ancient America* (London: Thames and Hudson, 1987), 241.
38. Roland W. Force and Mary Tefft Force, *The American Indians* (New York: Chelsea House, 1991), 26.
39. Ronald C. Schirmer, "Prehistoric Plant Use in the Red Wing Locality," *Institute for Minnesota Archaeology Newsletter* 13, no. 1/2 (March/June 1998): 4–6, 14.
40. Guy E. Gibbon, "The Middle Mississippian Presence in Minnesota," chapter 11 in *Cahokia and the Hinterlands: Middle Mississippian Cultures of the Midwest,* ed. Thomas E. Emerson and R. Barry Lewis (Urbana: University of Illinois Press, 1991), 207–20.
41. Jared Diamond, *Guns, Germs and Steel* (New York: Norton, 1997), 78, 89.
42. Bill Thomas, *American Rivers: A Natural History* (New York: Norton, 1978), 150.
43. Walter Havighurst, *Voices on the River: The Story of the*

Mississippi Waterways (New York: Macmillan, 1964), 277.
44. Ibid., 20.
45. William J. Petersen, *Steamboating on the Upper Mississippi* (Iowa City: State Historical Society of Iowa, 1968), 31.
46. Ibid.
47. Harry Sinclair Drago, *The Steamboaters: From the Early Side-Wheelers to the Big Packets* (New York: Bramhall House, 1967), 24–25.
48. The average life of a mid-1800s steamboat on the Mississippi has been estimated at between four and five years. See Louis C. Hunter, *Steamboats on the Western Rivers: An Economic and Technological History* (Cambridge, Mass.: Harvard University Press, 1949), 100–103.
49. Charles Dickens, *American Notes for General Circulation* (London: Chapman and Hall, 1842).
50. Petersen, *Steamboating*, 455.
51. Waters, *Streams and Rivers of Minnesota,* 220.
52. Havighurst, *Voices on the River,* 113.
53. Hunter, *Steamboats on the Western Rivers,* 234. Also Roald Tweet, "Rock Island Rapids" (Rock Island District publication, U.S. Army Corps of Engineers, April 1980), 1–3. The *Virginia* grounded at Rock Island in 1823, but after a tense two days, high water freed it.
54. William Cronon, *Nature's Metropolis* (New York: Norton, 1991), 297.
55. Erik F. Haites, James Mak, and Gary M. Walton, *Western River Transportation: The Era of Early Internal Development, 1810–1860* (Baltimore: Johns Hopkins University Press, 1975), 12.
56. William H. Goetzmann, *Exploration and Empire* (New York: Knopf, 1966), 5.
57. Stephen H. Long, "Voyage in a Six-oared Skiff to the Falls of St. Anthony in 1817," Collections of the Minnesota Historical Society 2 (1860–1867, reprinted 1889), 9–88.
58. The other two were Fort Winnebago at the Fox-Wisconsin River portage and Fort Howard at Green Bay, Wisconsin.
59. Todd Shallat, *Structures in the Stream: Water, Science and the Rise of the U.S. Army Corps of Engineers* (Austin: University of Texas Press, 1994), 118–27.
60. George Merrick, *Old Times on the Upper Mississippi: The Recollections of a Steamboat Pilot from 1854 to 1863* (St. Paul: Minnesota Historical Society Press, 1897), 100.
61. Shallat, *Structures in the Stream,* 127.
62. William H. Goetzmann, *Army Exploration in the American West, 1803–1863* (New Haven, Conn.: Yale University Press, 1957), 3–21.
63. John A. Anfinson, "The River We Have Wrought: The Upper Mississippi River, 1823–1940," unpublished manuscript.
64. Raymond H. Merritt, *The Corps, the Environment, and the Upper Mississippi River Basin* (Washington, D.C.: U.S. Government Printing Office, 1984), 13.
65. Lucille Kane, *The Waterfall that Built a City* (St. Paul: Minnesota Historical Society Press, 1966).
66. Marquis W. Childs, *Mighty Mississippi: Biography of a River* (New Haven, Conn.: Ticknor and Fields, 1982), 98–99. See also Capt. Ron Larson, *Upper Mississippi River History: Fact, Fiction, Legend* (Winona, Minn.: Steamboat Press, 1994), 13.
67. Shallat, *Structures in the Stream.*
68. Merrick, *Old Times on the Upper Mississippi,* 224.
69. Christine Whitacre, ed., *Gateways to Commerce* (Denver: National Park Service, 1992), 18.
70. *Laws of the United States Relating to the Improvement of Rivers and Harbors*, vol. 1 (Washington, D.C.: U.S. Government Printing Office, 1913), 152–53.
71. The first officer assigned to St. Paul was Major General G. K. Warren, a Union hero at the Battle of Gettysburg.
72. *Annual Report*, Corps of Engineers, 1875, Appendix CC, 454.
73. John Anfinson, "Henry Bosse's Priceless Photographs," *Ramsey County History* 27, no. 4 (Winter 1992–93): 4–9.
74. Anfinson, "The River We Have Wrought," chapter 3. *Annual Report*, Corps of Engineers, 1896, p. 1748.
75. Roald D. Tweet, *A History of the Rock Island District Corps of Engineers* (Rock Island, Ill.: U.S. Army Engineer District, 1975), 40–44.
76. Mark Twain, *Life on the Mississippi* (New York: Harper, 1882), 142.
77. Hunter, *Steamboats on the Western Rivers,* 638.
78. Merritt, *The Corps, the Environment, and the Upper Mississippi,* 13.
79. Ibid.
80. Army Corps of Engineers, *Annual Report*, 1881, Appendix U, 1679.
81. "Endless Frontier," *Time,* July 30, 1951, 48–51.
82. John Barry, *Rising Tide: The Great Mississippi Flood of 1927 and How It Changed America* (New York: Simon and Schuster, 1997), 89.
83. "The Memorial of the Legislature of the State of Minnesota," House Executive Document No. 58, 1867, 17.
84. Eugene Ostroff, *Western Views and Eastern Visions* (Washington, D.C.: Smithsonian, 1981), 8.
85. This point is made by Jean-Claude Lemagny and André Rouillé, eds., *A History of Photography: Social and Cultural Perspectives* (Cambridge, U.K.: Cambridge University Press, 1986), 27.
86. Ibid., 26.
87. John Wood, *The Scenic Daguerreotype: Romanticism and Early Photography* (Iowa City: University of Iowa Press, 1995).
88. Peter Bacon Hales, "American Views and the Romance of Modernization," chapter 5 in *Photography in Nineteenth Century America,* ed. Martha Sandweiss (New York: Abrams, 1991), 205.
89. Photographer Charles Savage, in his 1870s "Views of Great West from the Missouri River to the Pacific Ocean," and editor Edward L. Wilson's essay, "Views in the Yosemite Valley," in *Philadelphia Photographer* (April 1866, 107) are examples.
90. Hales, "American Views," 209.
91. Merritt, *The Corps, the Environment, and the Upper Mississippi,* 31.
92. Ibid.
93. Howard Bossen, "A Tall Tale Retold: The Influence of the Photographs of William Henry Jackson on the Passage of the Yellowstone Park Act of 1872," *Studies in Visual Communication* 8, no. 1 (Winter 1982): 98–109. For the opposite view, see Clarence Jackson, *Picture Maker of the Old West* (New York: Charles Scribner's Sons, 1947), 143–58. Clarence Jackson was William's son.
94. Lemagny and Rouillé, *History of Photography,* 51.
95. Rosalind Krauss takes issue with critics and scholars who make "art" out of photographs taken on government expeditions. She said photographers like Timothy O'Sullivan never intended their work to provide aesthetic pleasure but only to provide information. See Rosalind Krauss, "Photography's Discursive Space: Landscape/View," *Art Journal,* Winter 1982, 511.
96. Weston J. Naef and James N. Wood, *Era of Exploration: The Rise of Landscape Photography in the American West, 1860–1885.* (Boston: Albright-Knox Art Gallery, distributed by the New York Graphic Society, 1975), 63, 174, 222.

97. Vicki Goldberg, ed., *Photography in Print: Writings from 1816 to the Present* (New York: Touchstone, 1981), 169.
98. Hales, "American Views," 208–9.
99. Esthelle Jussim and Elizabeth Lindquist-Cock, *Landscape as Photograph* (New Haven, Conn.: Yale University Press, 1985), 35.
100. Lemagny and Rouillé, *History of Photography*, 26.
101. William C. Darrah, *Stereo Views: A History of Stereographs in America and Their Collection* (Gettysburg, Pa.: Times and News Publishing Co., 1964), 6.
102. Sandra S. Phillips, Richard Rodriguez, Aaron Betsky, and Eldridge M. Moores, *Crossing the Frontier: Photographs of the Developing West* (San Francisco: Chronicle Books, 1996), 23.
103. Alexander Mackenzie to James Greenleaf, School of Mines, Columbia College, New York City, February 5, 1894. National Archives Regional Office, Chicago, Record Group 77, Letterbook No. 3, 782.
104. Ralph W. Andrews, *Photographers of the Frontier West* (Seattle: Superior Publishing, 1965), 113. The trunk of a giant sequoia, the General Noble, was displayed in the rotunda of the government building.
105. Julie K. Brown, *Contesting Images: Photography and the World's Columbian Exposition* (Tucson: University of Arizona Press, 1994).
106. Ibid., 56–57. According to Corps records, Bosse's cyanotypes, not his black and whites, were exhibited in Chicago. See Memo from the Chief of Engineers, Washington, D.C., October 19, 1899, National Archives Regional Office, Chicago, Record Group 77, Letterbook No. 13, Entry 1661.
107. Major Mackenzie to M. Meigs, October 31, 1892, National Archives Regional Office, Chicago, Record Group 77, Letterbook No. 1, Entry 1652, 258.
108. Major Mackenzie to Captain W. L. Marshall, March 27, 1893, 138; Major Mackenzie to Captain Marshall, April 1, 1893, 154, National Archives Regional Office, Chicago, Record Group 77, Letterbook No. 1, Entry 1652.
109. Major Charles Townsend to Montgomery Meigs, March 13, 1903, 603; Major Jas. S. Lusk to Brig. Gen. G. L. Gillespie, Chief of Engineers, April 1, 1903, 634–35, National Archives Regional Office, Chicago, Record Group 77, Letterbook No. 11, Entry 1652.
110. From U.S. Commission to the Paris Exposition of 1900 to Willard A. Smith, Director of Civil Engineering and Transportation, Chicago, Ill., January 18, 1900, National Archives Regional Office, Chicago, Record Group 77, Letterbook No. 4, Entry 1661, 382. Also from U.S. Commission to the Paris Exposition of 1900 to Willard A. Smith, Director of Civil Engineering and Transportation, Chicago, Ill., February 8, 1900, National Archives Regional Office, Chicago, Record Group 77, Letterbook No. 5, Entry 1661, 2.
111. As quoted in Mike Ware, *Cyanotype: The History, Science and Art of Photographic Printing in Prussian Blue* (London: Science Museum and National Museum of Photography, Film and Television, 1999), 12. Original taken from P. H. Emerson, *Naturalistic Photography for Students of the Art* (London: Sampson, Lowe, Marston, Searle and Rivington, 1889).
112. As quoted in Ware, *Cyanotype*, 12. Original taken from R. Child Bayley, *The Complete Photographer*, rev. 10th ed. (London: Methuen, 1932), 392.
113. Since only seven negatives survive—and none earlier than 1885—it is difficult to say whether Bosse used wet or dry plate photography throughout his career. The remaining negatives are dry plates.
114. Mike Ware, "The New Cyanotype Process," *Ag+ Photographic* 7 (1995): 74–81.
115. Ware, *Cyanotype*, 11.
116. Larry J. Shaaf, *Sun Gardens: Victorian Photographs by Anna Atkins* (New York: Aperture, 1985). See also Larry J. Shaaf, *Out of the Shadows: Herschel, Talbot and the Invention of Photography* (New Haven, Conn.: Yale University Press, 1992).
117. "The Late Sir John F. W. Herschel FRS: His Discoveries in Photography," *British Journal of Photography* 18 (May 19, 1871): 229–31.
118. As quoted in Ware, *Cyanotype*, 13. Original taken from J. A. Tennant, "The 'Blue-Print' and Its Variations," *The Photo-miniature* 1, no. 10 (January 1900): 483. Prussian blue was also used for dying wool, silk, and cotton. Some companies offered cyanotype-printed pillows, slipcovers, and draperies, and at least one company offered to take customers' negatives and print them on fabric. See Ware, *Cyanotype*, 65.
119. Ware, *Cyanotype*, 14–15.
120. Some of Bosse's unbound photographs are printed on cyanotype paper, but the Rock Island and Dubuque sets were printed on regular drafting paper. The St. Paul, Mayo, and Mackenzie volumes were printed on the more expensive Johannot paper and did not have a Corps imprimatur. Ron Deiss and Michael Conner are among those who have speculated that these were printed on Bosse's own time or were made for personal gifts, or both.
121. Robert L. Craig and Mark Neuzil, "Views on the Mississippi: The Photographs of Henry Peter Bosse," paper presented to the Association for Education in Journalism and Mass Communication annual convention, August 10, 1996, Anaheim, Calif.
122. *Annual Report*, Corps of Engineers, 1875, p. 463.
123. Alberta Kirchner Hill, "Out with the Fleet," *Minnesota History*, September 1961, 286.
124. Ibid. The prices are from 1894.
125. Ibid.
126. Major A. Mackenzie to the Chief of Engineers, October 29, 1889, Army Corps of Engineers, Registers and Abstracts of Letters Received, 1881–1906. National Archives Regional Office, Chicago, Record Group 77, Book 5, Entry No. 1661, 190.
127. Ibid.
128. The River and Harbors Act of 1890 included a refuse section that could have slowed the sawdust problem, but it was so poorly written that it meant nothing and was not enforced. The act forbade dumping that would obstruct navigation, but it was up to the government to prove "obstruction," which was difficult to do on a river as large as the Mississippi. Not until the River and Harbor Act of 1899 did effective legislation pass Congress, closing the loopholes of the previous measures and empowering the Corps to arrest violators. See Albert E. Cowdrey, "Pioneering Environmental Law: The Army Corps of Engineers and the Refuse Act," *Pacific Historical Review*, August 1975, 331–49.
129. John Wood, "The Art of the Cyanotype and the Vandalous Dreams of John Metoyer," in *The Photographic Arts*, ed. John Wood (Iowa City: University of Iowa Press, 1997), 32–44.
130. Letter from Montgomery Meigs to Maj. Gen. Townsend, August 9, 1900. National Archives Regional Office, Chicago, Record Group 77, Letterbook No. 5.
131. For more on this point, see Abigail Solomon-Godeau, *Photography at the Dock* (Minneapolis: University of Minnesota Press, 1991), 103–12.

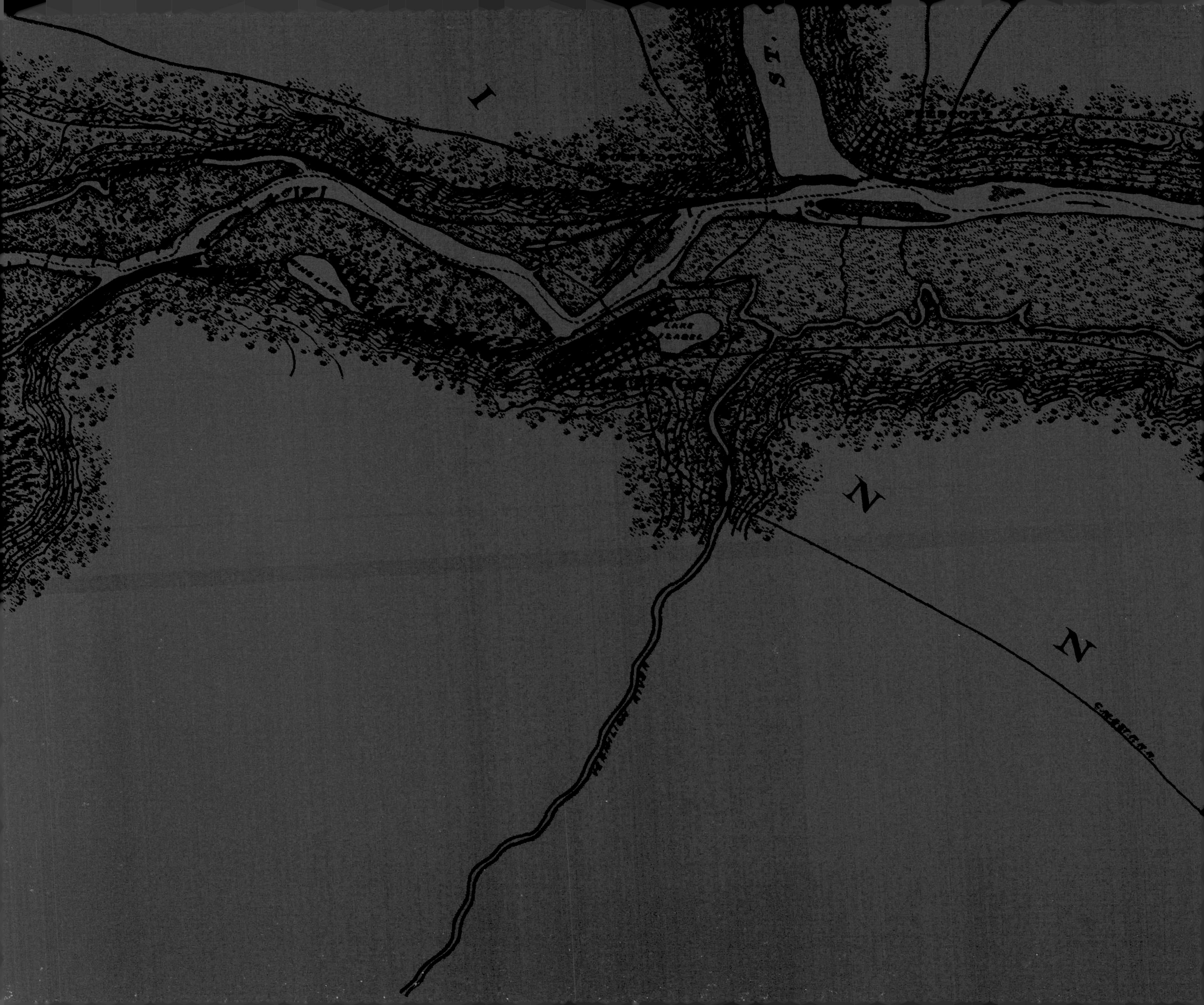

I
N
N

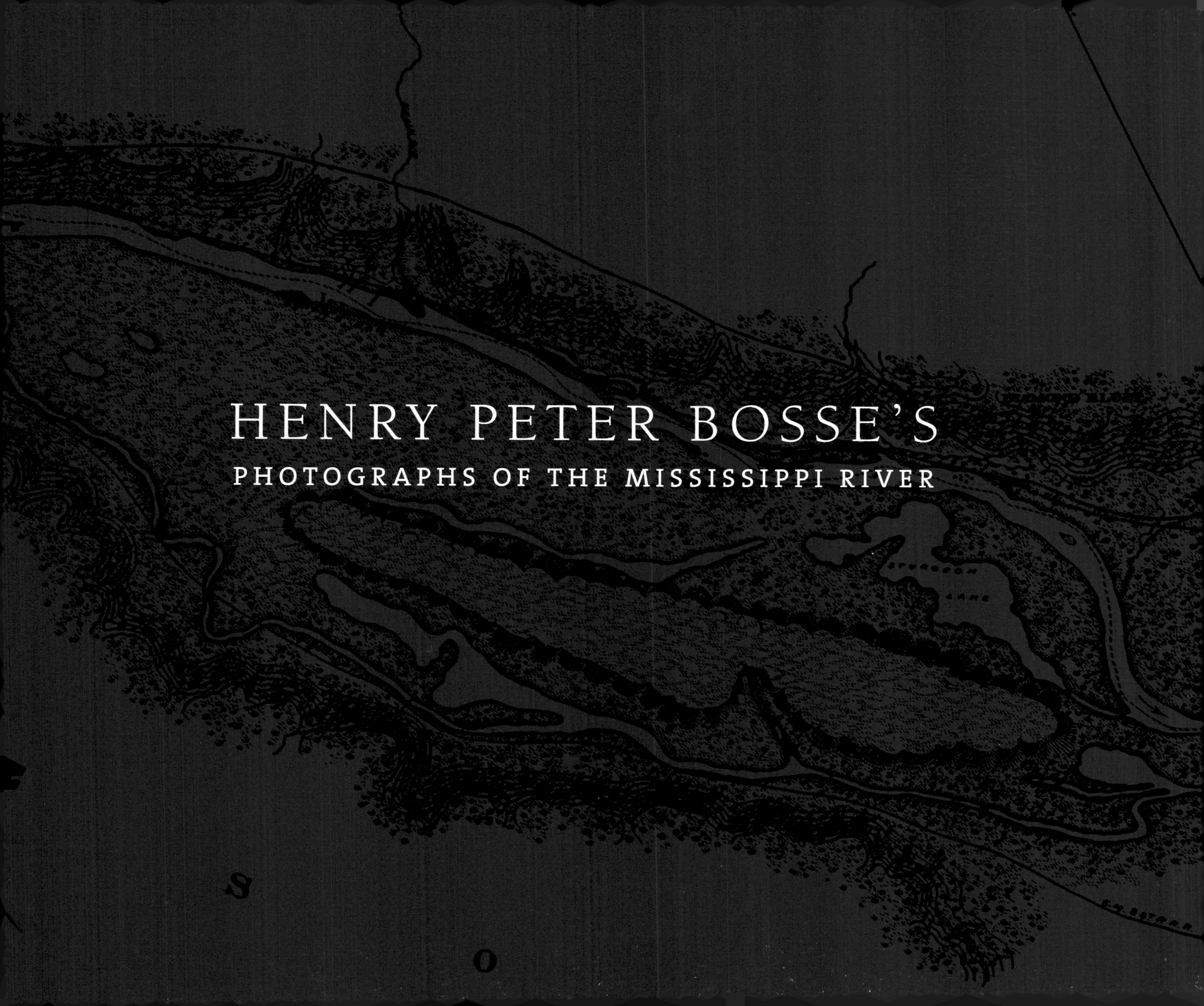

HENRY PETER BOSSE'S

PHOTOGRAPHS OF THE MISSISSIPPI RIVER

PLATE 1

Below the Falls of St. Anthony, Minneapolis, Minn., 1885

(MAYO FOUNDATION)

The Falls of St. Anthony, which featured up to a fifty-foot drop, were the upper limit of navigation on the Mississippi River during the nineteenth century, despite the best efforts of the Corps of Engineers and others. Steamboats loaded and unloaded at St. Paul because they were unable to navigate the steep falls, which became an important source of power for flour and lumber interests. • For much of the 1880s, low water (as evidenced by the riffles and mill debris in the foreground) hindered the floating of logs downstream for further milling. At the peak of lumbering, Minneapolis boasted twenty-seven sawmills across the falls. • By 1885, when Bosse took this photograph, the Tenth Avenue Bridge (foreground), the Stone Arch Bridge (middle ground), only two years finished in this picture, and the Hennepin Avenue suspension bridge (background), originally built in 1854, spanned the river. • The Corps did intensive work at the falls in 1882, 1885, and 1887, much of it to fix damage done by boom companies and mill companies. In 1868, William W. Eastman and John L. Merriam tried to tunnel under Hennepin Island up to Nicollet Island. The tunnel fell in and nearly caused the collapse of the entire falls. Between 1876 and 1880, the Corps worked to save and restore the cataract. After 1887, since navigation was not affected, the Corps did no work on the falls until 1937. With the completion of the lock and dam system in the 1960s, Minneapolis became head of navigation.

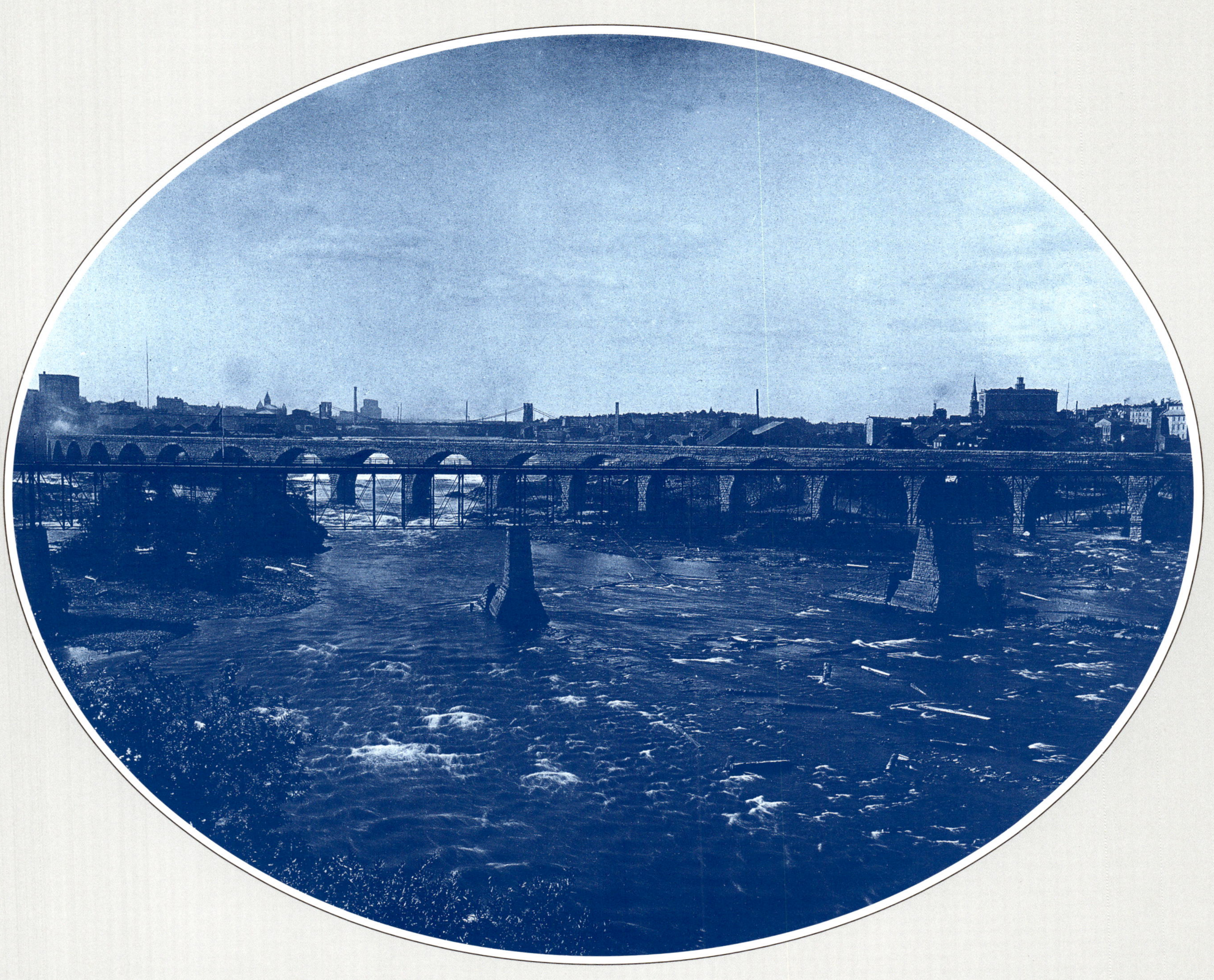

PLATE 2

Old Steamboat Landing at Minneapolis, Minn., 1890

(MAYO FOUNDATION)

PLATE 3

From Quarry at Riverside Park, (Minneapolis) looking up stream, 1890

(U.S. ARMY CORPS OF ENGINEERS, ROCK ISLAND DISTRICT)

PLATE 4

From opp. Riverside Park, (Minneapolis) looking up stream, 1890

(MAYO FOUNDATION)

All three of these photographs were taken on the same stretch of river near Riverside Park in Minneapolis in January 1890. These photographs are rare looks by Bosse at the river this far north in winter, because the Corps's Rock Island–based boats could not get past an iced-in Lake Pepin in other years. • Looking downstream from the old steamboat landing near what became the Washington Avenue Bridge (Plate 2), one gets a sense of the amount of pollution in the river. Lumber from mills in Minneapolis and elsewhere littered the shoreline; underneath the light covering of snow, the banks were often clogged with sawdust. Minneapolis sawmills processed 491 million board feet of lumber in 1894 alone. • Riverside Park was home to a limestone quarry, visible in the upper left of Plates 2 and 4. A few houses stood courageously on the flats on the east bank. 1890 was another low-water year, as seen by the exposed rocks and bars, and what remained of the main channel is on the inside bend in the photographs.

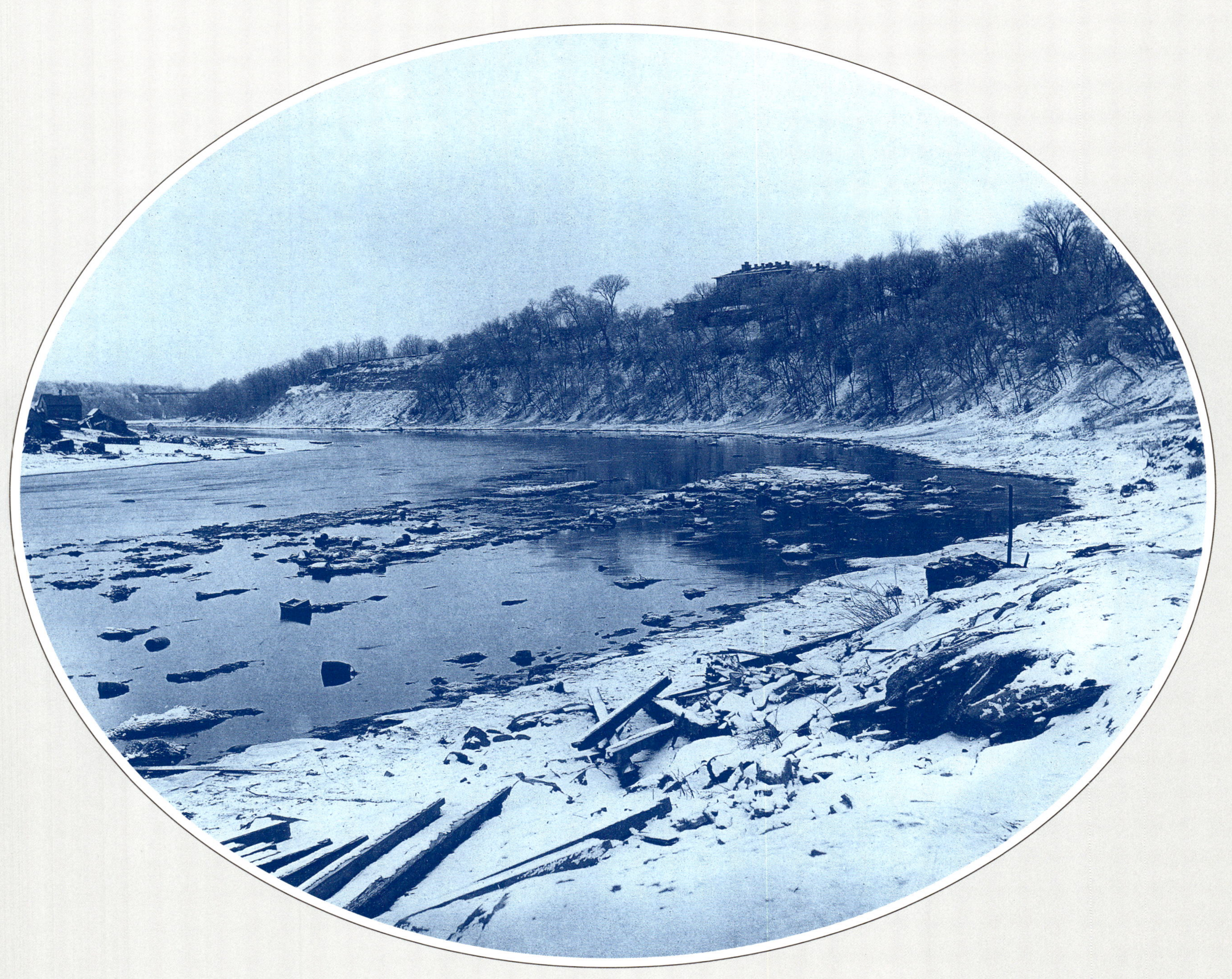

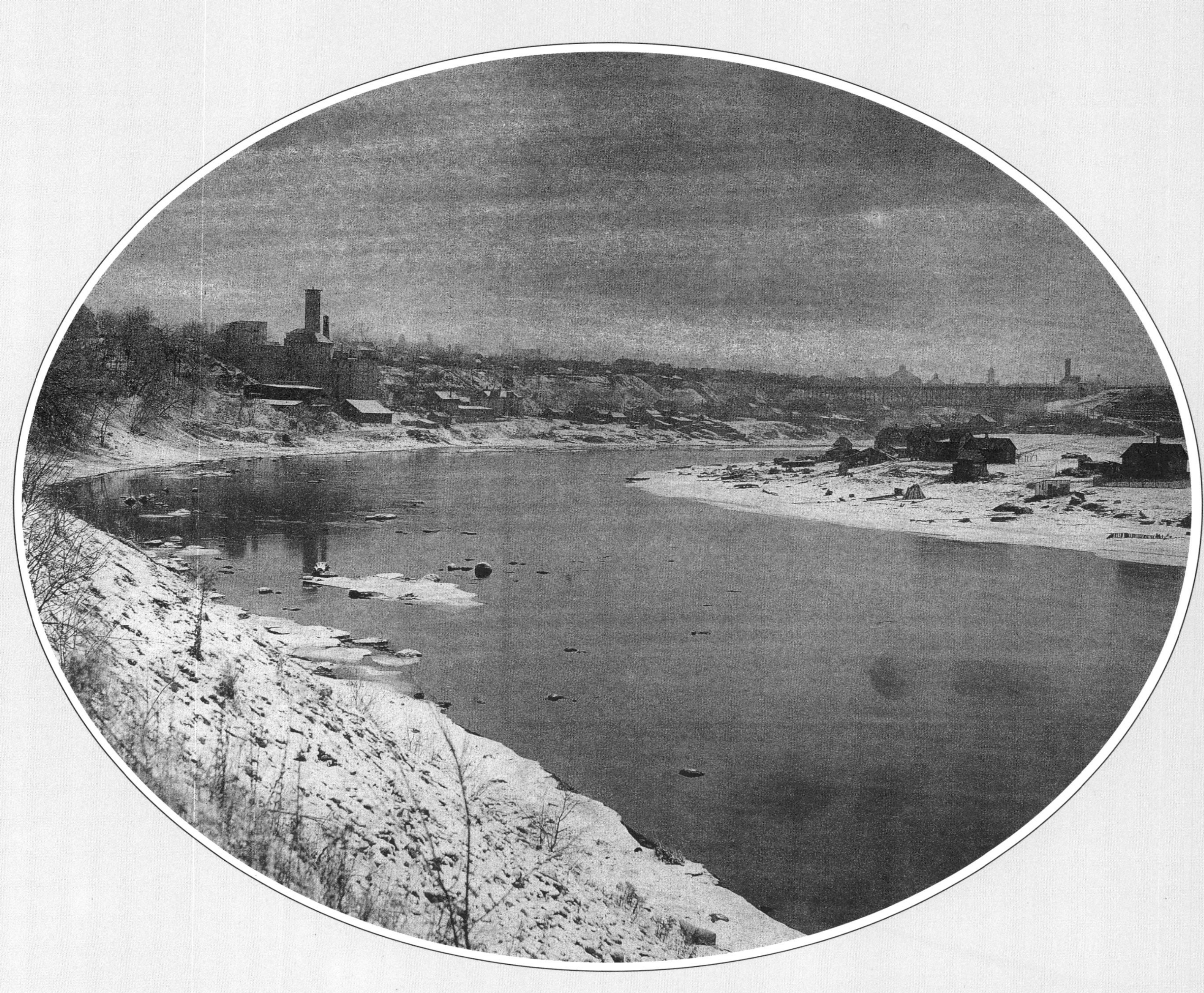

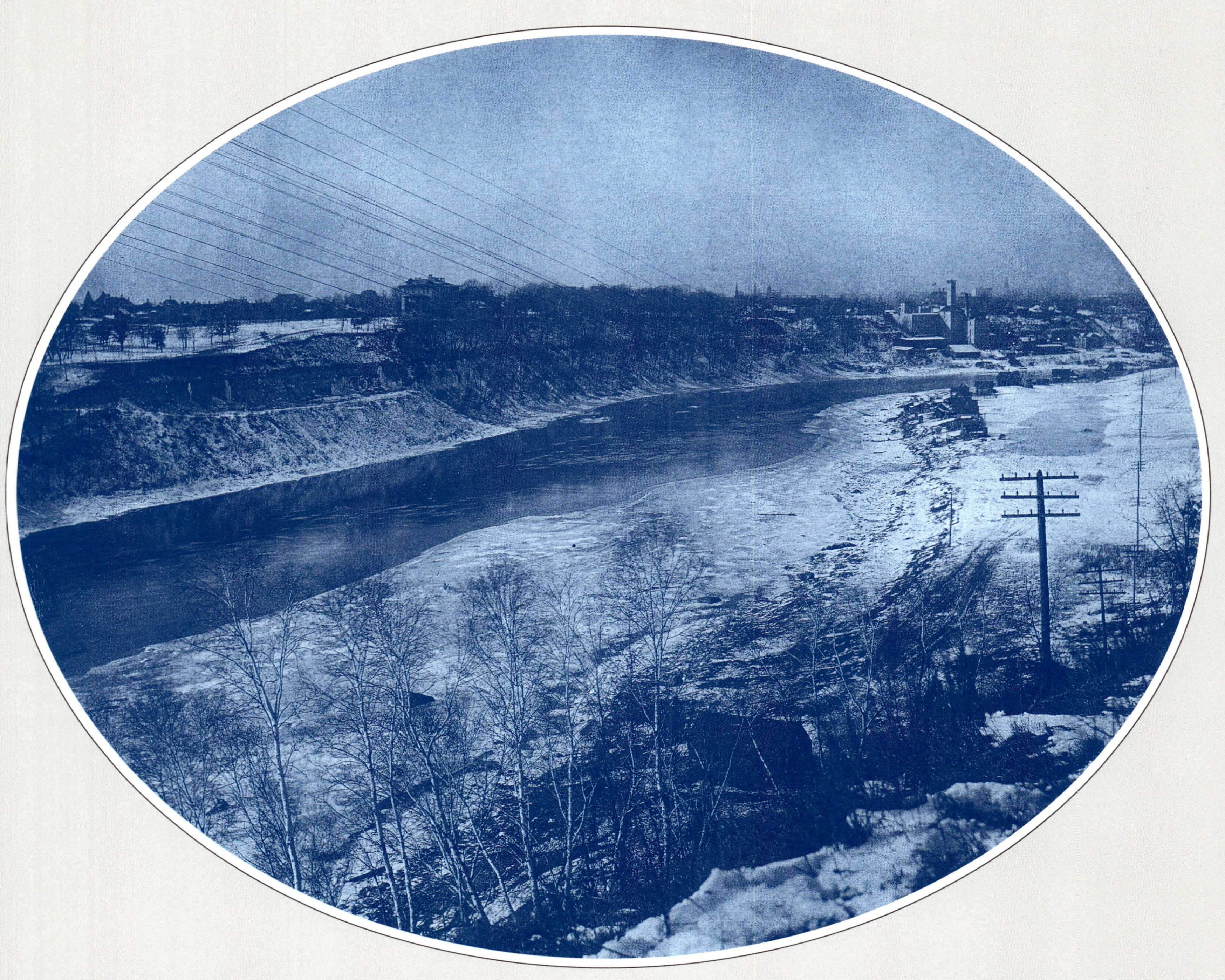

PLATE 5

Franklin Ave. Bridge, Minneapolis from left shore above, 1889

(U.S. ARMY CORPS OF ENGINEERS, ROCK ISLAND DISTRICT)

In the late 1880s, demand for bridges in Minneapolis grew louder. City bonds had been sold to pay for much early bridge construction, and the location of the spans was a source of controversy. By 1888, the hubbub was such that two more bridges were added to the city, one at Twentieth Avenue North and this bridge at Franklin Avenue. Bosse photographed the bridge in 1889, shortly after it was completed. • The original Franklin Avenue Bridge, a wrought iron truss and stone structure with a high center span, was replaced in 1919 by a concrete arch bridge designed by Cappelen and Oustad and still in use at the end of the century. In the early days of steamboat travel, tall stack steamers unhinged their chimneys to get through high span bridges like this one.

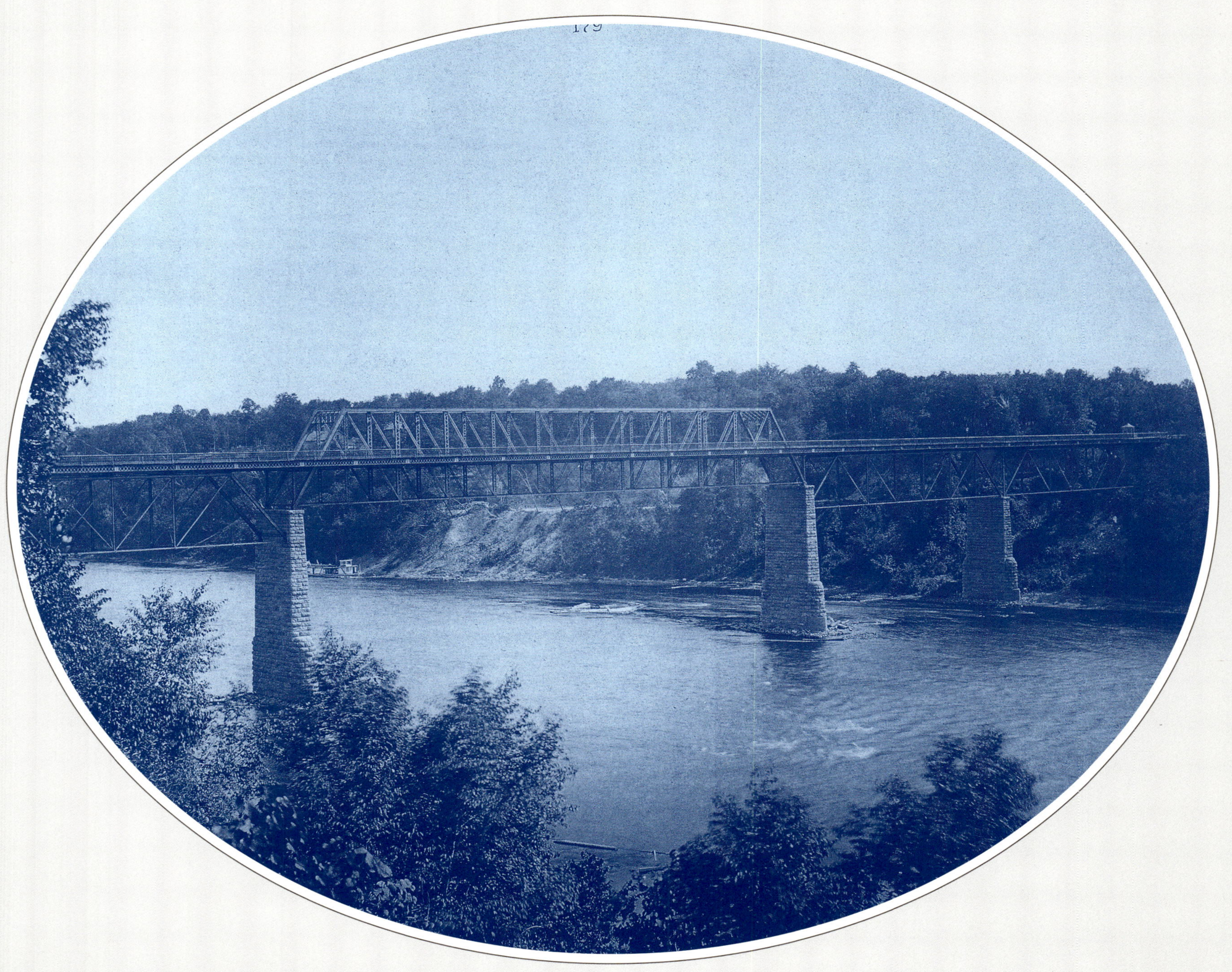

PLATE 6

C. M. & St. P. R.R. Bridge (Short line) at Minneapolis, Minn., 1889

(MAYO FOUNDATION)

The Chicago, Milwaukee & St. Paul Railroad Bridge was a short-line bridge at Minneapolis, built in the nineteenth century; it remained a railroad bridge site into the next century. Note the logs, barrel, and other debris in the river. The building of bridges in Minneapolis and St. Paul in the 1870s and 1880s led to much speculation and debate in the newspapers of the two towns. During the conflict over which bridges should be built and where they should be located, the newspapers began using the shorthand "Twin Cities" to refer to the communities.

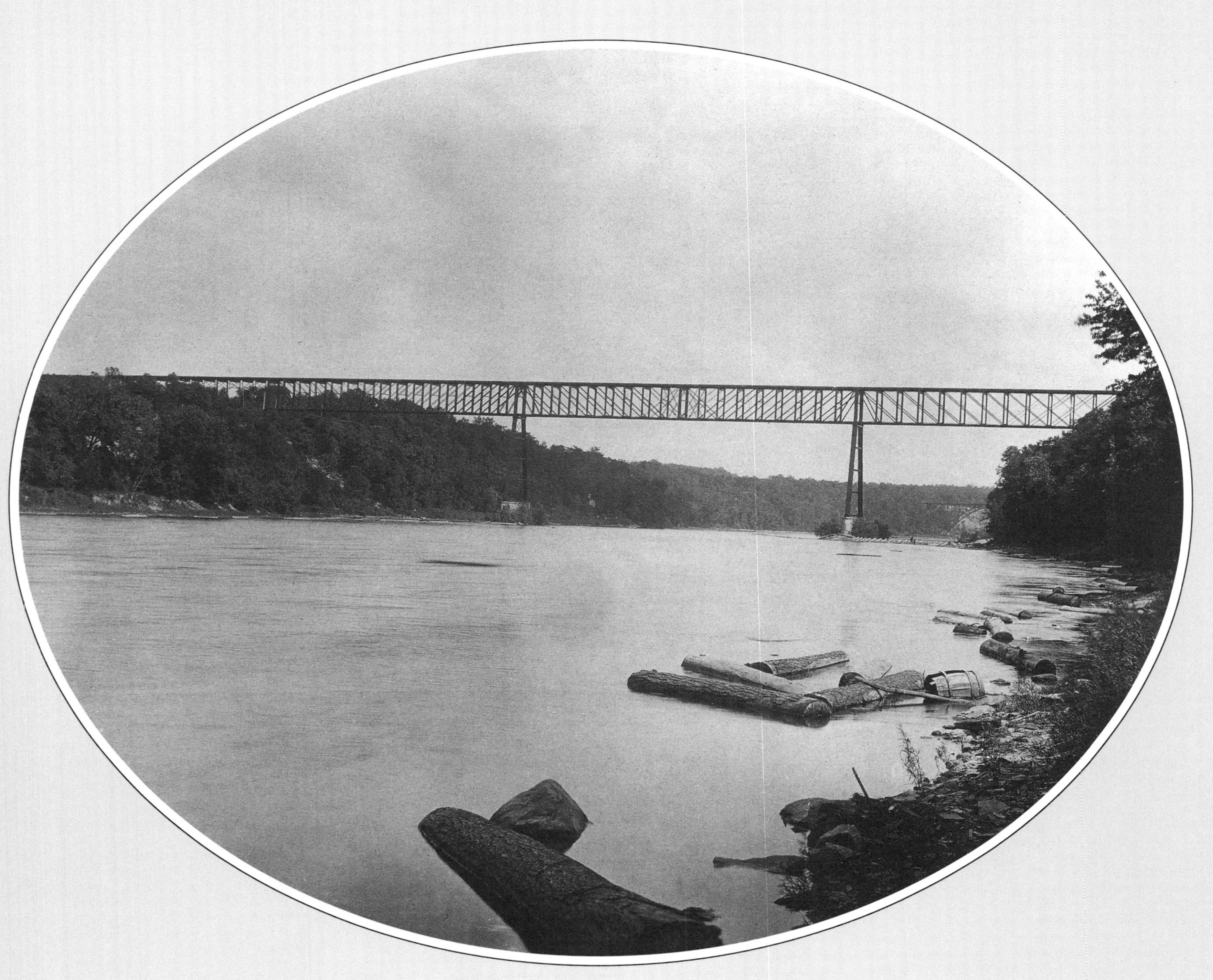

PLATE 7

Marshall Ave. Bridge—Minneapolis & St. Paul, 1889

(MAYO FOUNDATION)

Bosse took photographs of many of the engineering marvels of his era, including the Marshall Avenue Bridge connecting Lake Street in Minneapolis with Marshall Avenue in St. Paul. The bridge, designed by Joseph Sewall of St. Paul to be made entirely of wrought iron with a wooden deck, was only a year old in this photograph. At the time, it was the second-longest metal bridge in the United States (after the Eads Bridge in St. Louis, which was made of steel). • The contractor was the Wrought Iron Company of Canton, Ohio, for the superstructure and the J. F. O'Halloran Company for the substructure. Sewall took advantage of the cold winter of 1887–88 to begin construction—the frozen river made it easier to build. On January 19, 1888, the temperature reached minus forty-one degrees. This view is looking downstream.

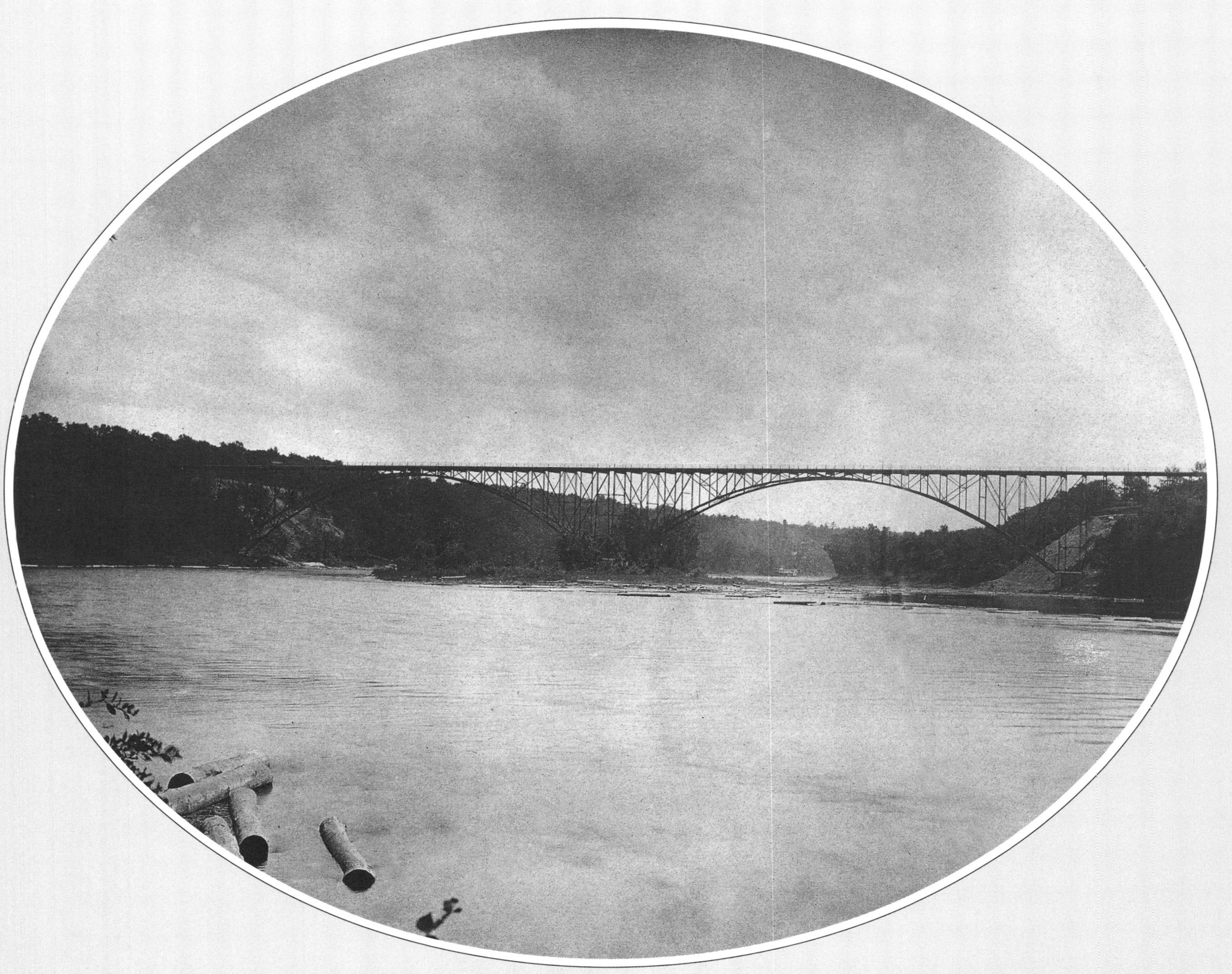

PLATE 8

Soldiers Home and mouth of Minne-ha-ha Creek, 1889

(MAYO FOUNDATION)

Bosse stood just downstream from the mouth of Minnehaha Creek to take this photograph of the creek's mouth and the building where veterans of the Indian wars and the Civil War and their families lived out their days. The Soldiers' Home was a new building in this photograph, having been completed the previous year. • Up the creek from the Soldiers' Home was Minnehaha Falls, which by the 1840s was one of the popular excursion points for visitors and wealthy residents of the area. Boats journeyed through the mouth of the creek to the base of the falls, where people disembarked and enjoyed picnics and parties. A bridge was built across the creek near this spot in 1908.

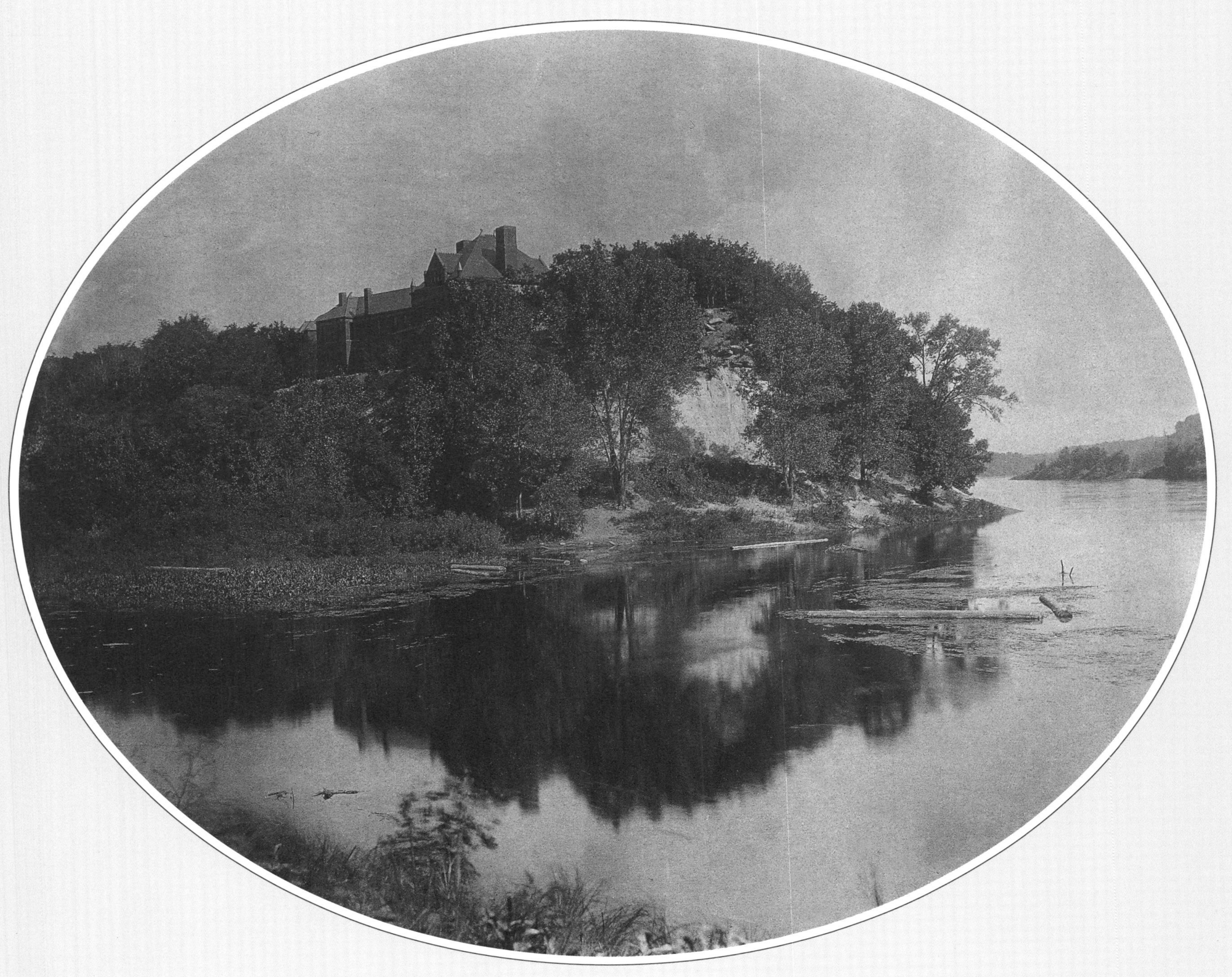

PLATE 9

Fort Snelling, Minn., 1889

(MAYO FOUNDATION)

Located on the bluffs at the confluence of the Mississippi and Minnesota rivers, Fort Snelling, originally called Fort St. Anthony, was considered a risky proposition in 1818 because its nearest supply and reinforcement station was seven hundred miles downstream in Missouri. • Keelboats were used by the Army to outfit the fort in its early years. The first steamboat to navigate the upper river, the *Virginia*, reached the fort from St. Louis in 1823, carrying supplies. Among its passengers when it launched were the Italian adventurer Giacomo Constantine Beltrami and the Sauk Indian chief Great Eagle, whose tribal members were forced to walk along the banks. Not far out of St. Louis, the chief quarreled with the *Virginia*'s pilot over the correct channel; when the pilot failed to heed Great Eagle's advice and the boat ran aground, the chief jumped overboard near Keokuk and joined his tribe, quitting the expedition in disgust.

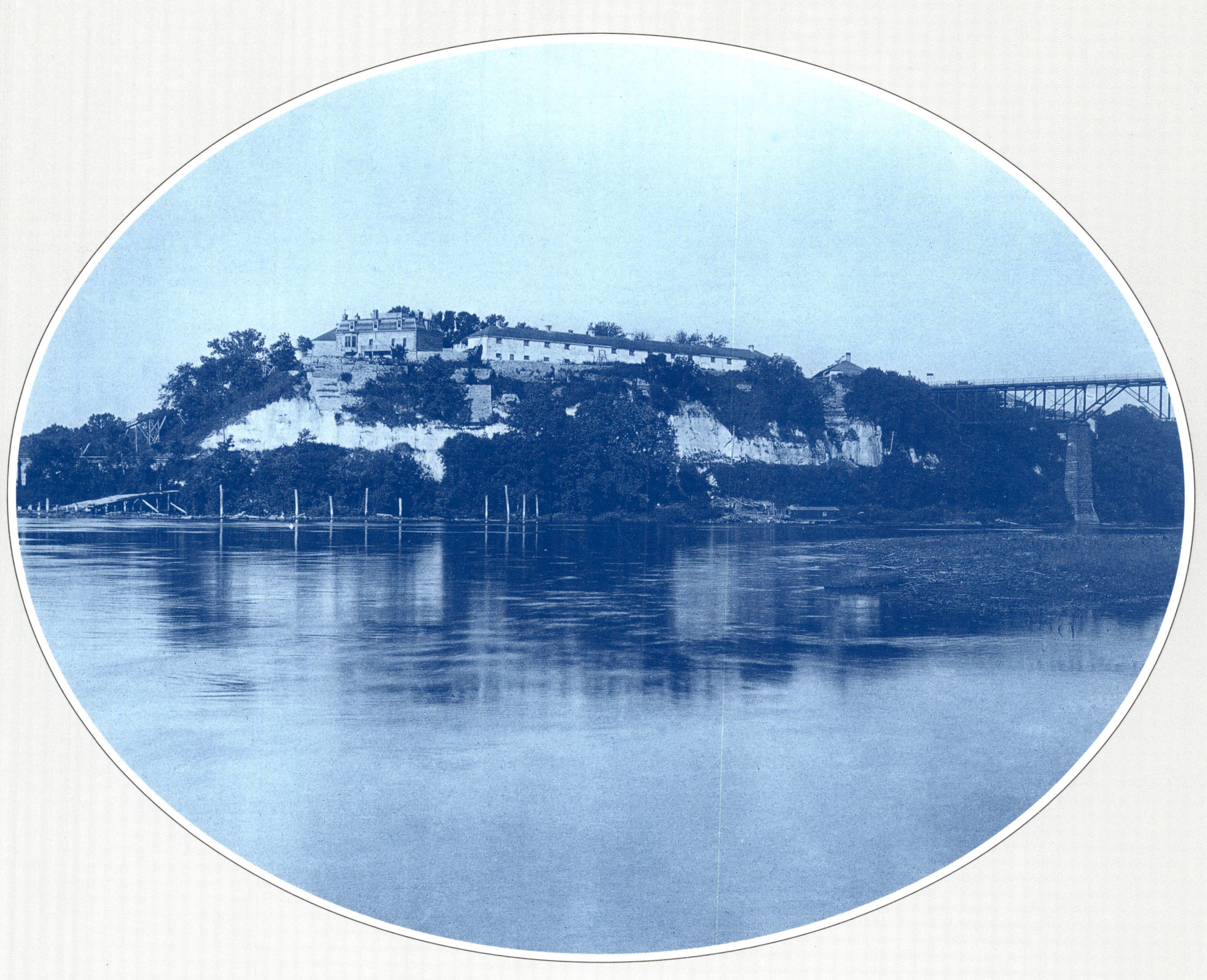

PLATE 10

Boom of St. Paul Boom Co., 1889

(MAYO FOUNDATION)

A boom was a location on the river where lumber companies would gather wood that they had floated downstream. The wood, either in logs or already milled, would be assembled into lumber rafts at the booms, picked up by a towboat, and pushed downstream for sale or further milling. The boom sites were recognizable by the pilings, seen here in low water, that helped fence in the logs as men tied them into rafts. Booms were usually located in slack-water areas, side channels, or sloughs so crews would not have to fight the current as they did their work. This view is looking downstream on the river between Fort Snelling and St. Paul. Lumber can be seen on the far shore.

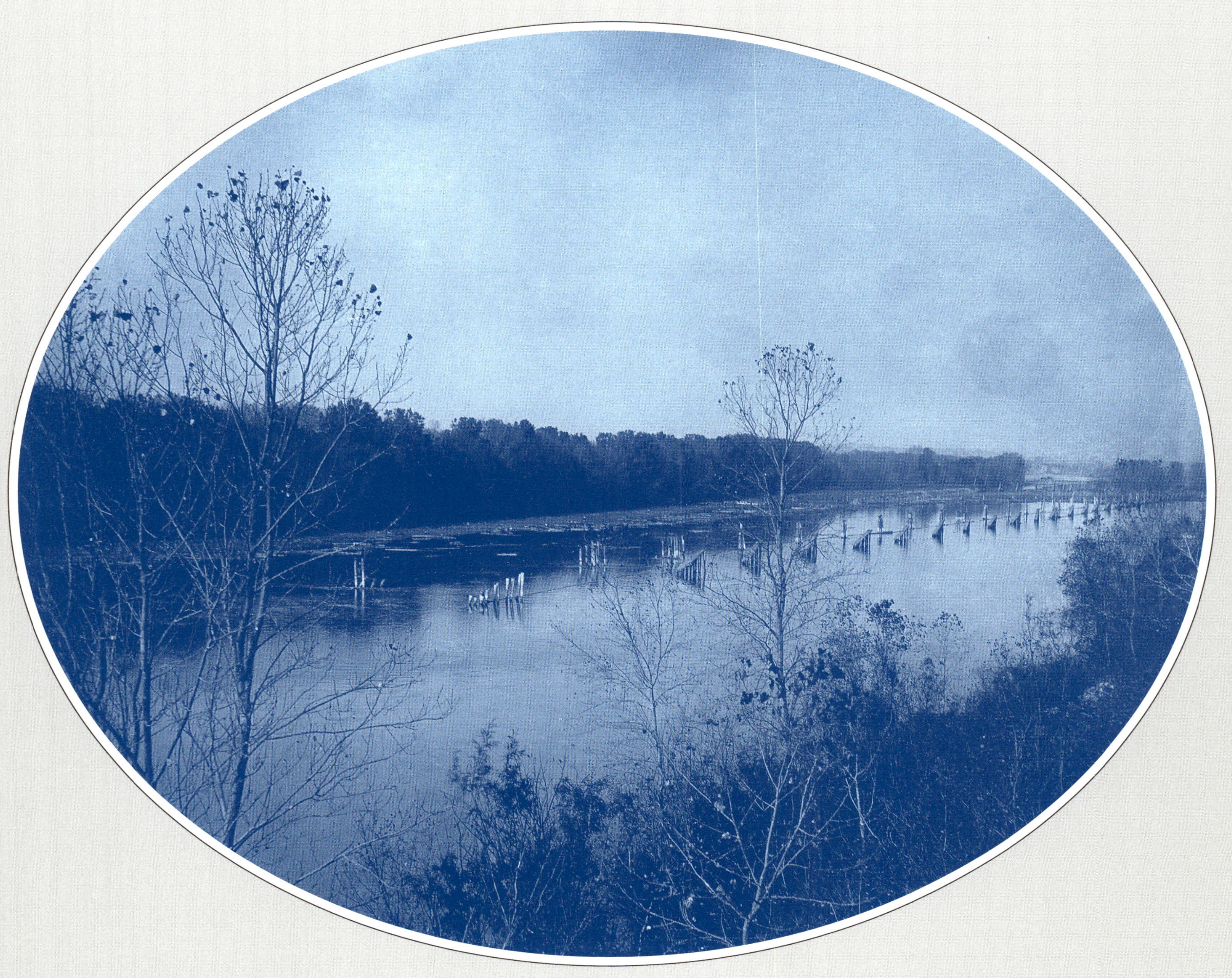

PLATE 11

Smith Ave. Bridge—St. Paul, Minn., 1889

(MAYO FOUNDATION)

The Keystone Bridge Company of Pittsburgh completed the Smith Avenue Wagon Bridge in May 1889, a few months before Bosse took this photograph. The bridge was designed to connect the West Seventh Street neighborhood in St. Paul to an undeveloped area near Cherokee Heights. The bridge replaced a ferry, which dumped passengers off at the flats below the bluff, operated since the 1850s by John Irvine. • At the time, the Smith Avenue Bridge was the longest and highest truss bridge in Minnesota at 2,770 feet long and 191 feet high at its upper end. Its 4 percent grade was unusually steep for the day and helped make it a striking structure. The High Bridge, as it came to be known, was a St. Paul landmark. It was abandoned in 1984 and replaced with a new bridge in 1985.

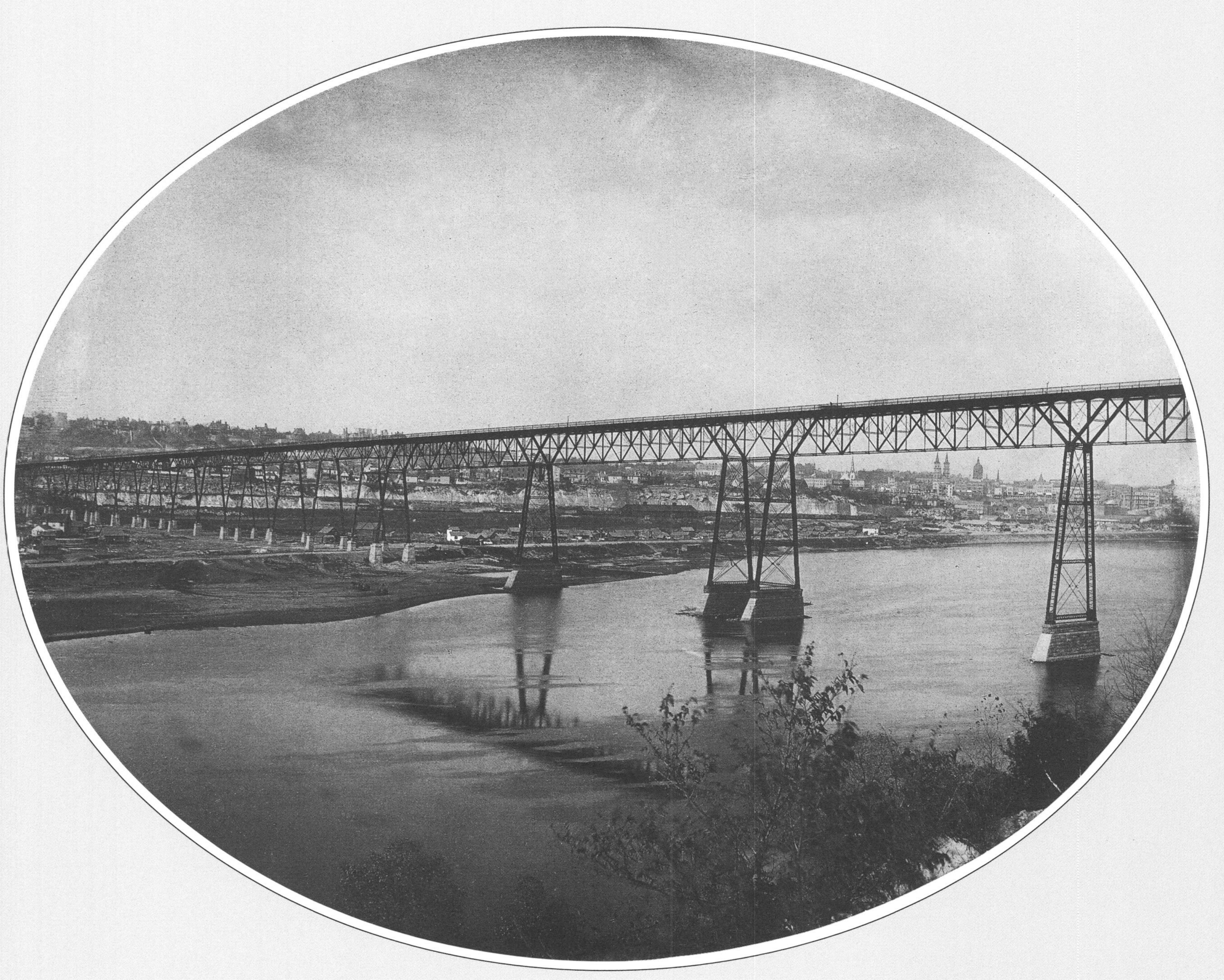

PLATE 12

St. Paul, Minn., 1885

(MAYO FOUNDATION)

The city of St. Paul boasted 41,473 people in 1880. Then came the great waves of immigrants—from Ireland, Germany, Poland, Italy, and elsewhere. By 1885, when this photograph was taken, its population had more than doubled to 111,397 people. Many of the immigrants lived on the flats—the floodplain, which offered little assurance that homes would stay dry from one season to the next. • The biggest advantage St. Paul held over Minneapolis was its location below the Falls of St. Anthony. That geography made St. Paul the last harbor for steamships heading from St. Louis and New Orleans and a major point of departure for ships going the other way. • The city was in a serious contest with Minneapolis (which had a population in 1885 of 129,200) for newcomers and the advantages that being a state's largest city brings. The rivalry intensified in 1890 with the indictments of twenty-eight Minneapolitans (and five St. Paulites) on charges of census fraud. Only two of the twenty-eight (and none of the five) were convicted and fined. • This photo was taken from a quarry in the vicinity of Cherokee Heights Park. The Wabasha Street Bridge, which hurried the development of the neighborhoods on the left bank, can be seen in the background.

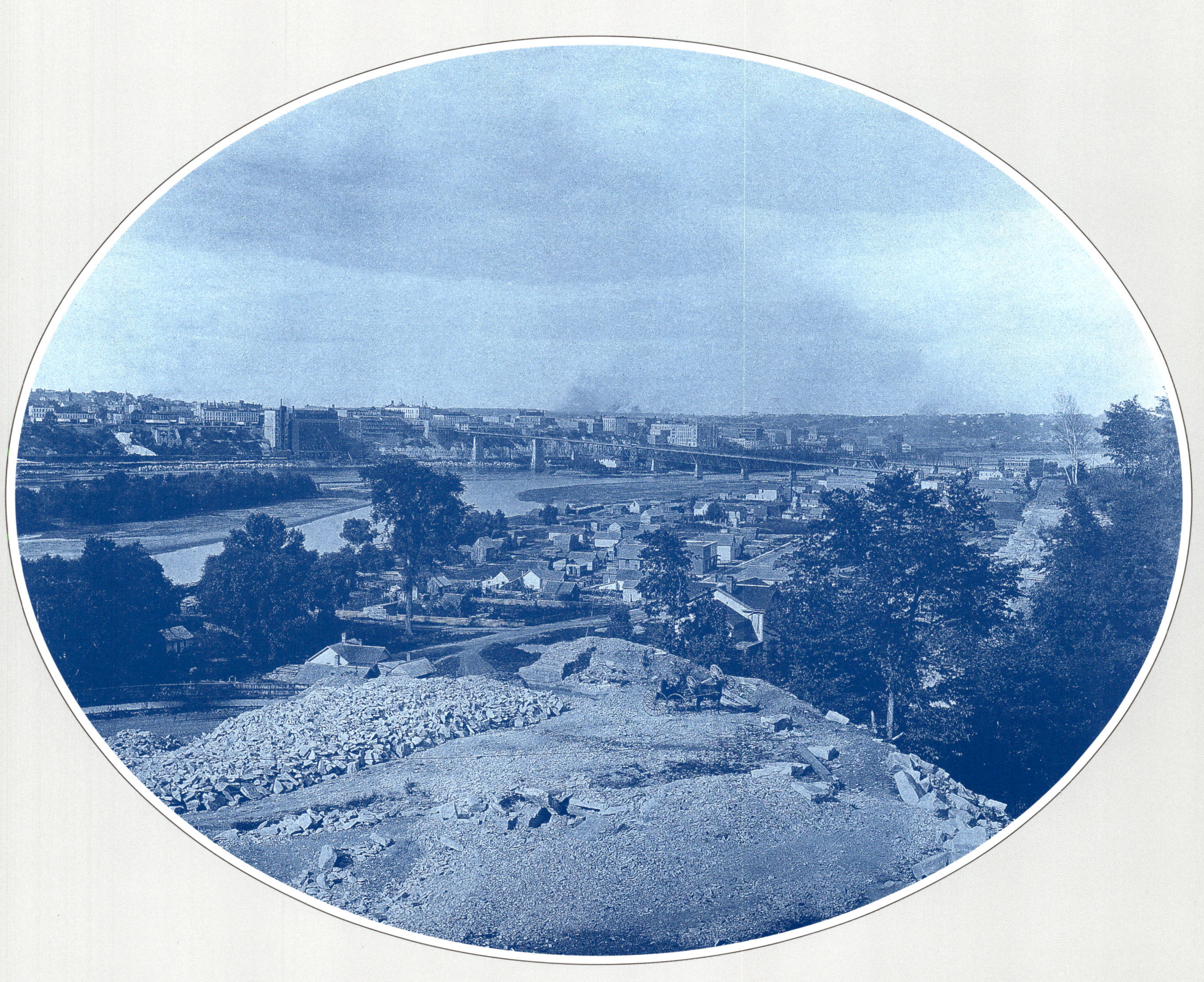

PLATE 13

U. S. Snagboat "J. G. Parke," 1885

(MAYO FOUNDATION)

When Captain Alexander Mackenzie took command of the Rock Island office of the Corps of Engineers in 1879, he commanded only one major working boat—the snag boat *General Barnard.* Mackenzie immediately sought to bolster his fleet to continue the work of constricting the channel, dredging and scraping the river, and pulling snags. Mackenzie took advantage of Henry Bosse's skills as a draftsman to have him complete the drawings for several new boats. The second snag boat Mackenzie added to the fleet was the *J. G. Parke*, a stern-wheeler (unlike his other snag boat, the *Barnard*, which was a side-wheeler). The smaller stern-wheeler *Parke*, built in 1882 for $18,750, could sometimes get to places that the *Barnard* could not reach. By 1882 Mackenzie had acquired four towboats, three steam launches, fifty-five stone barges, and "the necessary complement of quarter-boats, pile-drivers, & c."

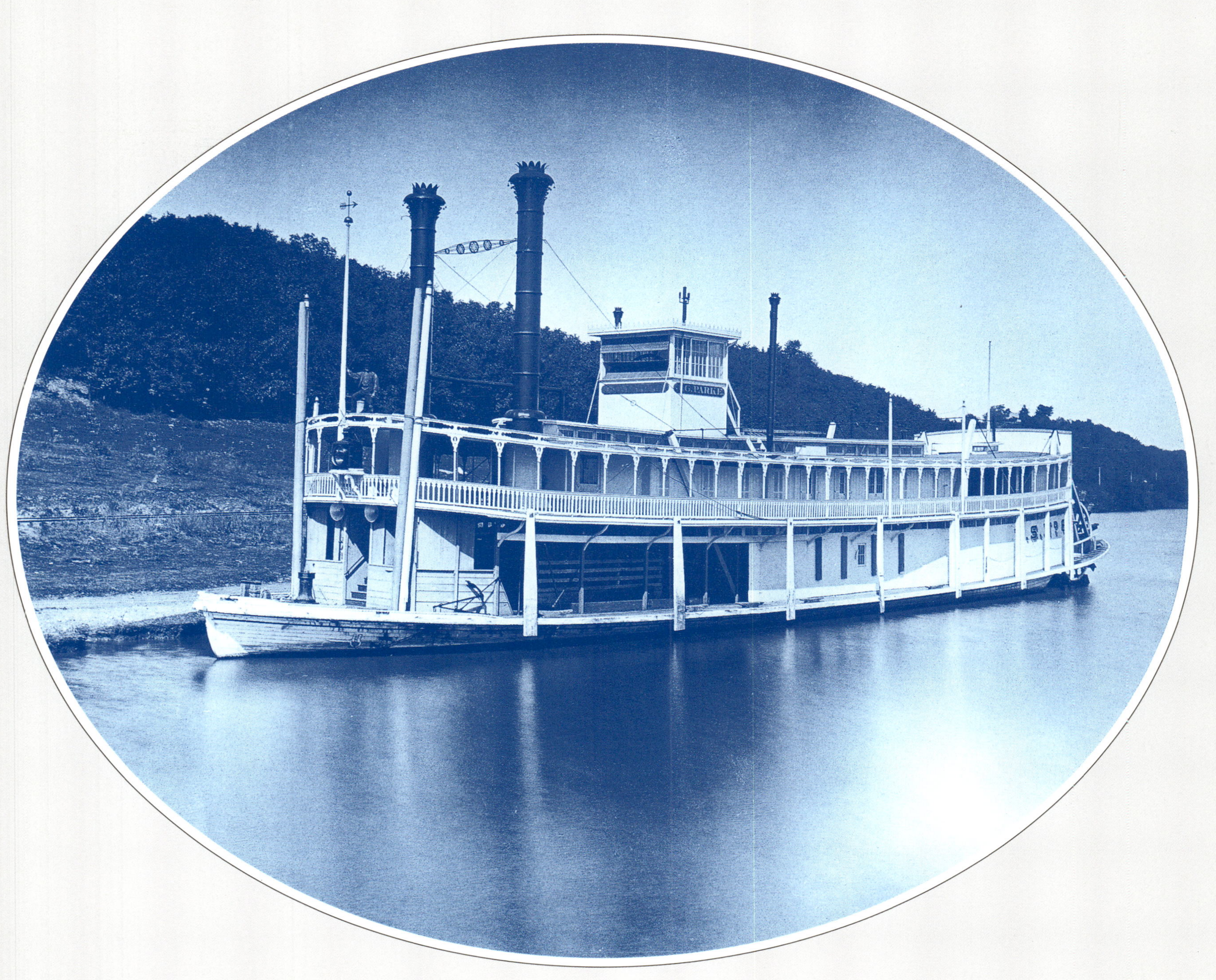
G. PARKE

PLATE 14

River at St. Paul, Minn. (from Dayton's Bluff), 1890

(MAYO FOUNDATION)

The industrial city of the late nineteenth century is well represented in this photograph, taken from the bluffs downriver from the St. Paul harbor. Another print of this image is dated 1891. Smokestacks belch and freight cars idle. Low water has exposed much of the right bank of the river, and the revetments can be seen lining the bank near the railroad tracks. Not much changed in that area—unlike other parts of the river—in the years to come. • The steeple in the photograph is the Ramsey County Court House, built in 1884. In 1862, the first railroad tracks were laid in St. Paul, a ten-mile stretch to St. Anthony. Twenty years later, fueled by men like James J. Hill, the city's trains had direct access to more than 3,100 miles of track. Hill became an outspoken opponent of navigation improvements on the Mississippi River primarily because he saw steamship lines as competition for his railroad empire. Ironically, the first locomotive delivered to Minnesota came via steamship. • Tucked out of sight behind the bridges is the Milwaukee and Northwestern Railroad bridge pier, which was built in 1885 but never authorized by the government. The pier was an unending source of frustration for riverboat pilots.

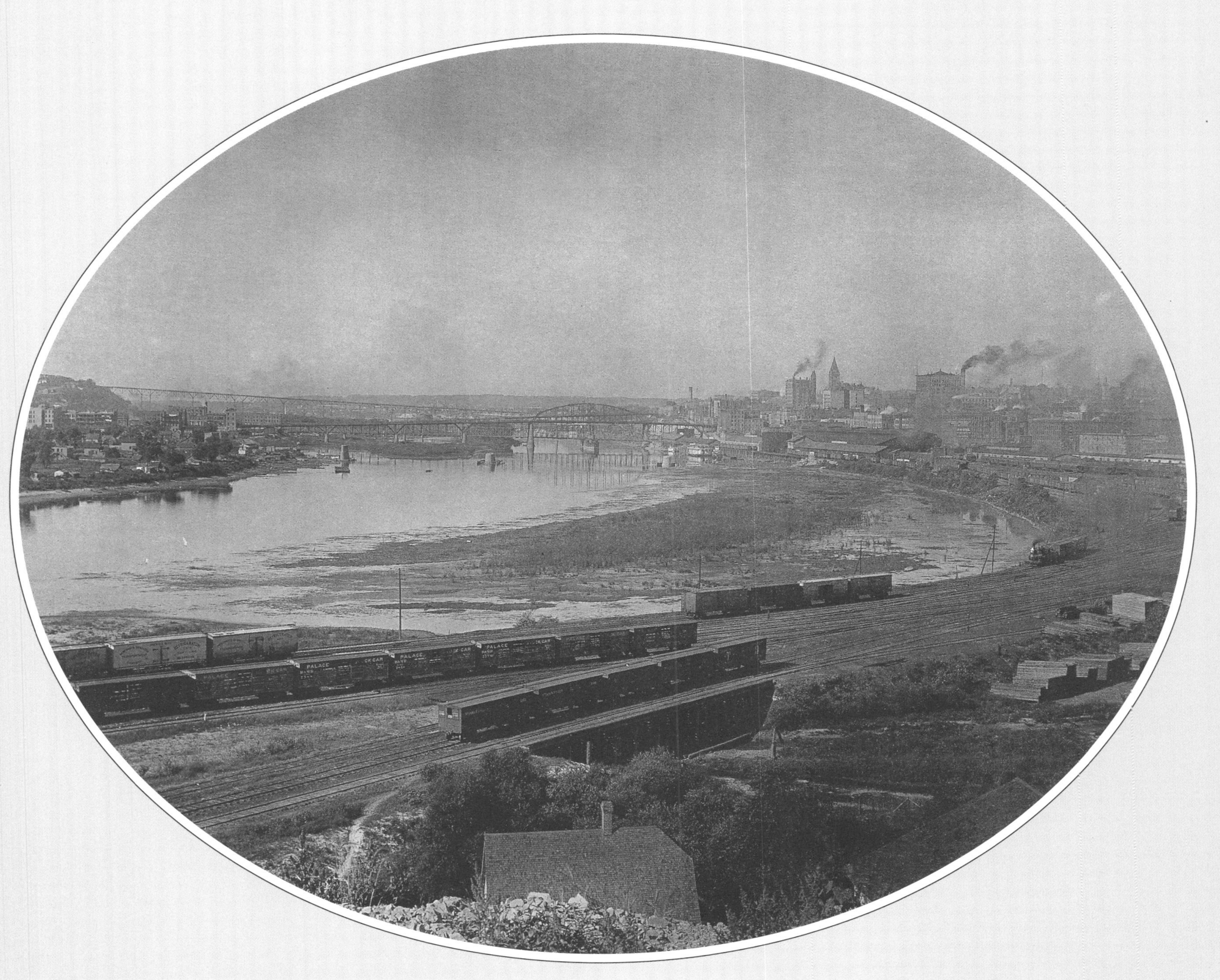

PLATE 15

Pigs Eye Island (from shore protection below), 1885

(U.S. ARMY CORPS OF ENGINEERS, ROCK ISLAND DISTRICT)

One way the Corps of Engineers attempted to speed up the current and reduce the amount of silt in the river (and thus save on dredging costs) was to build revetments like this one on Pig's Eye Island near St. Paul. The revetment, made up of rocks called rip-rap, was many small limestone boulders piled against a system of poles laid on the shore. Trees and grasses eventually grew between the rocks, taking root and supporting the entire structure. • Revetments were often placed around islands too large to remove or in the outside bend in the river, where the current was fastest and the erosion greatest. • Pig's Eye Island was named after Pierre "Pig's Eye" Parrant, a coarse fellow who sold whiskey, drank whiskey, and claimed to be the founder of St. Paul.

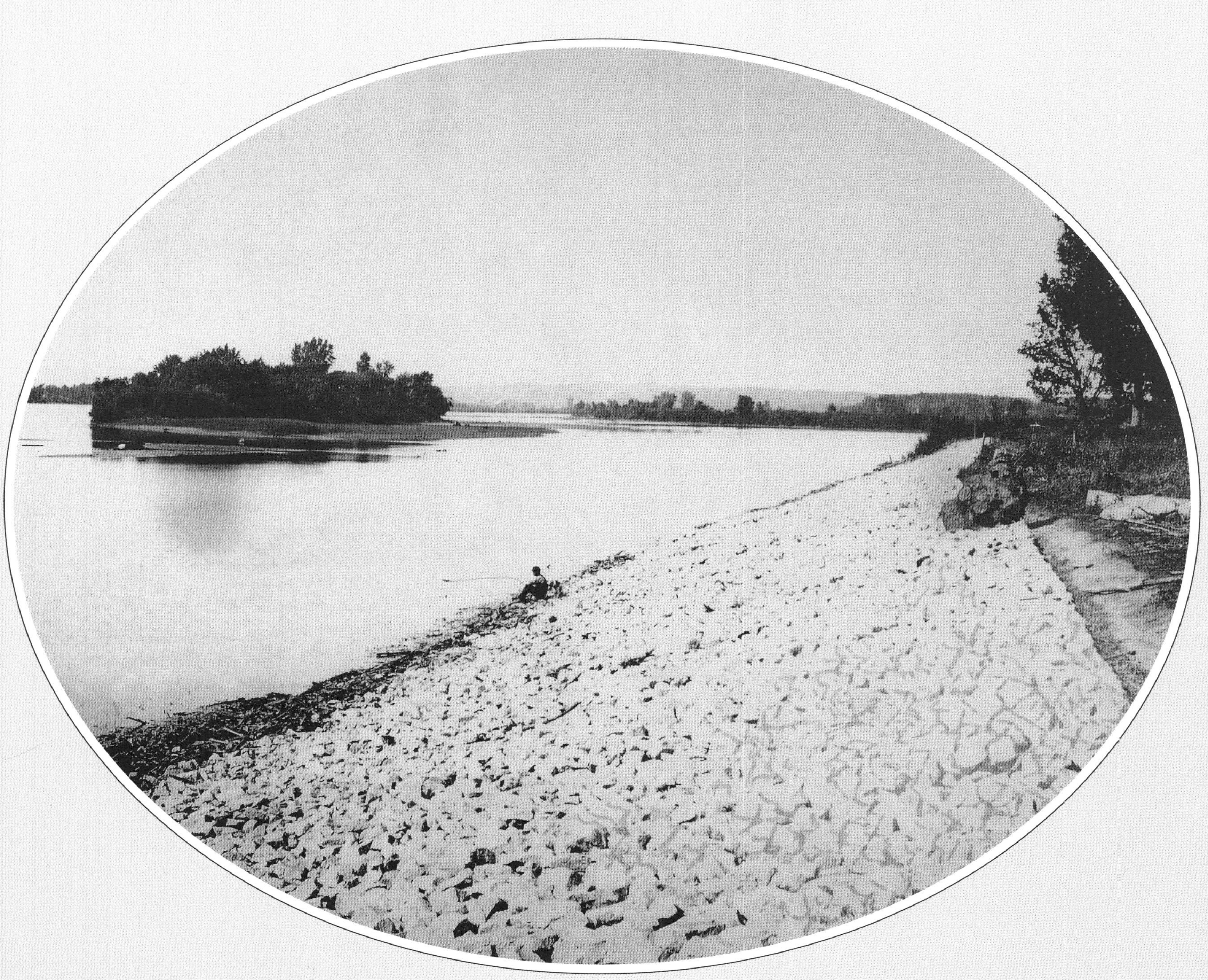

PLATE 16

Pine Bend, 1891

(U.S. ARMY CORPS OF ENGINEERS, ST. PAUL DISTRICT)

Perhaps nowhere are Bosse's skill as a photographer and the environmental effects of the efforts of the Corps of Engineers on the river so easily visible as in this photograph at Pine Bend, a spot between Hastings and Merrimac, Minnesota. A steep bluff on the left bank and miles of floodplain on the opposite shore provided the photographer with the classic landscape photograph. The wing dams and closing dam on the right bank show what happened after only a couple of decades of work constricting the big river. The smallish island in the middle ground is being enlarged by the wing dams on its main channel side; the side channel at the far right is closed by the upstream dam. It will slowly fill in as the island becomes attached to Grey Cloud Island, the larger land mass on the far right. • The dams forced the river into one main channel, which became scoured and flowed more quickly. The silt and sand formerly dumped all across the river had to go somewhere, so it ended up in the slack water behind the wing dams. Eventually, these areas became solid ground and first-growth willows and grasses took hold. The river, which was once wide and slow in these areas, was cut in half and accelerated. Fish and mussel habitats were damaged or lost altogether. Some of the land was reclaimed for farming, but the unpredictable nature of the Mississippi made that a risky business. After the lock and dam system was put into place starting in the 1910s, it became cost effective to reclaim some of the land behind the wing dams and closing dams for industrial property.

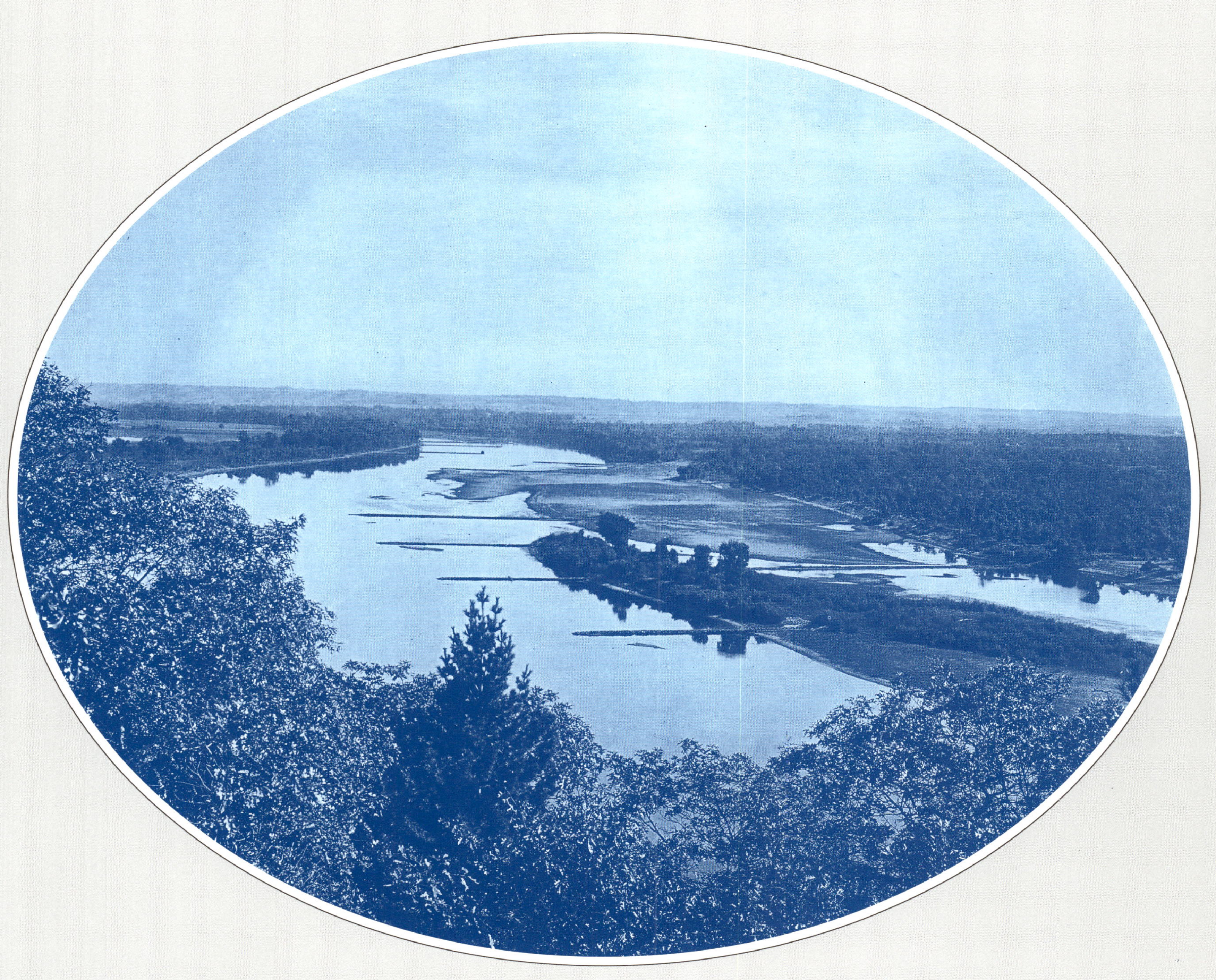

PLATE 17

Wingdams below Nininger, Minn., 1891

(MAYO FOUNDATION)

Wingdams below Nininger is perhaps Bosse's most famous photograph. One of his favorite techniques, putting a person or two in the middle ground, is represented in this picture. The subject was often A. J. Stibolt, the assistant draftsman in the Rock Island office, although Alexander Mackenzie, Bosse's supervisor, may have been a subject as well. Mackenzie's dog also shows up in several photos. • Nininger, a "city of tomorrow" platted in 1857, is important in Minnesota history because of its founder, Ignatius Donnelly, a leader of the young Republican Party and one of Minnesota's outstanding orators as a three-term congressman and longtime political figure on the national scene. He made the Grange a power in state politics fighting railroad interests in the 1870s and was a leader of the populist movement when he died in 1900. • Dreams die hard; author and historian Meridel Le Sueur, in her book *North Star Country*, said Nininger ended up "the ruin of a thousand houses in the wheat fields and only the pillared house of Donnelly standing by the river." • Franklin's Coulee was a deep gulch that dumped into the river between Hastings and Nininger. During the time this picture was taken, the Corps was attempting to constrict the river at this spot, a notoriously shallow point. • By the close of the twentieth century, the river near the coulee was one of the spots made wider, not narrower, by the engineers because Lock and Dam No. 2, completed at Hastings in 1930, included an earthen dam in what would have been the far left of this photograph. The pool behind the lock and dam widened the river considerably, rendering useless the wing dams above it—they became flooded under several feet of lower Pool 2.

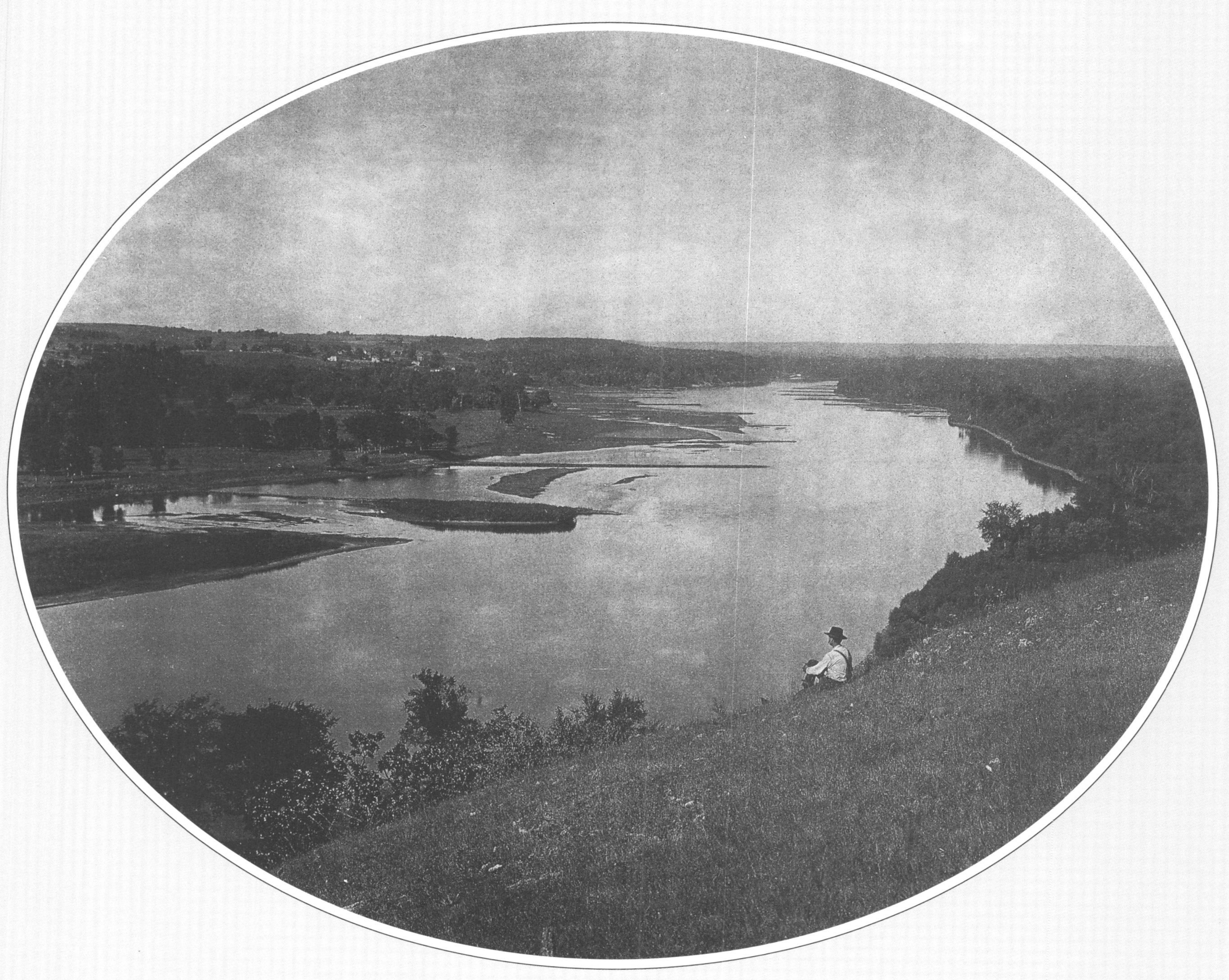

PLATE 18

Wingdams and Bar below Hastings, Minn., 1891

(MAYO FOUNDATION)

Hastings grew as a center of commerce in the 1850s and 1860s because it had a natural gravel bar boat landing on the river and a series of shallow rapids above town that prevented steamboats from making it all the way to St. Paul in low water. White settlers established a village in the area in the winter of 1818–19 when a boat bound for Fort Snelling got stuck at the site. The Dakota called the area "O-wo-bop-te," which has the unromantic translation of "the place we dug tipsinna [wild turnip]." • The Chicago, Milwaukee and St. Paul Railroad Bridge in the photograph is a swing bridge. Built between the Hastings landing and Point Douglas, the bridge connected the town to markets on the southern shore of Lake Michigan. • On a swing bridge, boats have priority over trains, and in the days before radio communication, the ship's captain would blow his whistle to signal the bridge tender to open the swing. The bridge tender would respond with one long blast on his whistle if the bridge was opening; four short blasts meant a train was crossing. • The system was not infallible. If the wind was wrong, it was difficult for both sides to hear the whistles. Savvy captains picked up a trick: The bridges were nesting habitat for pigeons, and when the span moved, so did a few dozen birds. The pigeons provided a visual signal that the swing was opening. • A spiral bridge, one of only three like it in the world, was built at Hastings in 1895 and torn down in 1951.

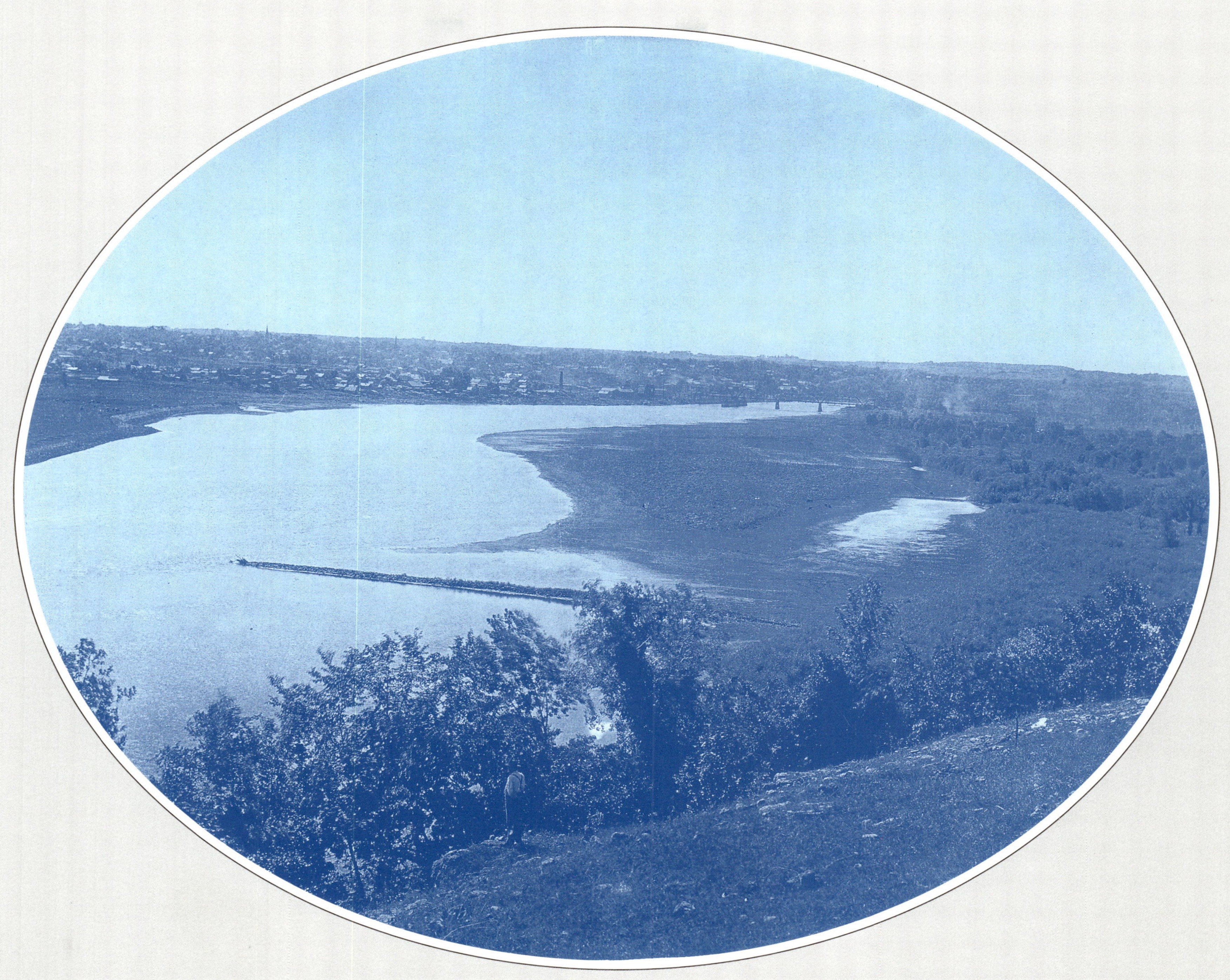

PLATE 19

Mouth of St. Croix Riv, 1885

(MAYO FOUNDATION)

PLATE 20

Prescott, Wis., 1885

(MAYO FOUNDATION)

PLATE 21

Raftboat "Ten Brook," 1885

(MAYO FOUNDATION)

The St. Croix River was an important commercial route for lumbering interests in Minnesota and Wisconsin in the latter part of the nineteenth century. White pine was floated downriver from the northern forests of both states to the Mississippi. • The first steamboat on the tributary was the *Palmyra* in 1838, and it carried materials to erect the first mill in the river valley near Stillwater, Minnesota. There were more than 100 mills on the St. Croix by the late 1800s. • The town of Prescott, Wisconsin, grew up at the mouth of the St. Croix (upper left in Plate 19). Rafts were floated to Prescott and made into larger rafts for the trip downriver. The riverbank at right in Plate 19 remains a popular swimming and picnic area. Point Douglas, from which this photo was taken, was a steamboat landing. • In the 1850s, the first timber rafts were floated down the Mississippi to sawmills and markets to the south. The rafts were made up of cribs—sixteen- by thirty-two-foot sets of logs roped together. Fifteen or sixteen cribs were joined to make a string; eight to ten strings were placed side by side and the raft was complete, held to the boat by guy lines and winding engines. • In the early days, the rafts were self-propelled, with tough crews ("fiddling, song-singing, whisky-drinking, breakdown-dancing rapscallions," Mark Twain called them) manning oars and sweeps at the bow and stern. Steamboats were first employed as early as the 1840s to assist the rafts through tricky waters; eventually, the steamers became the power source for the raft itself. Some rafts employed a small steamboat at the bow of the structure to move the bow from side to side for steering in rapids or tricky currents. • The *Ten Broeck* (misspelled by Bosse on the print) was built in Stillwater in 1882 for the rafting firm of Gillespie and Harper of Stillwater. The ship's design was interesting because it contained three boilers and had an unusually low profile to reduce wind effect. The well-known Walter A. Blair was the ship's captain. The Le Claire Navigation Company purchased the boat in 1886, and it wound up working on the Tennessee River. It burned at Cairo, Illinois, in November 1904.

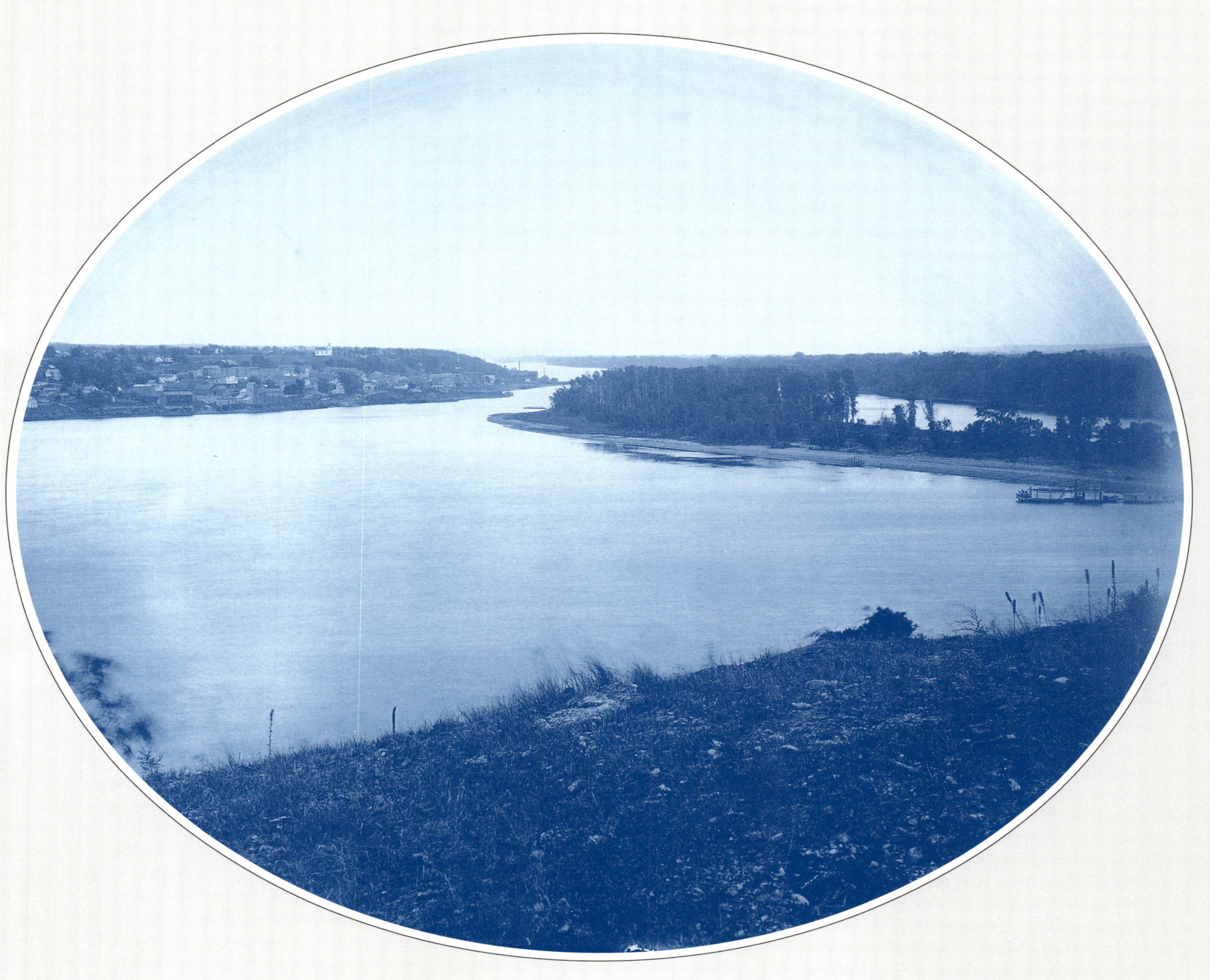

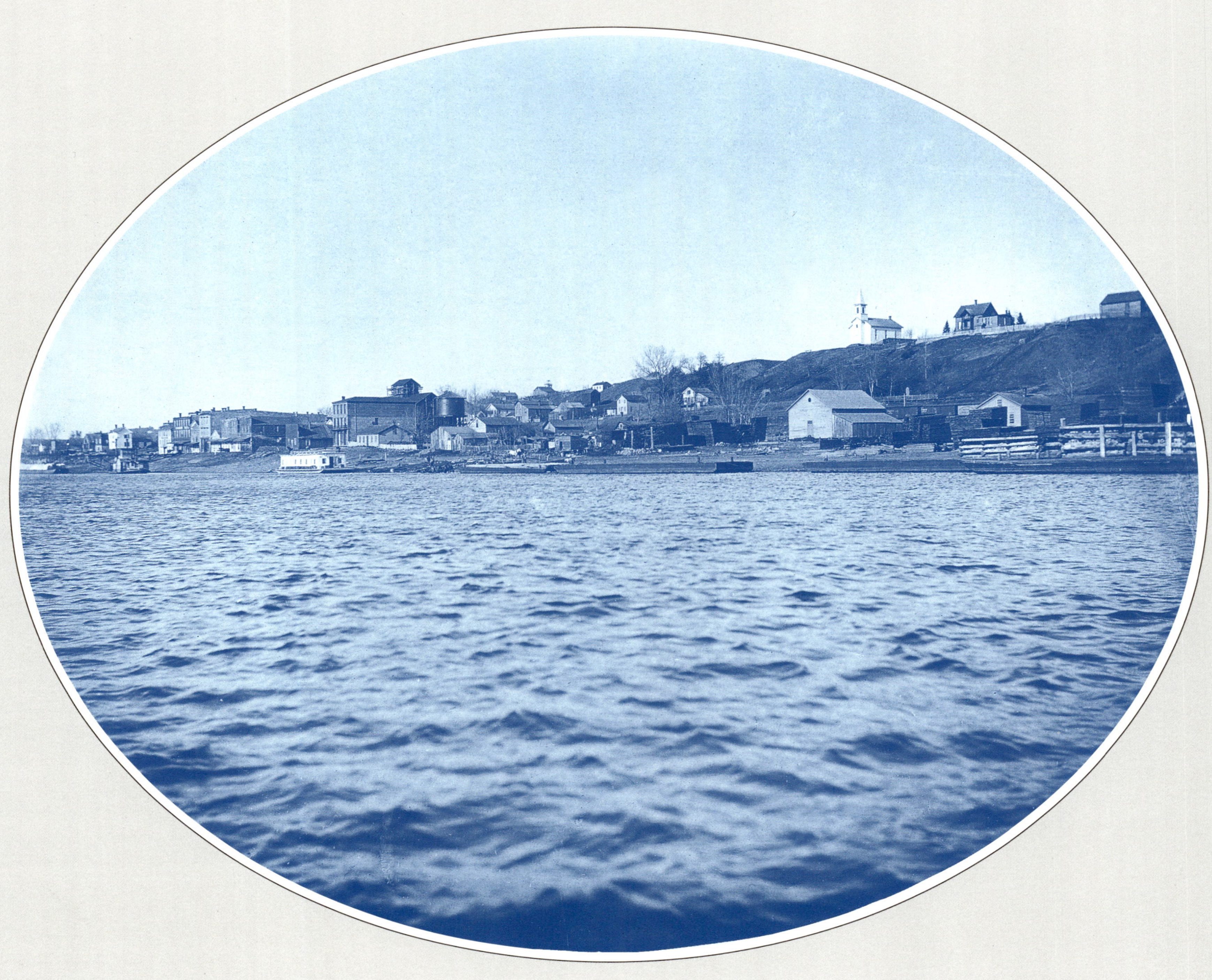

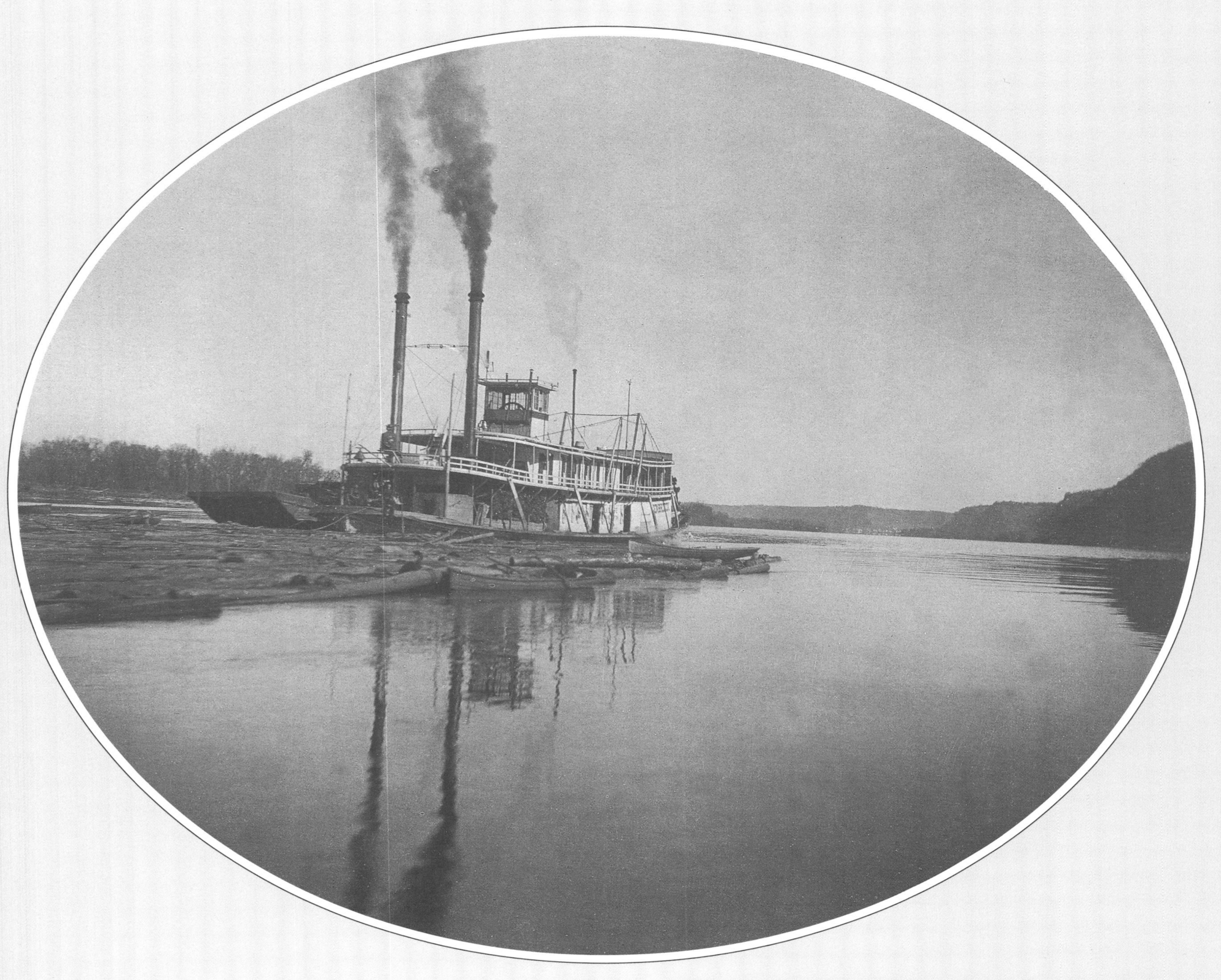

PLATE 22

Wreck of Excursionboat "Seawing" (capsized during a severe thunderstorm on Lake Pepin, July 13, 1890, causing a loss of 99 passengers.), 1891

(MAYO FOUNDATION)

More than two hundred people had paid fifty cents each for a leisurely thirty-mile trip down the Mississippi River from Red Wing to Lake Pepin and back on July 13, 1890, aboard the *Seawing*. More were scheduled to take the trip, but an itinerant preacher at the landing warned several passengers off the boat, telling them it would be destroyed by storm. Captain David M. Wethern, who owned a general store in Diamond Bluff, was the skipper. • On the return trip, a storm blew across the lake; passengers and crew watched in horror as a wall of low, rolling clouds rushed at them. The *Seawing* tipped to forty-five degrees, tottered on its side for a moment, then crashed on its top. Those thrown into the water were lucky; those trapped in the cabin had almost no chance. Some people struggled to swim in the stormy seas, pelted by hailstones, and others grabbed onto the hull. Tragically, the ship was flipped again, sending more people into Lake Pepin. One hundred and fifteen passengers survived; the exact death toll was never known, but it was at least eighty-five and perhaps as high as one hundred and included the captain's wife. The wreck, shown here with its top deck torn off, was towed to Diamond Bluff, salvaged in 1891, and returned to service.

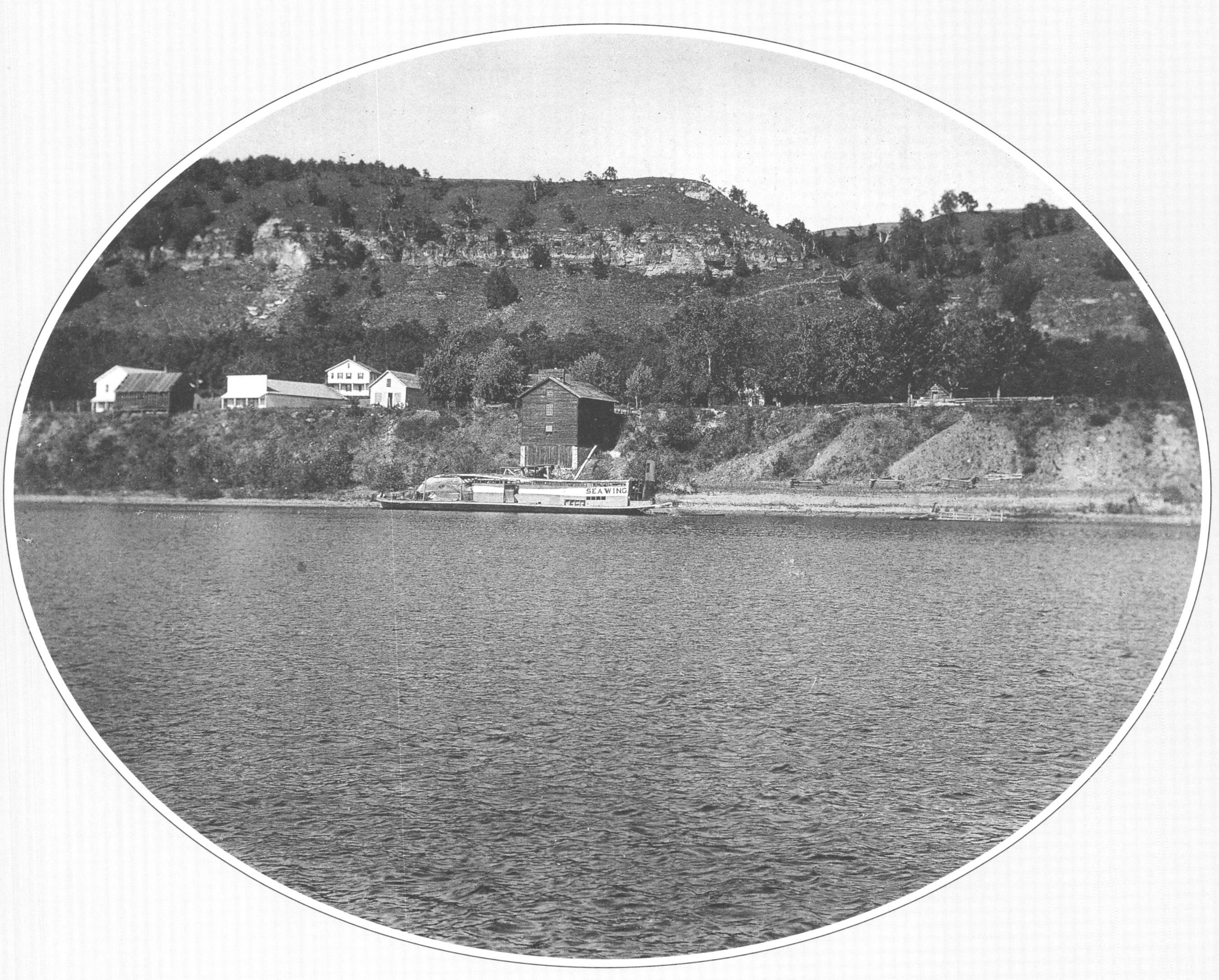
SEA WING

PLATE 23

Redwing, Minn. and Barn bluff, 1891

(MAYO FOUNDATION)

Red Wing (misspelled Redwing by Bosse), a thriving community by the 1890s, benefited from an accident of geography: the river at Red Wing was often open in the spring while Lake Pepin, downstream, was still iced in. Packet boats from St. Paul and the Minnesota River would pick up freight and passengers in Red Wing and deliver them to the Twin Cities before the big steamers could make it all the way upriver. • The city was plagued by floods because of its topography; at normal channel the river was six hundred feet wide, but a flood could cause the Mississippi to extend two and a half miles across the valley. • A horrible fire aboard the steamer *Galena* in the middle of a night in 1854 forced many passengers, mostly immigrants, into the water in their nightclothes. At least five were killed. • Barn Bluff, formerly called Mountain of the Grange, was the site of a Dakota village. Henry David Thoreau climbed Barn Bluff in 1861 and wrote glowingly of the grandeur and beauty of the region. The bluff is listed on the National Register of Historic Places.

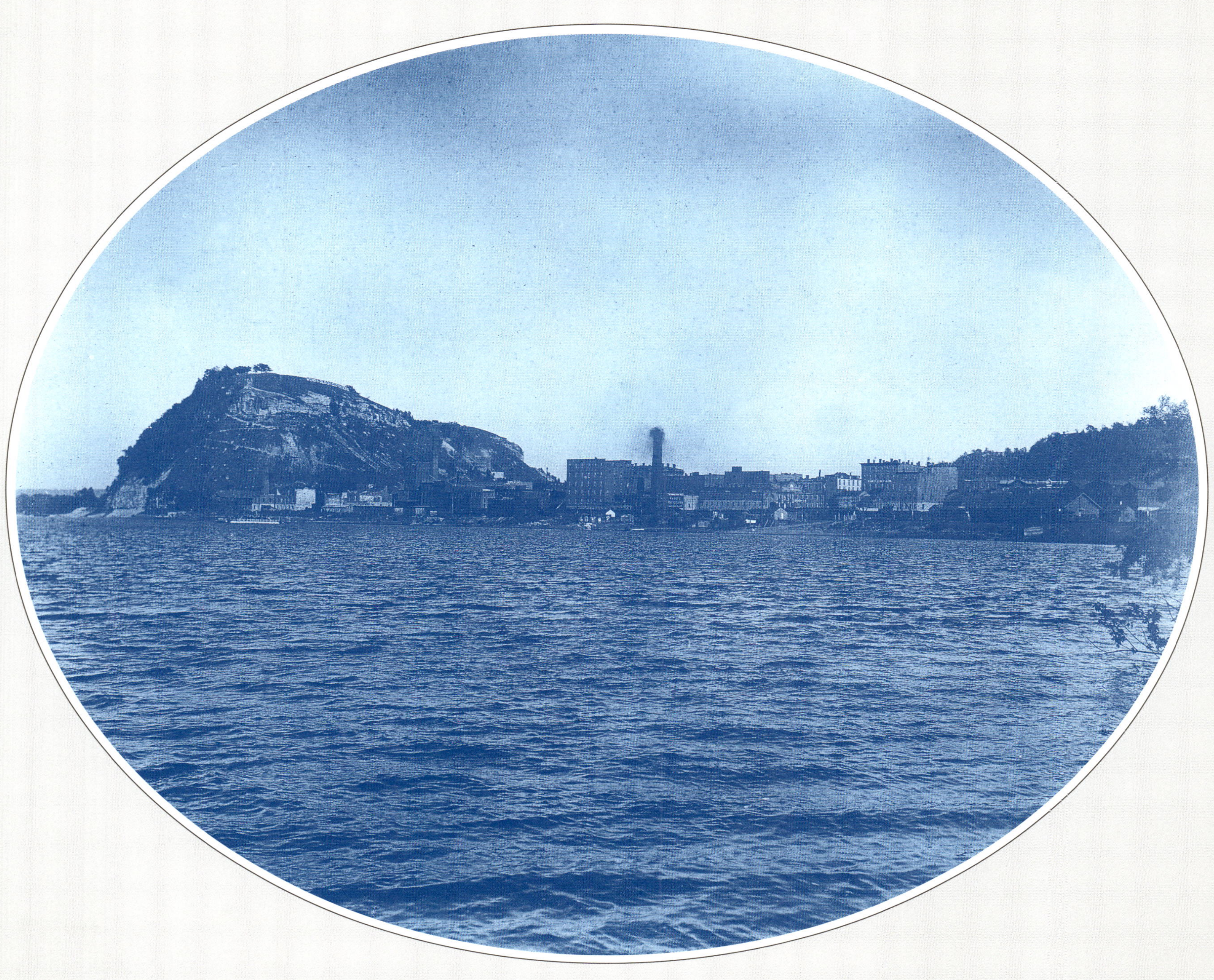

PLATE 24

From point "No Point" looking down stream, across Lake Pepin, 1885

(U.S. ARMY CORPS OF ENGINEERS, ROCK ISLAND DISTRICT)

The wide, flat expanse of Lake Pepin can be seen in this photograph, taken from the upriver side of the lake. Lake Pepin, one to two miles wide, became the bane of many boats journeying on the Mississippi. Its surface, open to the wind, often had a rough wake, and the lake was usually one of the first spots on the upper river to ice up in the winter and the last spot to thaw in the spring. • The river's edge at the lake was also the site of one of the early white settlements on the river, a fort established by the French soldier Nicholas Perrot in 1689. Perrot eventually made his way back downriver and is thought to have been among the first whites to mine lead in the Galena-Dubuque region. The community in the middle ground in this photograph is old Frontenac, established as a trading post in 1839 by James "Bully" Wells. Point No Point got its name from the fact that to a person in a boat coming upriver the bluff looks like a point, but it is simply a long, sweeping bend and not a point at all.

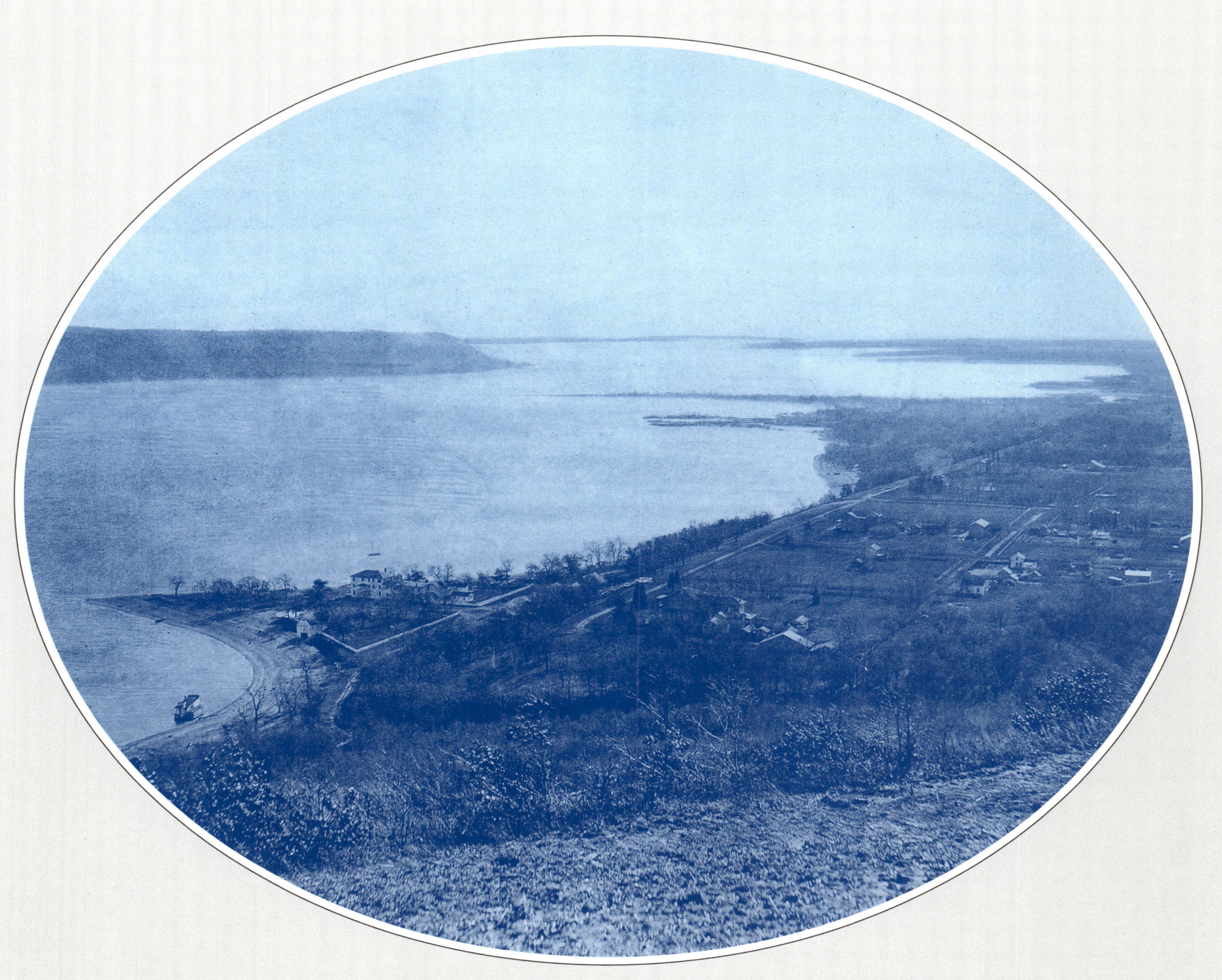

PLATE 25

Mouth of Chippewa River, 1885

(MAYO FOUNDATION)

The Chippewa River empties into the Mississippi at the downstream end of Lake Pepin. Sediment carried by the Chippewa over the centuries blocked off the big river, creating a natural wing dam, and backed up the Mississippi to form the twenty-two-mile-long lake. When the Corps of Engineers began experimenting in earnest with wing dams and closing dams on the Mississippi, this location was among the first and most intense objects of its attention. Two long jetties stretching from the mouth of the Chippewa are visible in the photograph. • It looks like Bosse or his assistant chopped down a few trees for a better vista. Fresh stumps and fallen branches can be seen in the foreground. • A massive log harbor at Beef Slough was built seven miles downstream from here in the 1860s to collect hundreds of thousands of white pine logs; by 1890, five years after this photograph, the boom was closed because of silting.

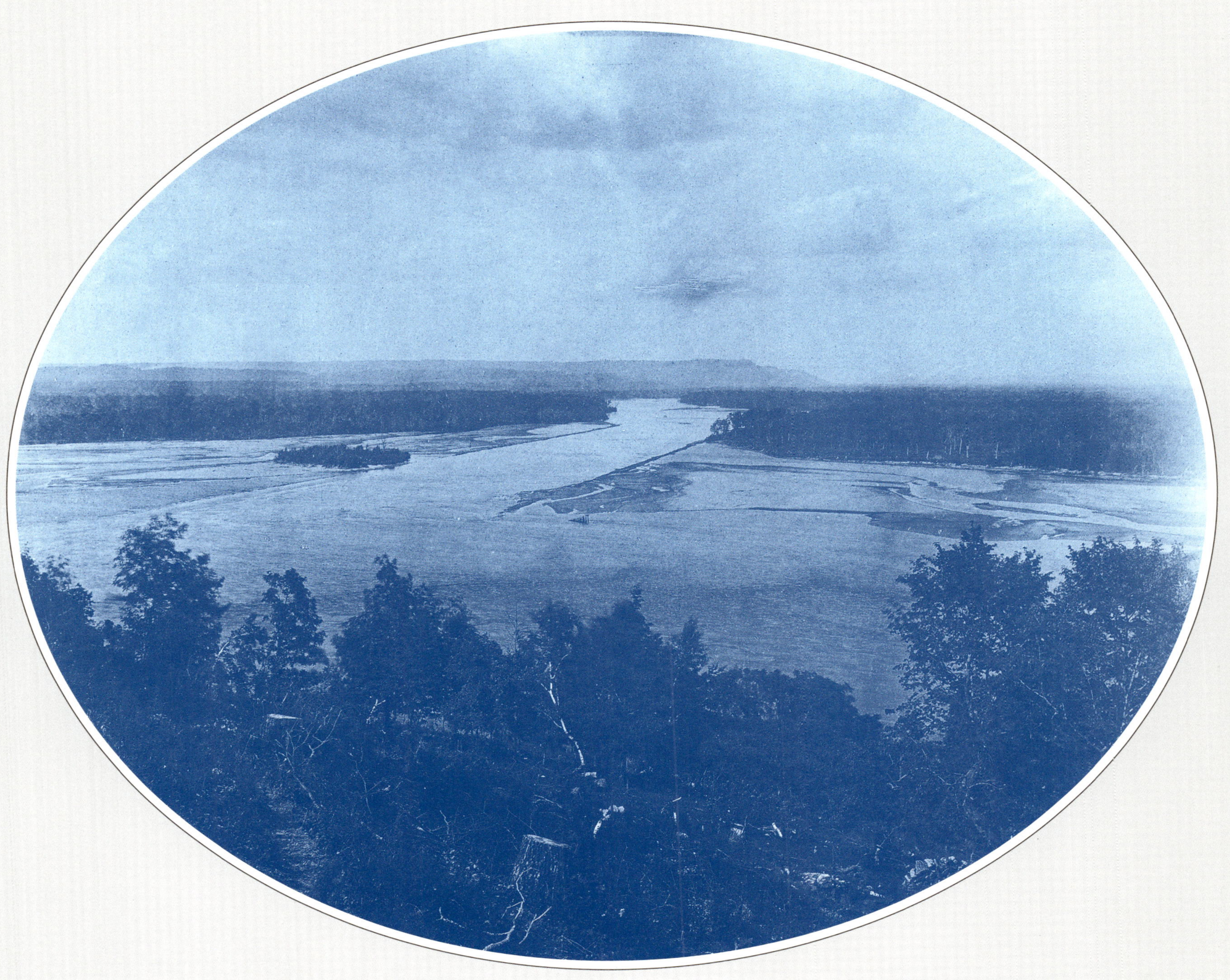

PLATE 26

From Quarry at Read's Landing, Minn. looking down stream, 1889

(MAYO FOUNDATION)

Read's Landing, near the mouth of the Chippewa River on the south side of Lake Pepin, served as a loading and unloading point for steamboats working both the Mississippi and the Chippewa. Steamboats began regular routes on the Chippewa from Read's Landing in the 1850s after immigrants began to settle the area. The landing was also the site of a quarry above the town, from which limestone was cut for wing dams. This photograph was taken from the quarry, looking downstream. • This pontoon bridge floated on the river and could be opened relatively easily for steamboat passage. The pontoons, made of wood, were also opened to allow ice floes to pass. The Chippewa Valley and Superior Railway built the bridge in 1882 over the furious objections of pilots, including Captain Joseph Buison, who collected fifty-one signatures from fellow rivermen in opposition to the bridge. Lumberman J. M. Turner countered Buison's effort, calling the petition "a sham and a fraud" and accusing the pilot of favoring a bridge at Wabasha, where Buison owned a home.

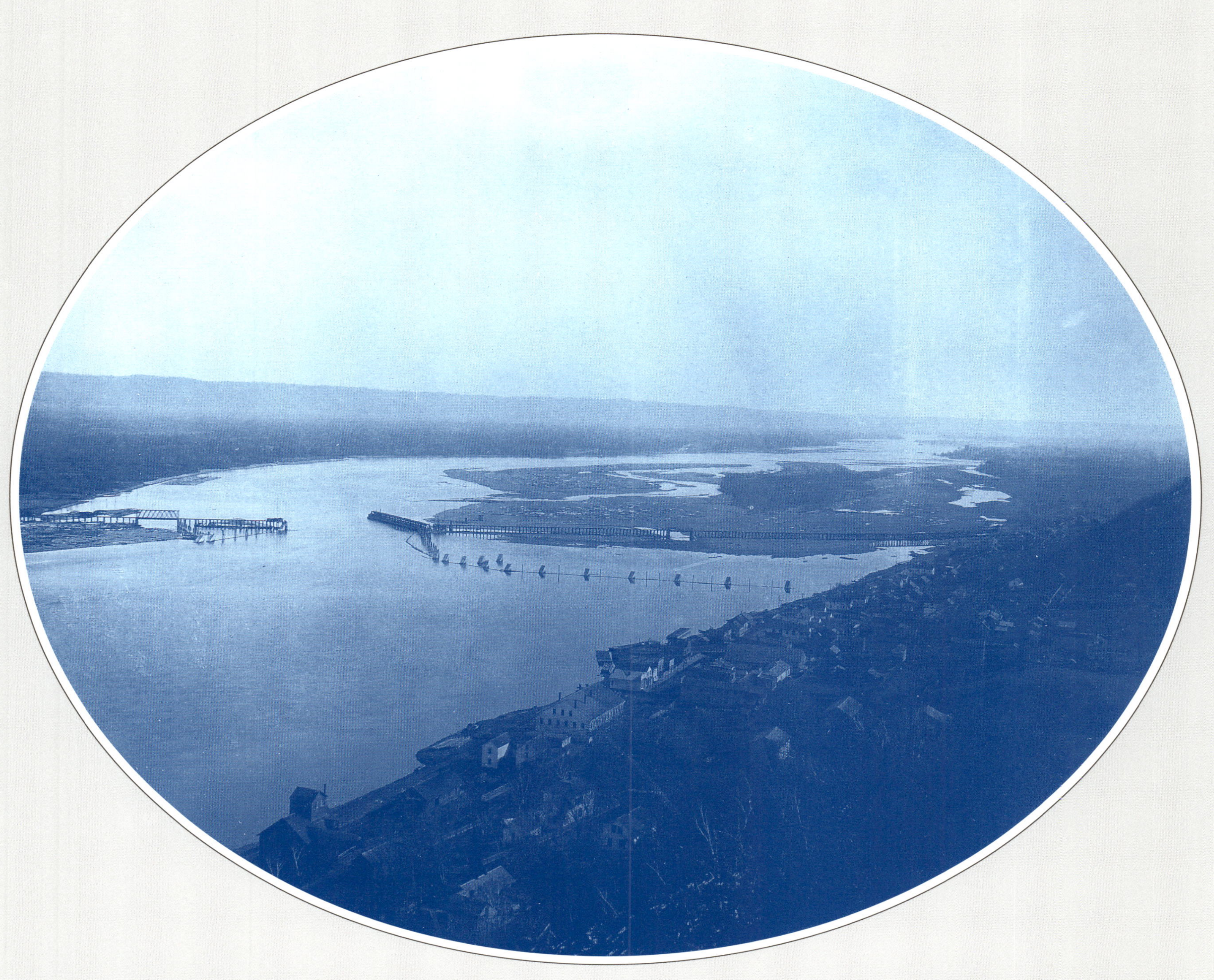

PLATE 27

Boatyard at Wabasha, Minn., 1891

(MAYO FOUNDATION)

The landing at Wabasha, a short distance upstream from the mouth of the Zumbro River, became an important docking point for steamboats and barges under the jurisdiction of the Corps of Engineers because of the amount of dam construction that went on near that stretch of the Mississippi. A boatyard at Wabasha supplied parts, repaired boats, and built new vessels. Samuel Peters and his son specialized in stern-wheelers at the yard, which was swept by fire on December 2, 1907. Five stern-wheelers were destroyed in the blaze, but the boatyard was rebuilt and continued at that site for another two decades. What was left of the place was buried under water when the lock and dam system was installed in the 1930s. • Among the more unusual cargoes carried by raft down the Mississippi River was a Catholic church, which was shipped in 1842 by an enterprising priest from Mendota Heights to what later became Wabasha.

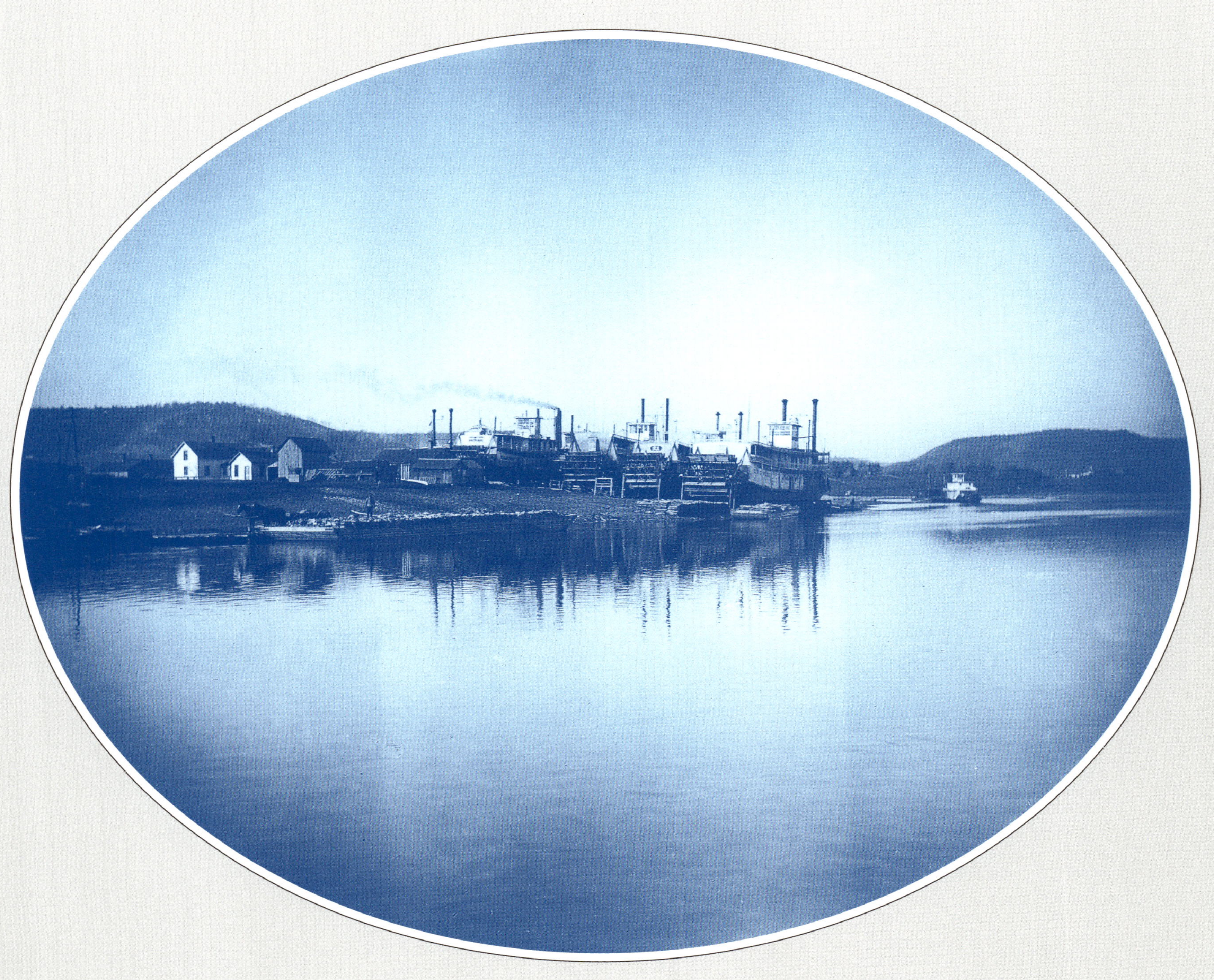

PLATE 28

From bluffs at Alma, Wis looking down stream, 1891

(MAYO FOUNDATION)

Two Swiss immigrants settled in the area that became Alma, Wisconsin, in 1848. Both men made a living selling wood to steamboats for fuel. Early steamboat pilots called the Alma area Twelve Mile Bluff and used the bluff as a navigational landmark. Two streets were built at the base of the bluff and the town grew up around them. • The railroad arrived in Alma in 1885, a few years before this photograph was taken. By then the community had a brewery (its first industry) and several cigar factories. Nearly fifteen hundred people lived in Alma when nearby Beef Slough was used as a boom in the 1880s. • In 1935, Lock and Dam No. 4 was completed on this spot. During the cold months, the highly oxygenated water rushing through the tainter gates and roller gates does not freeze and attracts fish. Migrating tundra swans and roosting bald eagles feeding on the fish frequent the area in winter.

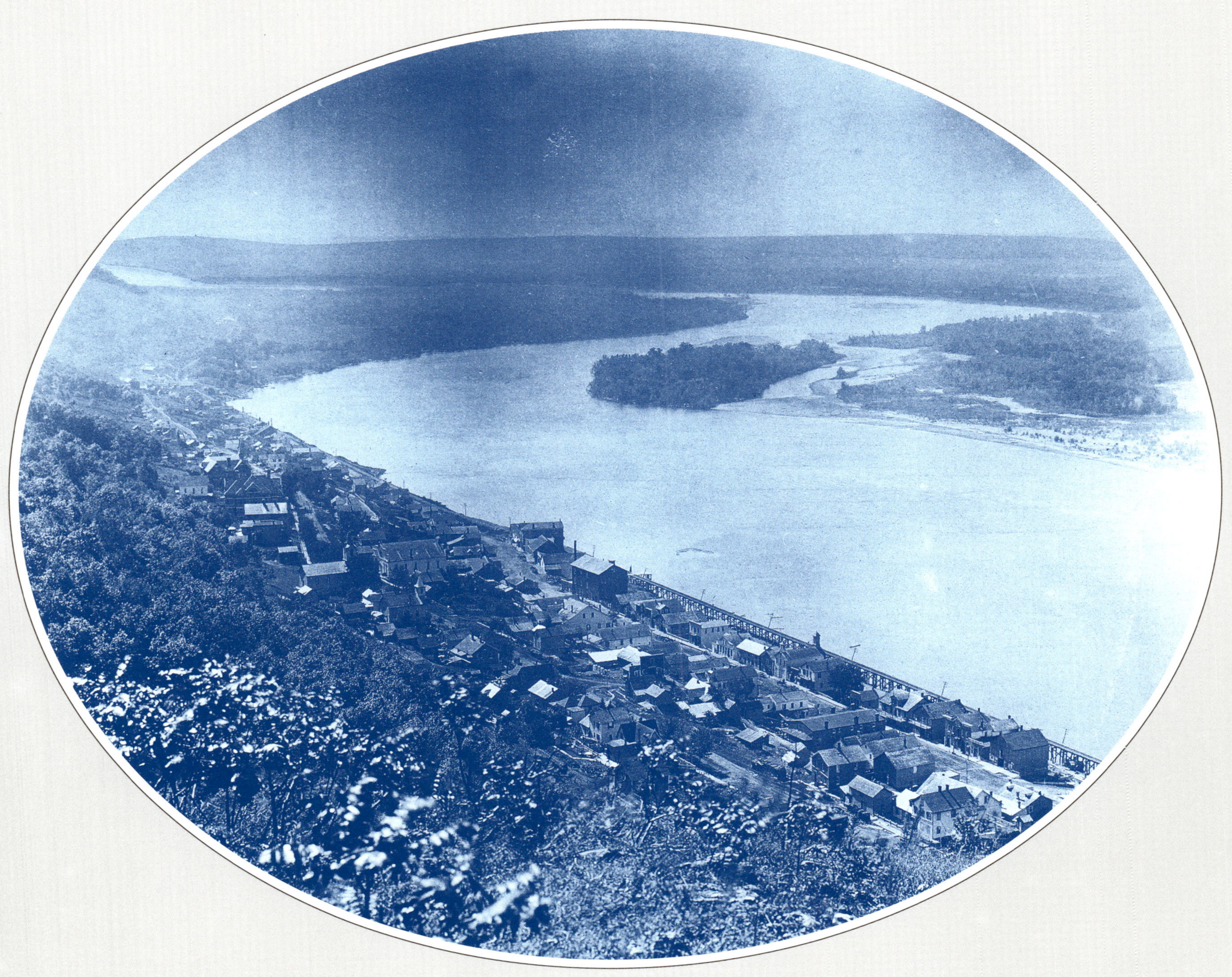

PLATE 29

Minneiska, Minn., 1885

(MAYO FOUNDATION)

The wing dam in the foreground and the person sitting at its end direct the eye to the community of Minneiska, tucked beneath the bluffs on the west bank of the river. The wing dam points to the white church nestled on the hillside. If the notes on map Sheet No. 5 are correct, Bosse took this photograph on July 25 or 26, 1885, from the point of an unmarked island at the mouth of the Whitewater River. • Minneiska was the location of a swinging boom where lumber was collected and bound for shipping downstream. In 1884, the year before this photograph was taken, a hired dredge had successfully removed a small tow head—the head of an island—that had damaged several rafts, at a cost of three hundred and fifty dollars. The Corps used its Minneiska experience to ask Congress for money for its own dredge in its annual report. The Corps purchased the dredge *Phoenix* in 1885. • In the tricky twenty-mile stretch of river between Minneiska and Read's Landing, 257 wing dams were built between 1866 and 1930. • Minneiska also has the distinction of being home to Putnam Gray, the man credited with inventing the Ferris wheel. Gray exhibited the design with his carnival in Winona at the county fair in 1892; G. W. G. Ferris saw it, bought the rights to it, and renamed it after himself in time to display it at the World's Columbian Exposition in Chicago the following year.

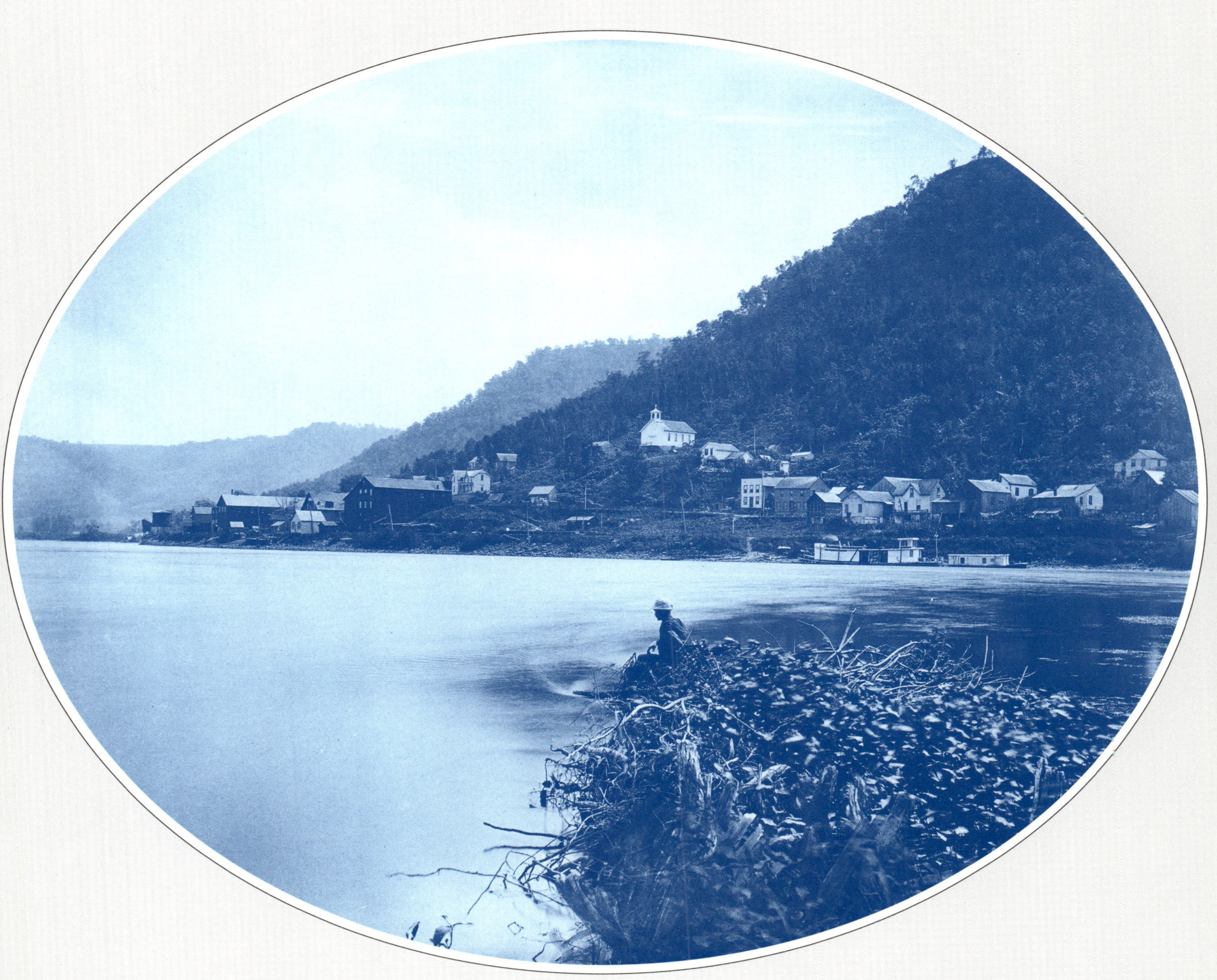

PLATE 30

From bluffs at Fountain City looking upstream, 1885

(MAYO FOUNDATION)

The size and strength of the Mississippi River are evident in this photograph, although it is likely that Bosse tried to improve on nature's geology by painting in a few more bluffs in the background. Dwarfed by the river is a steamboat pushing a load of wood downstream. These log rafts could reach up to four acres in size and carry enough lumber to build a frontier village complete with wooden sidewalks. The boats depended more on the current than on horsepower to move the rafts and advanced at a rate of about four miles per hour. In the left middle ground of the photograph, more log rafts waiting their turn are tied up at the bank. Lumber companies often used side channels and sloughs to construct these crafts because they were deep enough to float the logs but out of the main channel and its tricky currents. The Corps established a boatyard near here at Fountain City in 1889 and contracted with a local quarry to supply rocks for dams.

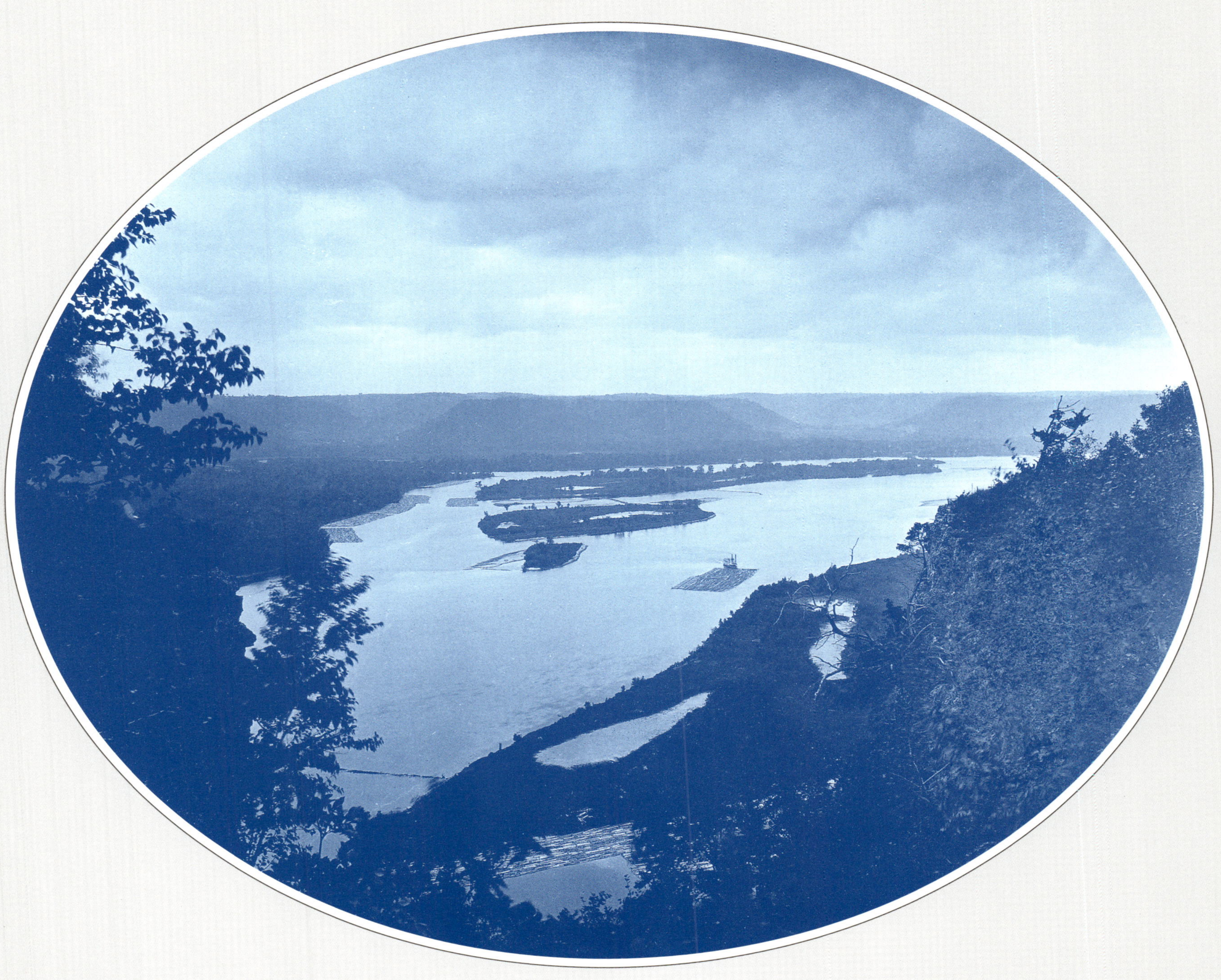

PLATE 31

Levee at Winona, Minn., no date

(U.S. ARMY CORPS OF ENGINEERS, ROCK ISLAND DISTRICT)

The one-time Sioux village of Winona grew to the nation's fourth-largest grain market and the Mississippi River's second-largest lumber milling center by the end of the nineteenth century. By 1870, Winona was Minnesota's third-largest city after St. Paul and Minneapolis. The city's geography gave it an advantage. The nearest stream navigable by steamboat to the west was the Minnesota River, 120 miles away. This left the intervening space available to wagons from Winona, and trails sprang up across the rich farm belt in southern Minnesota. The first timber mill in the city opened in 1855; eventually the Laird, Norton Company mills became one of the largest operations on the entire Upper Mississippi. The Winona and St. Peter Railroad, which eventually ran to the Missouri River in South Dakota, cemented Winona's economic hold on the southern part of the state by the early 1880s. • Originally called Montezuma by white settlers, Santee Sioux Chief Wa-ba-sha's former village was renamed after his daughter, We-no-nah ("Chief's first-born daughter") in the late 1850s, but the name was spelled incorrectly on the application papers. Upstream from Winona is Maiden Rock, where oral history has it that We-no-nah threw herself into the jagged rocks 150 feet below after her family refused to allow her to unite with a hunter from her tribe. Instead, her family had arranged a union with a warrior, whom she did not love; she preferred death to a loveless future.

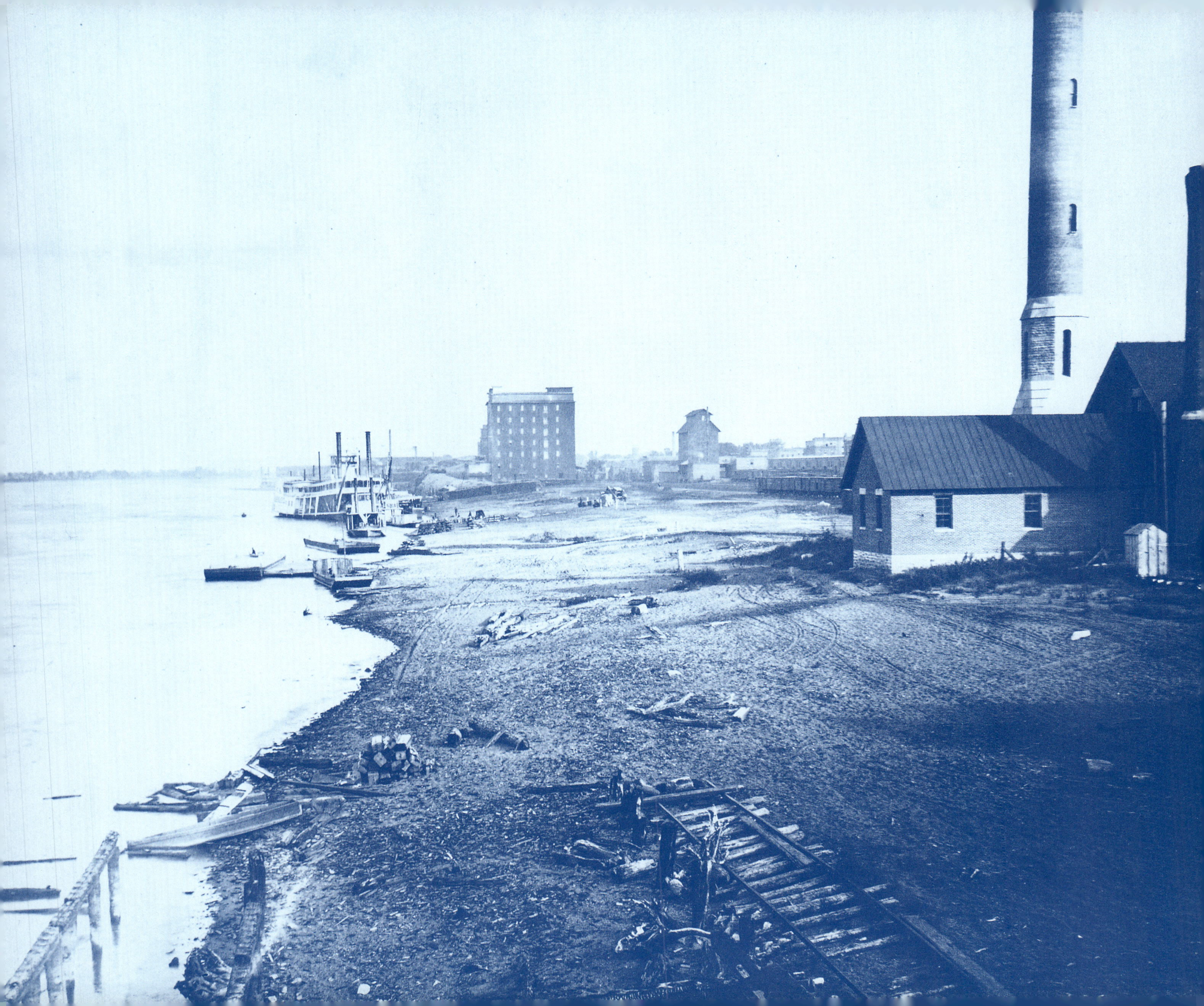

PLATE 32

Wagon Bridge at Winona, Minn., 1892

(MAYO FOUNDATION)

There are three bridges in this photograph, one of the latest Bosse prints known to exist. • The wagon bridge at Winona was built during the years 1891–92, at the time this photograph was taken. One can see the toolboxes, sawhorses, and other items left behind by workers in the foreground of the photograph. The bridge is of the "high-fixed" variety, which means that its spans did not move open and shut—it was simply built high enough to allow steamboats to pass beneath it. The wagon bridge was torn down and replaced during World War II. • The Chicago and Northwestern Railroad Bridge in the background was a swing-span bridge, constructed in the early 1870s as part of the Congressionally authorized bridge program that included structures in several cities along the river. The high railroad bridge in the foreground, built for the Winona and St. Peter Railroad, was famous among river pilots and others because the first train to use it snagged on unaligned rails and several flatcars loaded with limestone plunged into the river.

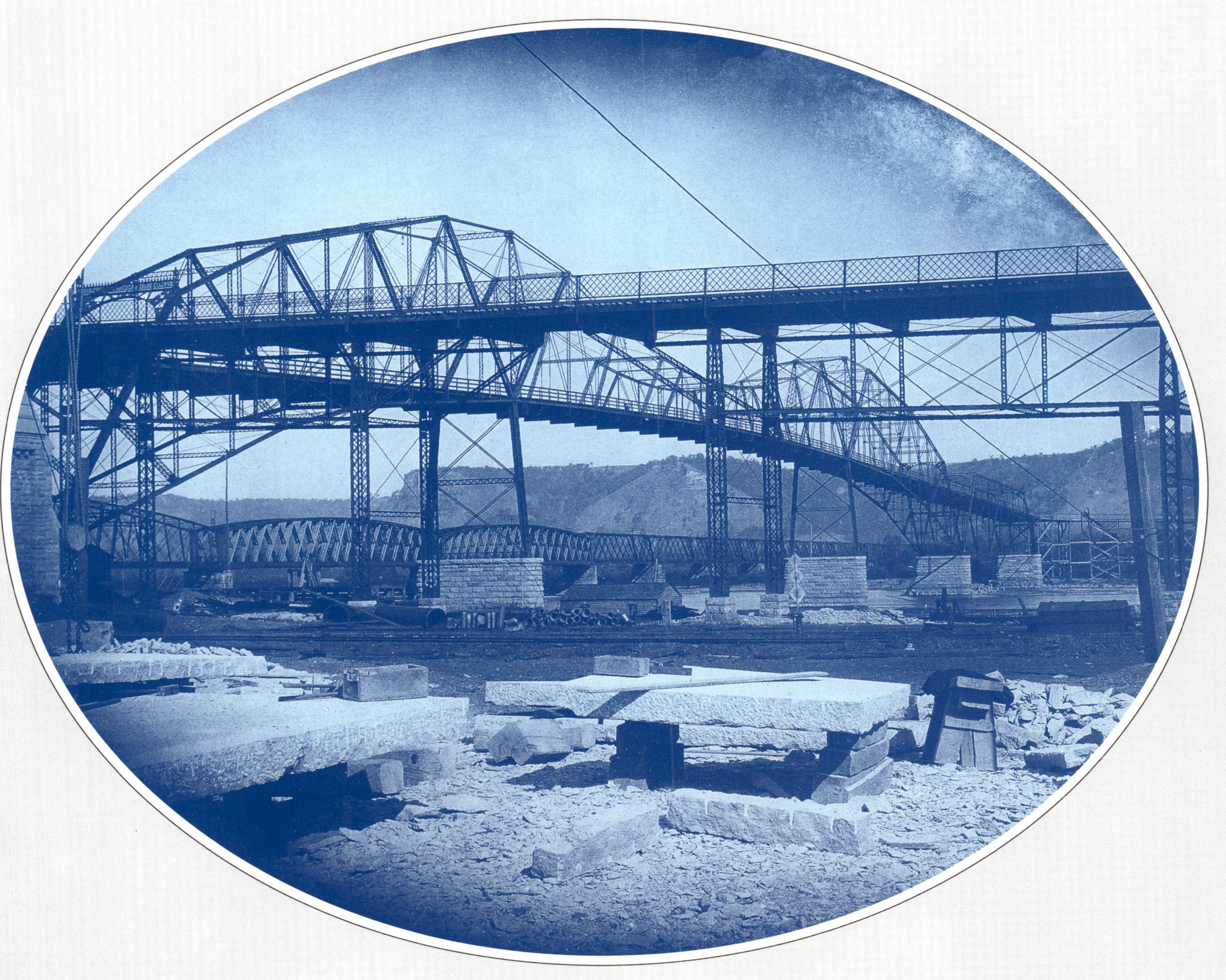

PLATE 33

From bluffs at Trempealeau, Wis. looking down stream, 1885

(MAYO FOUNDATION)

The bluff in the distance north of Trempealeau, one of the highest points on the upper river, was a memorable landmark for early travelers. The Italian adventurer Giacomo Beltrami, writing in 1823, said: "Amid a number of delightful little islands, encircled by the river, rises a mountain of conical form equally isolated. You climb amid cedars and cypresses, strikingly contrasted with the rocks that intersect them, and from the summit you command a view of valleys, prairies, and distances in which the eye loses itself. From this point I saw both the last and first rays of a splendid sun gild the lovely picture." • The Dakota called it *Pah-hah-dah*, or mountain separated by water. The French called it *la montagne qui trempe à l'eau*, or the mountain that dips into the water. The English adapted it to Mount Trempealeau.

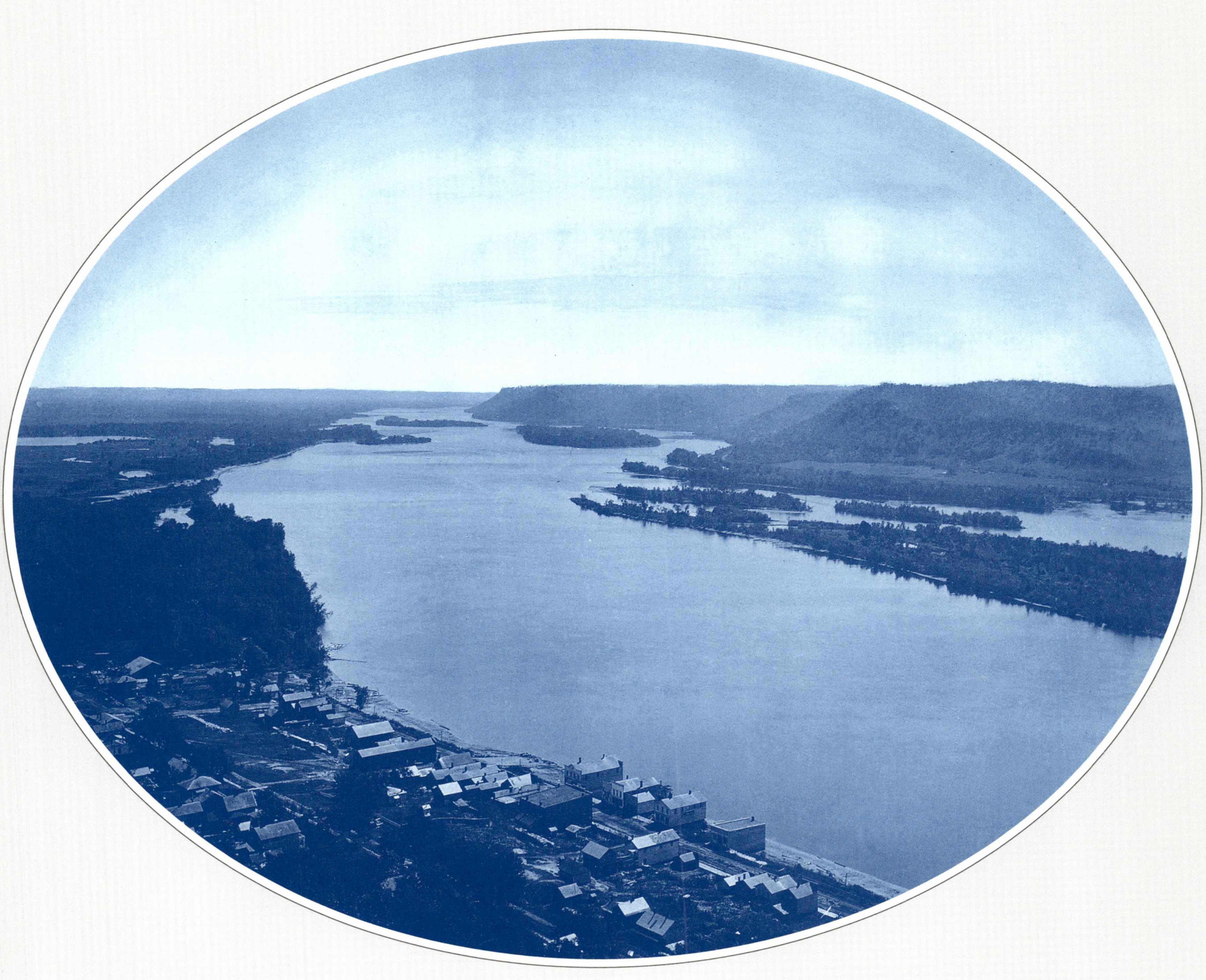

PLATE 34

Queen's Bluff, 1885

(MAYO FOUNDATION)

Bosse's superior at the Corps of Engineers during most of his career was Alexander Mackenzie, who later became chief of engineers in Washington, D.C. Mackenzie used the *General Barnard* as his office when he was away from Rock Island, where the Corps had regional headquarters. Mackenzie often traveled with his dog, a spaniel, and it could be Mackenzie and dog posed here in this image at Queen's Bluff. • Queen's Bluff, about twelve miles south of Winona, was originally called Pike's Tent. It is the highest bluff overlooking the upper river, at 1,244 feet above sea level. The artist George Catlin drew Pike's Tent, Fort Snelling, Pike's Peak near McGregor, Iowa, and Maiden Rock at Lake Pepin on several trips up the river from 1829 to 1835. "The Upper Mississippi, like the Upper Missouri, must be approached to be appreciated," he wrote from Fort Snelling in 1835. He preferred to travel by canoe, while his wife rode along on a steamboat.

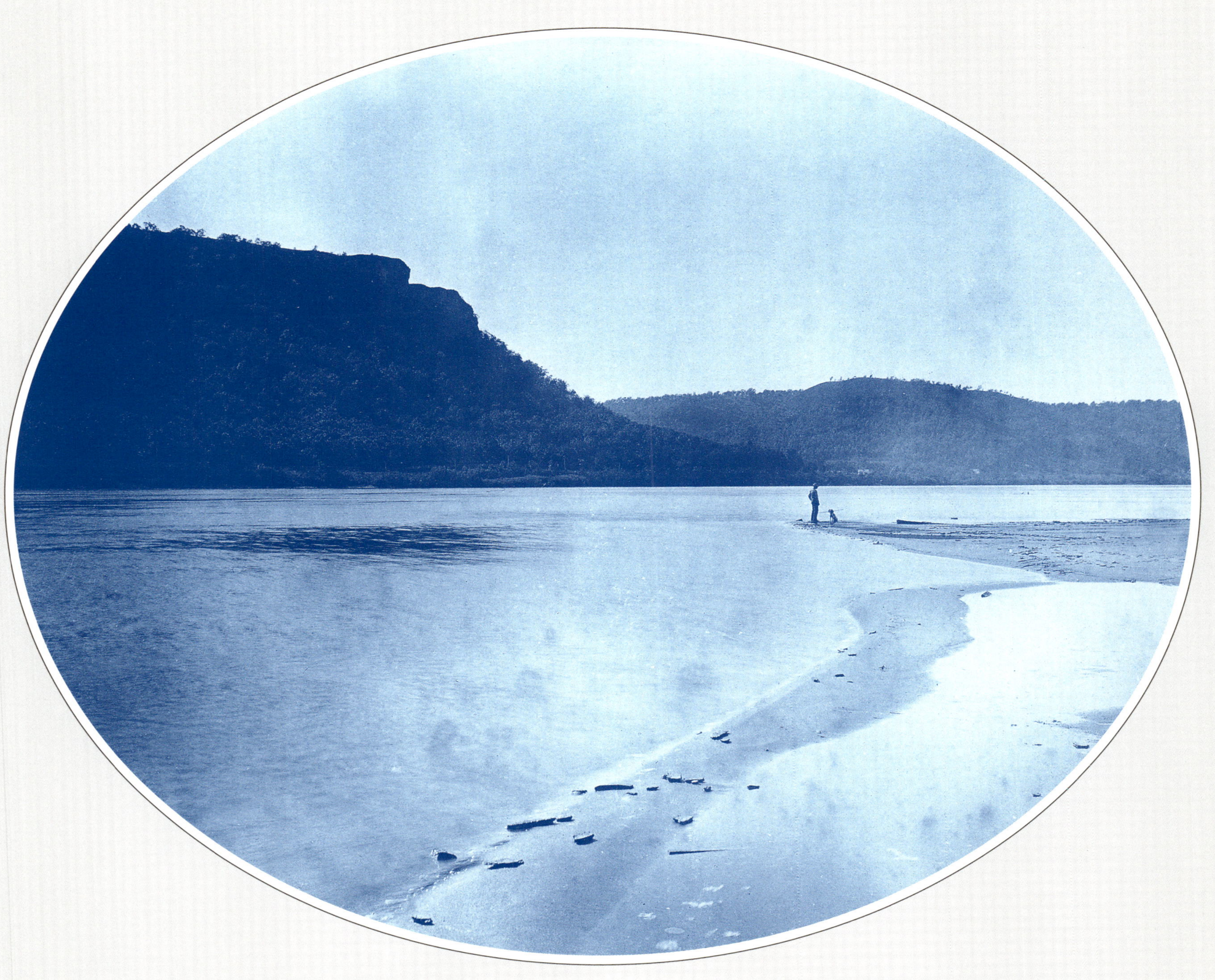

PLATE 35

Levee at La Crosse, Wis., 1891

(MAYO FOUNDATION)

The future site of La Crosse was a trading post for French fur traders and Winnebago Indians in the 1700s partly because the area was accessible by three rivers—the Mississippi, the Black, and the La Crosse. The city dates its founding to 1841, when a nineteen-year-old entrepreneur from Prairie du Chien built a trading post on an island near the present-day city. Among the trader's wares was timber for steamboat fuel. By 1857, regular packet service was available to St. Paul for seven dollars (with cabin) or four dollars (on deck). When the railroads arrived on the river a few years later, prices dropped considerably, and by the turn of the century a ride to St. Paul, even with inflation, was still less than five dollars for a spot on the deck. • Logging on the Black (sometimes called Sappah) River began as early as 1836. A sawmill opened in La Crosse in 1852, taking advantage of the three-rivers location. Others followed, and by 1880 there were thirteen mills in the growing city. • The University of Wisconsin at La Crosse, with a nod to the area's rich river history, holds a collection of some 44,000 steamboat and river photographs.

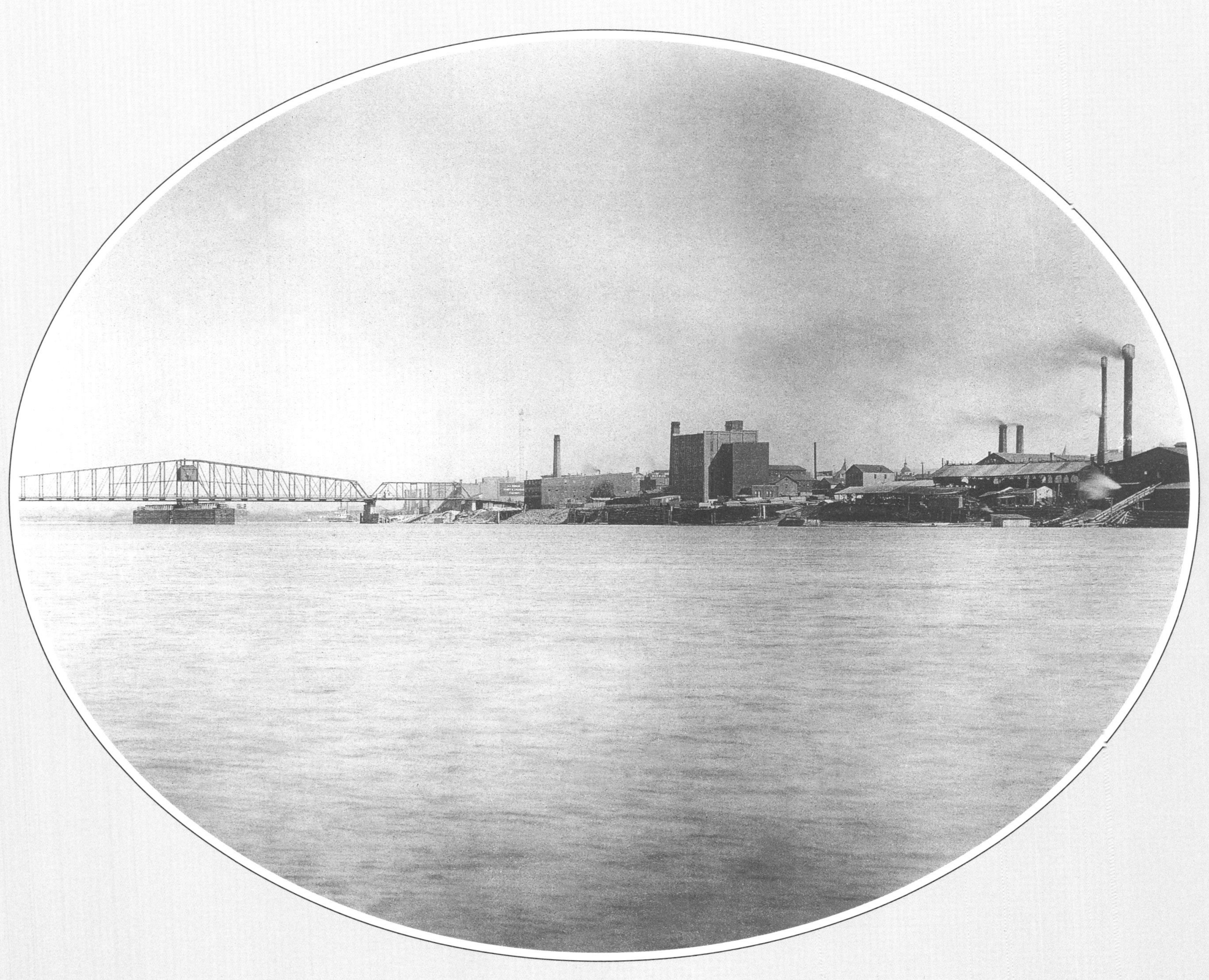

PLATE 36

Wagon Bridge at La Crosse, Wis., 1891

(MAYO FOUNDATION)

In the 1890s, La Crosse, with a population of 30,000, owned and controlled more steamboats than any other river city—sixty-six, totaling 5,139 tons. Perhaps because of the dominance of the steamboat industry, La Crosse's bridges were known as some of the least troublesome on the river. • Steamboat captains constantly complained about bridges interfering with their work, but La Crosse, along with St. Paul and St. Louis, usually escaped such carping. A railroad swing bridge was the first span constructed at La Crosse, in 1875–76. • Because of the city's large population, the steamship industry, and the nature of the river, more than sixty wing dams were built in the latter part of the nineteenth century in the five-mile stretch of river from La Crosse to Brownsville, Minnesota.

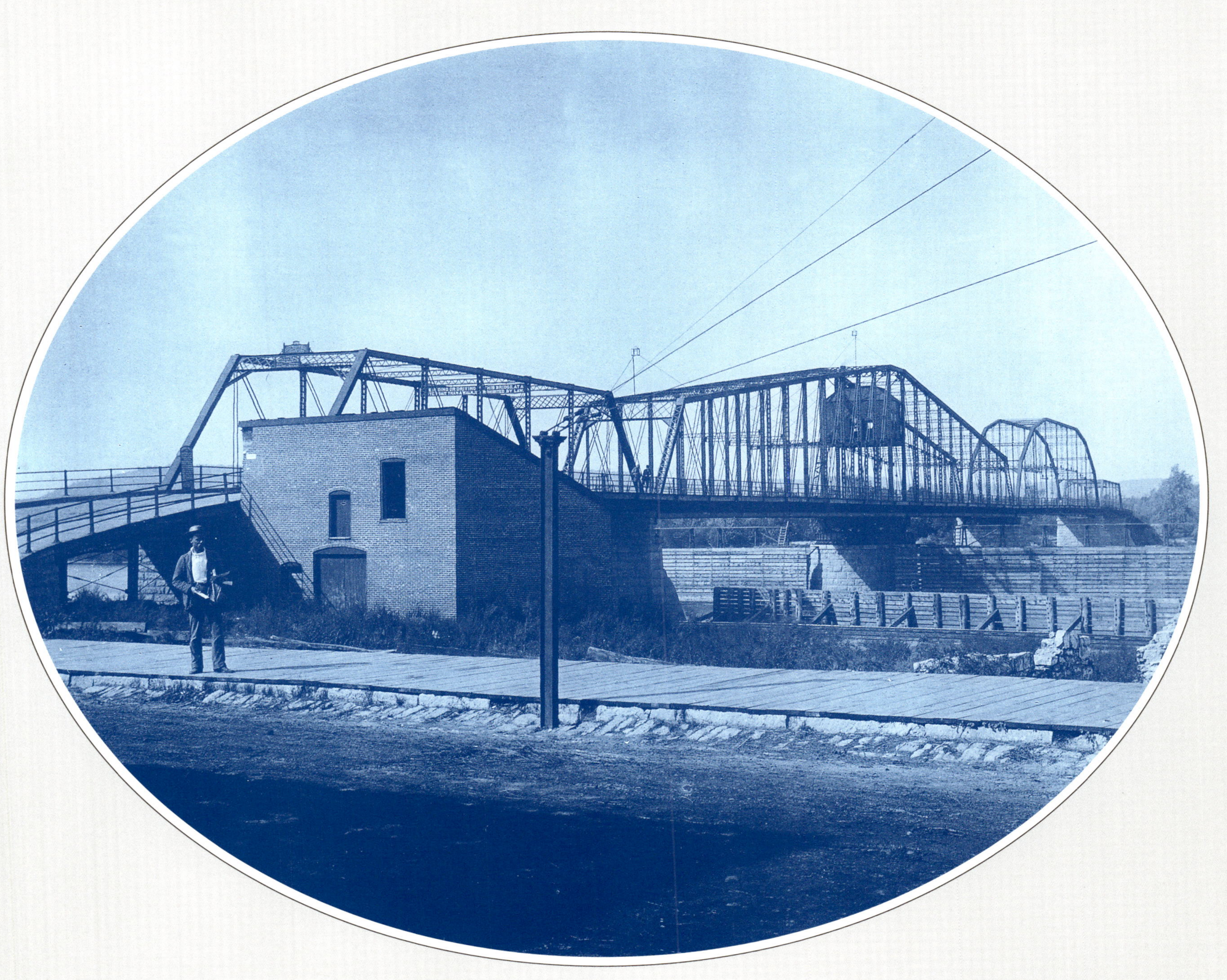
DING OR DRIVING
HIS BRIDGE AT A
THAN A WALK
BY LAW.

PLATE 37

Bar in front of La Crosse, Wis., 1891

(MAYO FOUNDATION)

This ferry, the *Warsaw*, operated at La Crosse, Wisconsin, from 1871 until at least 1886 and perhaps later. The boat was built in 1871 in Madison, Indiana, as a center-wheel ferry, complete with a stout rail to keep livestock on board. The *Warsaw*, 123 feet long and 36 feet wide, moved to Wisconsin to replace the *Thomas McRoberts* in the ferry business. • On March 23, 1880, under the guidance of a Captain Day, the *Warsaw*, which had a wooden hull, caught fire in midstream. With flames shooting from the deck, Day maneuvered the ferry to a nearby island and beached it. All hands jumped off safely and the crew managed to extinguish the fire without losing the ship. The *Warsaw* was towed to the P. S. Davidson Yard in La Crosse for repairs and in fifty days was back in service. In the meantime, the *Silver Lake* and a barge were called into ferry duty as replacements to make the run to the Minnesota side.

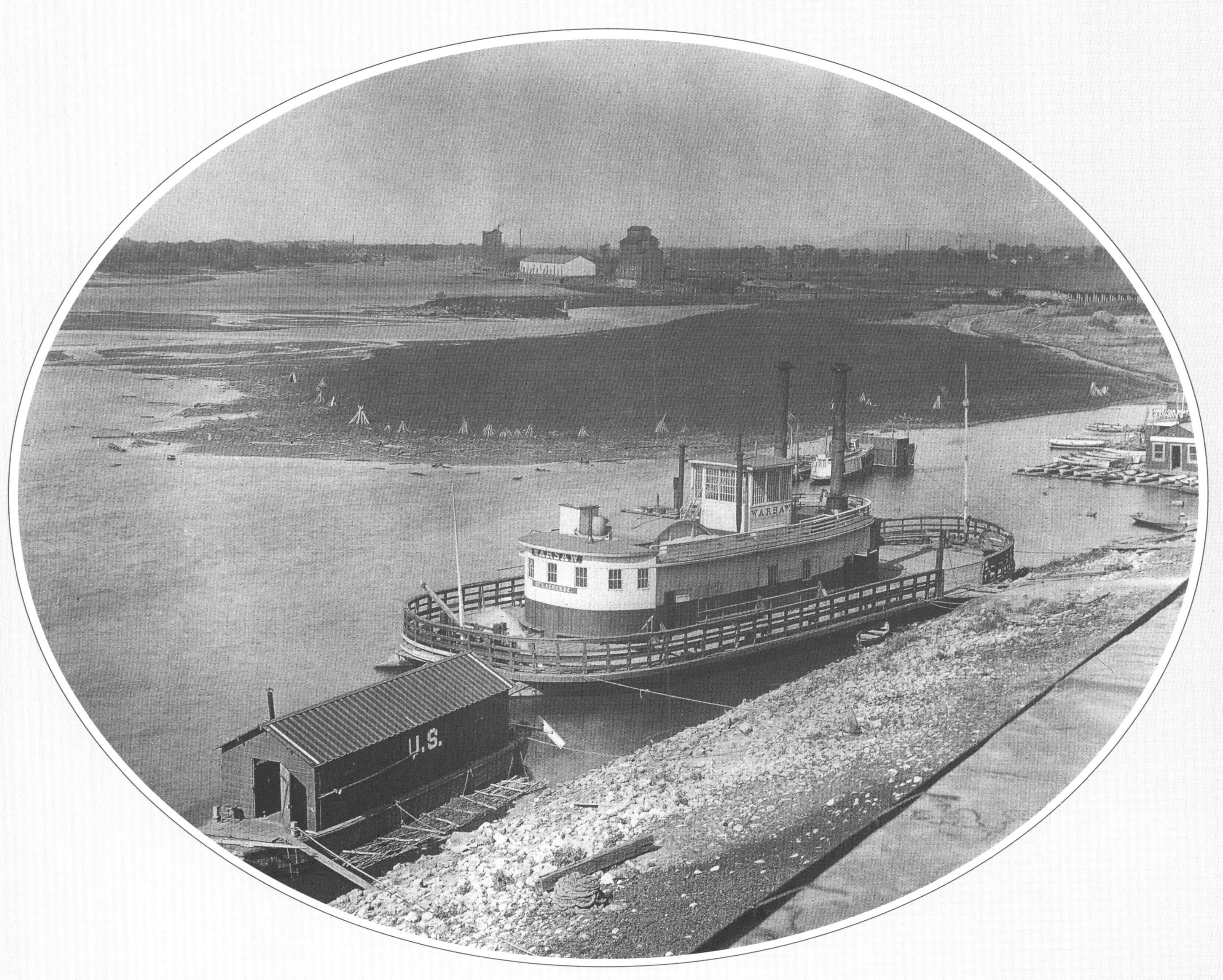
WARSAW
WARSAW
OF LACROSSE.
U.S.

PLATE 38

Genoa, Wis., 1891

(U.S. ARMY CORPS OF ENGINEERS, ST. PAUL DISTRICT)

Lead mining in the region of Dubuque and Galena brought scores of immigrants to the Midwest, including Italians. In 1848, a number of Italians left Galena and traveled to an area called Bad Axe City, named after a creek a few miles to the south that was the site of bloody battles between whites and Winnebagos and Sauks. After settling in, the villagers remapped the town and renamed it after the city in Italy. • Genoa, Wisconsin, populated mainly by fishermen and farmers, became known for the huge flocks of passenger pigeons that roosted on islands in the Mississippi. Like settlers elsewhere, the citizens of Genoa killed the birds for food and sport with nets and guns.

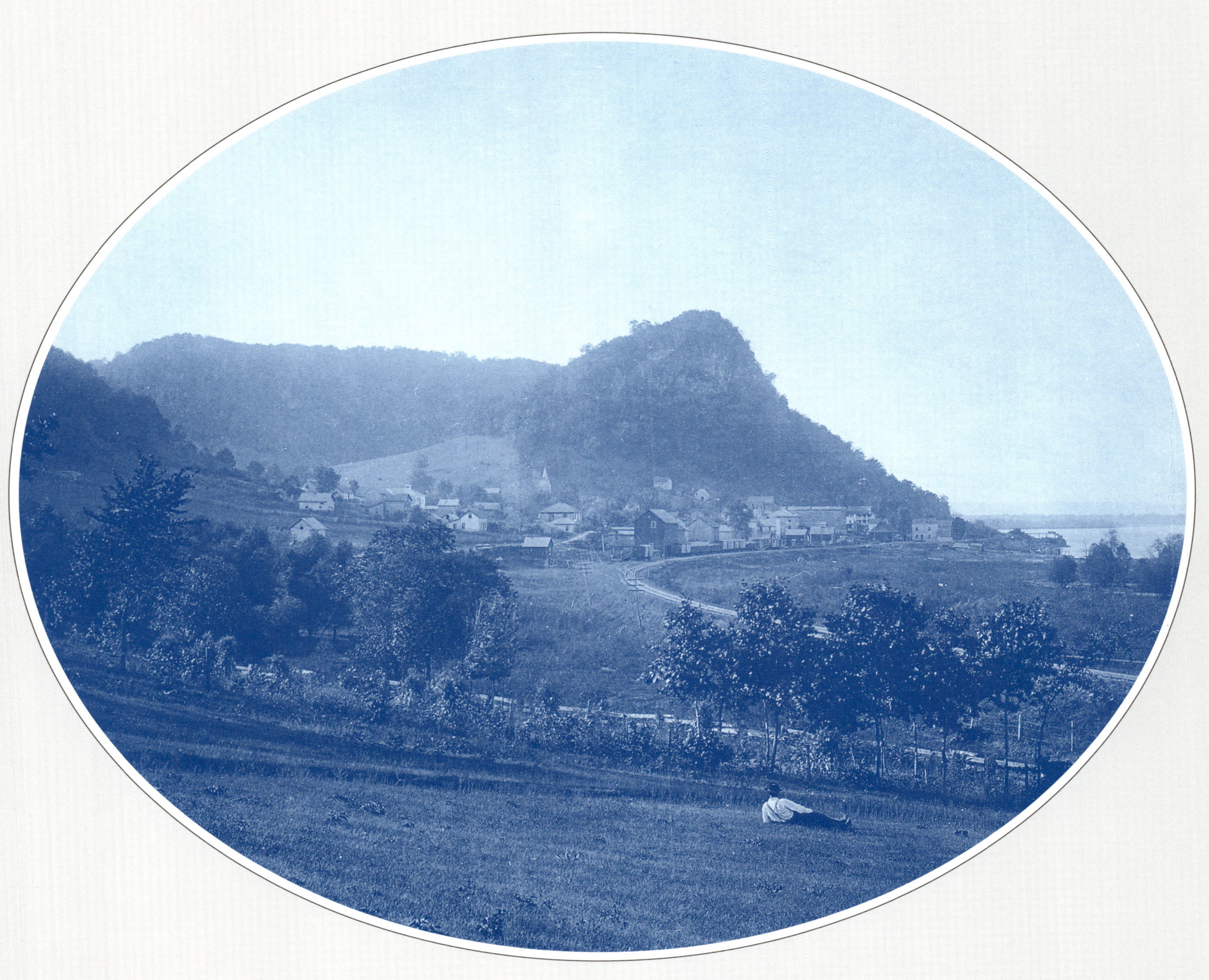

PLATE 39

De Soto, Wis., 1891

(MAYO FOUNDATION)

Early French traders established a post at Winneshiek's Landing, later known as De Soto, named after the early Spanish explorer. The French, who worked for John Jacob Astor's American Fur Company, swapped goods for furs from Chief Winneshiek. The legendary leader of the Winnebago is reportedly buried on the bluff overlooking the river. • The village was laid out in 1854 and designed as a colony closed to all except New Englanders. That effort ended when a large sawmill was established at De Soto in 1857. The mill cut an average of 50,000 board feet of lumber per day and employed fifty people, most of whom were not society's elite. • Bosse may have taken this photograph because the site was being considered for a dam. A dam was built at De Soto in 1894, but it caused sewage and disease to back up into the town's harbor. The dam was demolished in 1904.

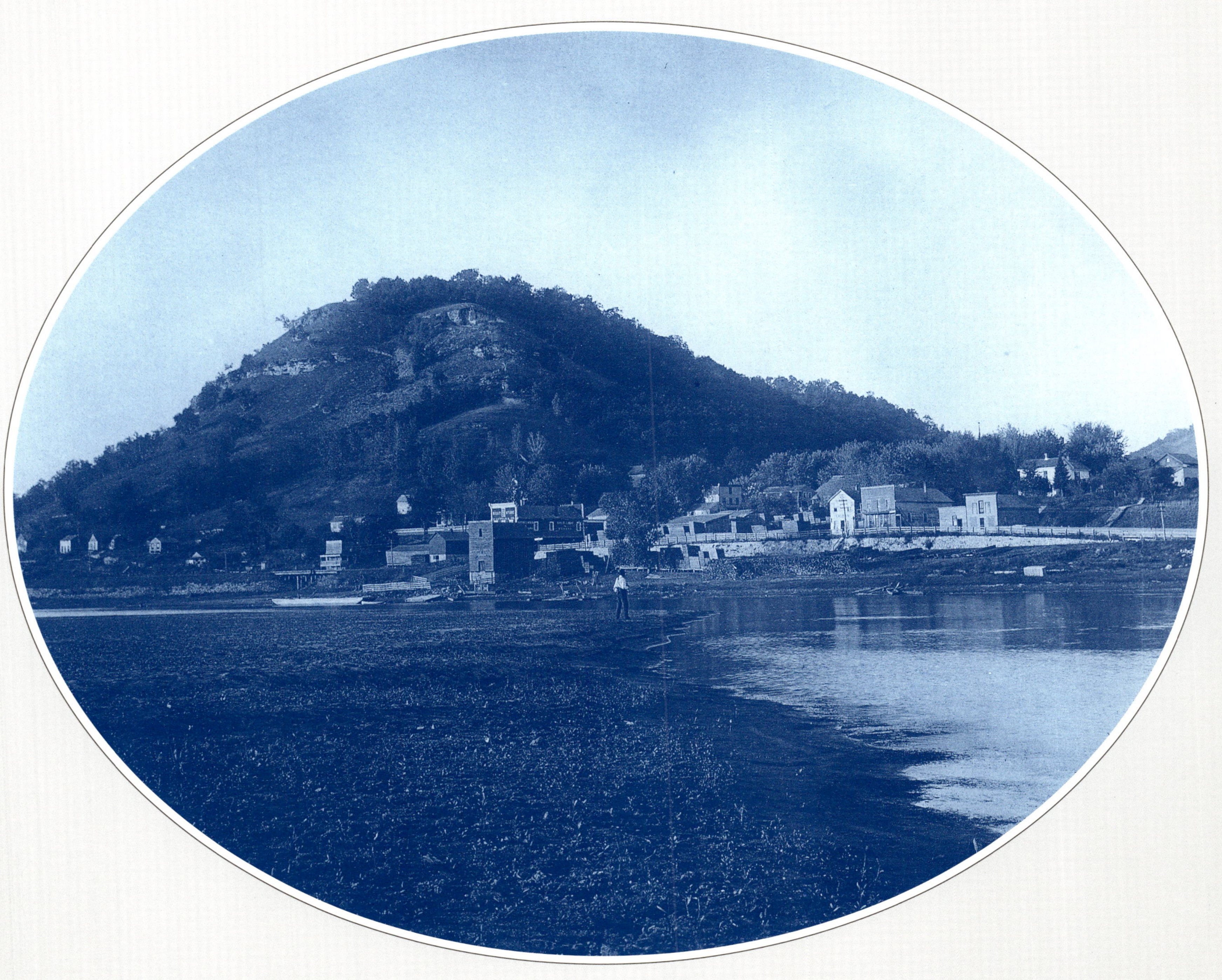

PLATE 40

U.S. Steamlaunch "Elsie" towing brush, 1889

(MAYO FOUNDATION)

PLATE 41

Construction of Rock & Brush Dam, 1891

(MAYO FOUNDATION)

PLATE 42

Construction of Rock & Brush Wingdam, 1891

(MAYO FOUNDATION)

Dams made of rock and brush were used to constrict the Mississippi River into a single channel. The technology, perfected in Germany, had not worked on other rivers in the United States mostly because those rivers had rock beds or hard gravel bottoms. The silt, sand, and sawdust of the Mississippi proved to be the perfect cement for wing dams and closing dams. • Willow trees, which grew in abundance near the river, were cut and woven by hand into mats called fascines, which were loaded onto barges and pushed into place with steamboats like the steel-hulled *Elsie*, brand new when this photograph was taken. The fascines were lowered into the water between two or more barges; limestone cut from nearby quarries was thrown onto the mats to make them sink. The process was repeated until the dam was built to the desired height. The work was best done at low water; the crews were idled during high water and floods. Eventually the government exhausted nature's supply of willows and a planting program was started.

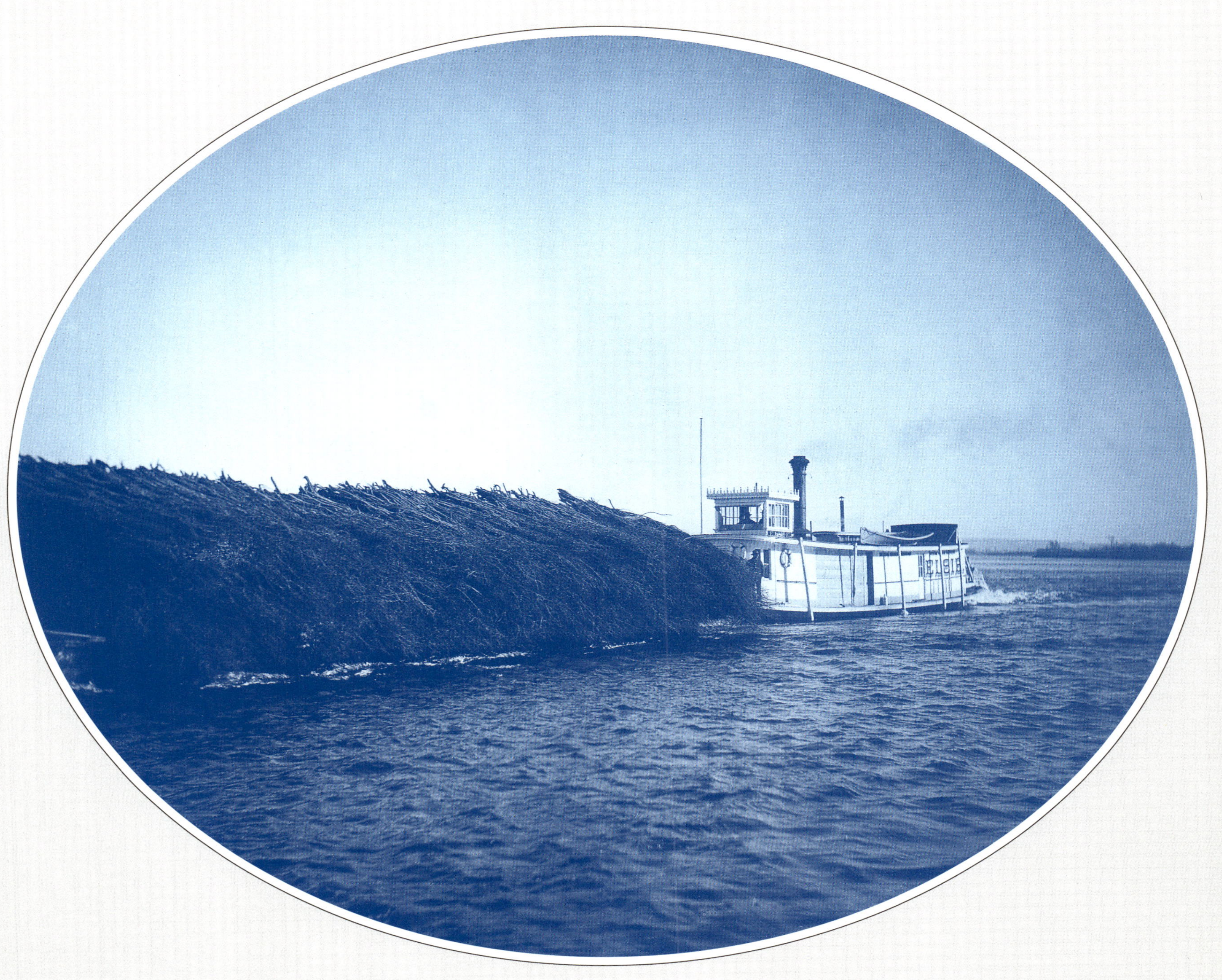
ELSIE

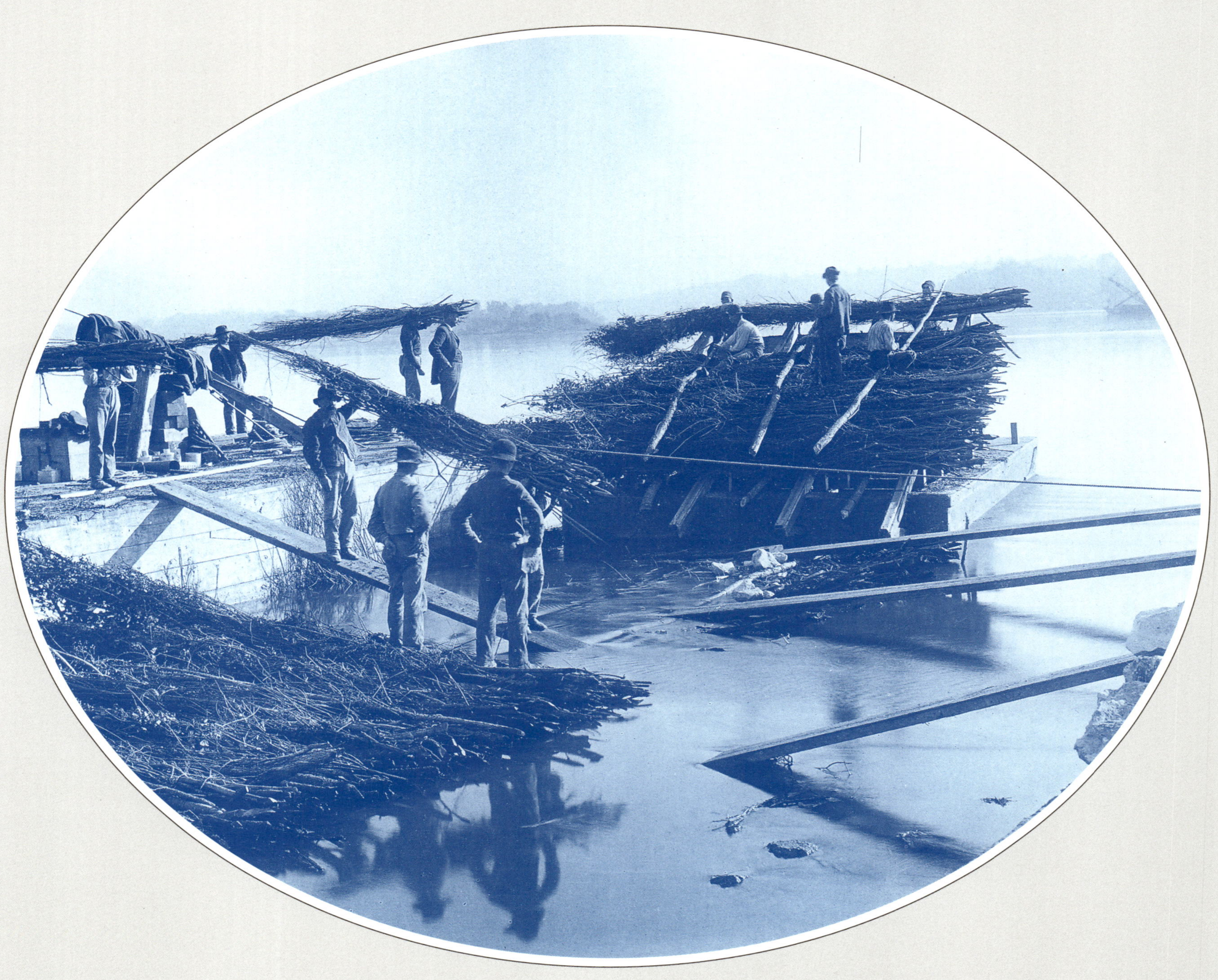

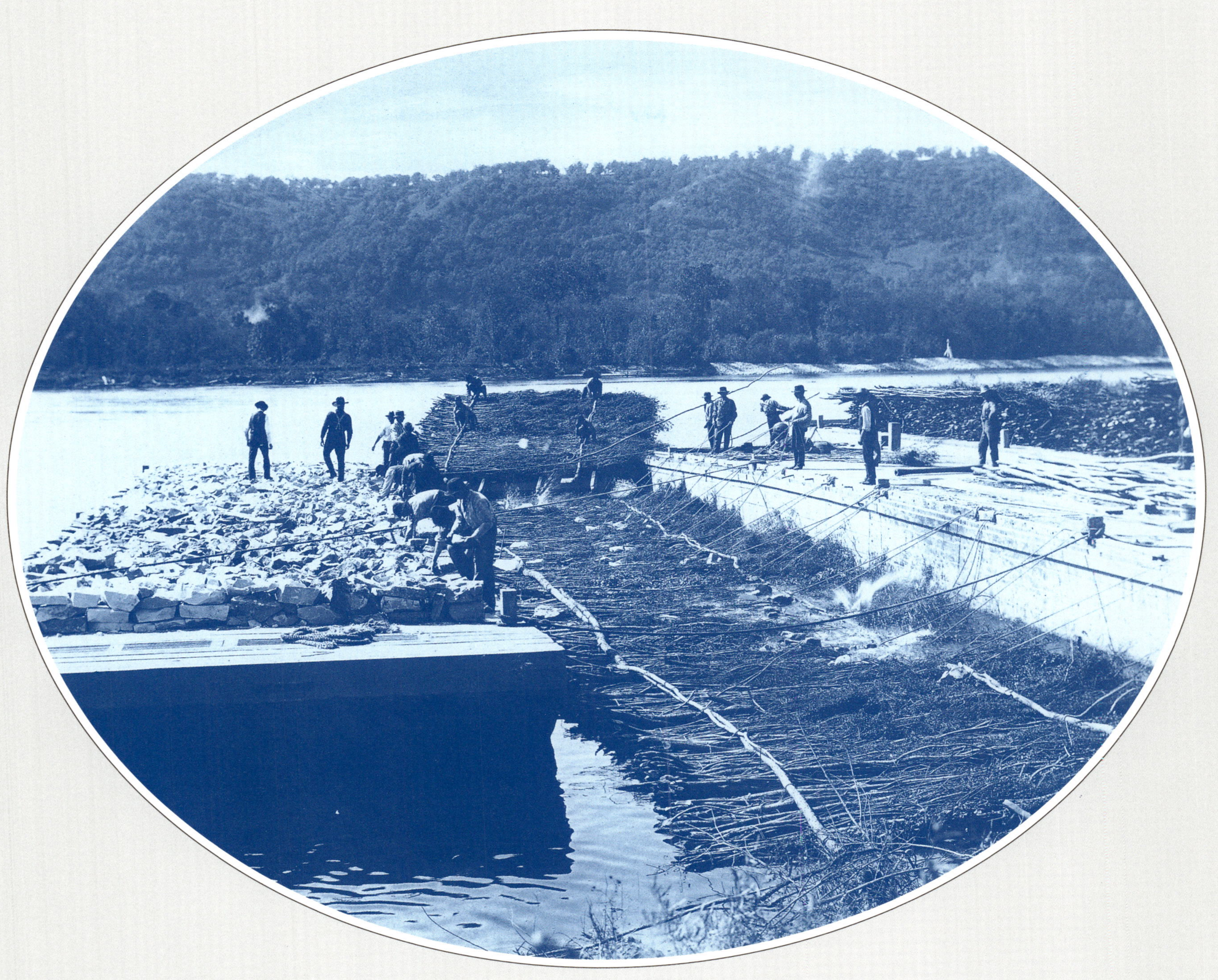

PLATE 43

Floating Palace, no date

(MISSISSIPPI RIVER MUSEUM)

This photograph, undated and not marked with a location, is of a private barge. The well-appointed vessel served as a resting place and entertainment center for its owners and their guests. A dory and a skiff helped guests move around the river. Note the dog and man standing near the entrance. • Such vessels were not uncommon up and down the river. Card playing, singing, whiskey drinking, and other activities were enjoyed aboard the boats, which were often moored. Some of the less well fitted boats were used as hunting and fishing clubs. Mark Twain recalled that the term "floating palace" was applied to the fancier packet steamboats, which ran the river carrying passengers on regular trips.

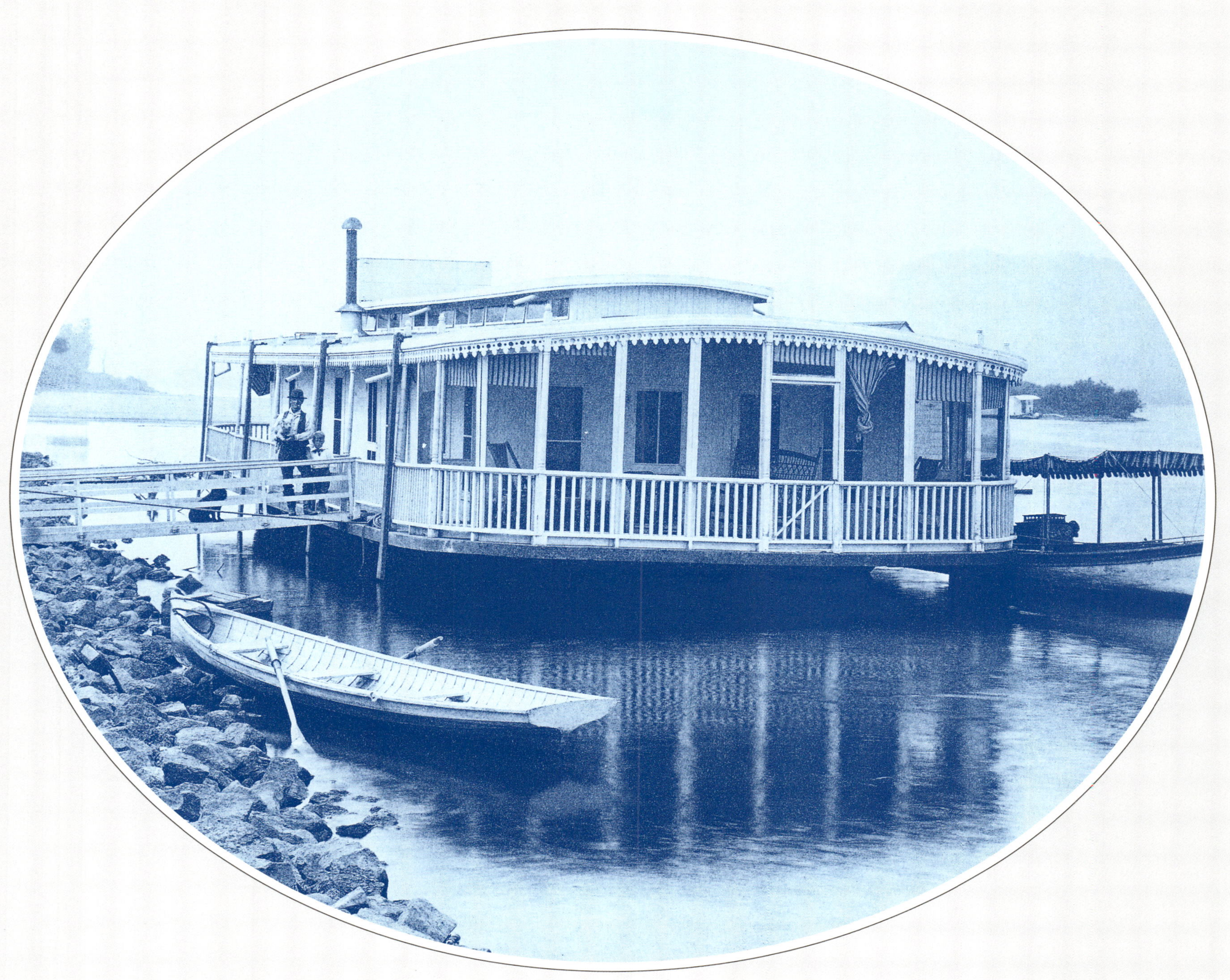

PLATE 44

Old Ponton Bridge at N. McGregor, Ia., 1885

(MAYO FOUNDATION)

McGregor and North McGregor (renamed Marquette in 1920), Iowa, were important shipping communities for steamboats and railroads. Alexander McGregor and Thomas Burnett, who ran a ferry across the river from Prairie du Chien, Wisconsin, founded McGregor in 1837. The region grew with white settlement and the lumber business on the river; by 1867, McGregor boasted 5,500 people. Among its citizens were the Ringling brothers, four of whom were born here and in 1884 created a "wagon show" that became the start of the Ringling Brothers Circus. • The pontoon railroad bridge seen here was completed in 1873–74; temporary pontoon bridges had been built before, but some historians believe this may have been the first permanent structure of its type. The Fleming Sawmill and Lumber Company is in the middle ground, with the owner's white mansion standing in the distance. The bridge was dismantled in 1961.

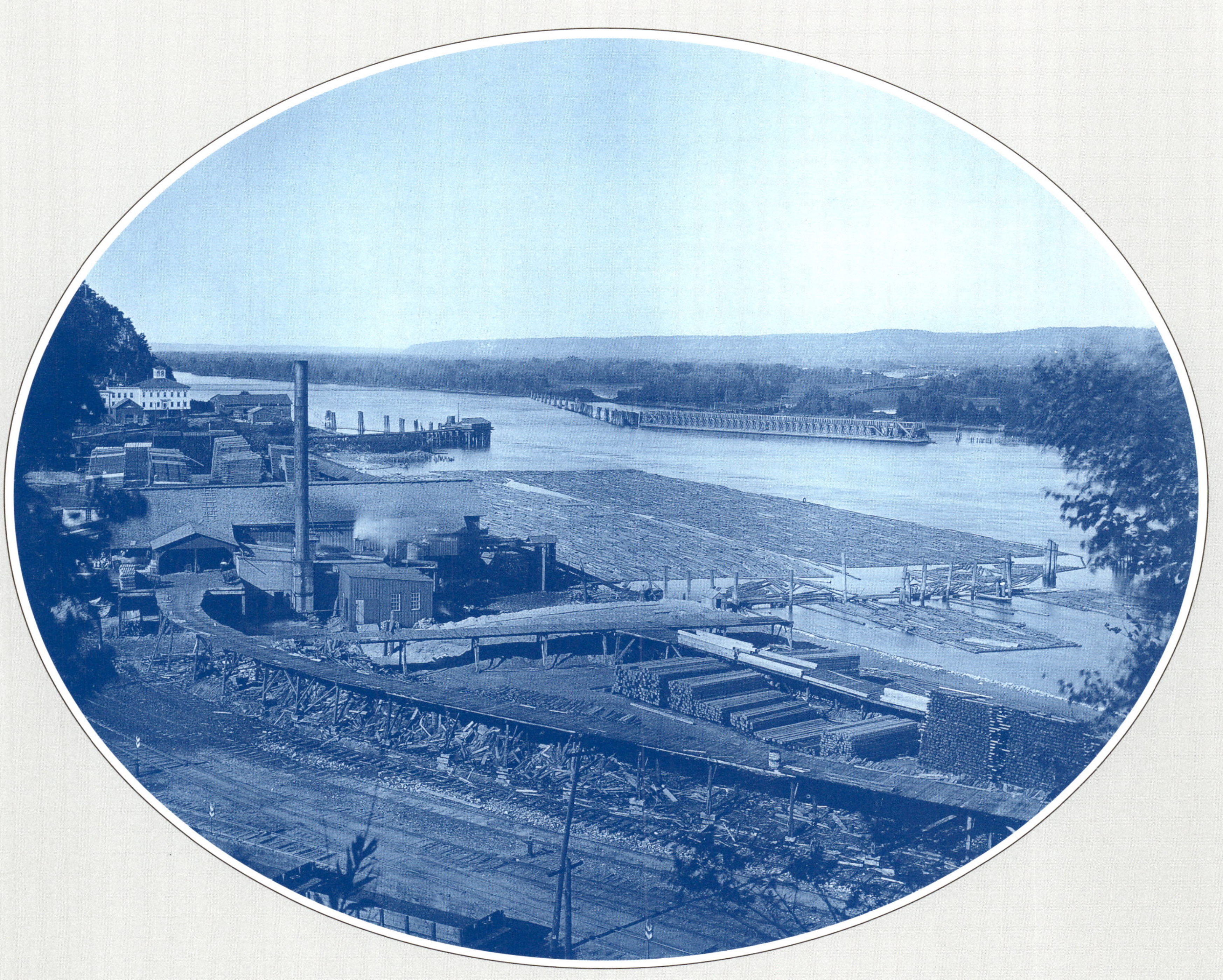

PLATE 45

Eagle Point, 1885

(MAYO FOUNDATION)

The shipyard at Eagle Point, north of Dubuque, was constructed in 1871 by the firm of Johnson and Gaylord. Diamond Jo Reynolds moved to Dubuque in 1874 and bought the yard to build and repair his boats. Reynolds, born in New York in 1819, was one of the Mississippi River's best-known entrepreneurs in the second half of the nineteenth century. • Reynolds, who owned a tannery, a railroad, and a flour mill, among other businesses, got into shipping when he ran into trouble getting a fair price for hauling his hides and grain from the Minnesota Packet Company in the 1860s. He built his own boat, the *Lansing*, and began a notable career as a riverman. In 1871, after acquiring several boats, he changed the name of his business to the Diamond Jo Line. • In addition to building boats at Eagle Point, Reynolds employed a large number of skilled mechanics and a crew of expert divers to salvage wrecks. One boat, the *Pittsburgh*, a 700-ton stern-wheeler, was badly damaged in a storm in St. Louis. Reynolds salvaged it and renamed it the *Dubuque*. • Reynolds amassed a personal fortune of an estimated $12 million; he died in 1891 inspecting copper mines he owned in Arizona.

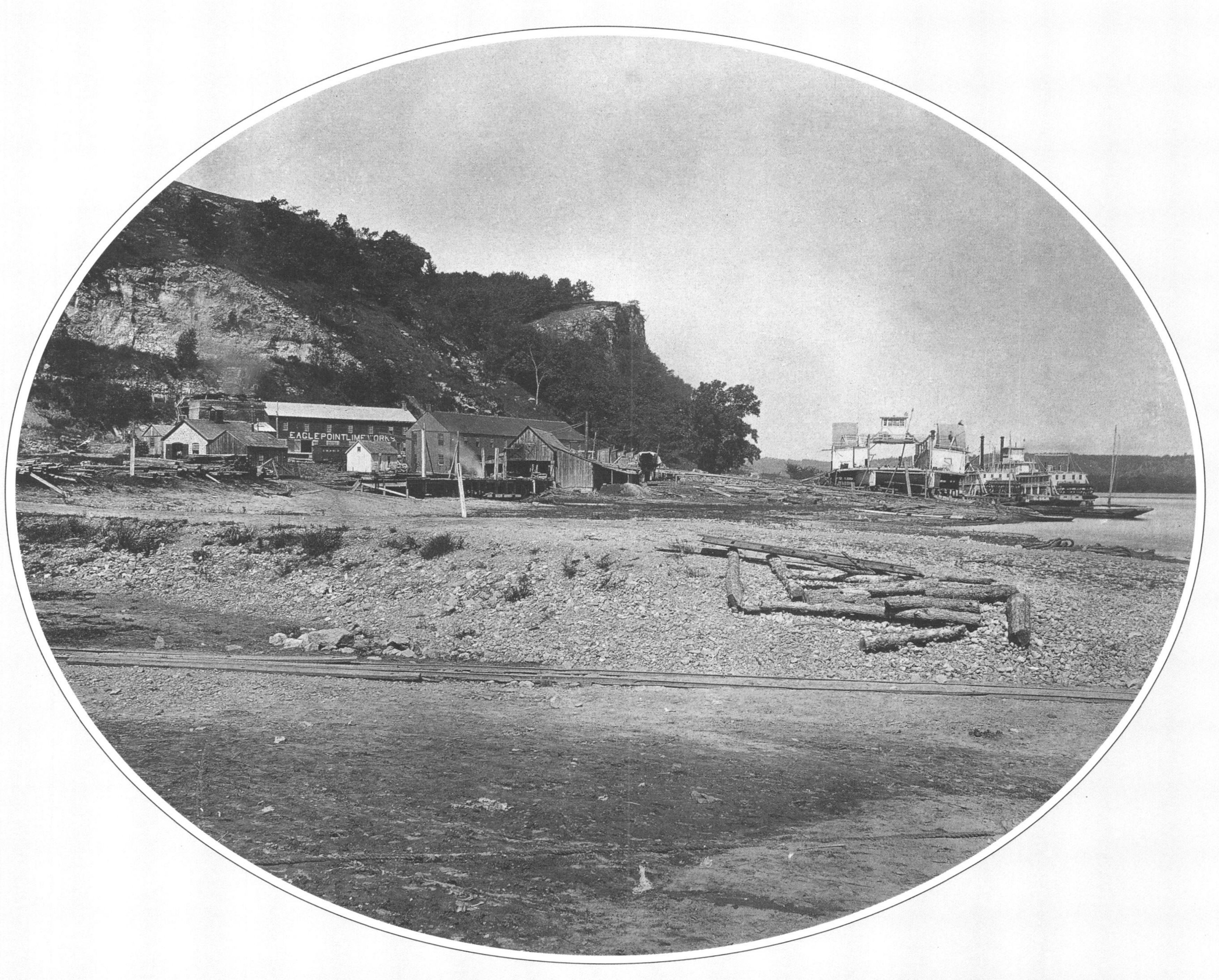
EAGLE POINT LIME WORKS

PLATE 46

Harbor at Dubuque, Ia., with hull of "Windom," no date

(MISSISSIPPI RIVER MUSEUM)

The city of Dubuque was home to a thriving boat-building industry in the nineteenth and early twentieth centuries. One of the more noteworthy boats manufactured in Dubuque in the 1890s was a ship built of steel for the U.S. Treasury. Variously known as the *Windom*, the U S S *Windom*, and the *William Windom*, the ship was a revenue cutter, launched in 1896 and named after a Minnesota senator and two-time secretary of the treasury. • The hull of the ship can be seen in this undated photograph taken from the hills overlooking the harbor in Dubuque. Built by the Iowa Iron Works, the *Windom* was ordered in 1891 but various delays and its unusual design drew out its construction for several years. The ship was moved to New Orleans in 1896 for finishing because it drew too much water to navigate the upper river. Once finished, it patrolled the east coast for several years. The *Windom* served in the Spanish-American War and was decommissioned in 1930. • A city founder, Julien Dubuque, was a French fur trapper who came to the area in the 1780s. Lead was discovered nearby, and through the subsequent lead trade became an important commercial commodity in the early nineteenth century. The area was fought over by several nations, including Mesquakie, Sioux, Fox, Sauk, France, England, Spain, and the United States. Four national flags—those of England, Spain, France (twice), and the United States—have flown over the region.

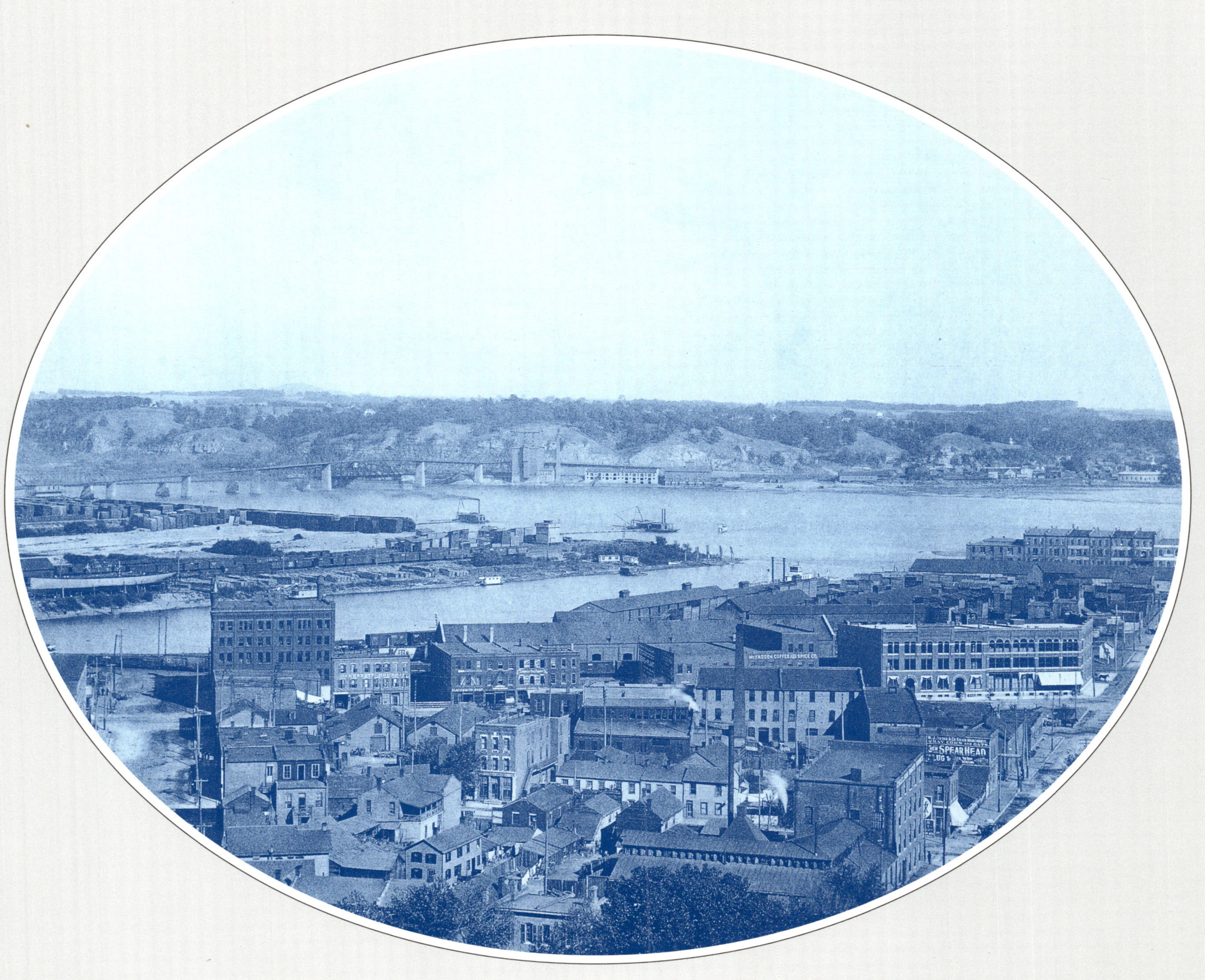
McFADDEN COFFEE AND SPICE CO.
HAY, CORN AND OATS
SPEARHEAD

PLATE 47

Locks, Galina River—Looking down stream, no date

(MISSISSIPPI RIVER MUSEUM)

The locks on the Galena River (misspelled in Bosse's caption) were built between 1890 and 1892 and rebuilt in 1895–96. The city of Galena, famous for its lead mines and the home of General Ulysses S. Grant, sat several miles upstream from the mouth of the river; getting boats in and out of town was a constant problem. In addition to dredging, the Corps built a wing dam downstream from the lock in 1890 to try to keep the channel clear and added eight more wing dams in 1892. A closing dam at the head of Stone Slough, near the mouth of the Galena, was another attempt at improving the river for navigation. The railroad bridge belonged to the Chicago, Burlington and Northern Railroad. The locks were abandoned in 1925. • Across the river and upriver from Galena, a small stream called Tête du Mort Creek flows into the Mississippi. Oral histories from the area have it that the bluffs near the creek were the site of a fierce battle between the Sioux and the Sac. The Sac used canoes to blockade the river as they surrounded a Sioux camp. The victorious Sac tossed the bodies of their enemies over the bluff, where years later French fur traders found bleached bones along the creek bed. Thus the name, which translates to "head of the dead."

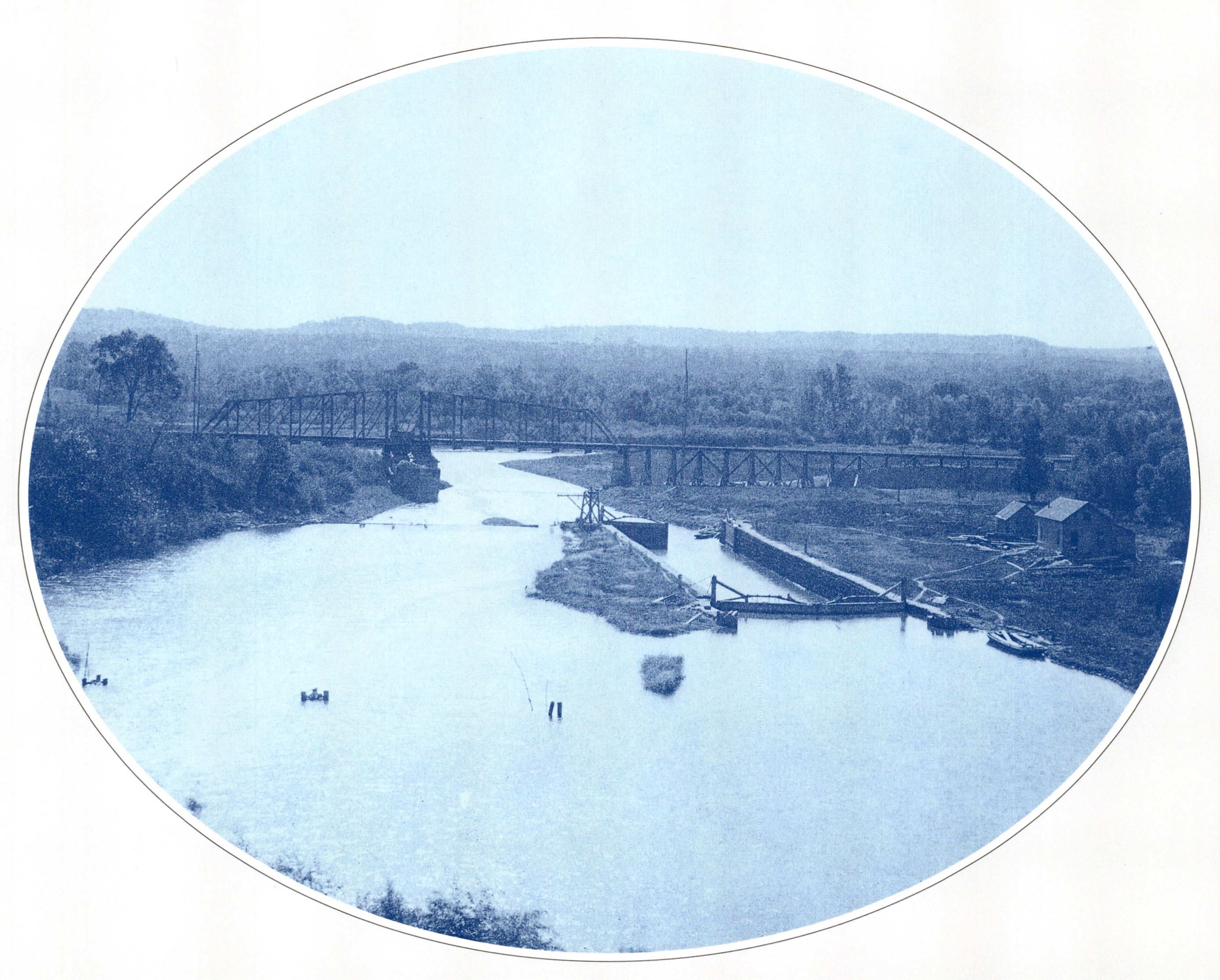

PLATE 48

Raftboat "W. J. Young," 1888

(MAYO FOUNDATION)

Raft boats like the *W. J. Young* moved huge amounts of logs and timber downstream from the Mississippi tributaries in Wisconsin and Minnesota to mills in Winona, Dubuque, La Crosse, Fort Madison, and elsewhere. Although the deckhands seen on the raft appear in rather casual poses, the job of working a raft boat was dangerous and sometimes fatal. It was not unusual for steamboats like the *Young* to push up to 2.5 million board feet of lumber, and in at least one case a boat handled 10 million board feet on a trip. The raft in front of the steamer could cover several football fields. • The *Young* was built in Dubuque for Clinton, Iowa, sawmill owner W. J. Young in 1882. Note the cordwood stacked on its deck to feed the boilers. By 1895, the *Young* was retired from rafting and ran as a packet boat from Davenport to Burlington. By 1906, it was an excursion boat renamed the *Hiawatha* running the Ohio River. It burned at Louisville, Kentucky, on November 14, 19[illegible]1.

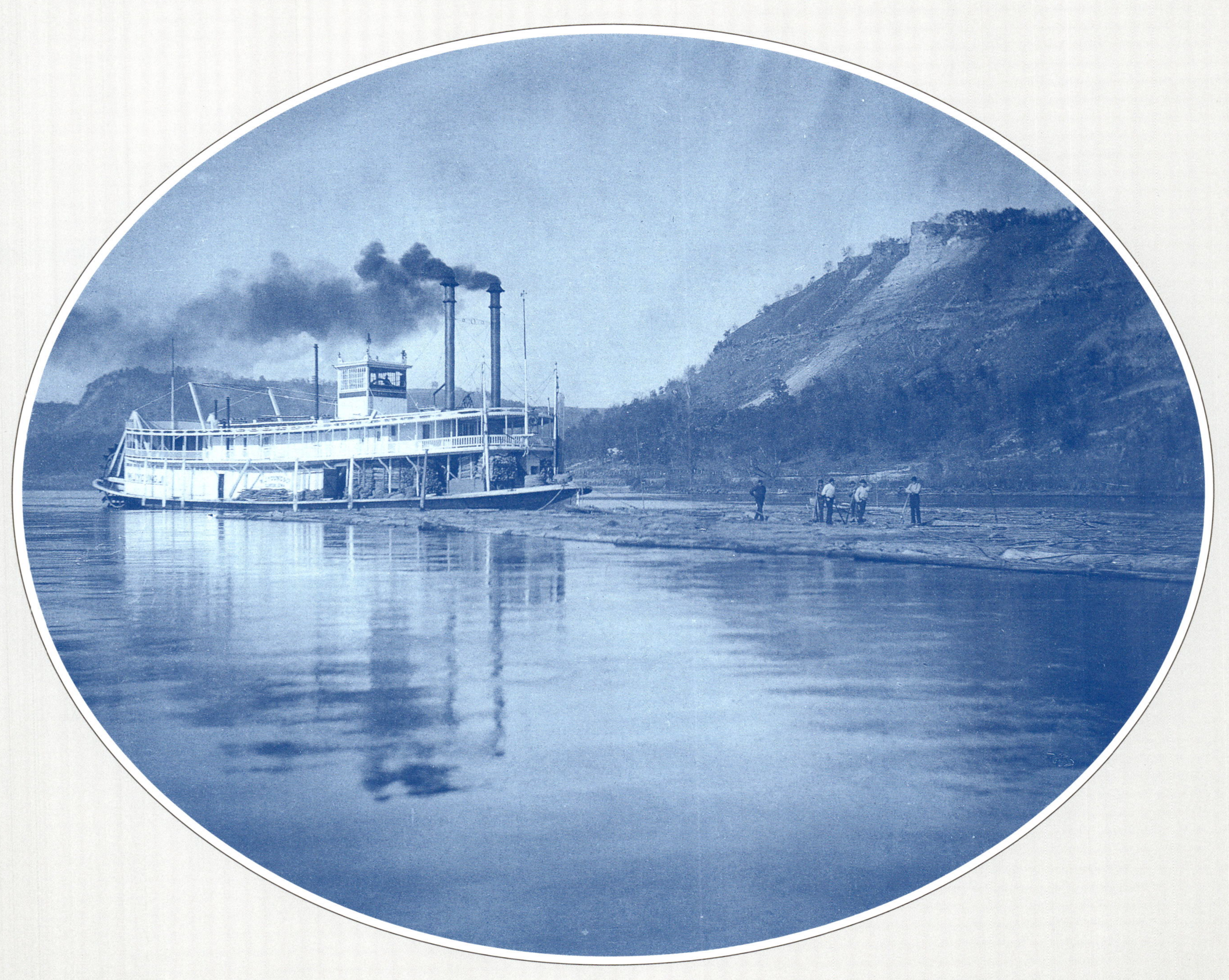

PLATE 49

Lamb & Son's Saw Mill, Clinton, Iowa, no date

(MISSISSIPPI RIVER MUSEUM)

The gritty skyline of Clinton, Iowa, foreboding and ominous, was marked by the smokestacks of one of the largest sawmills on the Mississippi River. The refuse from Lamb & Sons Sawmill and the W. J. Young sawmill was a principal reason Clinton earned the nickname Sawdust Town from river captains. When an east wind blew, as in this photograph, the smoke and soot blew over the town. Sawdust piled up along the riverbank, sometimes impeding navigation. The mill was located on Beaver Slough. • By 1894, after the peak of lumber production in the Great Lakes forests, Clinton was third only to Minneapolis and Winona, Minnesota, in board feet of lumber processed on the river. That year, Lamb & Sons, W. J. Young and Company, and the other Clinton mills chopped and cut 101,662,000 board feet of northern white and red pine and other lumber. Yet production had dropped nearly in half from 1892, and a few short years later, the boom time ended for Clinton and many other mill cities. The northern forests were depleted of pine, and mills began closing at a rapid rate. The stronger yellow pine from southern states like Arkansas and Louisiana eventually replaced white pine as the lumber of choice for building middle America.

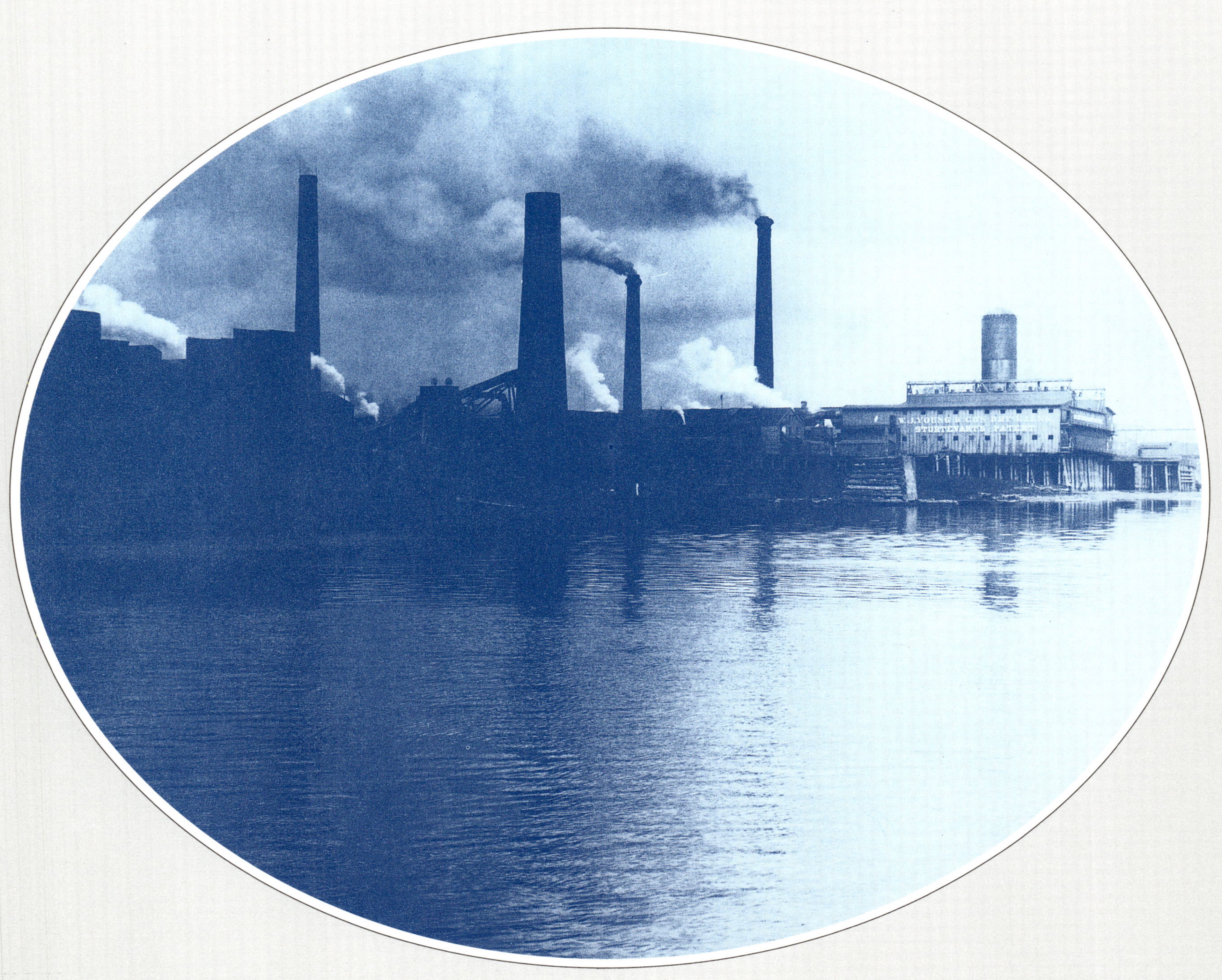
W. J. YOUNG & CO'S DRY
STURTEVANT'S

PLATE 50

Wagon Bridge at Fulton, Ill., 1891

(MAYO FOUNDATION)

The graceful geometric shapes of this high-fixed wagon bridge between Fulton, Illinois, and Lyons, Iowa, caught the photographer's eye. The bridge was brand-new when this picture was taken in 1891. The structure was built by a local concern created to make it, the Lyons and Fulton Bridge Company. The superstructure was made of steel and the deck was wood. The river was very narrow in this spot, making it a busy ferry crossing, but the bridge quickly put the ferry out of business. Lyons was annexed to Clinton, Iowa, in the 1890s. The bridge was torn down in the 1970s.

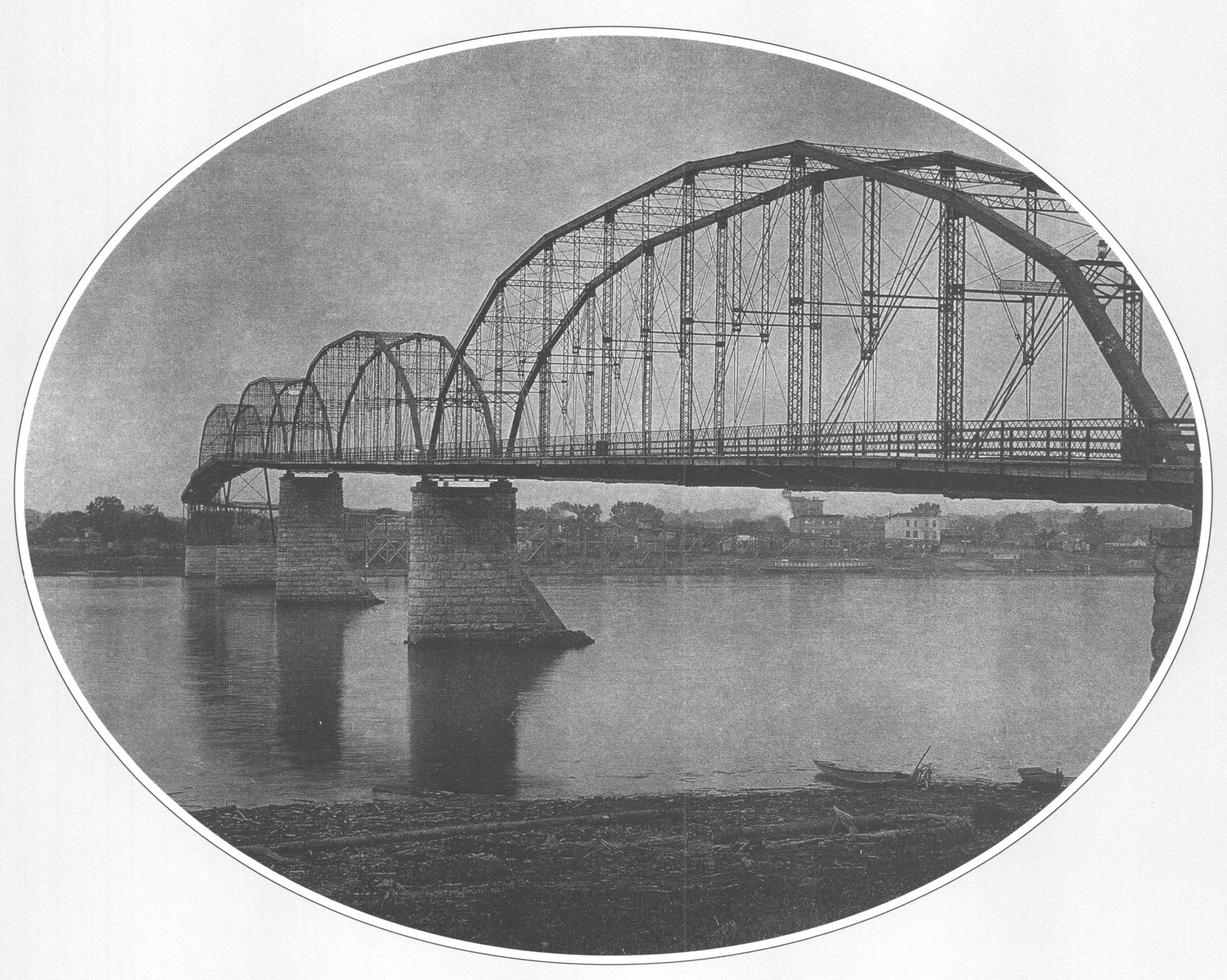

PLATE 51

Snagging Scene, 1885

(U.S. ARMY CORPS OF ENGINEERS, ROCK ISLAND DISTRICT)

The *General Barnard,* 218 feet long with a 37-foot beam, was one of the largest snag boats on the upper river. During its twenty-two years of service to the Corps, the *Barnard* removed 6,584 snags, 38 wrecks, and 73,935 leaning trees and pulled back another 1,621 trees. Corps records show that the *Barnard,* which Bosse probably used as a portable darkroom, traveled 130,732 miles. • The chain connected to the A-frame and block and tackle at the bow was called a Samson's chain because of its strength. Some of the equipment on the boat was salvaged and reused when the Corps replaced the *Barnard* with a new snag boat, the *Colonel A. Mackenzie,* in 1900. The rest was condemned and sent to the shipyard at Jefferson, Indiana, where it was sold at auction for one thousand dollars.

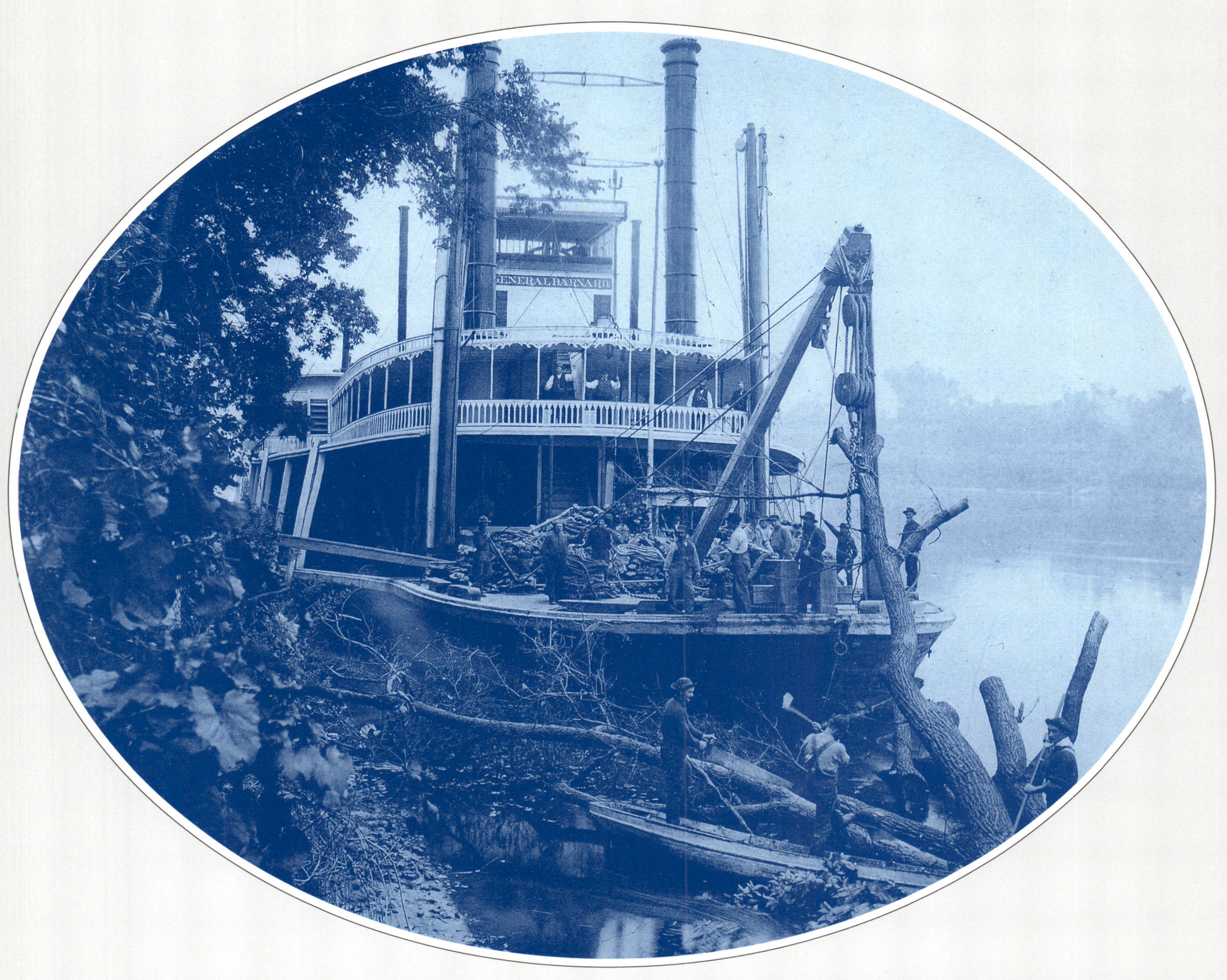
GENERAL BARNARD

PLATE 52

Ice Gorge at Rock Island, Ill., 1893

(MISSISSIPPI RIVER MUSEUM)

Ice gorges like this one formed when ice broke, often in the spring. They were a serious hazard to navigation, sometimes sweeping away moored boats, ferries, barges, and wharves. And, at least in this case, the ice got the better of a railroad. Steamboats took refuge in the winter in sloughs, creeks, or lagoons up and down the river to avoid the ice. Near Rock Island, the slough behind Arsenal Island was a safe harbor. • Sometimes boats were taken as far as Pittsburgh or St. Louis to avoid the ice, but even St. Louis was not always safe from the ice gorges. On December 13, 1876, ice destroyed the *Jennie Baldwin*, the *Bayard*, the *Rock Island*, and the *Davenport* in St. Louis and damaged four other ships. The newspapers reported that none of those ships were insured; three smaller steamers—the *Fannie Keener*, the *South Shore*, and the *Belle*—were also sunk but covered by insurance. In Dubuque, civic leaders successfully pushed for the construction of an ice harbor so ships could safely winter over by the 1880s.

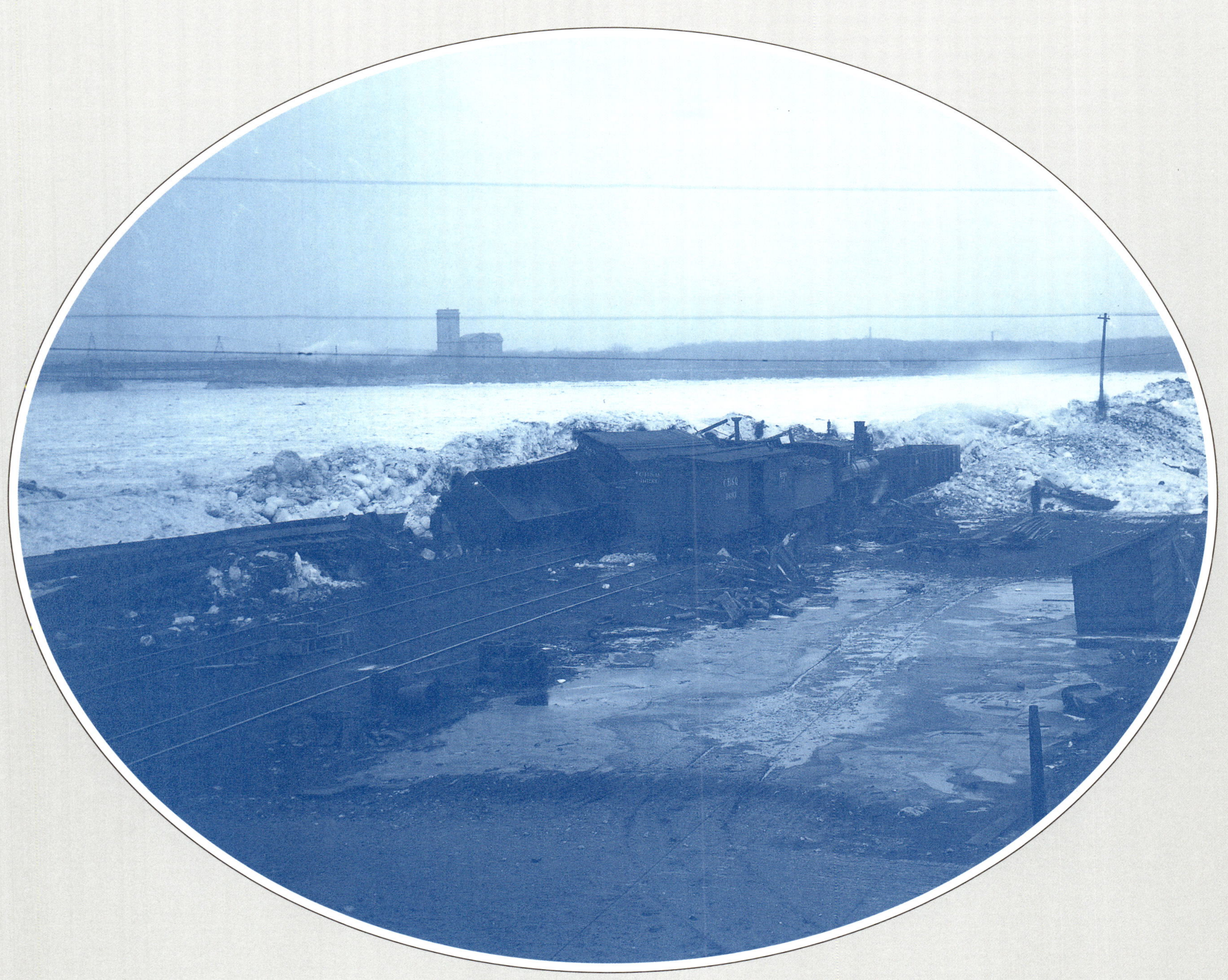

PLATE 53

U.S. Government Bridge at Rock Island, Ill., 1888

(MAYO FOUNDATION)

The government bridge at Rock Island connects Arsenal Island to Davenport, Iowa. It was built near the site of Fort Armstrong, the 1816 white settlement. Corps Major G. K. Warren, a Union hero at the battle of Gettysburg, designed and constructed the bridge in 1869–70. It was the only one of the first eleven Mississippi River bridges that was built by the government. • Part of the foundation of the old fort can be seen in the left foreground of this photograph, which Bosse took from the clock tower of the Arsenal headquarters of the Corps of Engineers. • The entire island, more than nine hundred acres, is owned by the government. A government bridge and the clock tower remain significant landmarks in the city. The back channel of the island, on the Illinois side, was dammed and used for water power for a sawmill and flour mill in the 1820s and 1830s. "Milltown" grew around the business; its name was changed to Moline in 1843, an adaptation of the French *moulin*, meaning mill. The negative for this photograph is one of only seven known to survive from the Bosse collection.

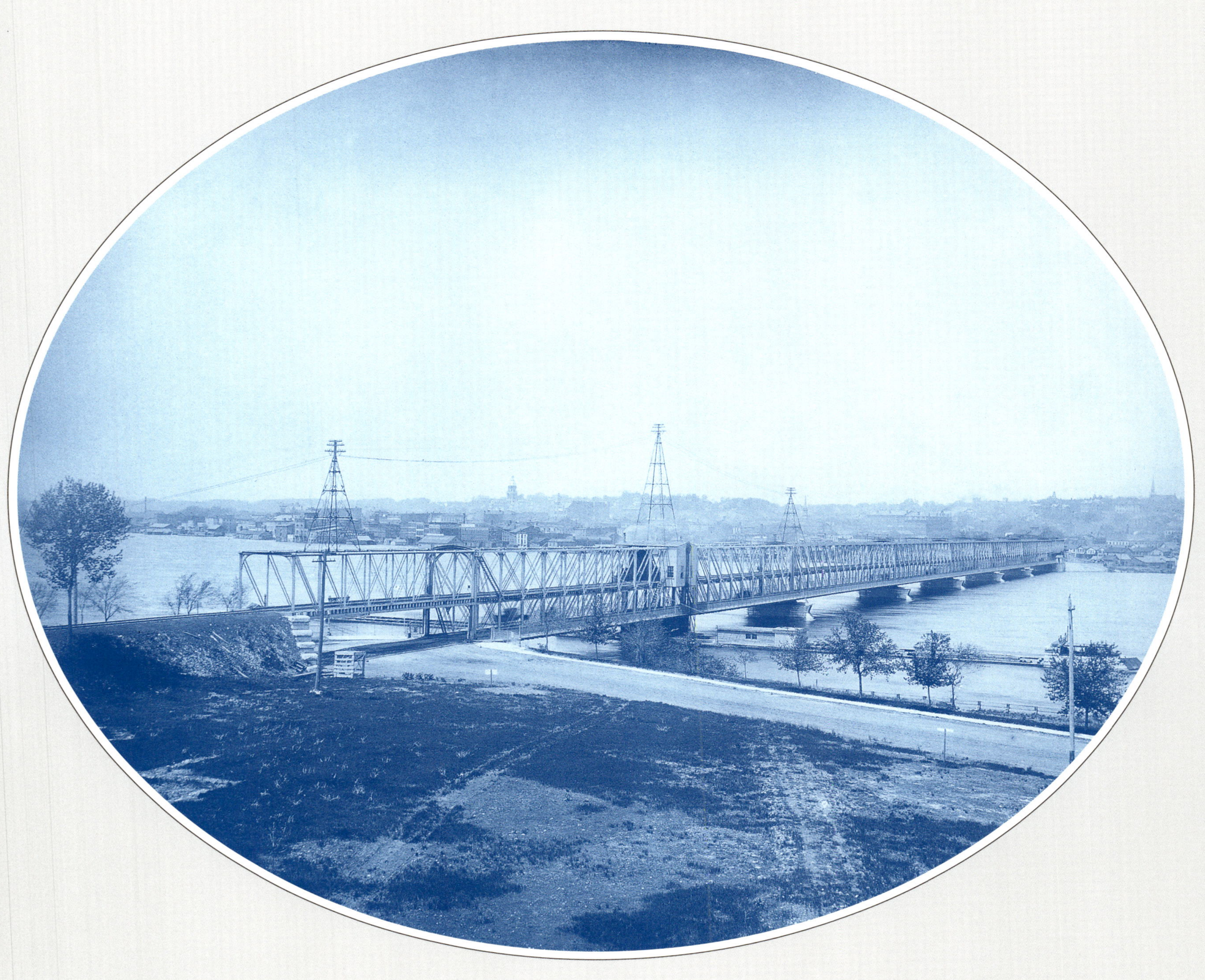

PLATE 54

Machine Shops of Rock Island Arsenal, 1885

(MAYO FOUNDATION)

The government complex at Arsenal Island, which grew to number about two hundred buildings, developed from the single structure at Fort Armstrong. Arsenal Island, in addition to being the home of the Rock Island district of the U.S. Army Corps of Engineers, served as a prisoner of war camp during the Civil War, a machine shop for military equipment, a weapons manufacturing plant, barracks, a graveyard, and offices. In the 1880s, several impressive buildings made from limestone quarried nearby were constructed. In this photograph, the workers have left jackets and tools on the stones in the front right.

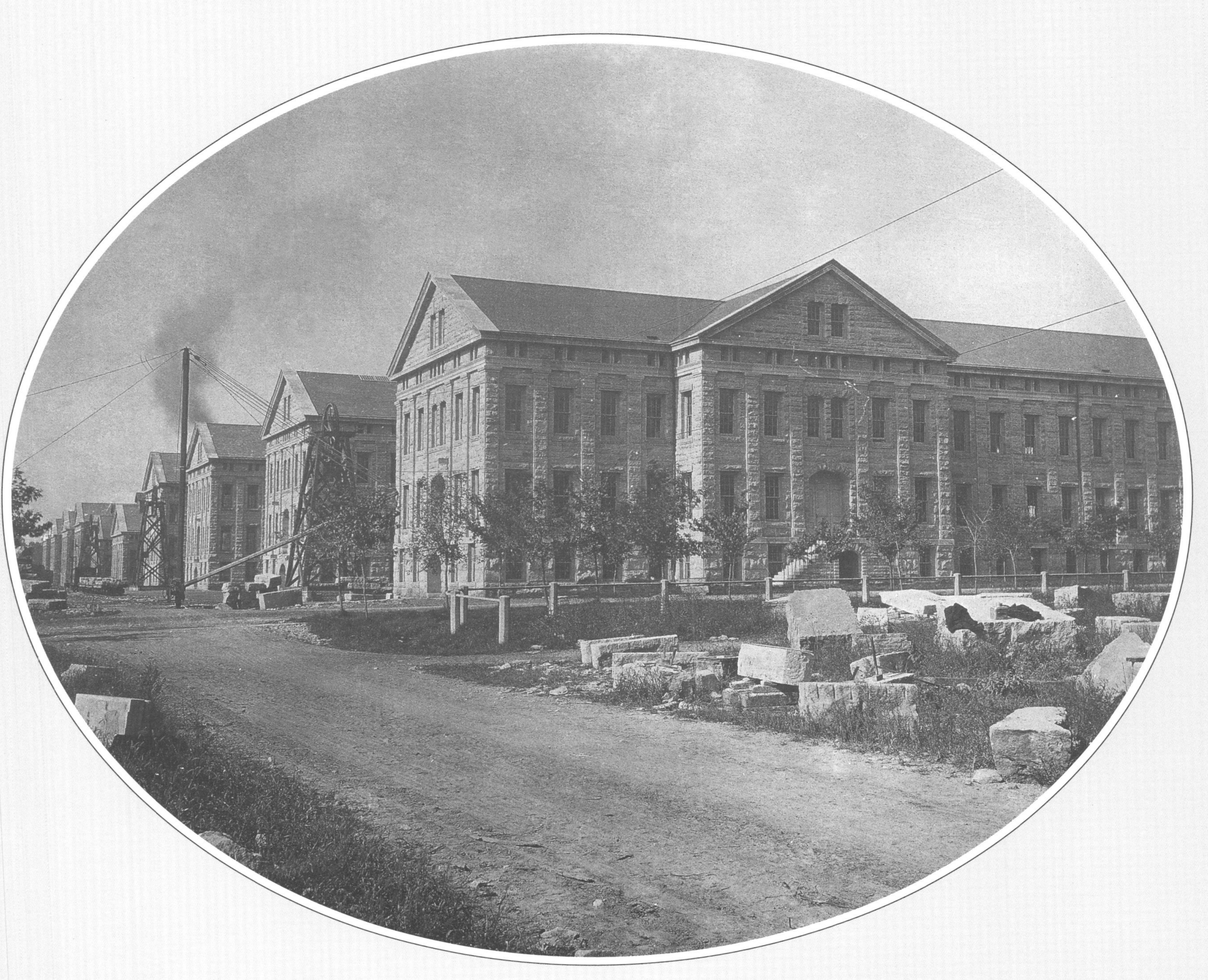

PLATE 55

Front St.—Davenport, during high water 1888, 1888

(U.S. ARMY CORPS OF ENGINEERS, ST. PAUL DISTRICT)

PLATE 56

Front St.—Davenport during High water 1888, 1888

(MAYO FOUNDATION)

PLATE 57

Second Ave.—Rock Island, Ill. during High water 1888, 1888

(MAYO FOUNDATION)

Bosse took a series of photographs during the spring flood of 1888 in his hometown of Rock Island as well as across the river in Davenport. The flood of '88 set records or near records from Dubuque south. In Plate 55, some of Davenport's downtown rooming houses, including Swanson's Boarding House and the Metropolitan, stand against the rising waters along Front Street. Note how the wooden sidewalk and planks in the foreground move the eye to the center of the photograph before trailing off into the floodwaters. • Bosse's picture of the flooded railroad tracks (Plate 56) may have been a subtle commentary on the fragility of rail lines too close to the river during floods. • By the summer of that year, the waters had receded and the river was again at low water, where it had been for much of the 1880s.

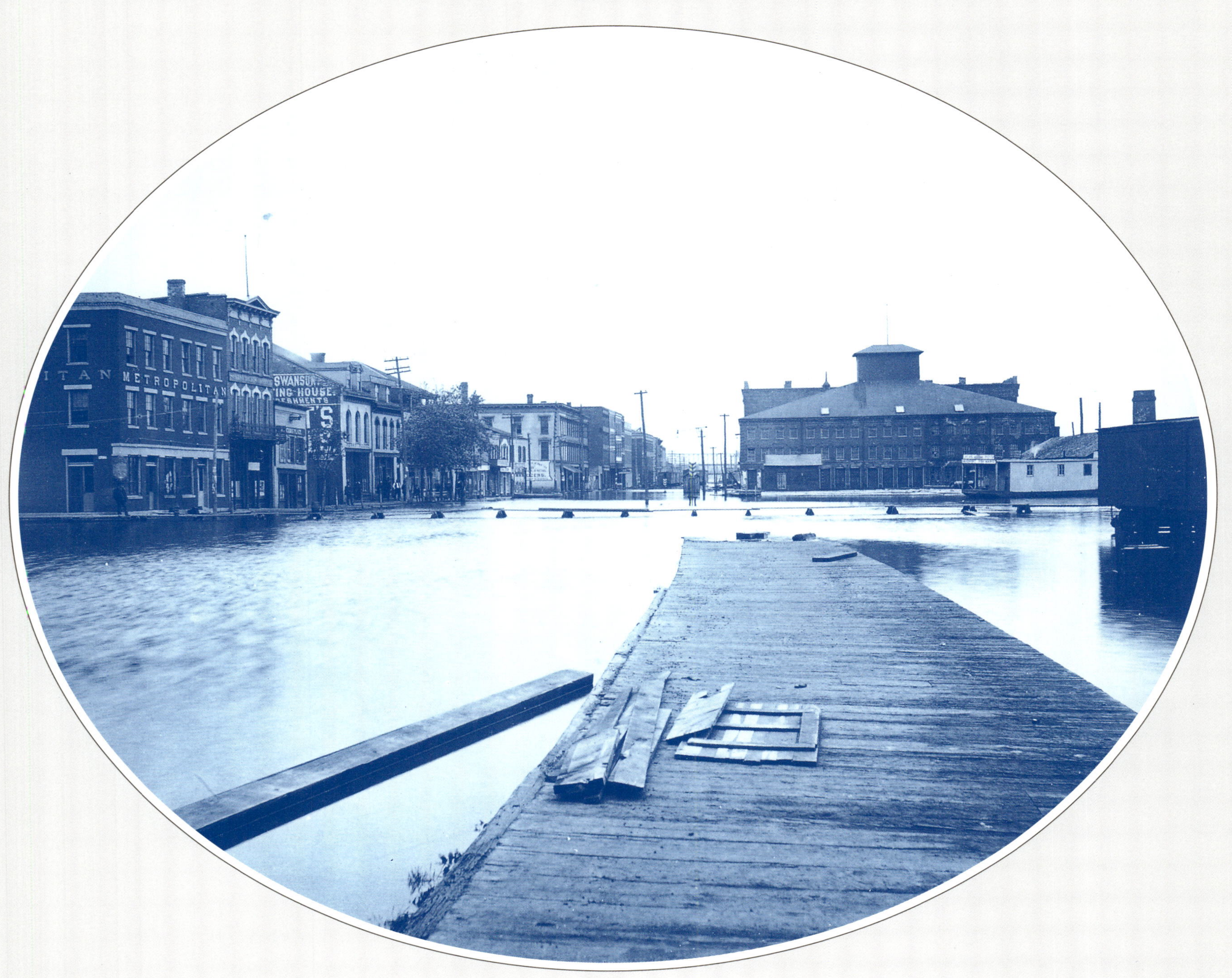
ITAN METROPOLITAN

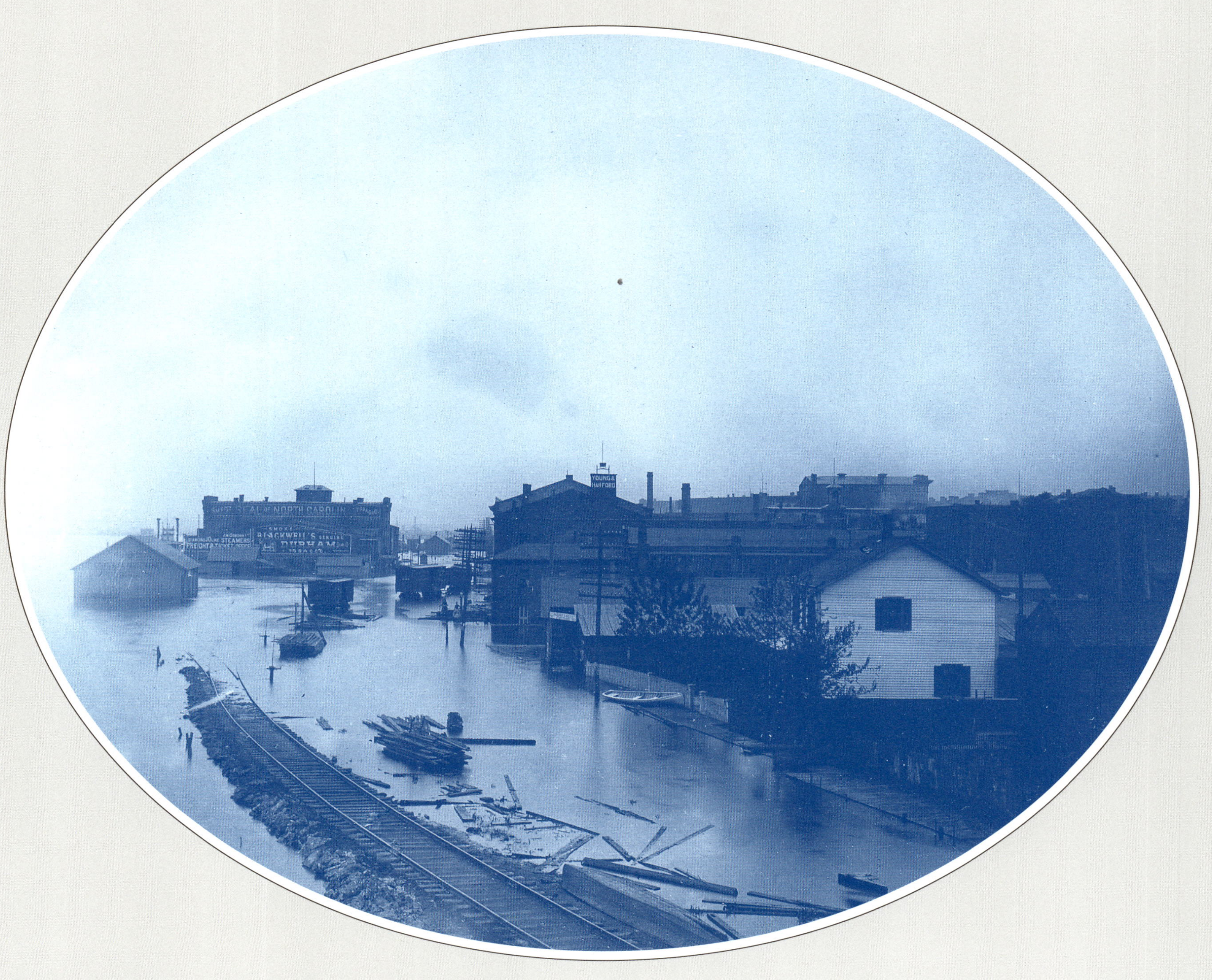
NORTH CAROLIN
SMOKE
STEAMERS
DURHAM
YOUNG &
HARFORD

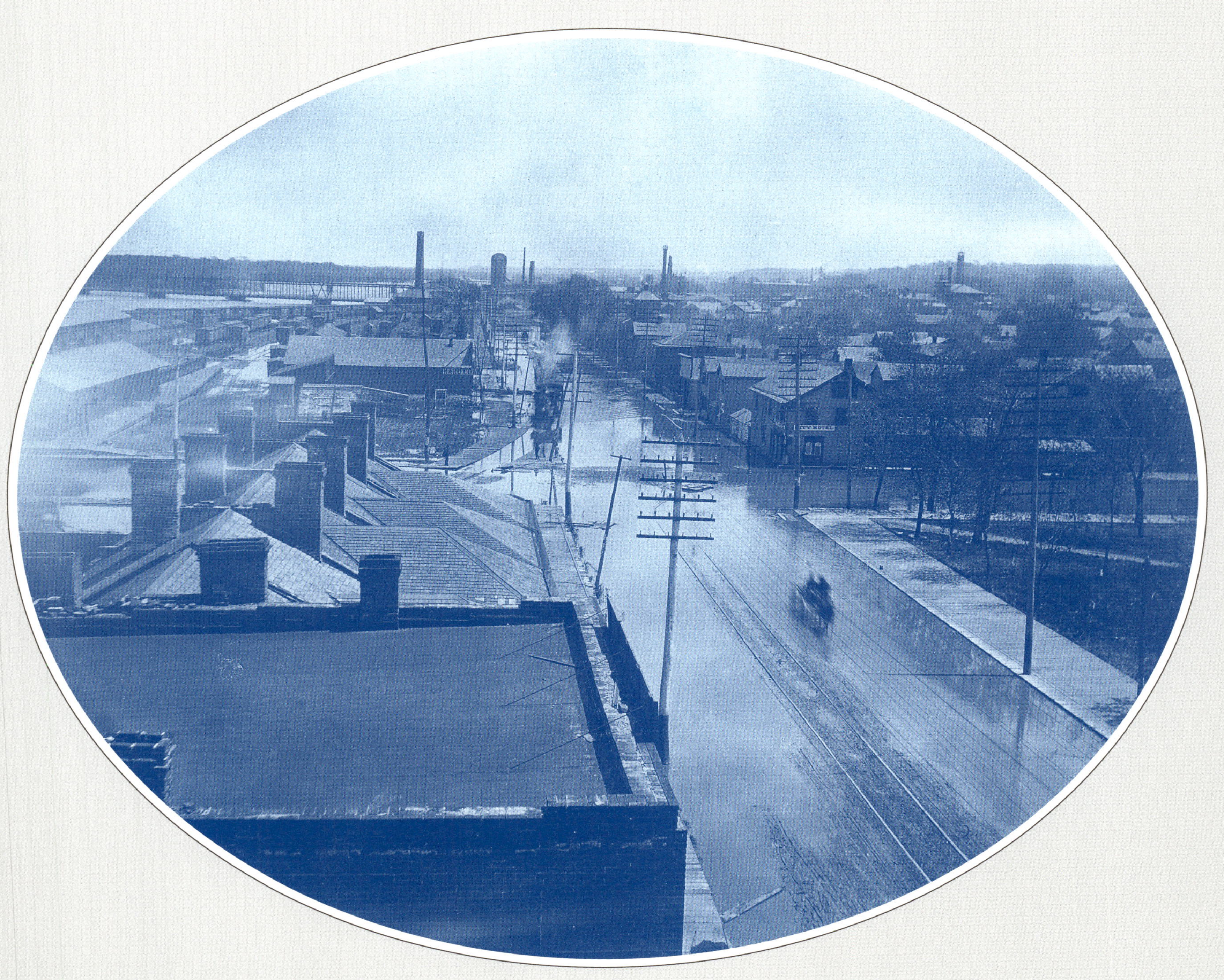

PLATE 58

Kahlke's Boatyard—Rock Island, Ill., no date

(MISSISSIPPI RIVER MUSEUM)

PLATE 59

Raftboat in construction (Boatyard of Kahlke Bros, Rock Island, Ill.), 1891

(MAYO FOUNDATION)

PLATE 60

Boatyard of Kahlke Bros, Rock Island, Ill., 1891

(MAYO FOUNDATION)

The Kahlke Brothers Boatyard at Rock Island was a major supplier and repair shop on the Mississippi in the late nineteenth and into the twentieth century. Brothers John and Peter Kahlke, German immigrants, began the business after the Civil War. The yard continued to operate under the Kahlke name until it closed in the early 1960s. • Plate 60, printed in March 1892, was acquired by the Kahlke brothers from the Corps and used on company letterhead for several years. The shop was not far from Bosse's home on Seventh Avenue, and he photographed several scenes there over the years. • More than 10,000 steamboats were built in the United States between 1811 and 1900, including these at the Kahlke yards. Western steamboats were built with a broad, flat hull that drew little water and was relatively easy to dislodge from a spit. The keel usually was constructed first, then the hull. When the boat was finished, it was pushed and pulled down the rails into the water. Modern wooden-hulled ships are built with fewer ribs, or frames, because of the advent of stronger laminated lumber.

Kahlke's Boat-Yard- Rock Island, Ill.

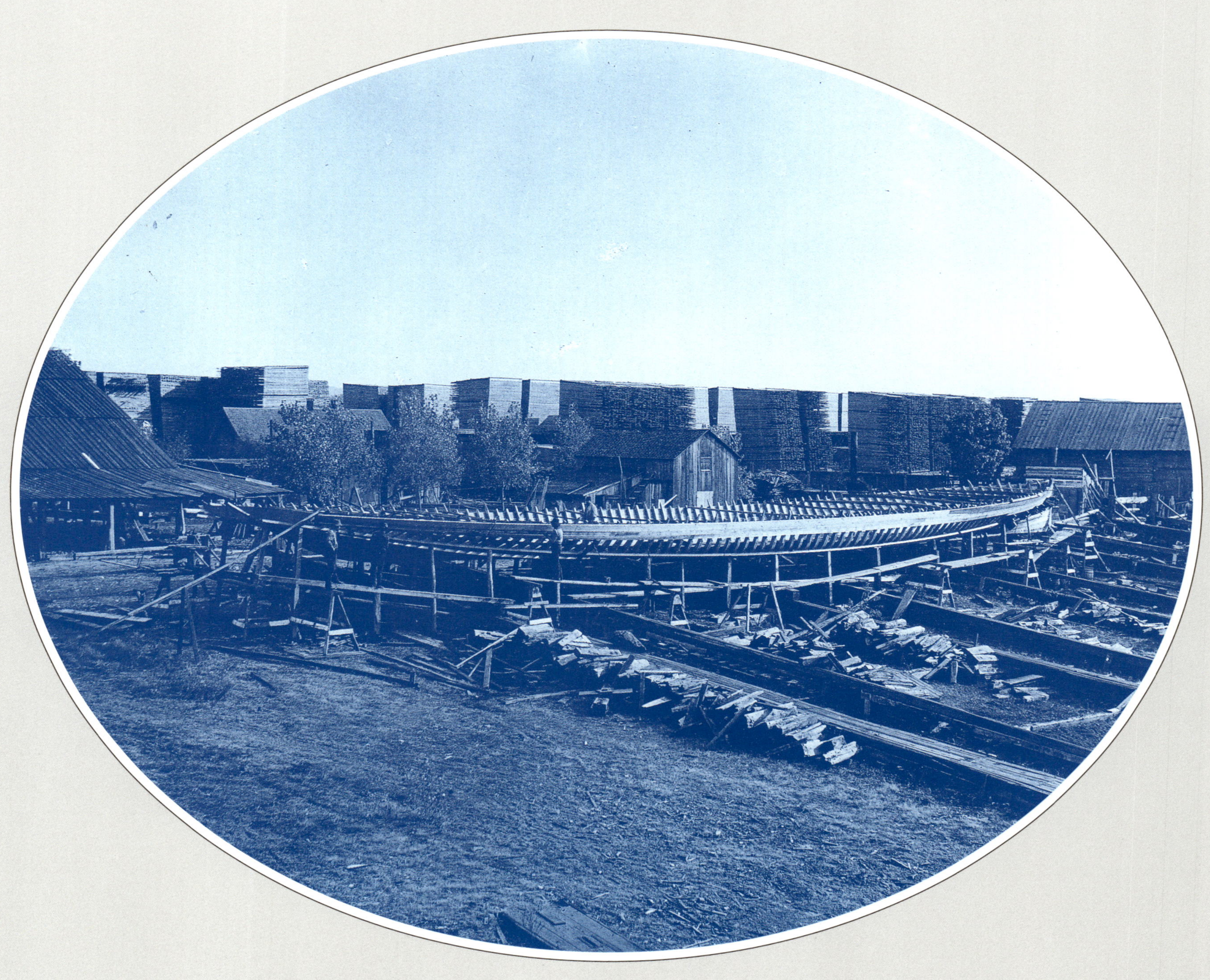

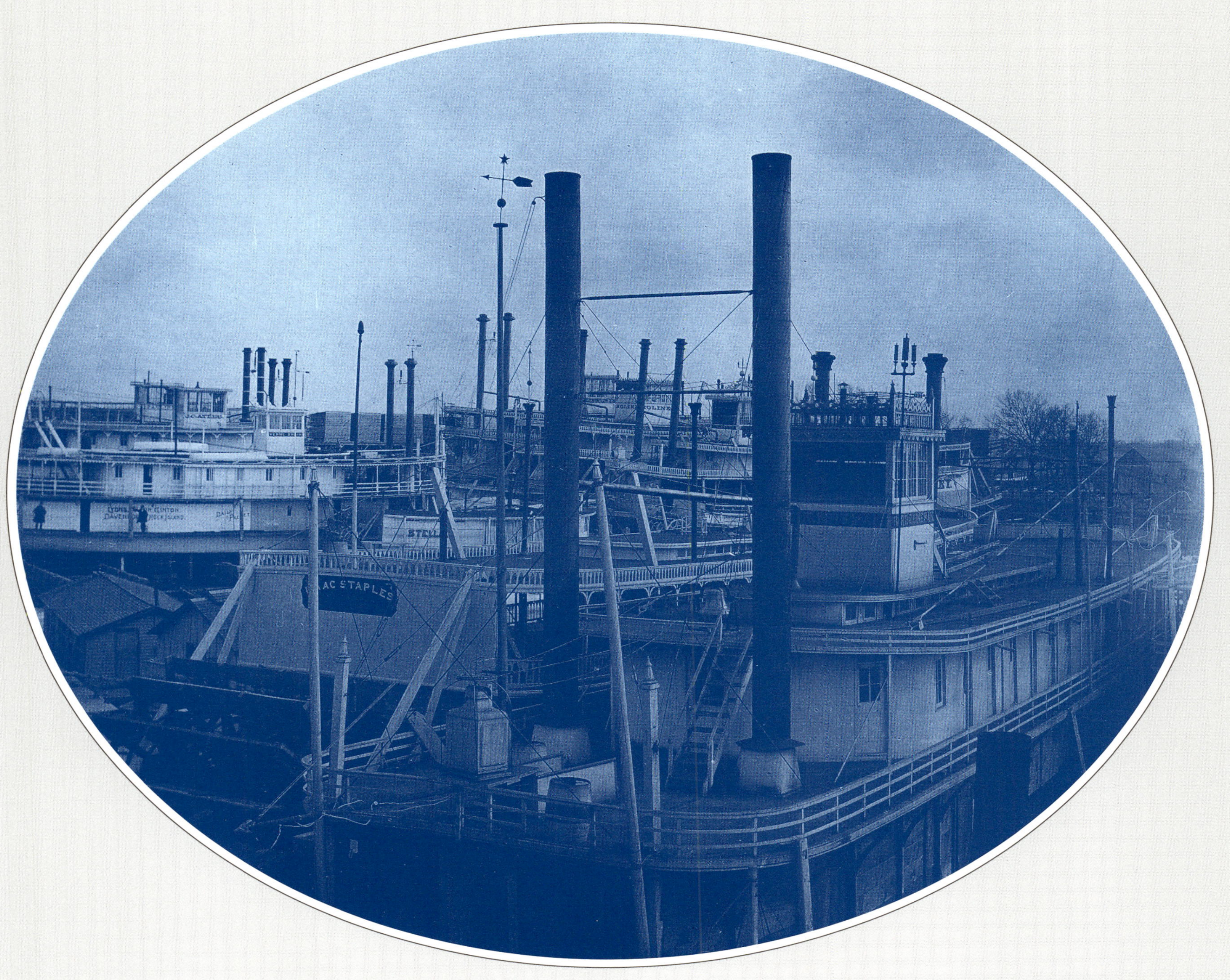
DAILY PACKET
STELL
AC STAPLES

PLATE 61

Muscatine, Ia., 1891

(U.S. ARMY CORPS OF ENGINEERS, ST. PAUL DISTRICT)

The Iowa port of Muscatine became one of the country's leading suppliers of fine buttons at the turn of the twentieth century. Commercial fishermen caught clams and mussels from the river—some on beds so thick that the Corps of Engineers' dredges had difficulty penetrating them—and sold them to Muscatine button manufacturers like the Hawkeye Pearl Button Company. The shops turned out buttons on a specially designed lathe. By 1897, there were eleven button factories in Muscatine alone. • But the river's supply of mussels was not inexhaustible; overfishing and the environmental damage done by the constriction and nine-foot channel projects drove some species to extinction and others to the edge of annihilation. Fishermen began to exploit the Mississippi's tributaries for mussels, but the end was in sight. The introduction of plastic buttons in the middle of the twentieth century effectively ended the industry.

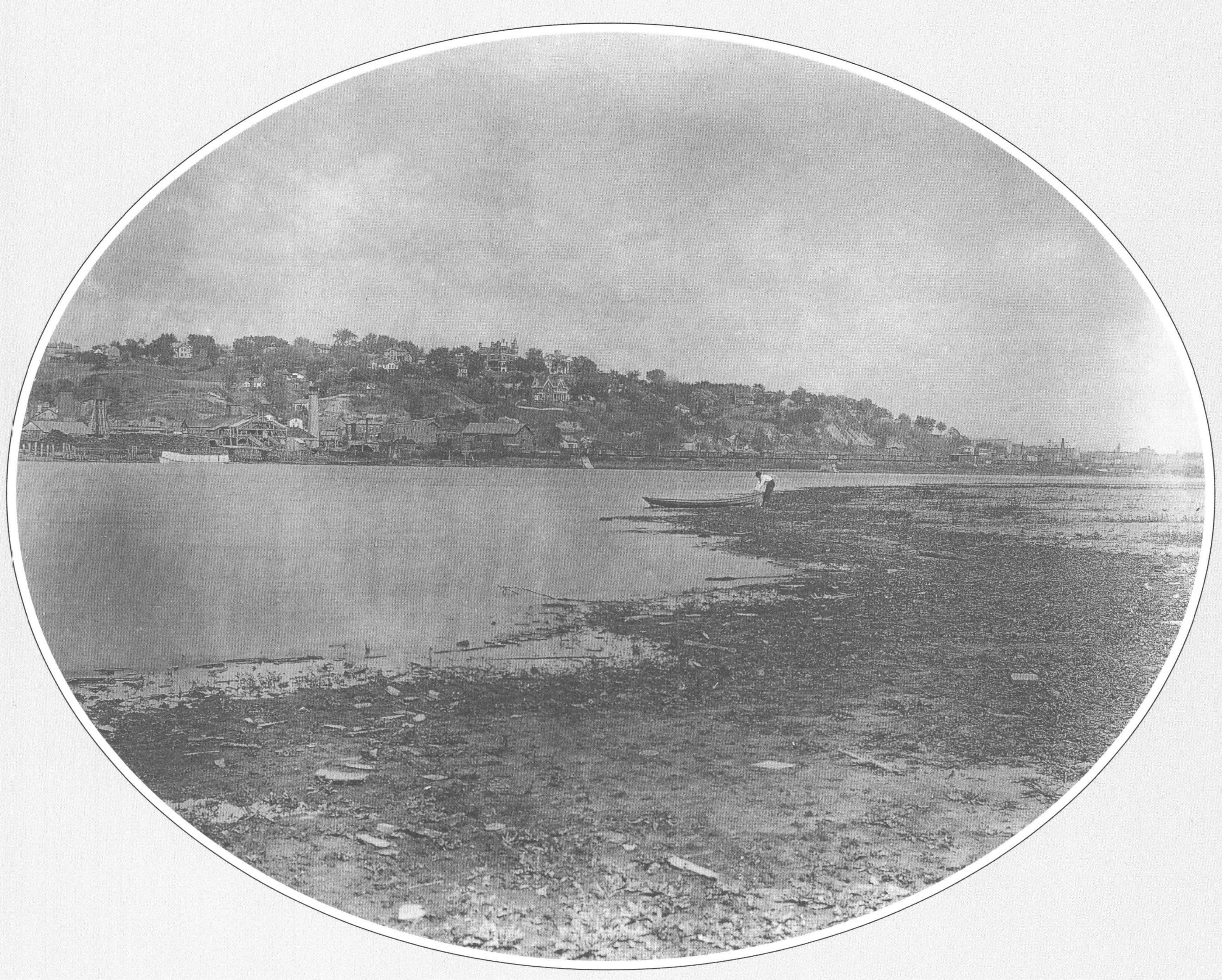

PLATE 62

Iowa Central R. R. Bridge at Keithsburg, Ill., 1889

(MAYO FOUNDATION)

The Iowa Central Railroad Bridge became an object of attention for the Corps of Engineers because of concerns about its danger to navigation. Keithsburg was a place for steamboats to stop and "wood up" with fuel for their boilers because the town and surrounding countryside contained thick stands of woods, so there was much river traffic near the bridge. (Big River State Forest was created south of town in the twentieth century.) • In Bosse's day, the city was also known for allowing nude bathing after sundown. Abraham Lincoln collected recruits in Keithsburg in 1832 when he led a militia of two thousand men to fight in the Blackhawk War. • The great flood of 1993 destroyed much of the northwest corner of town; many homes were removed and the region was replanted. • The area is home to a rare plant, the Patterson bindweed, discovered in 1873 by scientist N. H. Patterson near the town.

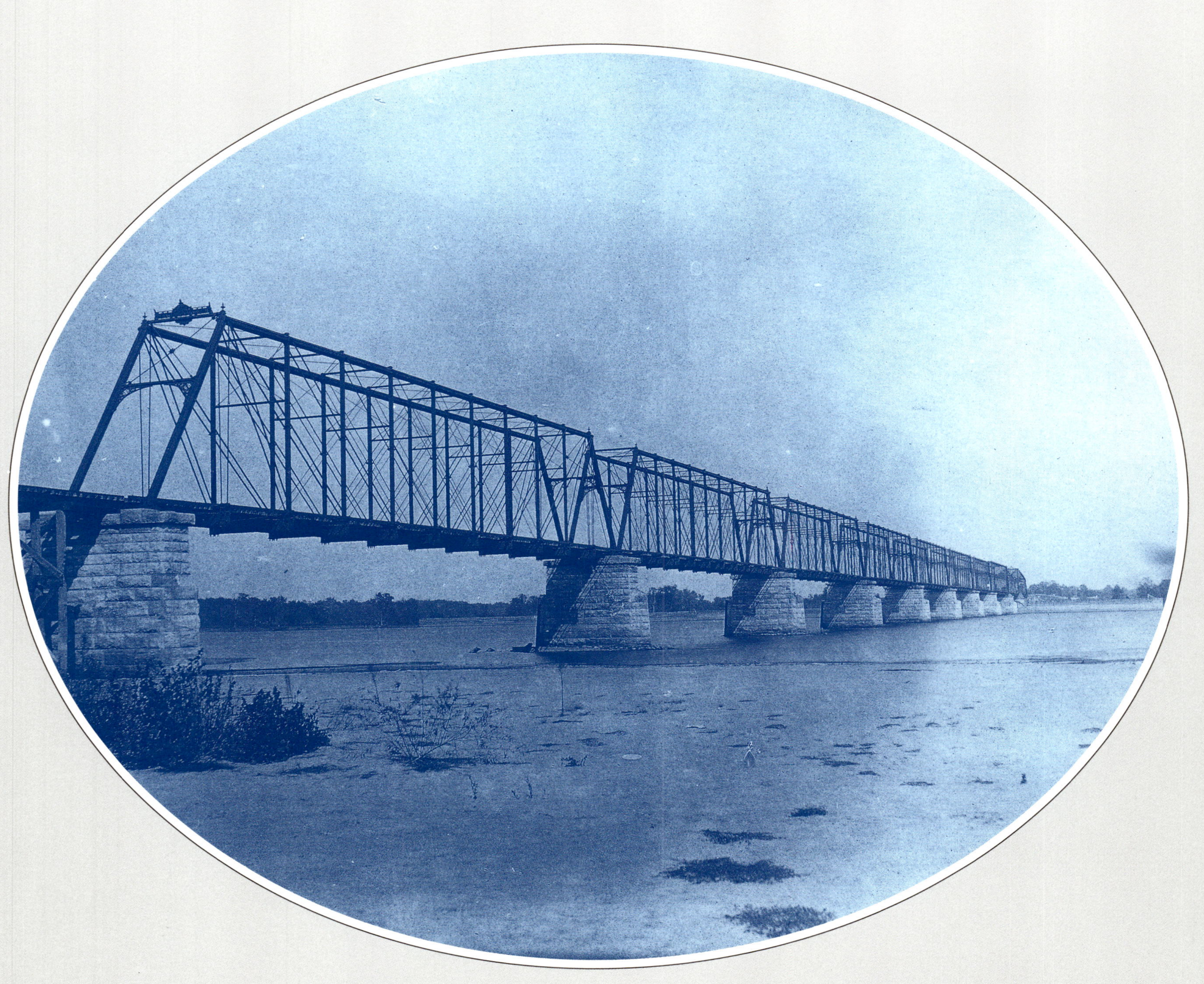

PLATE 63

Closing Dam—Whisky Chute, no date

(MISSISSIPPI RIVER MUSEUM)

The Corps of Engineers built closing dams like this one at Whiskey Chute, near Keithsburg, Illinois, to force the river into a main channel. Once the side channels were shut, most of the entire volume of water was funneled into a smaller space, increasing the current and flushing the river of sand and sediment. Where the river bottom was sand and silt, the system worked well. Where the bedrock was exposed, the river remained hazardous despite the often-increased water depth. • Closing dams often broke. The Corps tried several variations on the willow mat and limestone design, including driving piles deep into the muck to strengthen the structure. A pile dam system was used more extensively on the Missouri River than on the Mississippi, although Alexander Mackenzie, the Corps's man in charge of the river, favored the partially permeable pile and brush design for closing side channels. Closing side channels reduced the amount of sediment in the main river. "It is thought that on the lower portion of this district the amount of sediment is increasing," Mackenzie wrote in 1892, "and that more favorable results can be secured by pile and brush dams than has heretofore been thought possible." • The Whiskey Chute dam, finished in 1889, ran from Keithsburg Island to the Illinois shore in front of the town. A wing dam was constructed at the other end of the island in 1892. By the time the Corps was done working in the area, Whiskey Chute was closed off at both ends and became a lake.

Closing Dam - Whisky Chute.

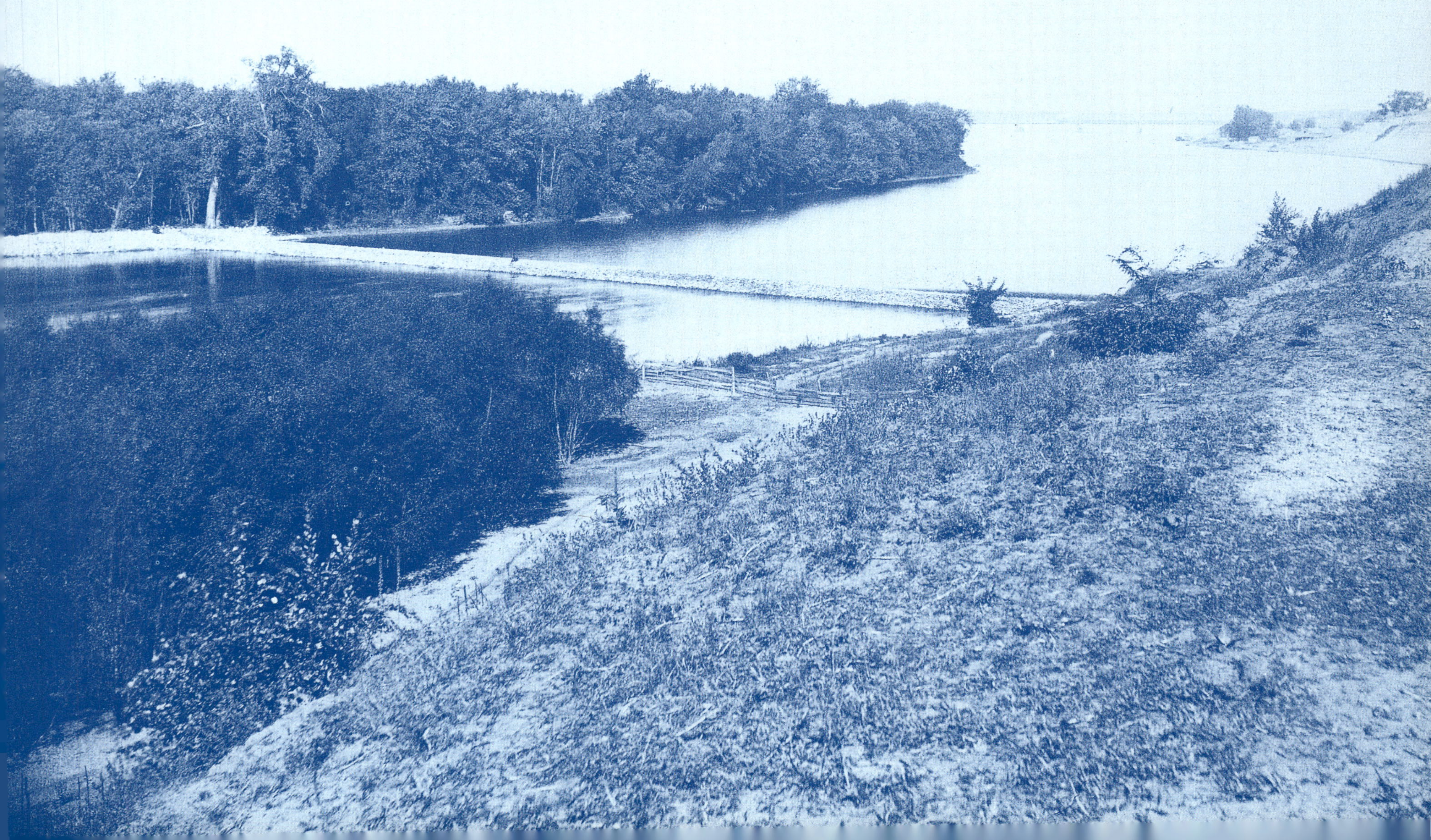

PLATE 64

Closing dam in Otter chute, 1889

(MAYO FOUNDATION)

Otter Chute, near Burlington, Iowa, also called Otter Slough, was a problem for steamboats because it drew away a good percentage of the river's flow from the main channel and occasionally shifted the main channel through it. The Corps of Engineers' solution was a series of dams, including this closing dam, to keep the flow out of Otter Chute entirely. Bosse posed two men, one holding a stadia rod, to give the dam some perspective. • The Corps experimented with closing dams in a serious way in 1873 with structures at Pig's Eye Island in Minnesota and Rollingstone Bar in Wisconsin; when the technology proved effective, hundreds were built from St. Paul to St. Louis. • The dam at Otter Chute blew out in the late 1880s; this is the repaired version, probably made with piles (oak or pine poles driven into the muck) to help support the willow mats and limestone.

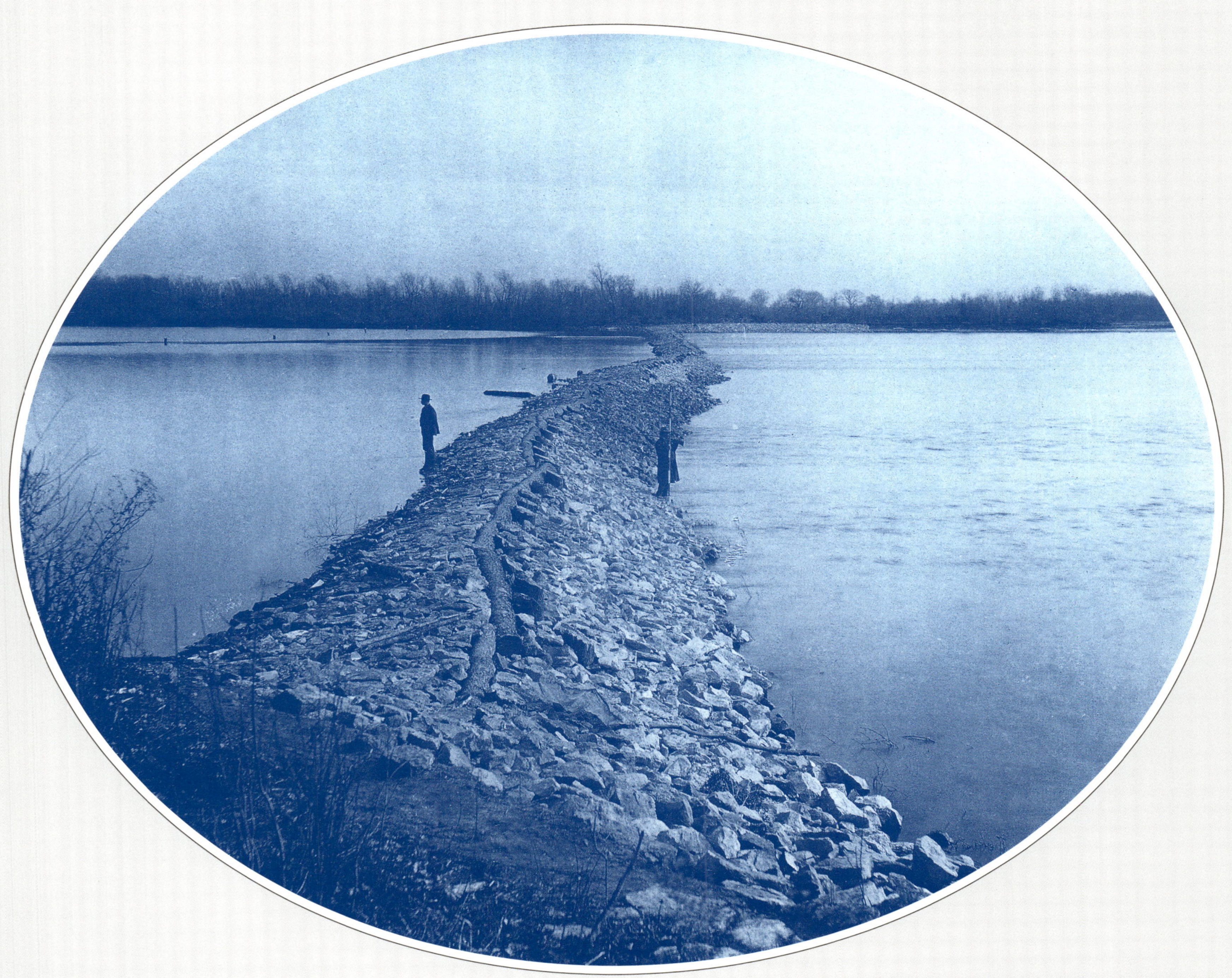

PLATE 65

Transfer Boat "Campbell," 1885

(U.S. ARMY CORPS OF ENGINEERS, ROCK ISLAND DISTRICT)

The railroads usually were regarded as the curse of the steamboat shipping industry—with good reason—but what is often overlooked is that many of the big railroads also owned boats. Transfer boats such as the *Campbell* were used to move railroad cars and engines across the river or longer distances, particularly in the days when few bridges existed. The Chicago, Burlington and Northern Railroad Company owned the *Campbell,* a side-wheeler. The *Campbell* was built in St. Louis in 1875 and used on the Missouri River as well. It was sold to the Ohio Valley Railroad in 1892 and moved to Evansville, Indiana.

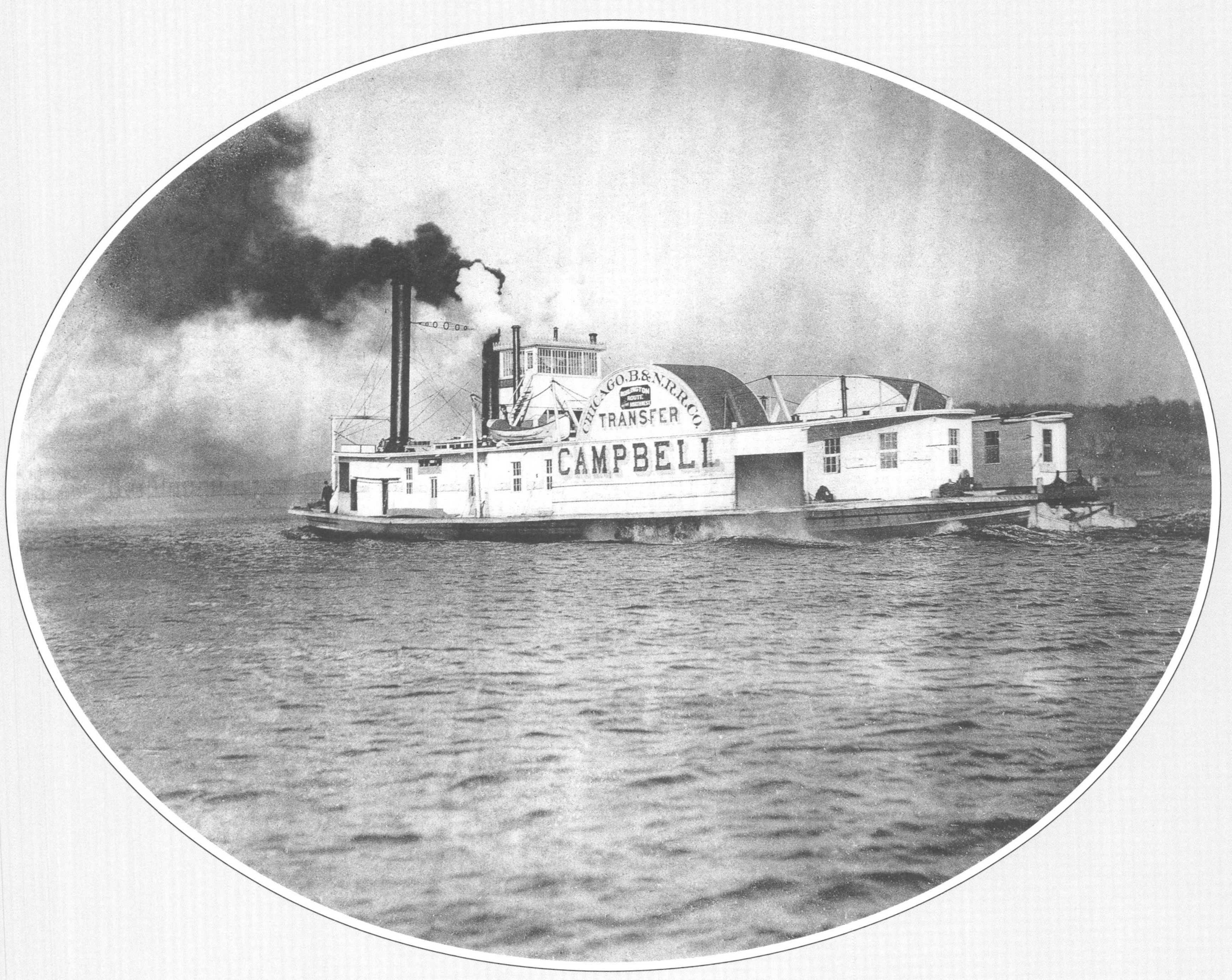
CHICAGO.B.&N.R.R.CO.
TRANSFER
CAMPBELL

PLATE 66

C. B. & Q. Ry Bridge at Burlington, Ia. (after reconstruction), 1891

(MAYO FOUNDATION)

The business elite in Burlington, Iowa, were among the most aggressive at lobbying Congress and influencing federal and state governments for transportation improvements. In 1866, under pressure from several river cities, Congress authorized bridges at Burlington, Quincy, Winona, Dubuque, Keokuk, Hannibal, and St. Louis. Burlington was more prepared to act than its competitors (plans were drawn in 1865), and the Chicago, Burlington and Quincy Railroad almost immediately began building this bridge. • The low, swing-span bridge was engineered by Max Hjortsberg of the railroad and built by the Detroit Bridge Iron Company. Upon completion in 1868, it became the first all-metal span across the Mississippi River, and this was one of only three railroad lines connecting Iowa to points east. Hjortsberg was able to use the soft riverbed at Burlington for driven pile formations rather than the more dangerous and expensive caisson design. (Caissons were structures built to keep water from flowing to the site while the foundations were being built.) The single-track bridge lasted only twenty-four years; a double-track bridge replaced it in 1892.

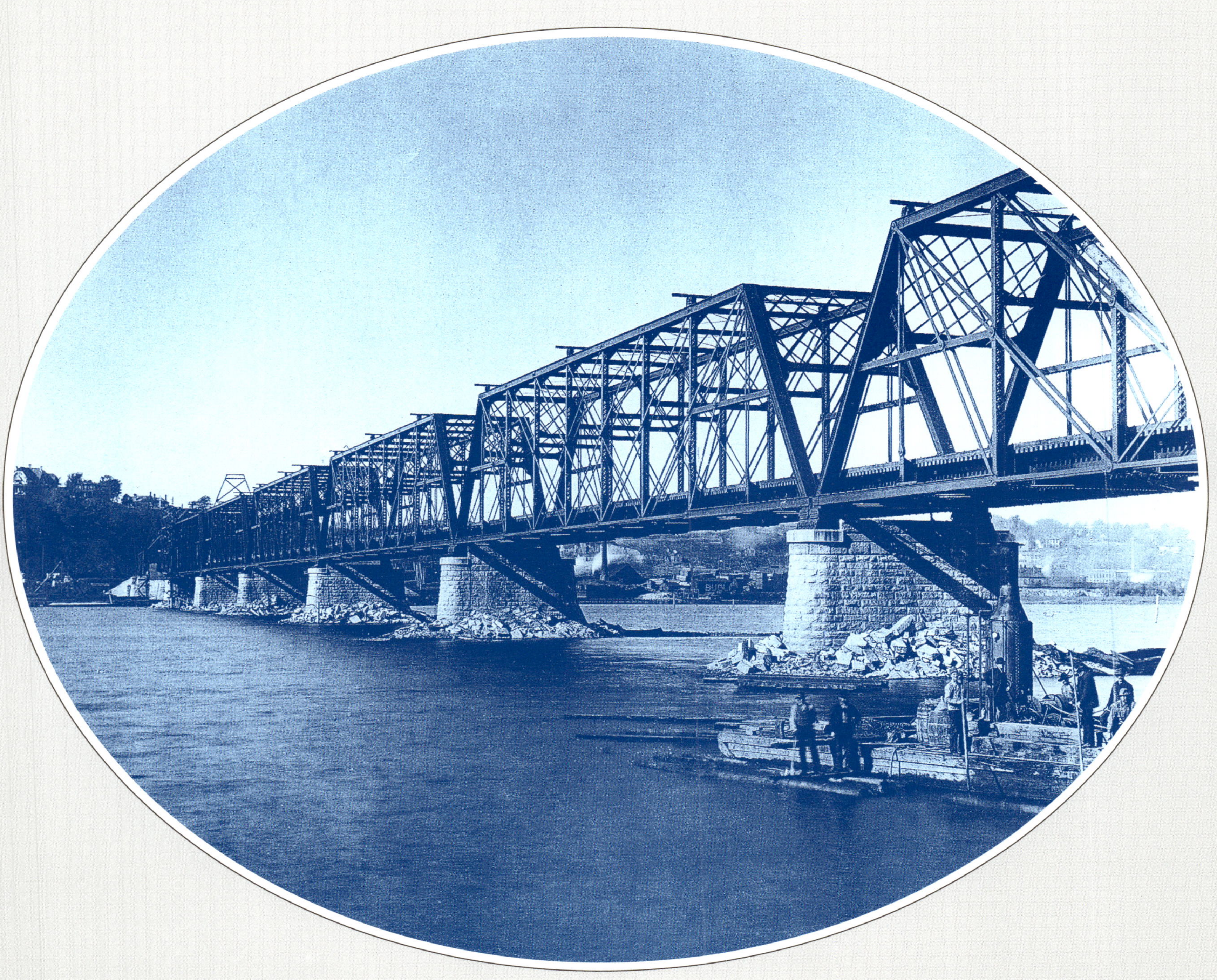

PLATE 67

River Front at Burlington, Ia., no date

(MISSISSIPPI RIVER MUSEUM)

Bridges at places like Burlington, Rock Island, and Quincy often were built by Chicago-based railroads. This meant that grain and other products shipped from Iowa, Nebraska, and points west often continued into the industrial city in Illinois rather than being transferred to barges bound for St. Louis or New Orleans. Merchants in St. Louis, in particular, felt the loss of river trade as the railroads expanded west. • Bosse took this photograph from South Hill, looking upstream. The Berry and Company sawmill is visible in the foreground, while farther north is the J. Dickie and Company sawmill and lumberyard. Burlington was named the first capital of the Iowa Territory in 1838 and remained an important agricultural and commercial port through the nineteenth century.

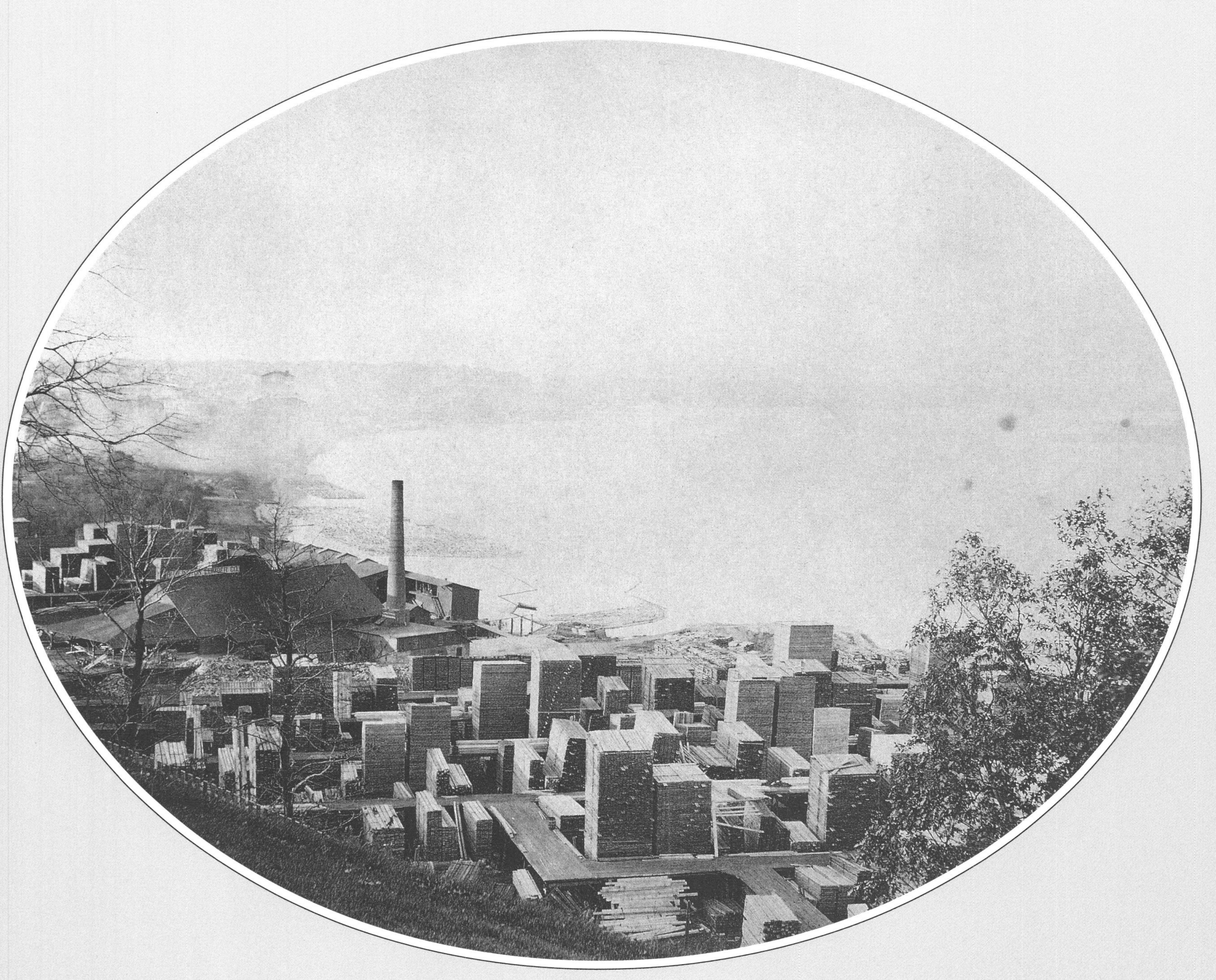

PLATE 68

Fort Madison, Ia., 1885

(MAYO FOUNDATION)

Fort Madison, at the time of this photograph, was one of the most important milling towns on the Iowa-Illinois border. Huge rafts of timber, mostly white pine, floated into town from the forests of Minnesota and Wisconsin to be cut, planed, and stacked for shipping to build Kansas City, Des Moines, Topeka, and other prairie towns. In 1879, there were seventy-three sawmills on the river between the mouth of the Chippewa and St. Louis. By the 1890s, the timber trade had started to dwindle as the forests were cleared; by 1913, the sawmill at Fort Madison was the only one left on the entire upper river. • In 1915, the *Ottumwa Belle,* piloted by Walter Hunter, guided the last lumber raft from Hudson, Wisconsin, down the St. Croix to the Mississippi to Fort Madison. The glory era of the timber industry in the Upper Midwest was over. Hunter died in 1962 at the port of Bellevue, Iowa, at age ninety-four. He had been a riverman since 1880.

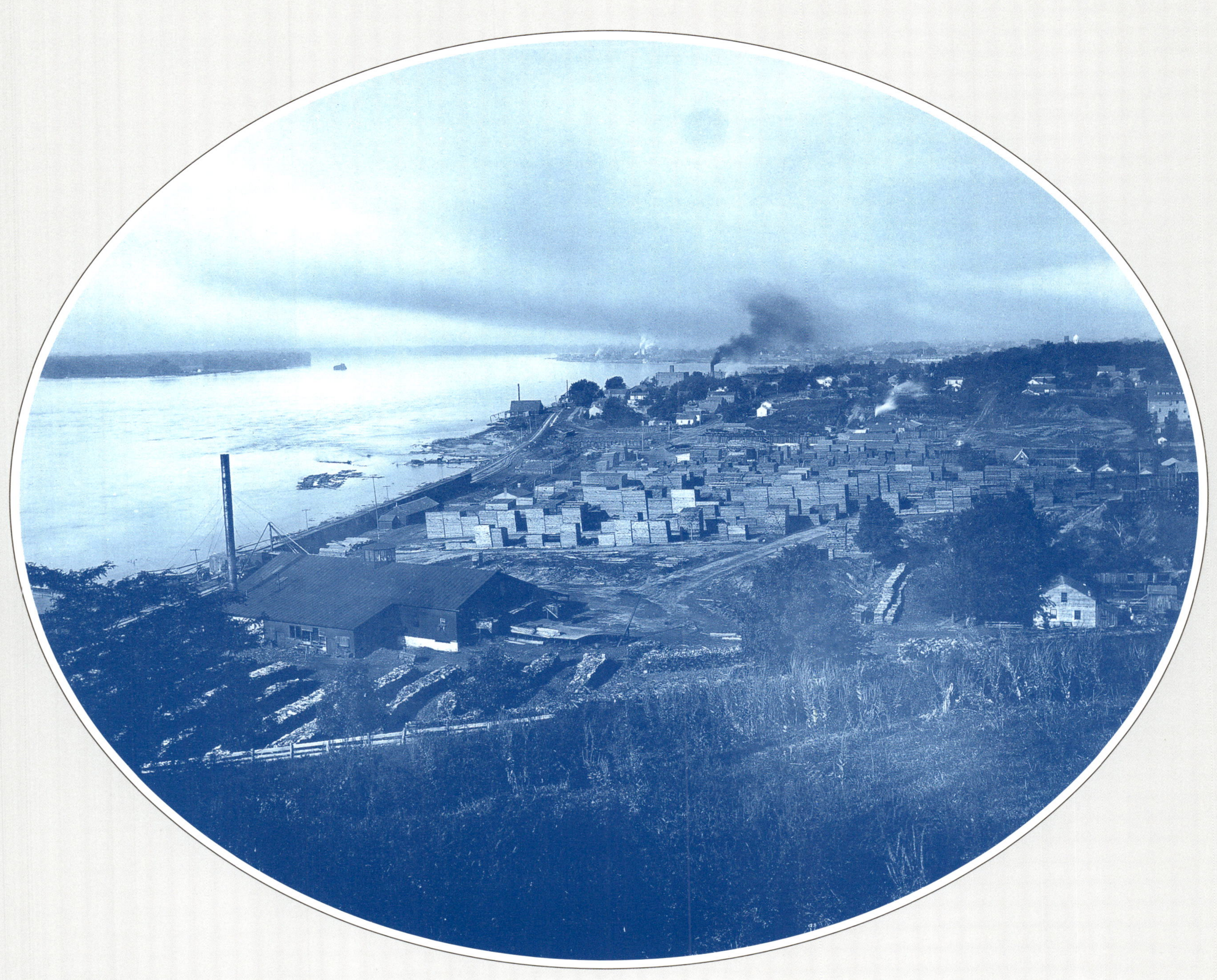

PLATE 69

Iowa State Penitentiary—Fort Madison, Ia., 1891

(MAYO FOUNDATION)

This is a rare Bosse photograph taken some distance away from the Mississippi River, yet it has all the marks of his style, including the model in the foreground. It was taken from an area called Black Hawk Heights, from which he could see the river if he swung his camera back around to the east. Bosse sometimes shot institutional buildings near the river, like this prison, the Soldiers' Home in Minneapolis, and the Rock Island Arsenal. The penitentiary was established in 1839 as a territorial prison. • One of the reasons it was convenient, if not always simple, for Bosse to shoot Mississippi River subjects was the availability of water. The cyanotype process, if the photographer was not using a treated paper, consisted of ferric ammonium citrate and potassium ferrocyanide applied to ordinary notebook paper with a brush, cloth, or sponge. The paper dried in the dark. When the time came to make a print, the paper was placed under a glass negative and exposed to the sun. The exposed paper was then washed in water to bring out the color and make the print permanent. Although Bosse used the cyanotype process extensively, he was not the only one experimenting with its look; Carleton Watkins, Henri Le Secq, Edward Curtis, Paul Haviland, and other photographers also produced cyanotype prints for public view.

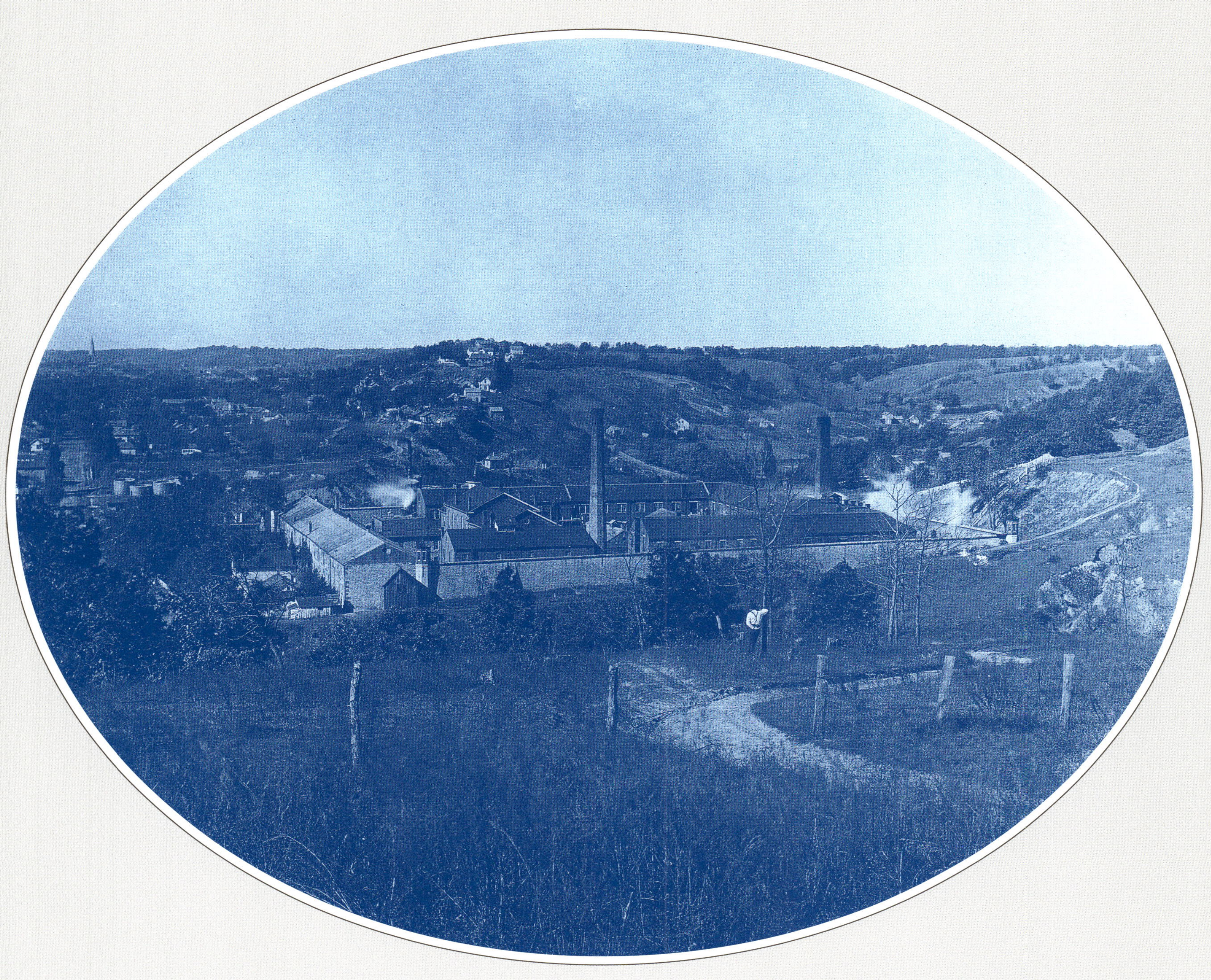

PLATE 70

Mechanic's Rock, 1889

(MAYO FOUNDATION)

Mechanic's Rock, two miles below the town of Montrose, Iowa, was named for an unfortunate ship that crashed and sank there in the early days of steamboat travel. Part of the dangerous Des Moines Rapids, Mechanic's Rock became a landmark for captains navigating that treacherous stretch of river. The low-water mark of 1864 was chiseled into the rock, thirty-two and a half inches below the top, to give captains and crews a visual reminder of water depth. The person in the picture is holding a stadia rod, a device used to measure river depth. Local history has it that a team of oxen moved the rock in the 1840s to get it out of the way of the navigation channel. It was flooded by the lock and dam system that went in at Keokuk, Iowa, in 1917. A team of divers failed to find Mechanic's Rock in the 1990s; it is possible that it was destroyed—or buried under tons of silt—by the Corps during work on the Des Moines Rapids.

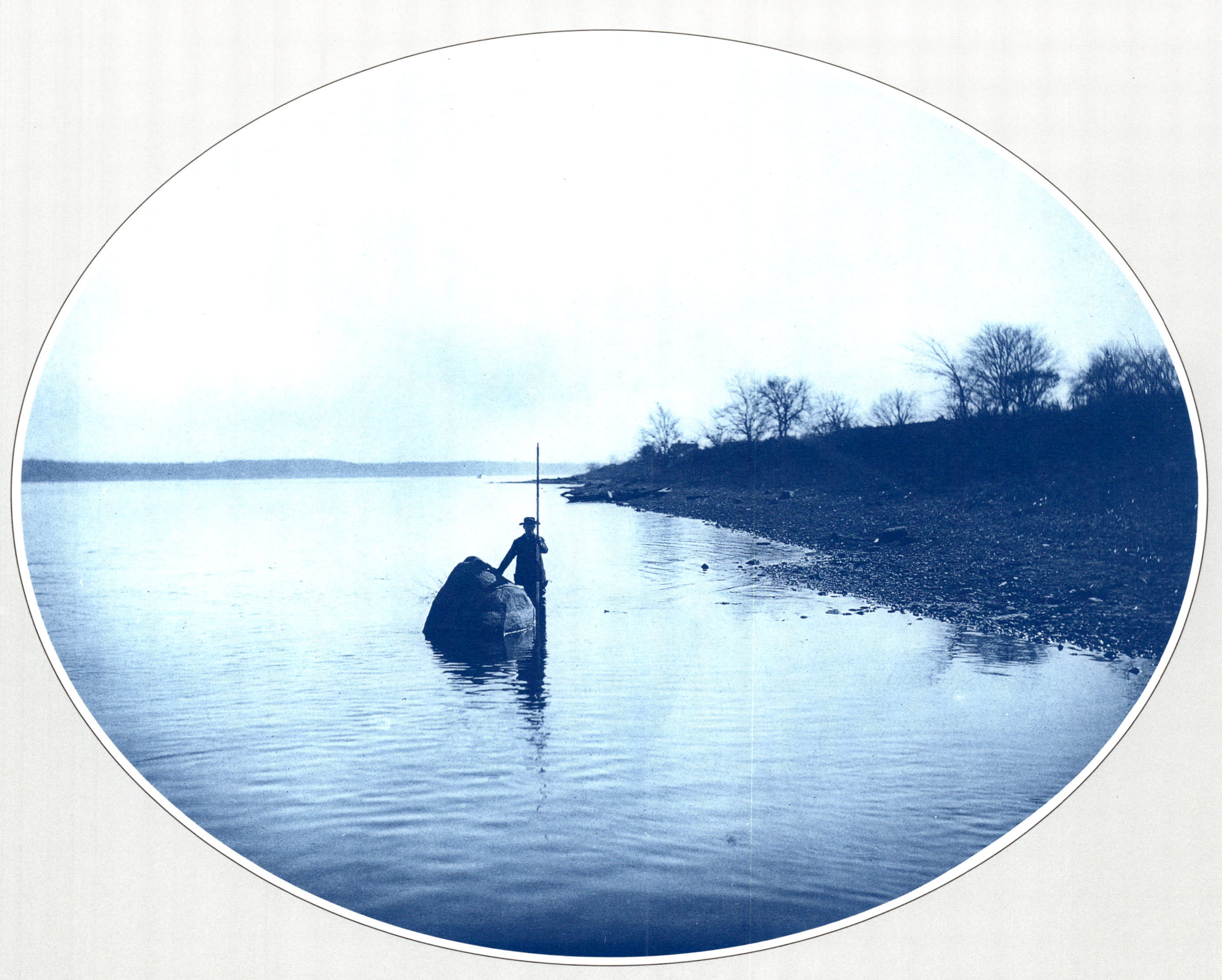

PLATE 71

U.S. Dredge "Phoenix," 1885

(U.S. ARMY CORPS OF ENGINEERS, ST. PAUL DISTRICT)

The photograph of the dredge *Phoenix* seems to embody the industrial age. The Corps had this boat built with congressional authorization after Rock Island district commander Alexander Mackenzie convinced his bosses that a dredge would save the government time and money as compared to hiring out the work. • Bosse's photographs at Minneiska (Plate 29), where a private dredge contracted for by the Corps removed a small island, were used to persuade the higher-ups of the necessity for a vehicle like this one. The *Phoenix*, which was not self-propelled, dug out islands, tow heads, sandbars, and other obstructions and dumped the spoil on another nearby barge. The spoil was used to fill in the spaces behind wing dams or was deposited on shore. Bosse made at least five prints of this photograph; in one, he brushed out the man standing on the bucket.

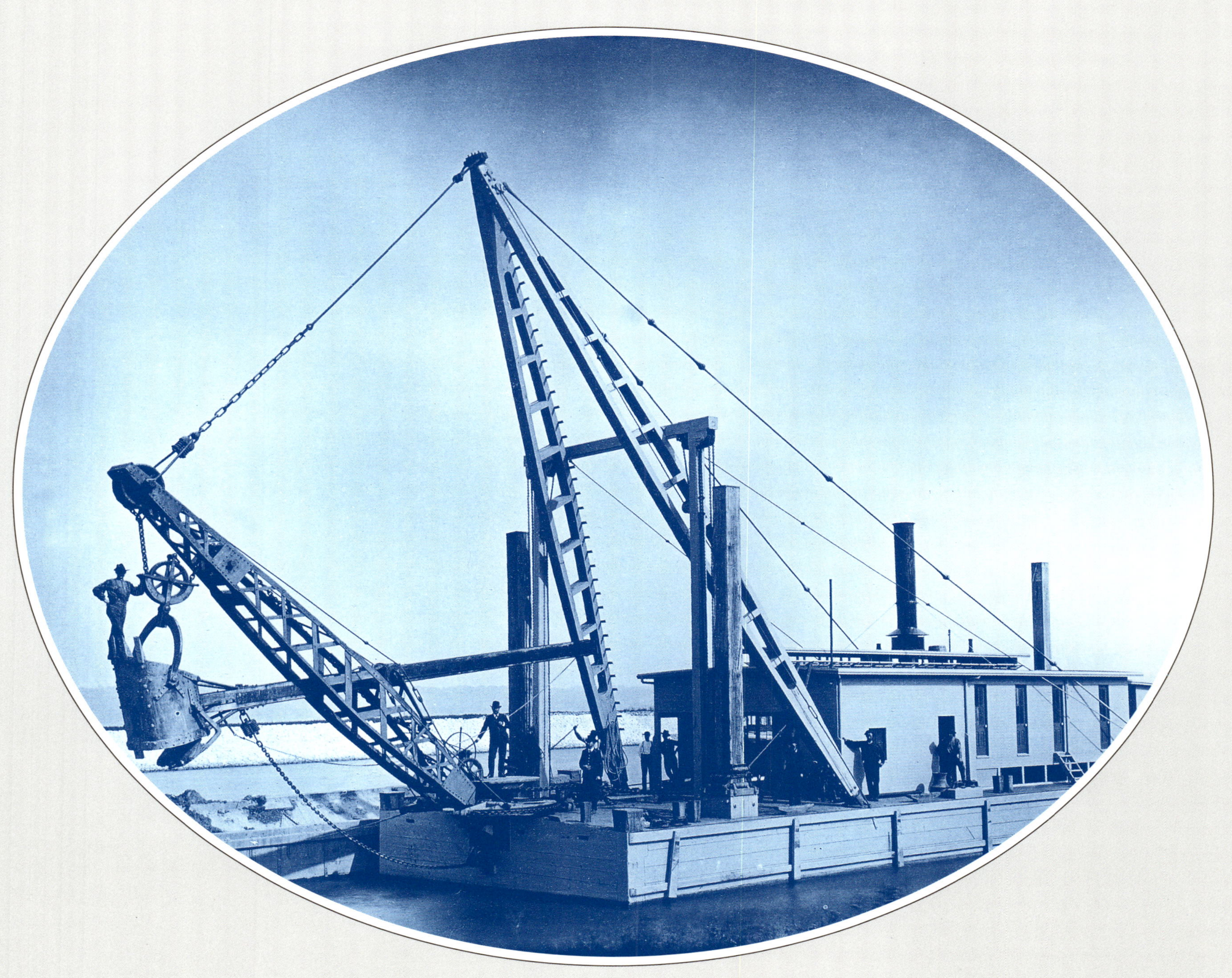

PLATE 72

Showing hole in "Vixen," no date

(MISSISSIPPI RIVER MUSEUM)

In another one of his life's ironies, Bosse shot a photograph of this steamboat, the *Vixen*, which would be renamed in his honor a few years after his death. The hole in the bow of the *Vixen* was big enough to force it into this dry dock, probably at the Des Moines Rapids, for repairs. It is an unusual photograph for Bosse, who preferred landscapes and less obvious documentary subjects. • The stern-wheel towboat *Vixen*, built in Dubuque in 1881, measured 100 by 19.5 by 3.8 feet at its maiden launch. It was the sister boat to the *Fury*, a well-known vessel on the upper river. The *Vixen* was renamed the *Henry Bosse* in 1908, almost five years after the photographer died at age fifty-nine. The stern-wheeler met a similarly untimely fate: it capsized off Keokuk, Iowa, in a severe storm in 1913, killing six men.

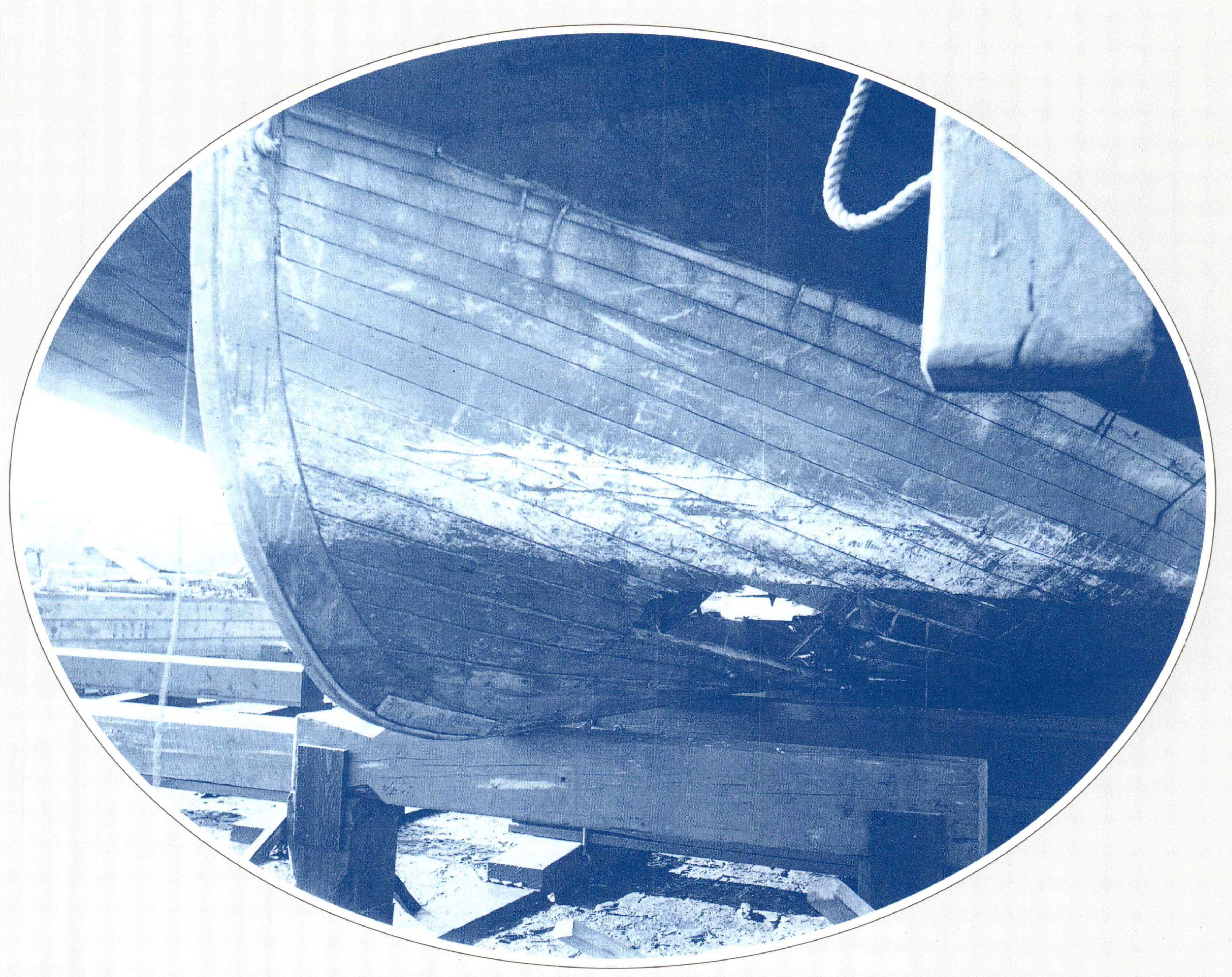

PLATE 73

Entrance to Guard Lock, 1889

(MAYO FOUNDATION)

PLATE 74

Middle Lock and Dry Dock, 1891

(MAYO FOUNDATION)

PLATE 75

Lower Lock, 1891

(MAYO FOUNDATION)

Nearly eight miles of rapids near the mouth of the Des Moines River between Montrose and Keokuk, Iowa, was the worst stretch of the Upper Mississippi River for shipping. A mass of hardened limestone formed a natural dam, but the surface of the river was so smooth and regular that it gave little notice of the dam's presence. Shippers often had to "break bulk"—that is, remove freight from one boat and put it on another—at the Des Moines Rapids, which greatly increased the cost of moving people and things. • Even shallow draft flatboats and barges took three to five days to navigate the rapids, as many were pulled by hand along the shore. The first work at the rapids, blasting and drilling, began in the 1830s under the supervision of Lieutenant Robert E. Lee. By the 1860s, the Corps settled on the solution of a 7.6-mile lateral canal with three locks around the rapids on the Iowa side. Work began in 1866 and was finally completed at a cost of $4.5 million in 1890, although the canal was open to traffic in 1877. Its three locks are pictured here.

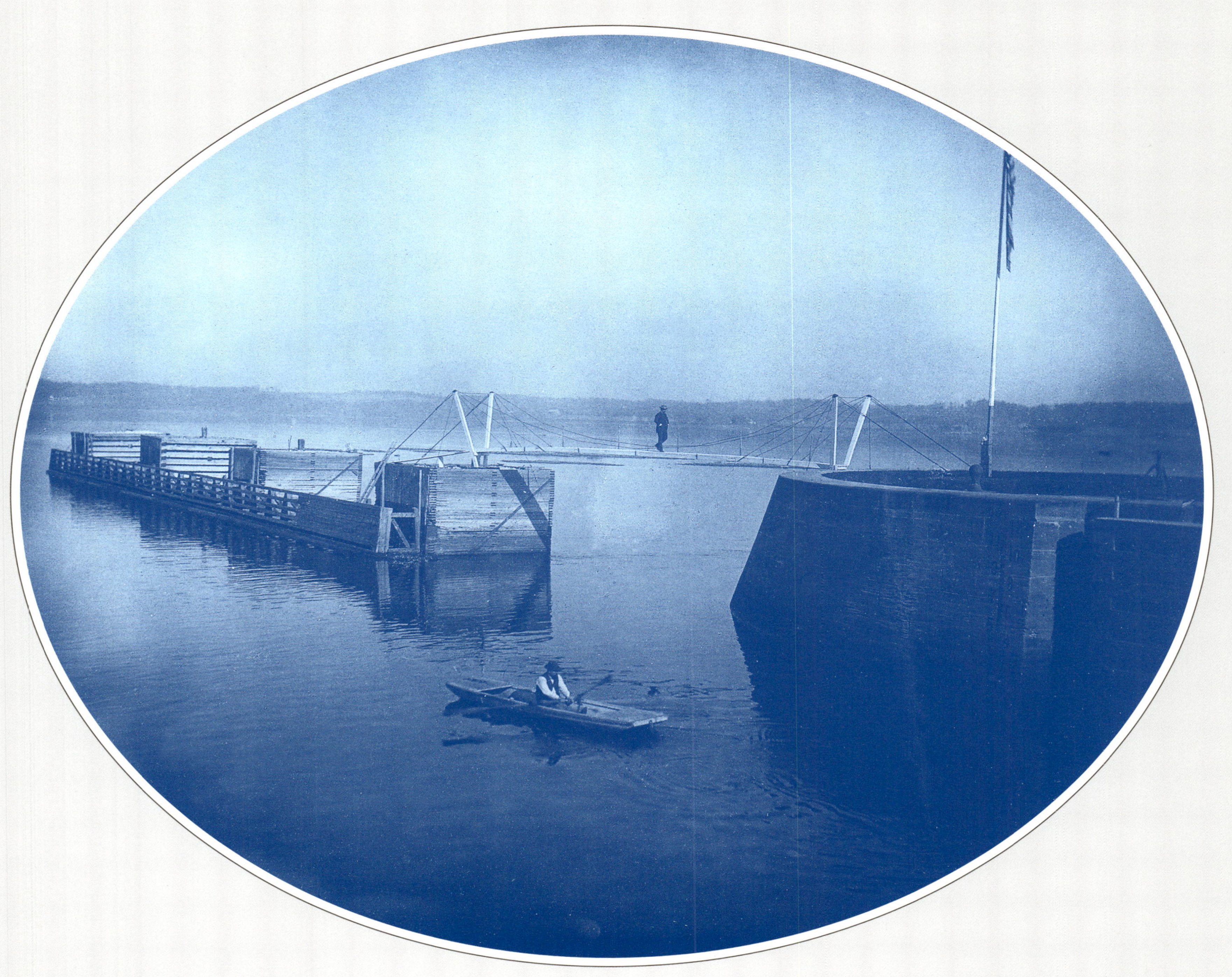

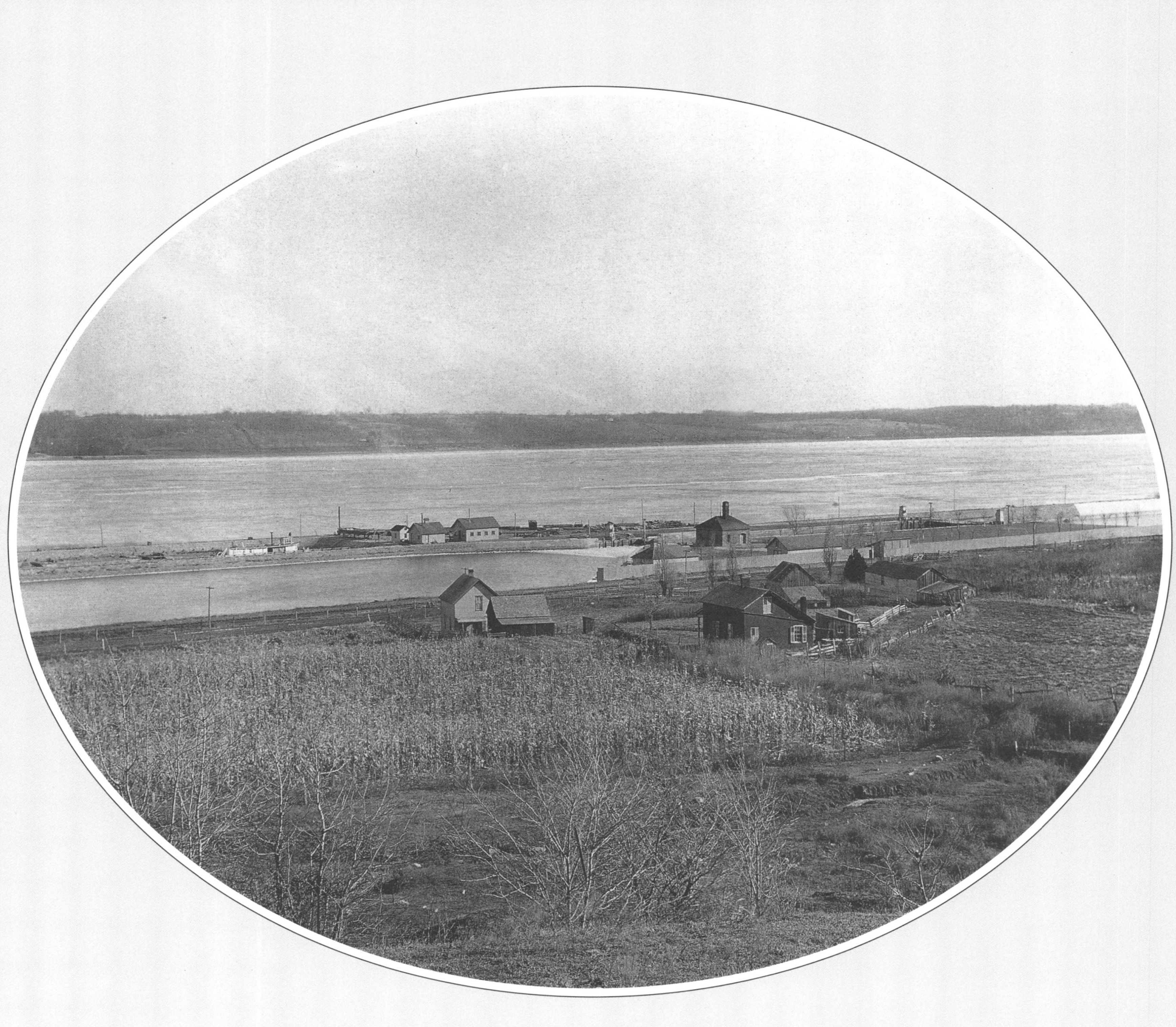

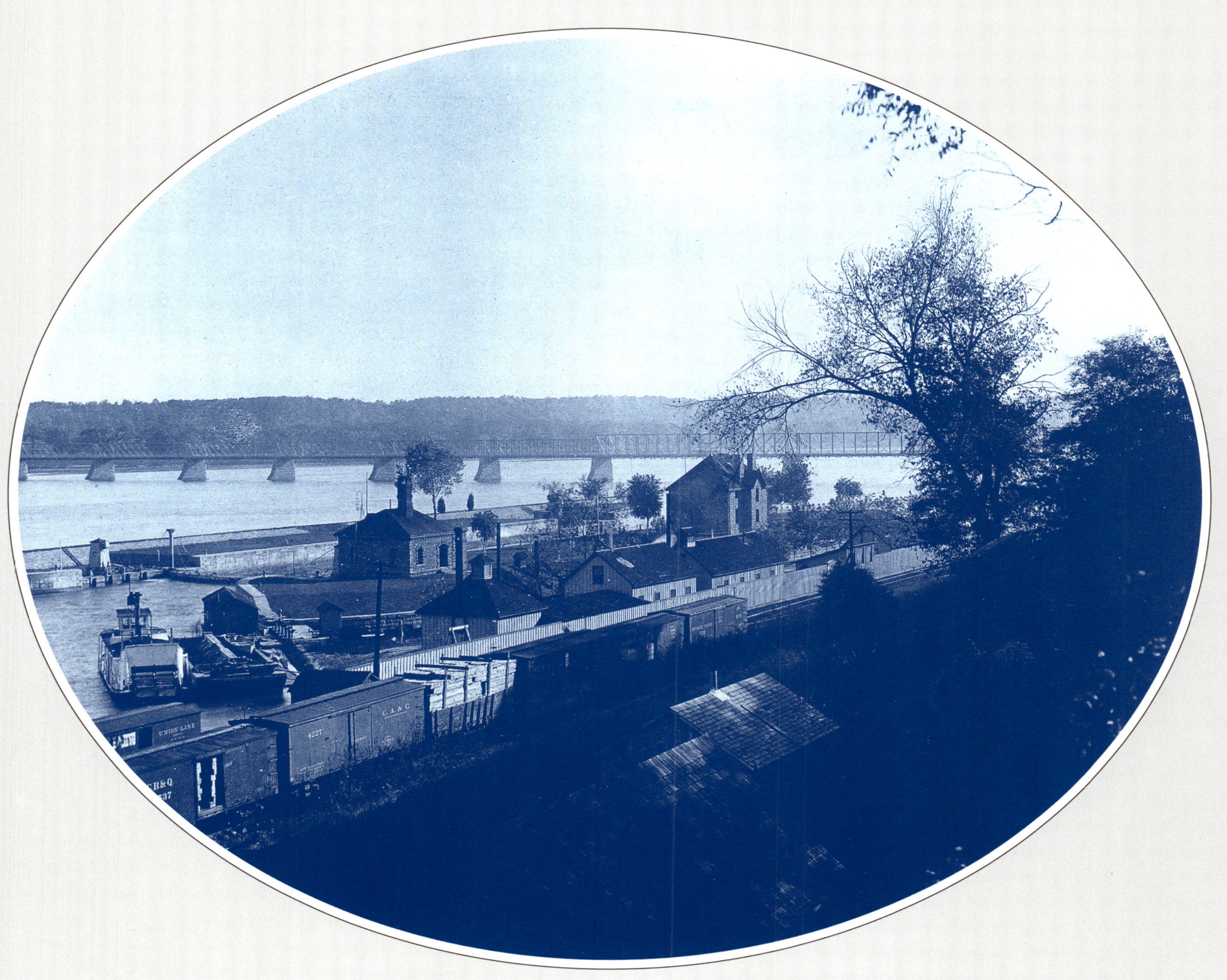
UNION LINE
4227
C. A. & C.
CB&Q

PLATE 76

U.S. Launch Lucia, no date

(MISSISSIPPI RIVER MUSEUM)

The *Lucia* was one of the longest-lasting steamboats on the Upper Mississippi River. In an era when a five-year-old steamer was a creaky veteran, the small stern-wheel towboat with a wood hull was in service for at least forty-five years, although here it sits in dry dock awaiting repairs. The *Lucia* tended dredges, picked up booms, moved buoys, rescued flood victims, towed barges, and worked the levees. • The *Lucia*, built in 1885 in Keokuk, Iowa, was christened after the daughter of the Rock Island district engineer, Alexander Mackenzie. One reason the stern-wheeler lasted so long was that the hull was rebuilt out of composite steel in 1907. The single-deck, one-stack towboat began life sixty-five feet long, but was rebuilt to seventy-eight feet with the new hull. The *Lucia*, operated by the Corps in the Des Moines canal, shows up in several Bosse photographs. With only a twenty-four-inch draft, it was a valuable boat in the Des Moines Rapids region. One of the *Lucia*'s engineers, Tom Noonan, died at his post during a tornado near the Keokuk bridge.

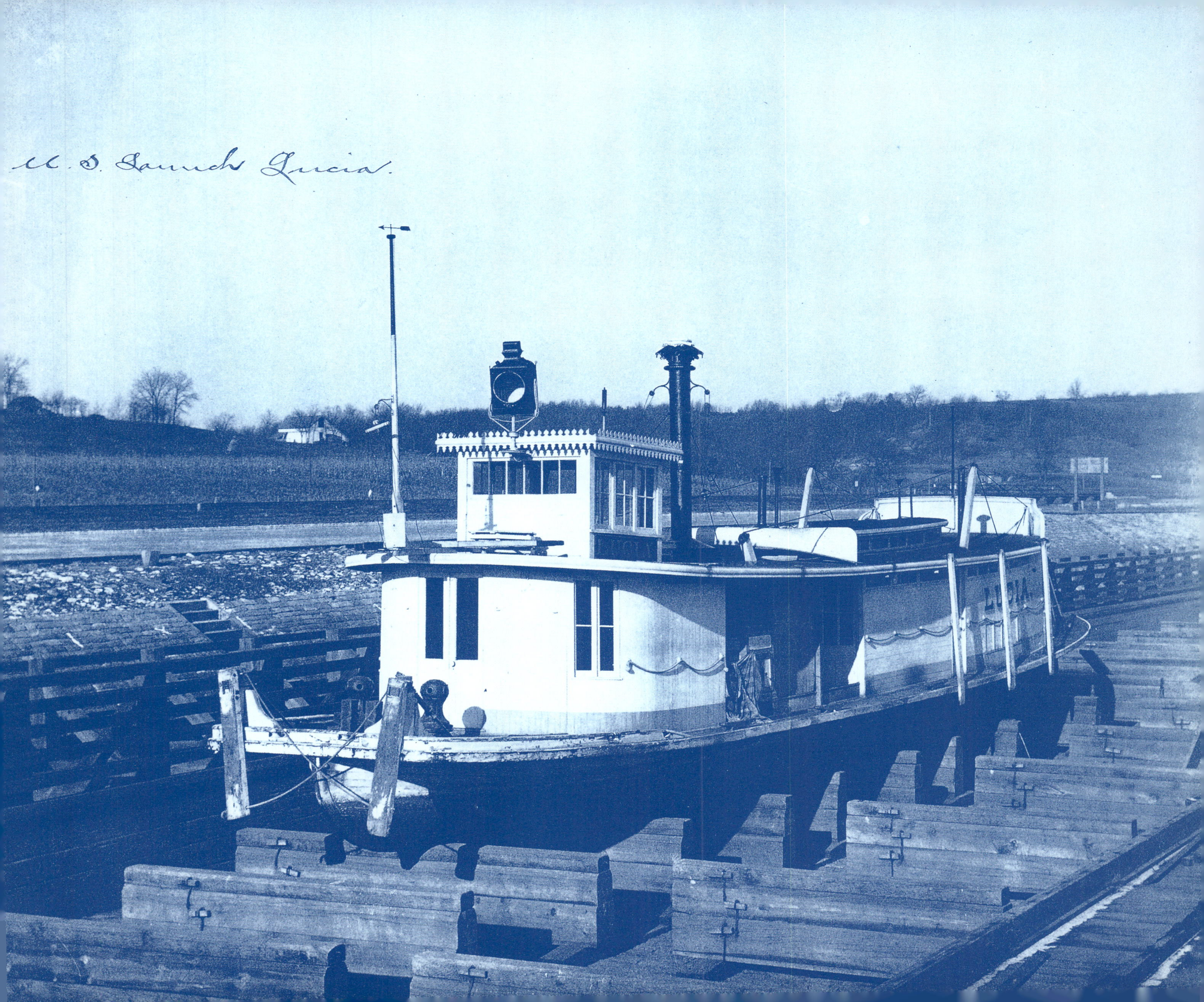
U. S. Launch Lucia.

PLATE 77

U.S. Steamlaunch "Louise," 1885

(MAYO FOUNDATION)

In addition to snag boats and dredges, the Corps ordered several smaller working boats for its river fleet. The *Louise* is an example of the smaller stern-wheelers used for a variety of tasks, including moving men and equipment. The Corps built the *Louise* at its Keokuk boatyard; the boat's small size meant that much of its work was done in the Des Moines Rapids Canal. The Corps also used these boats to push barges full of rocks or willow mats to crews working on dam construction projects. Their engines burned coal or wood. The *Louise* is docked here near Keokuk above the lower lock at the Des Moines Rapids Canal. It is one of many boats whose names begin with L; almost none start with the unlucky M—the thirteenth letter of the alphabet.

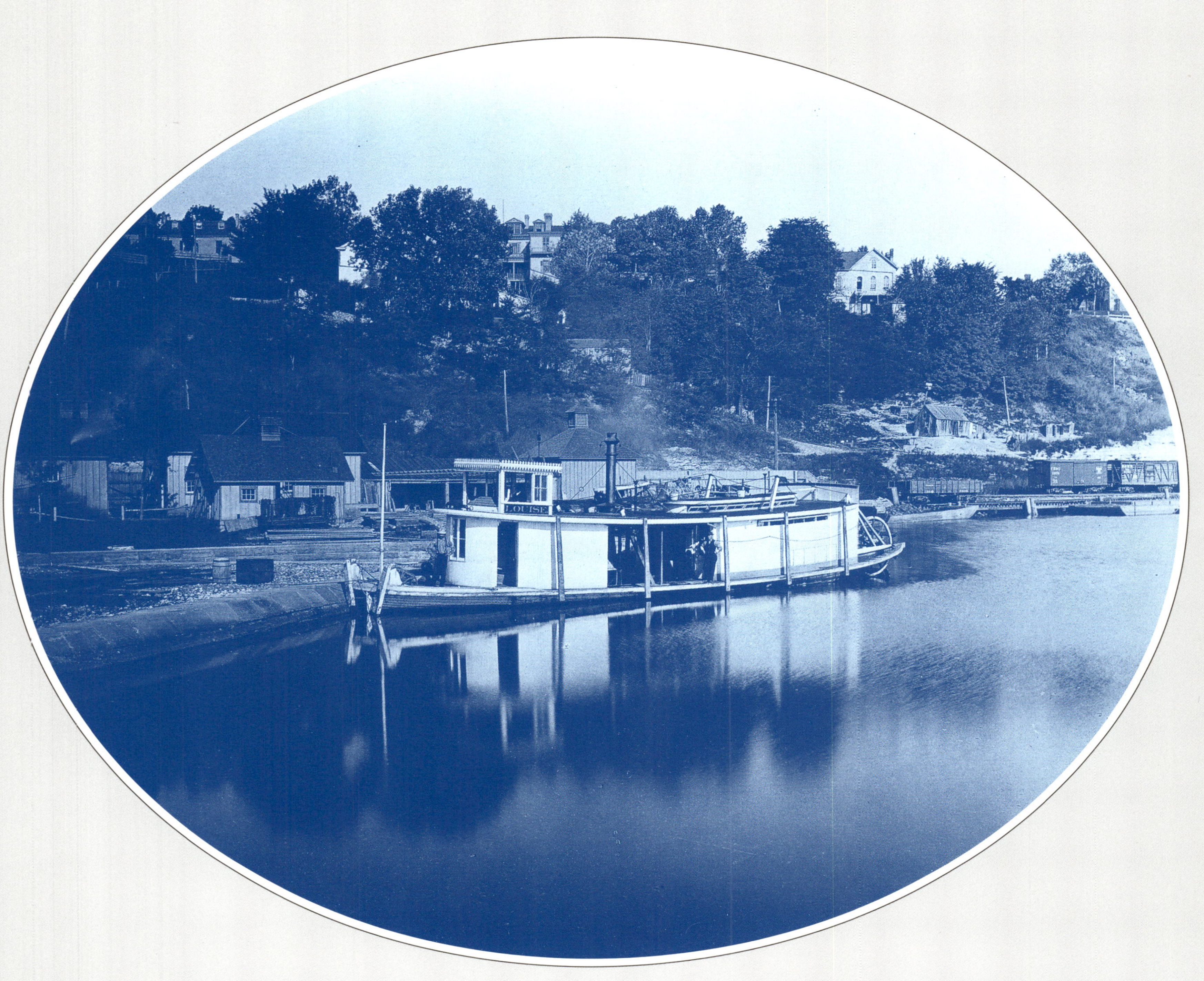
LOUISE

PLATE 78

C. B. & Q. R. R. Bridge at Quincy, Ill., 1885

(MAYO FOUNDATION)

In 1856, bridges were added to the river hazards of snags, rocks, rapids, chains, sandbars, eddies, leaning trees, wrecks, and current (or lack of current). An early example is this bridge at Quincy, Illinois. Quincy was the southern terminus for the Chicago, Burlington and Quincy Railroad. The town took its name from President John Quincy Adams. One of the Lincoln-Douglas debates in 1858 took place four blocks from the river. By the time of this photograph, fifteen railroads had bridged the Upper Mississippi. Looking back from sixty years later, William Faulkner wrote, "There were railroads in the wilderness now." This multispan swing bridge moved rail traffic across the river to Missouri.

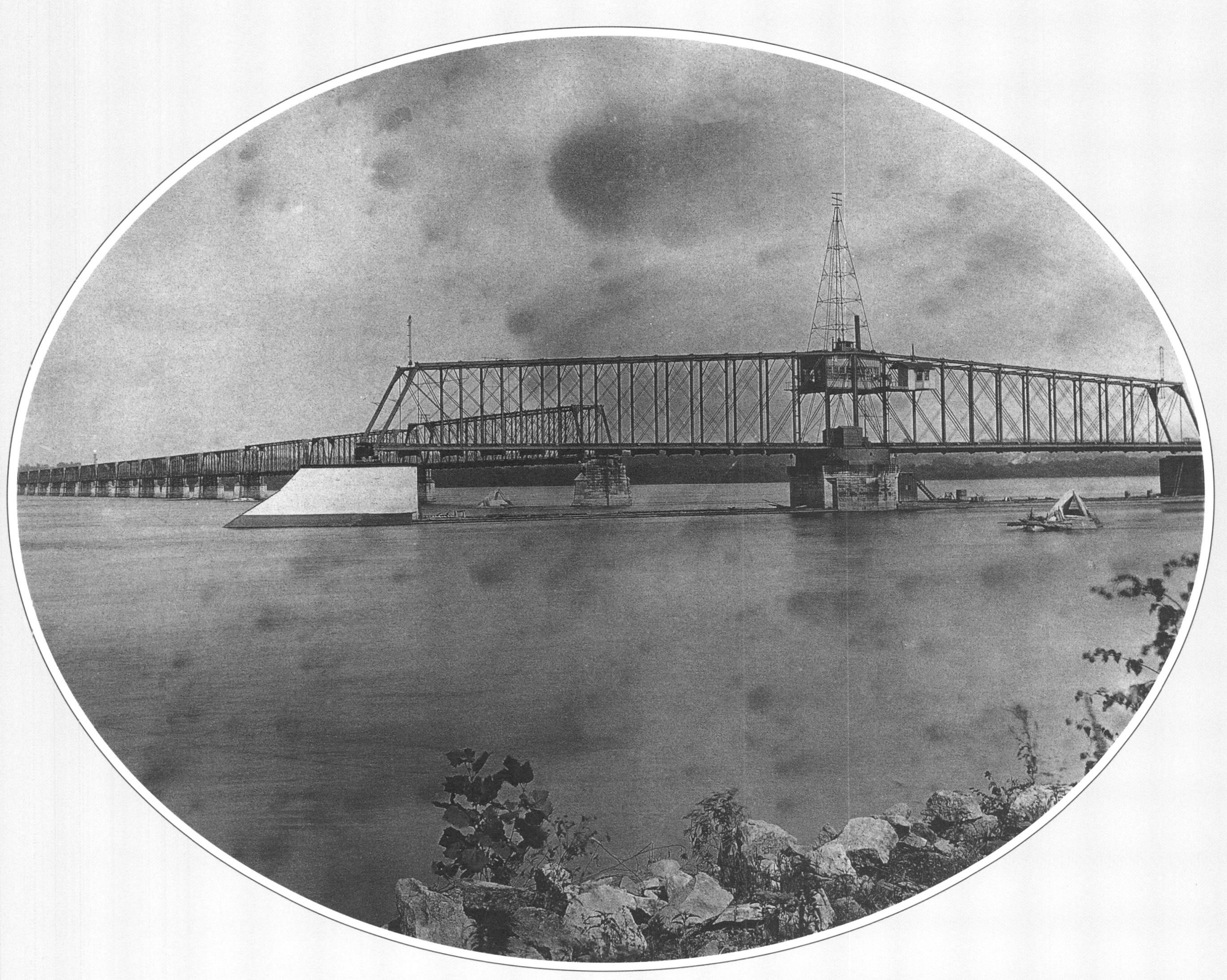

PLATE 79

Hannibal, Mo., no date

(U.S. ARMY CORPS OF ENGINEERS, ROCK ISLAND DISTRICT)

Hannibal is known throughout the world as the hometown of Samuel Clemens, who spent his river pilot days marking twain (a method of measuring the river's depth) on the lower Mississippi. Clemens moved to Hannibal as a preschooler in the 1830s as the city became known as a sawmill town. With the sawmills came pork packing, soap and candle making, coopering, rope making, and tanning. Boats laden with grain and hemp crowded the waterfront. • City entrepreneurs, including Clemens's father, were quick to invest in railroads and the building of railroad cars and locomotives when the technology reached eastern Missouri in the 1860s, and the area prospered from it. • A railway bridge was finished at Hannibal in 1871 for the Wabash Railroad. It began life as a center pivot bridge, but was converted to a lift bridge several decades later. The bridge doubled as a pedestrian, wagon, and, later, automobile bridge and was the town's only connection to the Illinois border until 1936, when an automobile bridge was dedicated by President Franklin Roosevelt.

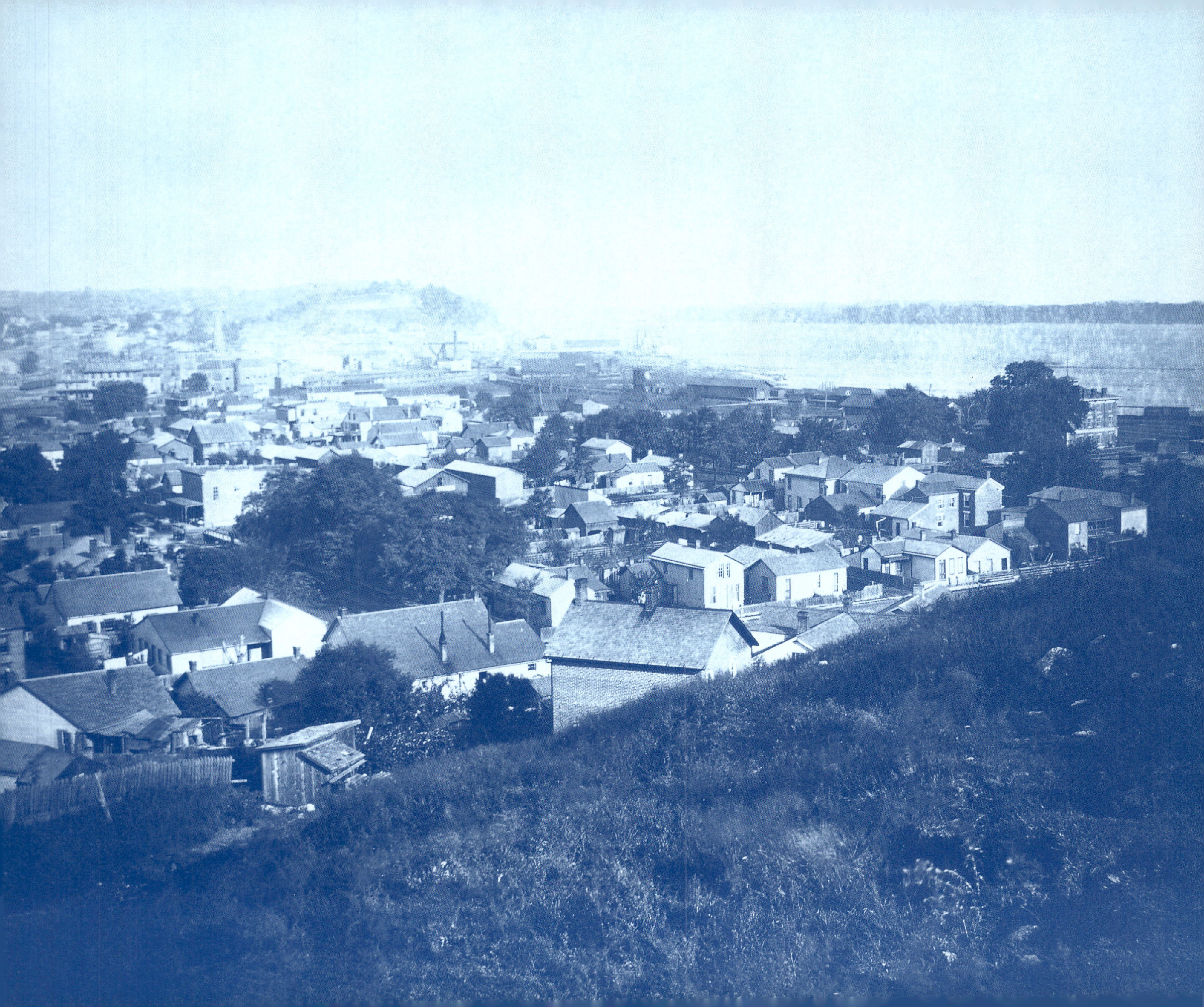

PLATE 80

Louisiana, Mo., 1885

(MAYO FOUNDATION)

The French explorers called the land near Louisiana, Missouri, *la terre des collines dorées*, or land of the golden hills. Whites first settled the area, about eighty miles from St. Louis, in 1808. The surrounding countryside became home to several tobacco and dairy farms, and the town shipped butter by the keg on the Mississippi. A typical shipper charged $1.75 per hundred pounds to send butter to the Minnesota frontier in the 1840s. Some of Louisiana's early settlers were Kentucky homesteaders who grew tobacco; by 1860 there were fourteen cigar factories in town. • Around the time of this photograph, taken from the hills south of town, Louisiana became known as an excursion town. Steamboats docked in places like Louisiana and took citizens for pleasure trips up and down the river, usually for twenty-five or fifty cents per passenger. The pleasure trips were a sign of the growing amount of leisure time people had at the end of the nineteenth century. Noix Creek can be seen in the foreground of this picture, taken facing north.

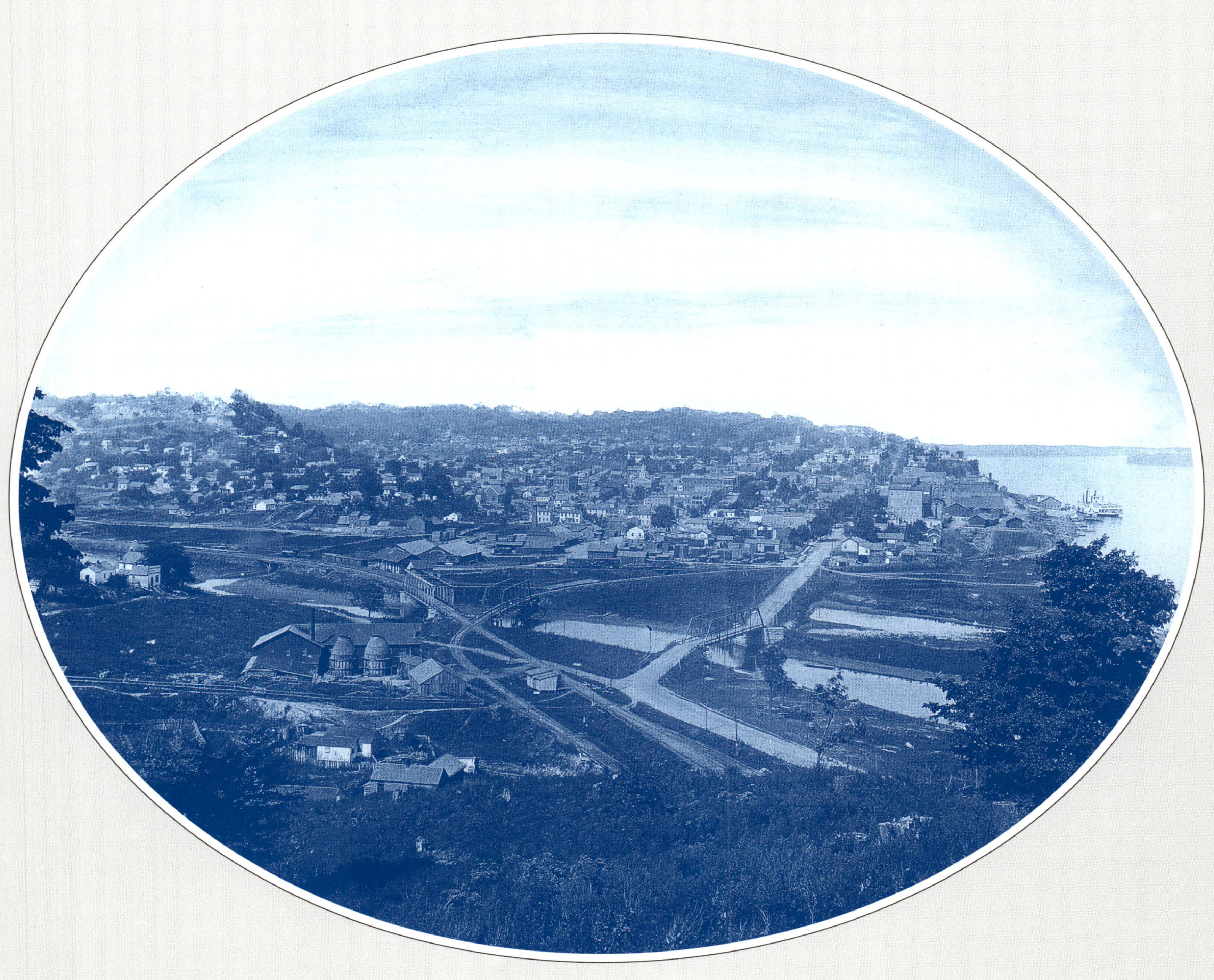

PLATE 81

Quarry at Grafton, Ill., no date

(MISSISSIPPI RIVER MUSEUM)

The Illinois River flows into the Mississippi at Grafton, Illinois, also the site of a large-scale limestone quarry that provided rock for rip-rap, wing dams, and closing dams to the Corps of Engineers. Owners of the quarry were the Grafton Stone and Transportation Company, with its main office in St. Louis. Quarrying in Grafton began in 1836, and the company employed hundreds of men throughout its lifetime. Stone from the quarry was used in the Eads Bridge piers in St. Louis and other Mississippi River structures. • The men who worked on (and sometimes in) the water got more money than those who worked in the quarries or cut and laid brush on the bank. In an 1877 report to the American Society of Civil Engineers, Edward P. North, who had been working in the granite-filled Thousand Islands region near St. Cloud, Minnesota, noted that his men earned nineteen and a half cents per hour for working on the land and twenty-six and a half cents per hour for working in water. • The lower boundaries of the Upper Mississippi River have been defined in a couple of ways by the government. In some of the earlier maps, Grafton was considered the "end" of the upper river; by the turn of the twentieth century, Cairo, Illinois, and the mouth of the Ohio River several miles downstream past St. Louis generally were considered the southernmost boundary of the upper river. Father Jacques Marquette and Louis Joliet, on their return trip from exploring the river in 1673, journeyed from the Mississippi up the Illinois River from the future site of Grafton. Robert Cavalier, the sieur de la Salle, and Father Louis Hennepin, who was a cartographer, had passed this way downstream four years earlier, establishing trading posts and exploring the Illinois country.

Quarry at Grafton, Ill.

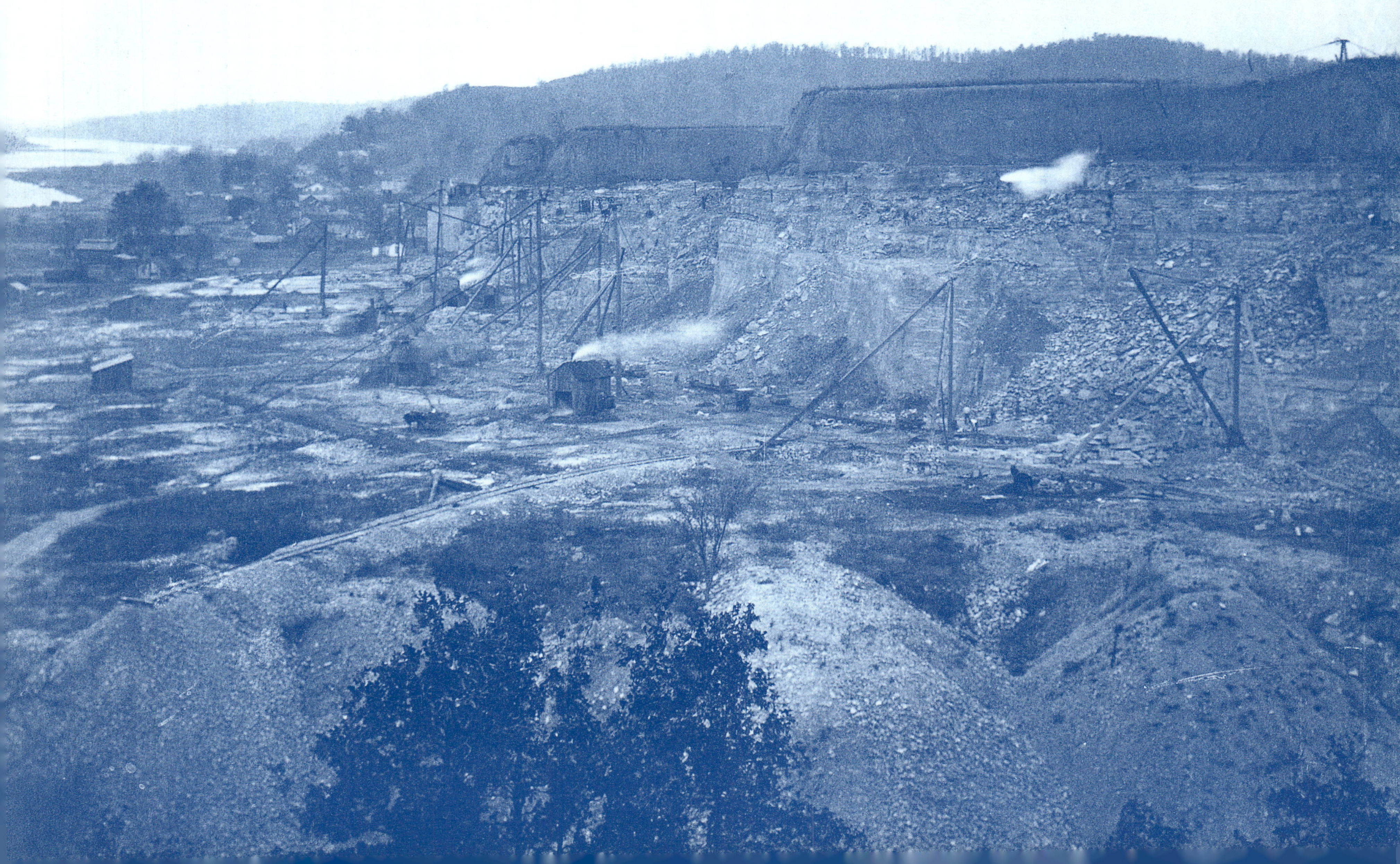

PLATE 82

Alton Bridge, no date

(MISSISSIPPI RIVER MUSEUM)

The historic city of Alton, Illinois, site of a Lincoln-Douglas debate and home of the martyred abolitionist newspaper editor Elijah Lovejoy, became the spot for an experiment with a camera. Bosse did not possess a panorama-style camera, as did so many of his contemporaries who worked for the government. Instead, he used his eleven-by-fourteen camera four times to create this panoramic view of Alton Bay and the bridge. The edges of the prints were carefully aligned and glued to give the viewer the impression of a single frame. • Panorama photographs were favored by galleries and collectors, but Bosse was not in the business of selling his pictures. In a few instances, the Corps sold Bosse prints to those who asked. In 1894, James Greenleaf of the School of Mines at Columbia College in New York wrote Alexander Mackenzie asking for prints of the river. Mackenzie offered the photographs to Greenleaf "not mounted, not to exceed 40 cents each—or even cheaper if you want a large number." • Alton, home to 10,000 people in 1890, was said to have the best harbor on the east bank of the river with a solid rock surface for steamers to land. A company of private investors built the railroad bridge over the river to try to lure some traffic from St. Louis. In 1892, near the time of this photograph, Franklin Olin founded the Equitable Powder Company in Alton to supply black powder for use in southern Illinois coal mines. Olin grew into one of the largest powder and ammunition companies in the nation. • Lock and Dam 26 was finished at Alton in 1938 and rebuilt in 1994 at the cost of more than one billion dollars. At the time of the rebuild, it was the nation's largest lock and dam.

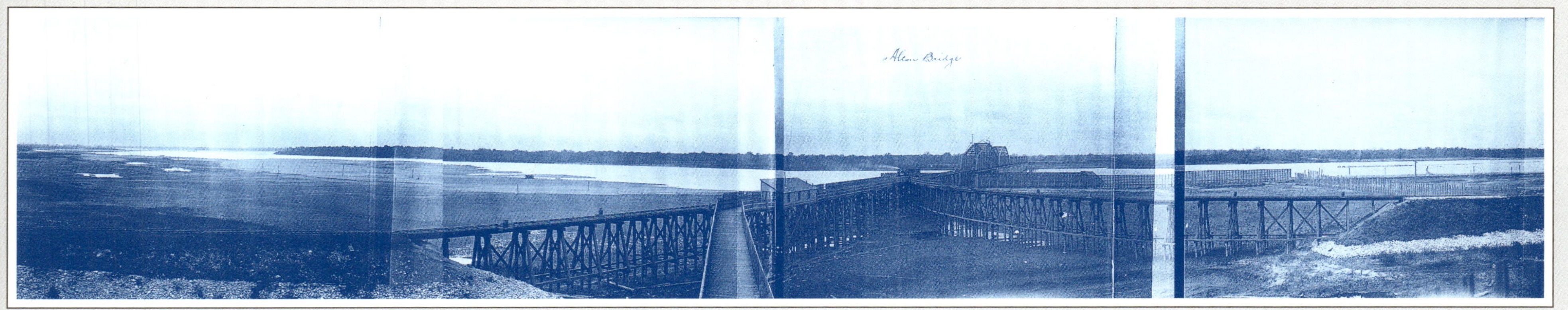
Alton Bridge

PLATE 83

Packet "St. Paul" (St. Paul, Minneapolis & St. Louis Packet Co.), 1885

(U.S. ARMY CORPS OF ENGINEERS, ROCK ISLAND DISTRICT)

The St. Paul, Minneapolis and St. Louis Packet Company (which was known by several names through various mergers and buyouts) featured the 300-foot-long wooden-hulled packet boat *St. Paul,* built in St. Louis in 1883. Steamboats were called packets or packet boats if they made regularly scheduled runs with passengers and freight. The *St. Paul,* which later ran under the Diamond Jo banner, cruised the river from St. Paul to Vicksburg, Mississippi, before finding a home in St. Louis as the *Excursion Queen St. Paul* in 1917 after a large dance floor was added. It moved on the Ohio River to Pittsburgh in 1937 and was rebuilt and renamed the *Senator* in 1939–40. The Coast Guard used it as a training boat during World War II; it was dismantled in 1953. • There were at least three boats called the *St. Paul* plying the river after the Civil War, although six-letter boat names were considered bad luck by rivermen. • The last working steam towboat on the Mississippi, the *Lone Star,* cooled down at Davenport in August 1967.

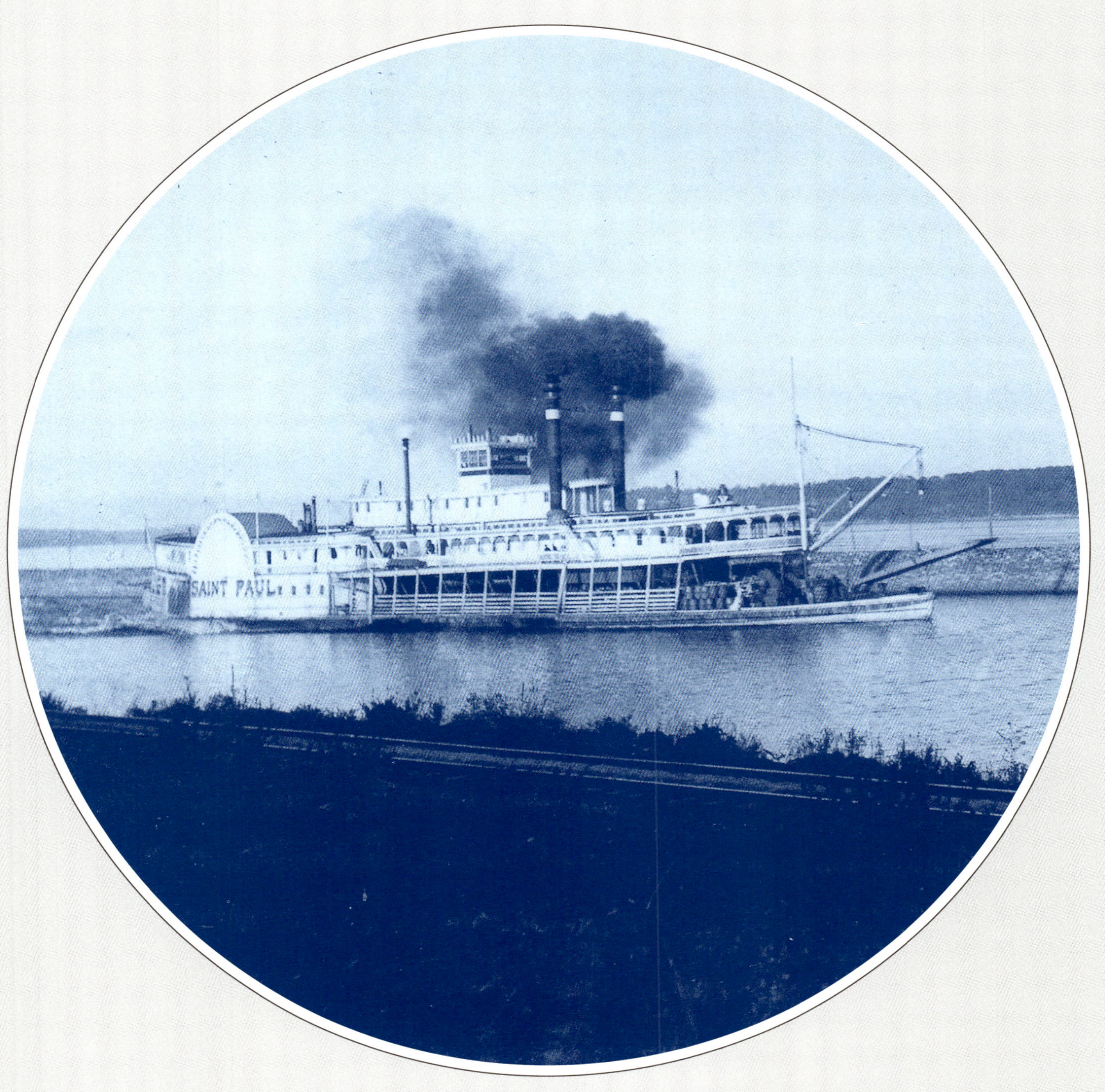
SAINT PAUL

PLATE 84

Bridge at St. Louis, Mo., no date

(U.S. ARMY CORPS OF ENGINEERS, ROCK ISLAND DISTRICT)

James Buchanan Eads, a visionary engineer, was more famous for steamboats than bridges in 1866 when St. Louis merchants asked him to chair a committee on building a railroad bridge in their city. During the Civil War, St. Louis lost millions of dollars in trade to arch rival Chicago, and a Mississippi River railroad bridge was seen as a partial remedy. • Eads designed the bridge himself, despite having no experience creating such structures. He made it out of three spans of steel, a revolutionary idea during a period when Britain banned the use of steel in bridges altogether, in part because it was too brittle and untested. • Two thousand men worked on twenty-four barges and boats for seven years, and thirteen died of what later became known as the bends (then named "caisson disease") from toiling on the piers 125 feet underwater. The bridge opened on July 4, 1874, with a crowd of three hundred thousand on hand.

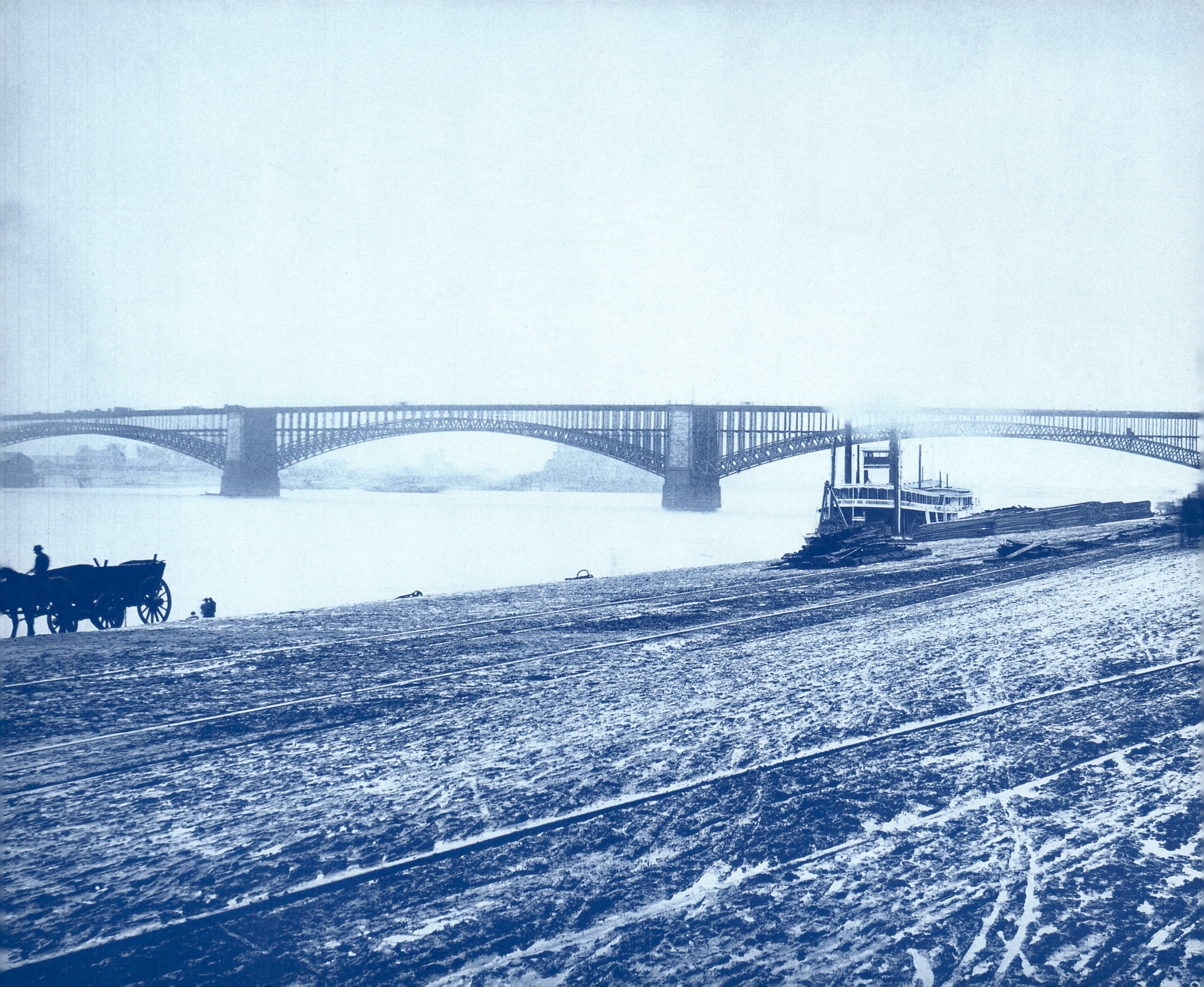

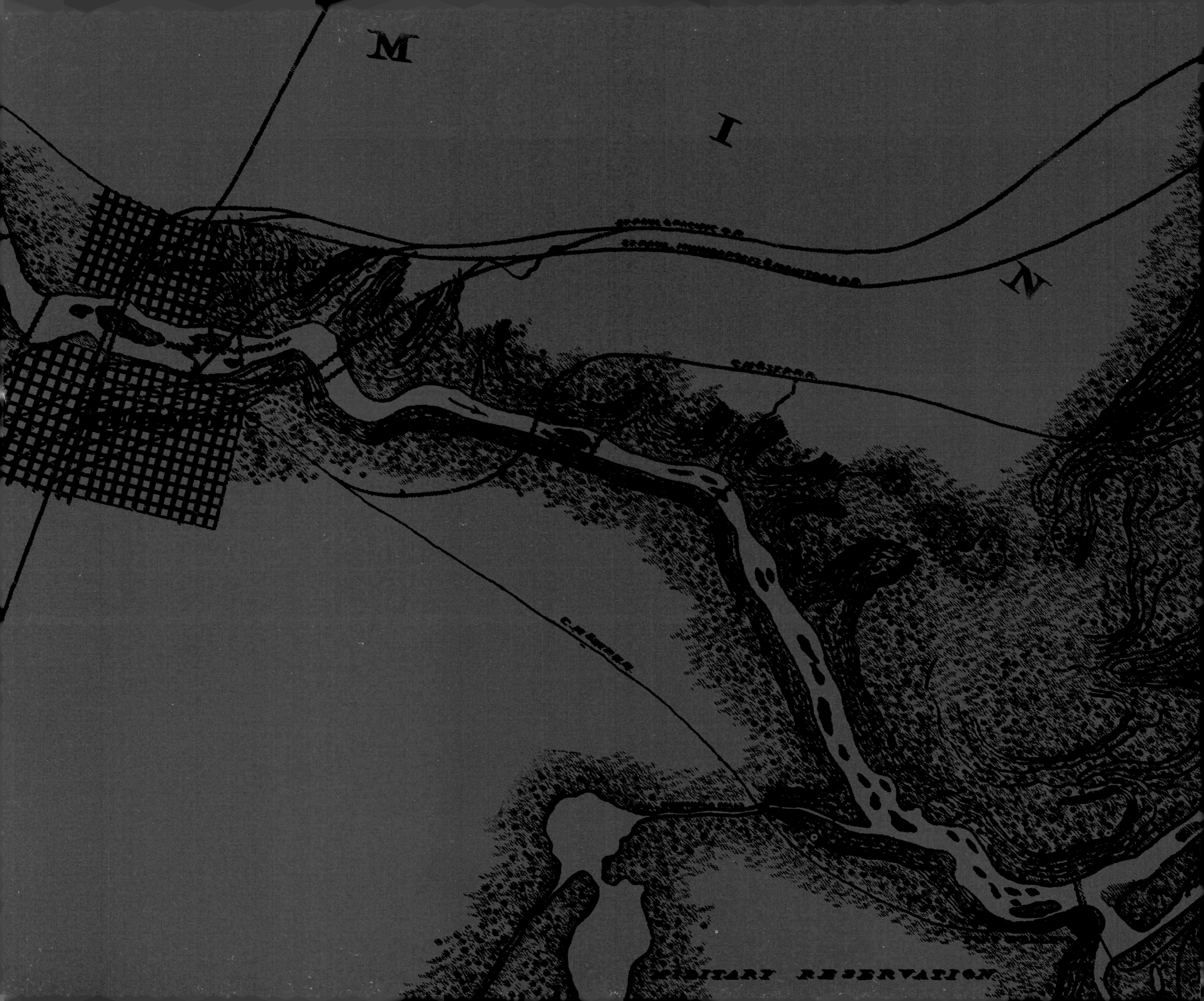
M
I
N
MILITARY RESERVATION

MAP OF THE MISSISSIPPI RIVER

FROM THE FALLS OF ST. ANTHONY TO THE JUNCTION OF THE ILLINOIS RIVER IN TWENTY SEVEN SHEETS

H. Bosse and A. J. Stibolt, 1887–1888

Henry Bosse and his assistant, A. J. Stibolt, drew these maps of the Upper Mississippi River from data gathered on an extensive survey of the river in 1878–79, although the map was not published until almost ten years later in Washington, D.C. It was the Corps's third attempt at a comprehensive map of the upper river, following and building on maps made from 1866 to 1870 and again in 1878. The Bosse map came on the heels of the authorization of the four-and-a-half-foot channel project by Congress; Bosse moved from St. Paul to Rock Island to oversee the project. Bosse's map, created under the direction of Rock Island district commander Major Alexander Mackenzie, may have been produced with the help of his photographs, although his oldest known dated picture is from 1883.

White settlers' mapping of the Mississippi River dates back to the French and Spanish in the 1600s. The Frenchman Joseph Nicollet produced what is arguably the most famous nineteenth-century map of the river and its "infinity of courses" in 1842 and 1843, using notes from his expeditions from St. Louis from 1836 to 1840. Nicollet's map wasn't detailed enough to be of use to a steamboat crew, and river pilots always claimed to rely less on maps than on experience and gumption anyway. Even the best maps couldn't accurately chart the Mississippi, with its ever-changing snags, sandbars, reefs, and sunken wrecks. "Two hundred men, on a hundred boats, groped their way in darkness," wrote Captain George Merrick of a typical night on the upper river in *Old Times on the Upper Mississippi*, "amid known and unknown terrors, up and down the windings of the great river, without having for their guidance a single token of man's helpful invention."

The first comprehensive Corps maps of the upper river came under the direction of Major General G. K. Warren, who ordered a Mississippi River Basin map that included the Red River, the Minnesota, and tributaries as far south as Arkansas. Warren and his men spent four years in reconnaissance work before producing the map, which also used the work of railroad companies and other government units. At two inches to the mile, Warren's map, he boasted, was "brought together with a nearer approach to accuracy than has before been reached; in many cases as near as ever will be practicable." On the shifting Mississippi, that practicality lasted only eight years, when Rock Island Corps commander Lieutenant Colonel F. U. Farquhar ordered it updated with a new map drawn by Bosse's predecessor, F. S. Eastman. At a scale of one inch per mile, Eastman's map became the basis for Bosse's work. The map was updated again in 1901, 1903–05, and 1915 before the lock and dam system made it obsolete in the 1930s.

The maps that follow are reprints of the 1887–88 map drawn by Bosse and Stibolt. Listed in the margins of each map are the photographs from the plate section of this book that were taken in the area represented on the map. Familiar towns and physical features are also listed in upstream to downstream order as a reference for the reader. Sheets 5, 6, and 7 have handwritten notations from Bosse or his assistant marking the date and sometimes time of day and weather when the photographs were taken from that spot. Included in the notes on Sheet 5 is the Minneiska, Minnesota, photograph location (Plate 29).

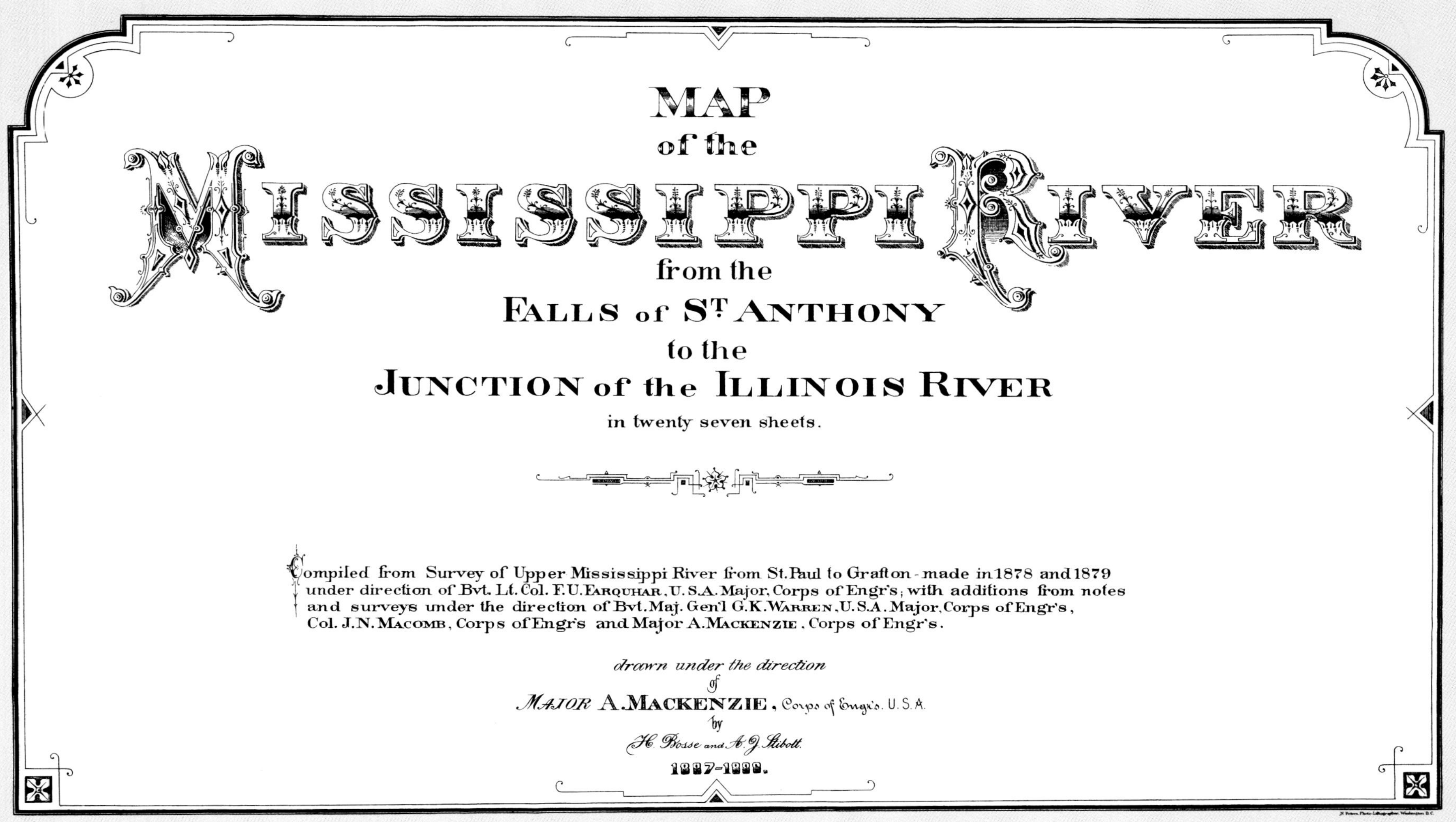

MAP
of the
MISSISSIPPI RIVER
from the
FALLS of S^T ANTHONY
to the
JUNCTION of the ILLINOIS RIVER
in twenty seven sheets.

Compiled from Survey of Upper Mississippi River from St. Paul to Grafton - made in 1878 and 1879 under direction of Bvt. Lt. Col. F. U. Farquhar, U. S. A. Major, Corps of Engr's; with additions from notes and surveys under the direction of Bvt. Maj. Gen'l G. K. Warren, U. S. A. Major, Corps of Engr's, Col. J. N. Macomb, Corps of Engr's and Major A. Mackenzie, Corps of Engr's.

drawn under the direction
of
Major A. MACKENZIE, Corps of Engr's. U. S. A.
by
H. Bosse and A. J. Stibolt.
1887–1888.

TITLE PAGE

INDEX SHEET AND TABLE OF DISTANCES IN MILES BY STEAMBOAT CHANNEL

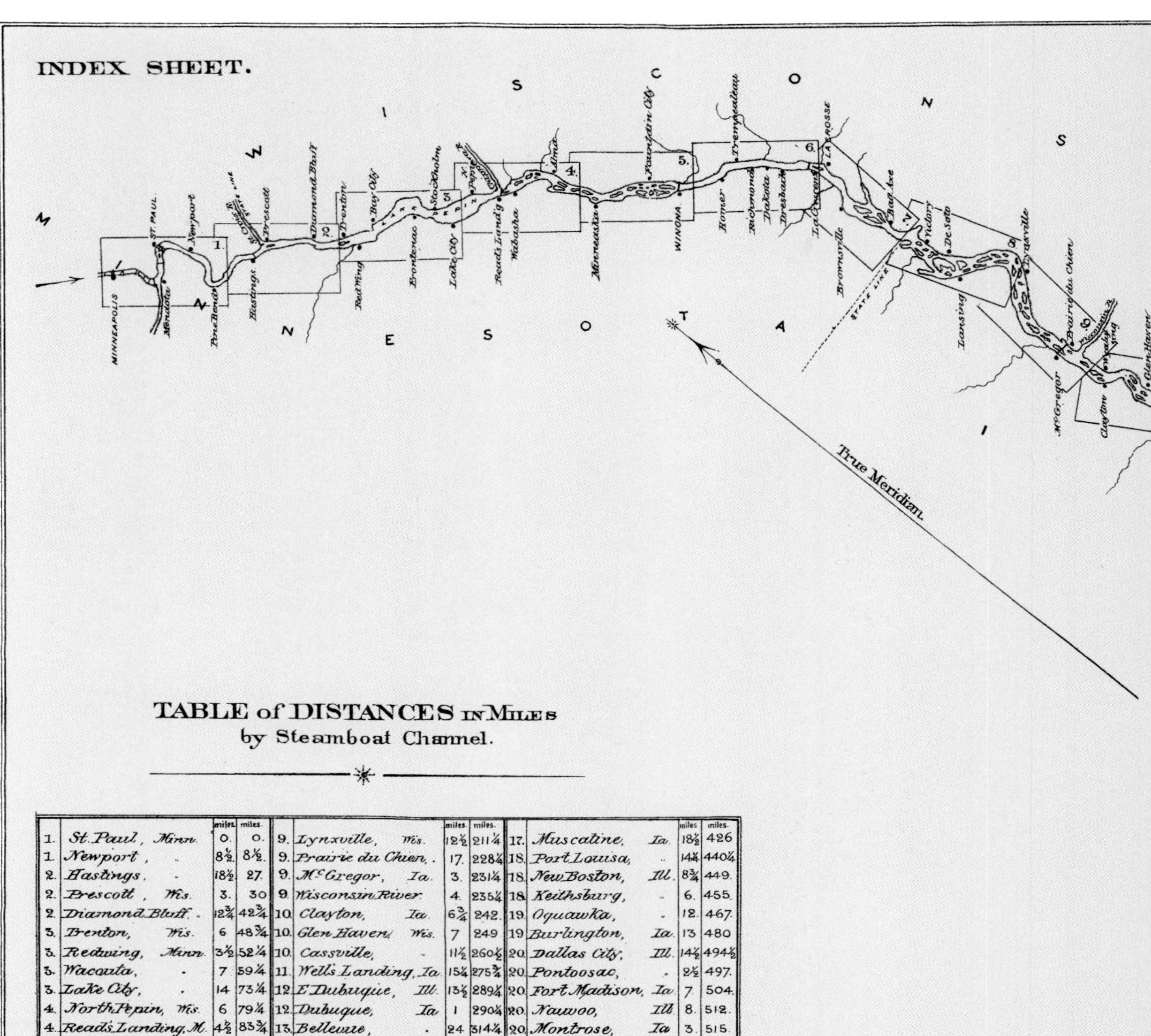

TABLE of DISTANCES IN MILES
by Steamboat Channel.

		miles.	miles.
1.	St. Paul, Minn.	0.	0.
1.	Newport, ..	8½.	8½.
2.	Hastings, -	18½.	27.
2.	Prescott, Wis.	3.	30
2.	Diamond Bluff. -	12¾	42¾
3.	Trenton, Wis.	6	48¾
3.	Redwing, Minn	3½	52¼
3.	Wacouta, -	7	59¼
3.	Lake City, .	14	73¼
4.	North Pepin, Wis.	6	79¼
4.	Read's Landing, M.	4½	83¾
4.	Wabasha, Minn	2¾	86½
4.	Alma, Wis.	9	95½
5.	Minneiska, Minn	10	105½
5.	Mt. Vernon, .	2¾	108¼
5.	Fountain City, Wis.	9	117¼
5.	Winona, Minn	7½	124¾
6.	Trempeleau, Wis.	12¾	137½
6.	Dresbach, Minn	10½	148.
7.	La Crosse, Wis.	8	156.
7.	Brownsville, Minn	10	166
7.	Warner's Ldg, Wis.	7¾	173¾
7.	Bad Axe, -	5	178¾
8.	Victory, -	8¼	187
8.	De Soto, -	6¾	193¾
8.	Lansing, Ia.	5	198¾

		miles.	miles.
9.	Lynxville, Wis.	12½	211¼
9.	Prairie du Chien, .	17.	228¼
9.	Mc Gregor, Ia.	3.	231¼
9.	Wisconsin River	4.	235¼
10.	Clayton, Ia.	6¾	242.
10.	Glen Haven, Wis.	7	249
10.	Cassville, ..	11½	260½
11.	Well's Landing, Ia.	15¼	275¾
12.	E. Dubuque, Ill.	13½	289¼
12.	Dubuque, Ia	1	290¼
13.	Bellevue, .	24	314¼
13.	Savanna, Ill.	20½	334¾
13.	Sabula, Ia	2½	337¼
14.	Lyons, .	16¾	354
14.	Fulton, Ill	1.	355
14.	Clinton, Ia	2½	357½
14.	Albany, Ill.	5¼	362¾
15.	Camanche, Ia	2.	364¾
15.	Cordova, Ill	9.	373¾
15.	Princeton, Ia.	1.	374¾
15.	Port Byron, Ill.	5½	380¼
15.	Le Claire, Ia.	½	380¾
15.	Hampton, Ill	6	386¾
16.	Davenport, Ia.	10	396¾
16.	Rock Island, Ill.	¾	397½
16.	Buffalo, Ia.	10	407½

		miles.	miles.
17.	Muscatine, Ia.	18½	426
18.	Port Louisa, ..	14¼	440¼
18.	New Boston, Ill.	8¾	449.
18.	Keithsburg, ..	6.	455.
19.	Oquawka, ..	12.	467.
19.	Burlington, Ia.	13	480
20.	Dallas City, Ill.	14½	494½
20.	Pontoosac, .	2½	497.
20.	Fort Madison, Ia.	7.	504.
20.	Nauvoo, Ill.	8.	512.
20.	Montrose, Ia	3.	515.
21.	Keokuk, ..	11½	526½
21.	Warsaw, Ill.	4½	531.
21.	Alexandria, Mo	½	531½
22.	Canton, .	19.	550½
23.	La Grange, .	7.	557½
23.	Quincy, Ill.	10	567½
24.	Hannibal, Mo.	20	587½
25.	Louisiana, .	28¾	616¼
25.	Clarksville, ..	10	626¼
26.	Hamburg, Ill.	14½	640¾
27.	Cap au Gris, Mo.	22.	662¾
27.	Grafton, Ill.	27.	689¾
	Alton, ..	16.	705¾
	St. Louis, Mo.	23	728¾

Numbers before the names are those of the sheets.

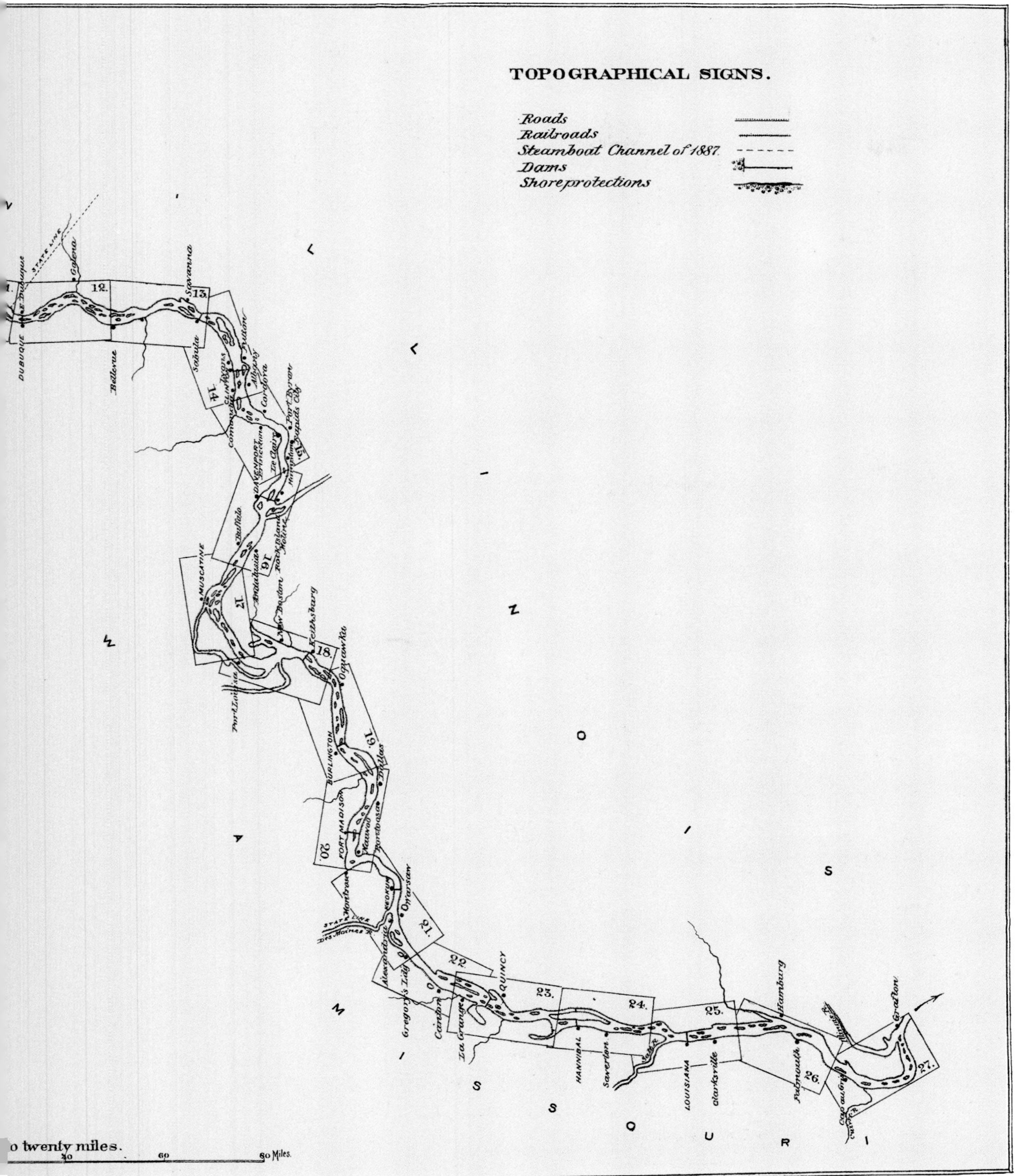

TOPOGRAPHICAL SIGNS.
Roads
Railroads
Steamboat Channel of 1887.
Dams
Shoreprotections
o twenty miles.
N. PETERS, Photo-Lithographer, Washington, D.C.

MAP 1
MINNEAPOLIS
FALLS OF ST. ANTHONY
MINNEHAHA FALLS
FORT SNELLING
MINNESOTA RIVER
ST. PAUL
DAYTON'S BLUFF
PIG'S EYE LAKE
PINE BEND

Below the Falls of St. Anthony, Minneapolis, Minn. (PLATE 1)

Old Steamboat Landing at Minneapolis, Minn. (PLATE 2)

From Quarry at Riverside Park, (Minneapolis) looking up stream (PLATE 3)

From opp. Riverside Park, (Minneapolis) looking up stream (PLATE 4)

Franklin Ave. Bridge, Minneapolis from left shore above (PLATE 5)

C. M. & St. P. R.R. Bridge (Short line) at Minneapolis, Minn. (PLATE 6)

Marshall Ave. Bridge—Minneapolis & St. Paul (PLATE 7)

Soldiers Home and mouth of Minne-ha-ha Creek (PLATE 8)

Fort Snelling, Minn. (PLATE 9)

Boom of St. Paul Boom Co. (PLATE 10)

Smith Ave. Bridge—St. Paul, Minn. (PLATE 11)

St. Paul, Minn. (PLATE 12)

River at St. Paul, Minn. (from Dayton's Bluff) (PLATE 14)

Pigs Eye Island (from shore protection below) (PLATE 15)

Pine Bend (PLATE 16)

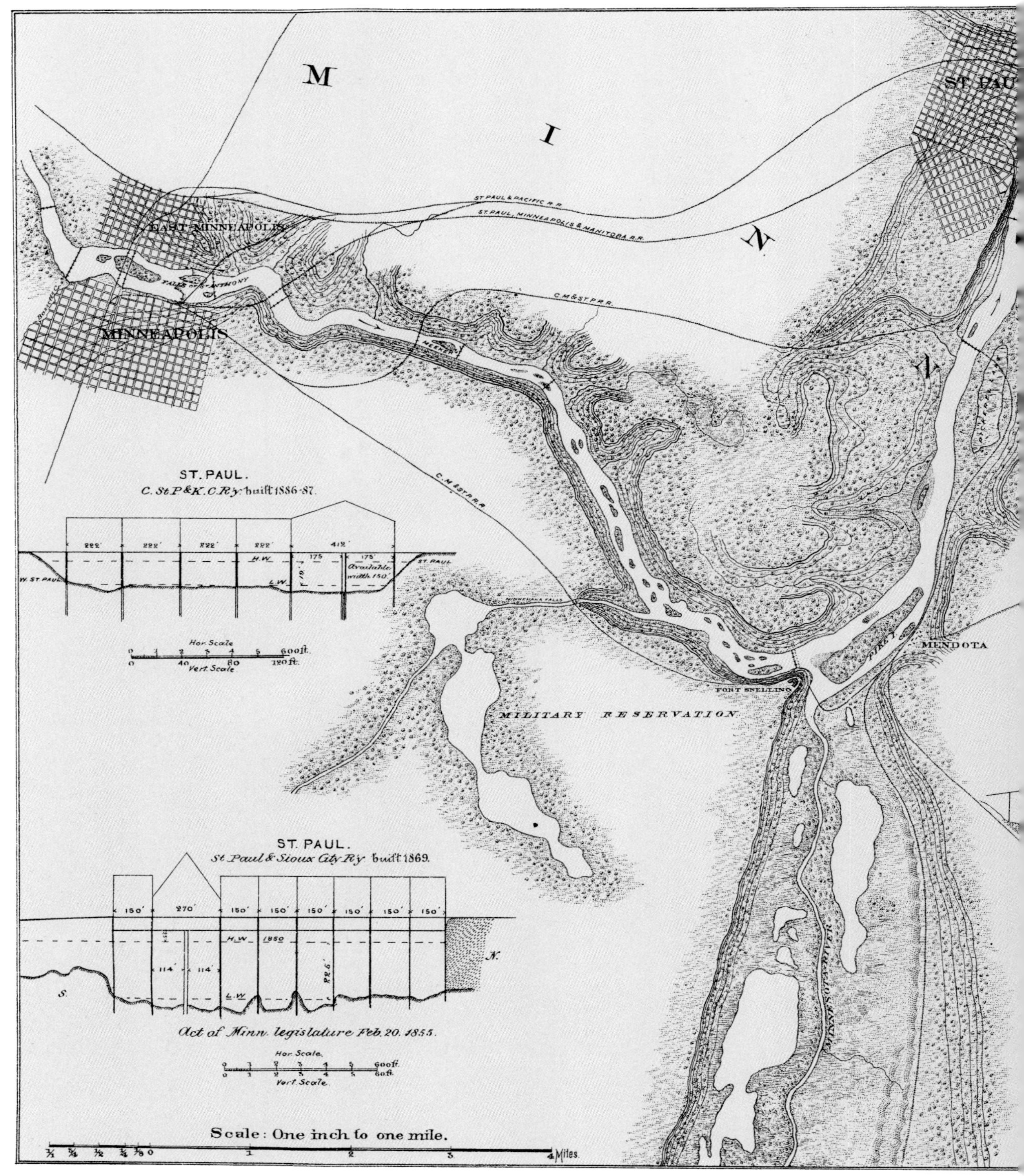

SHEET No. 1.

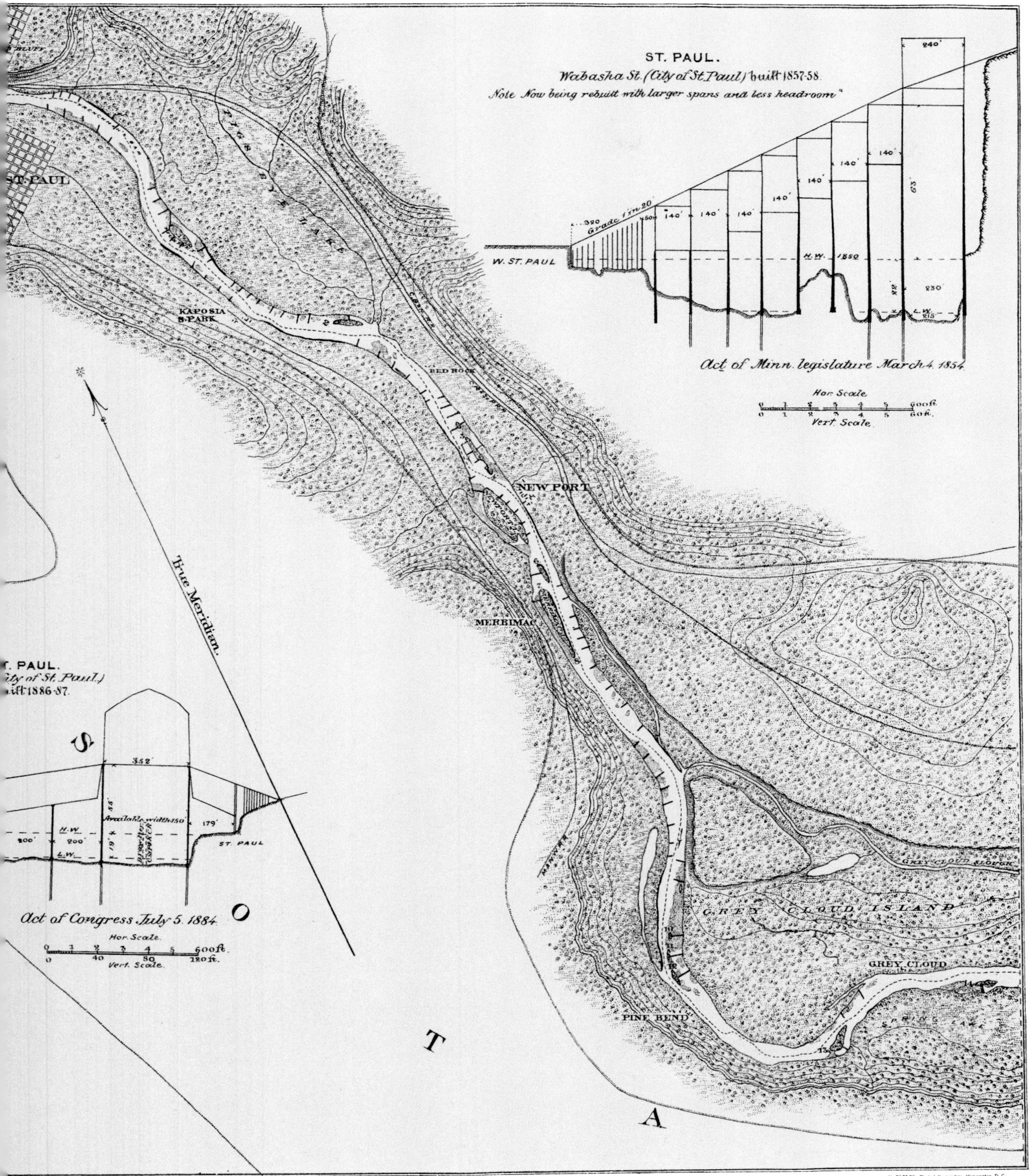

ST. PAUL.
Wabasha St. (City of St. Paul) built 1857-58.
Note Now being rebuilt with larger spans and less headroom"
W. ST. PAUL
Grade 1 in 20
H.W. 1850
L.W.
Act of Minn. legislature March 4. 1854
Hor. Scale
Vert. Scale
ST. PAUL
KAPOSIA
B. PARK
RED ROCK
NEW PORT
MERRIMAC
True Meridian.
T. PAUL.
ity of St. Paul.)
uilt 1886-87.
Available width 150'
H.W.
L.W.
ST. PAUL
Act of Congress July 5. 1884
Hor. Scale
Vert. Scale
GREY CLOUD ISLAND
GREY CLOUD
PINE BEND
S
O
T
A

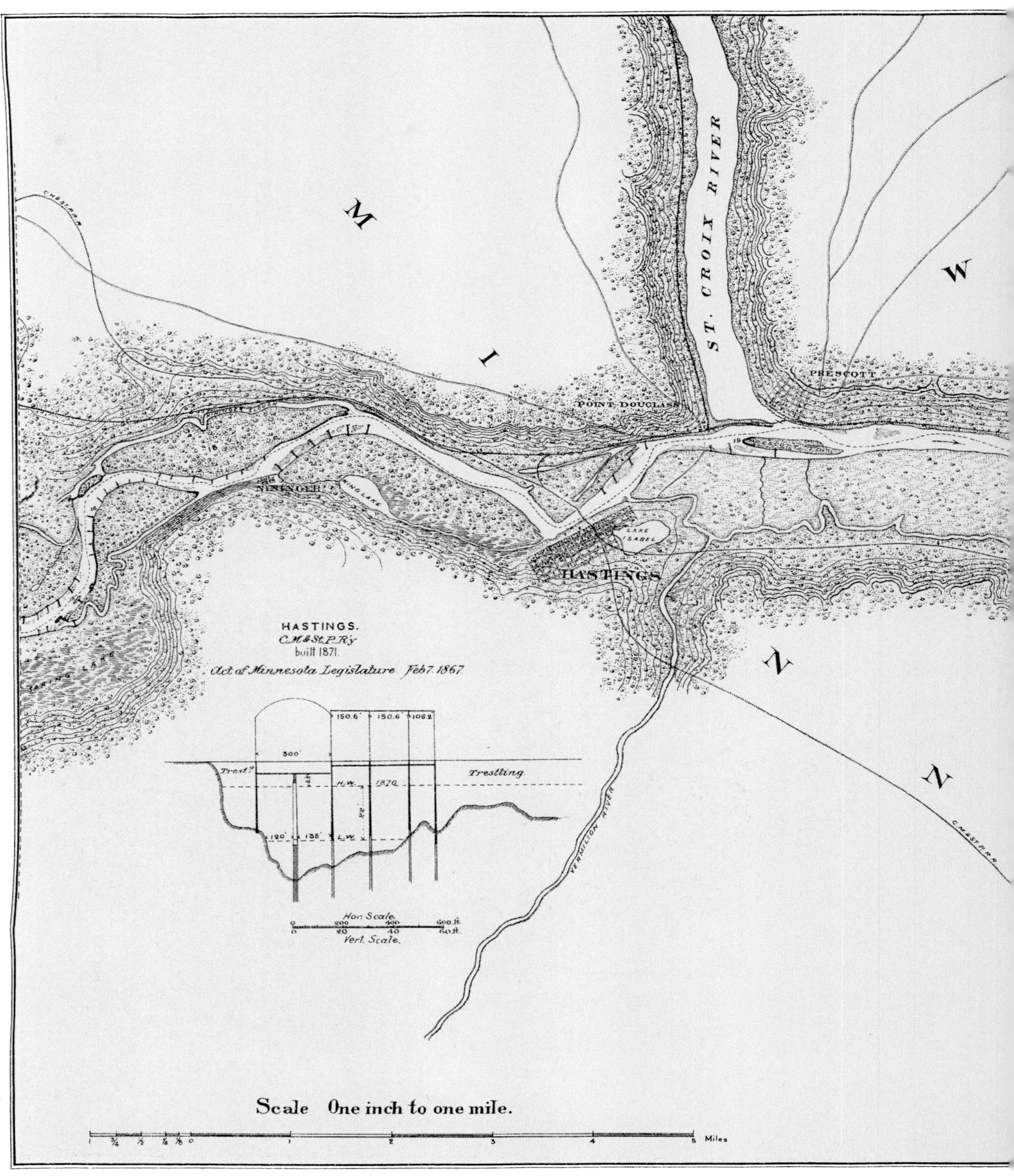

MAP 2
NININGER, MINNESOTA
HASTINGS, MINNESOTA
POINT DOUGLAS
ST. CROIX RIVER
PRESCOTT, WISCONSIN
DIAMOND BLUFF, WISCONSIN

Wingdams below Nininger, Minn. (PLATE 17)

Wingdams and Bar below Hastings, Minn. (PLATE 18)

Mouth of St. Croix Riv (PLATE 19)

Prescott, Wis. (PLATE 20)

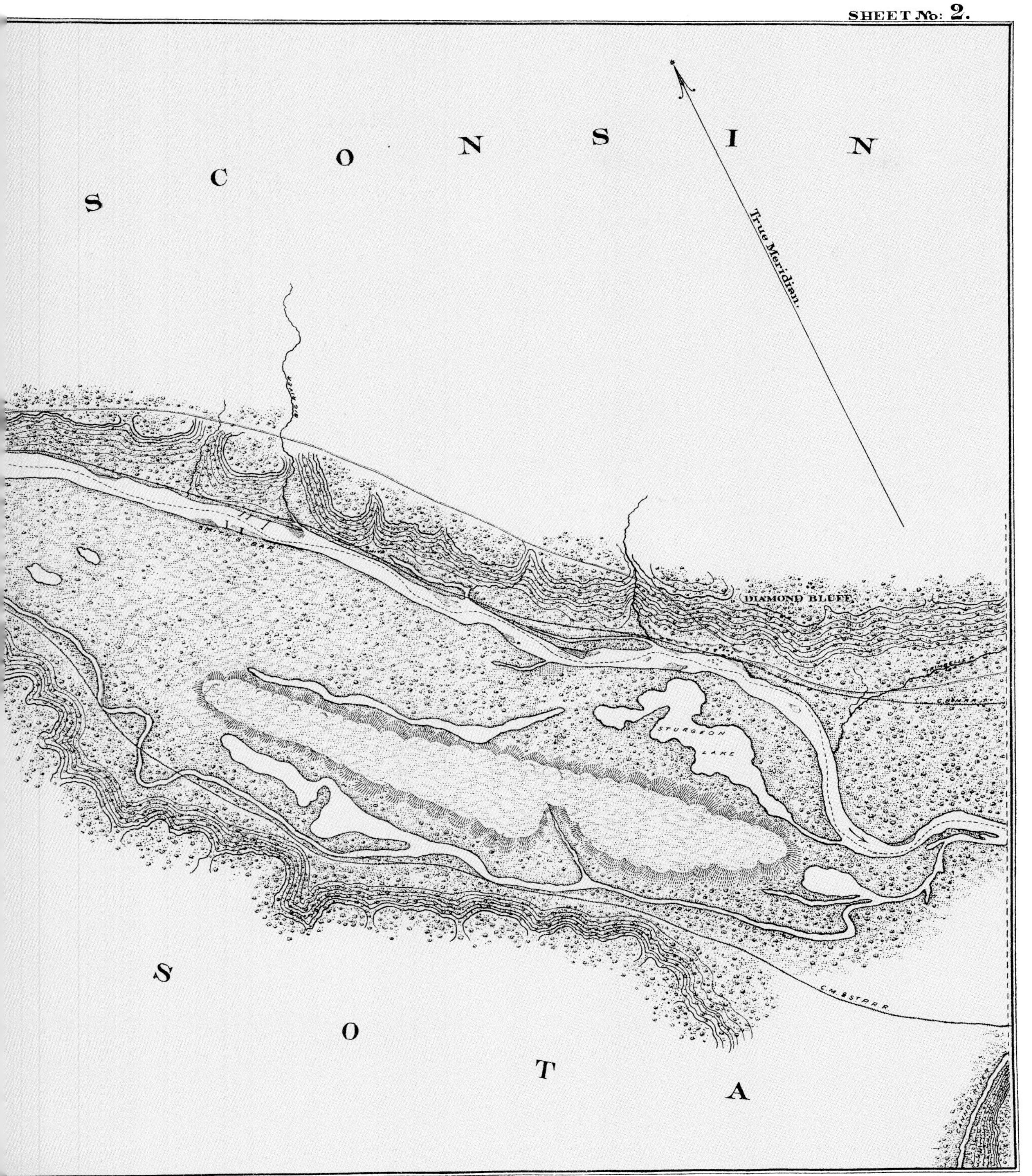
SHEET No: 2.
S C O N S I N
True Meridian.
DIAMOND BLUFF
STURGEON LAKE
C.M.&ST.P.R.R.
S O T A
CANNON
N. PETERS, Photo-Lithographer, Washington, D.C.

MAP 3
RED WING, MINNESOTA
BAY CITY, WISCONSIN
LAKE PEPIN
MAIDEN ROCK, WISCONSIN
POINT NO POINT
FRONTENAC, MINNESOTA
STOCKHOLM, WISCONSIN
LAKE CITY, MINNESOTA

Wreck of Excursionboat "Seawing" (capsized during a severe thunderstorm on Lake Pepin . . .) (PLATE 22)

Redwing, Minn. and Barn bluff (PLATE 23)

From point "No Point" looking down stream, across Lake Pepin (PLATE 24)

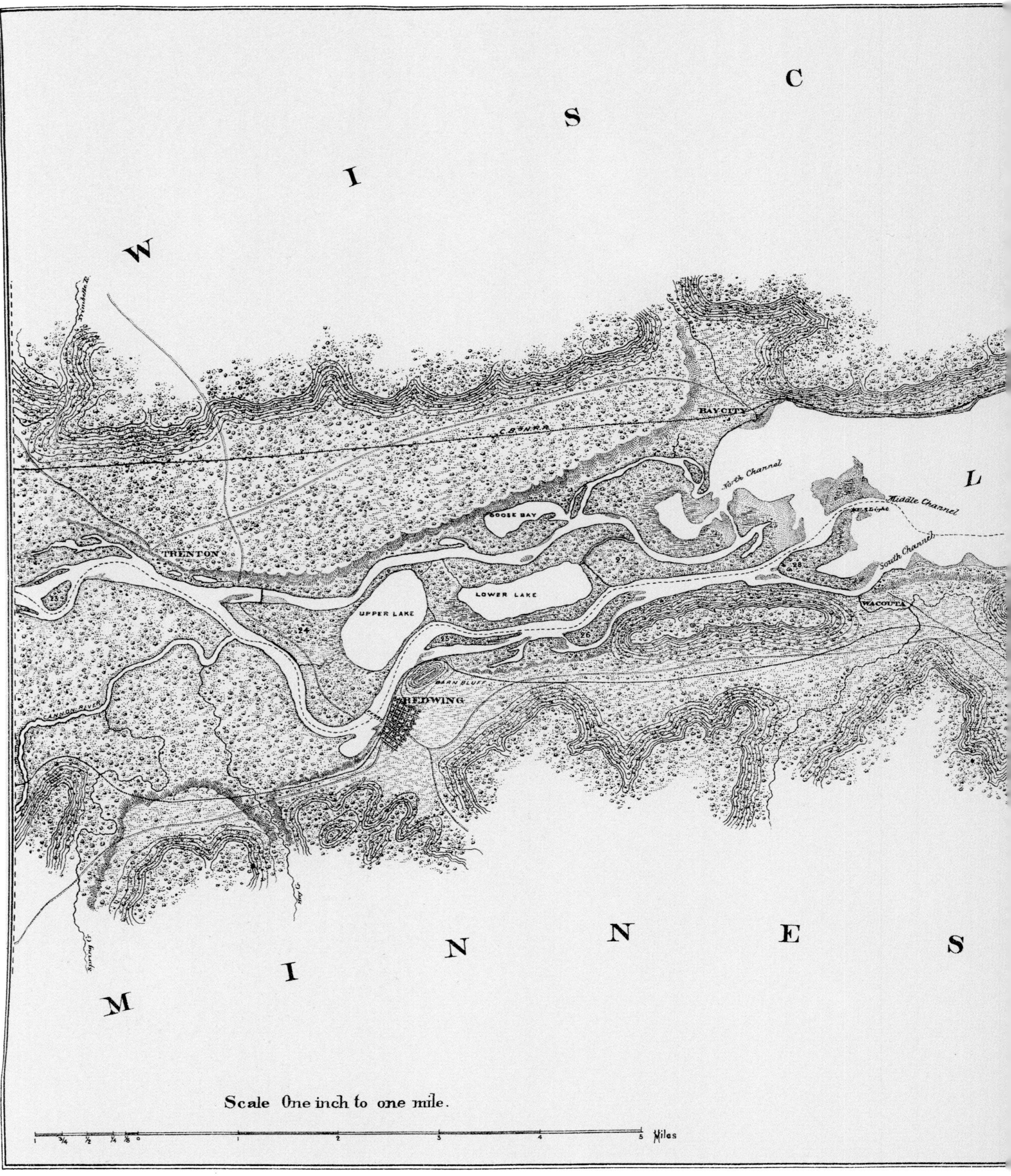

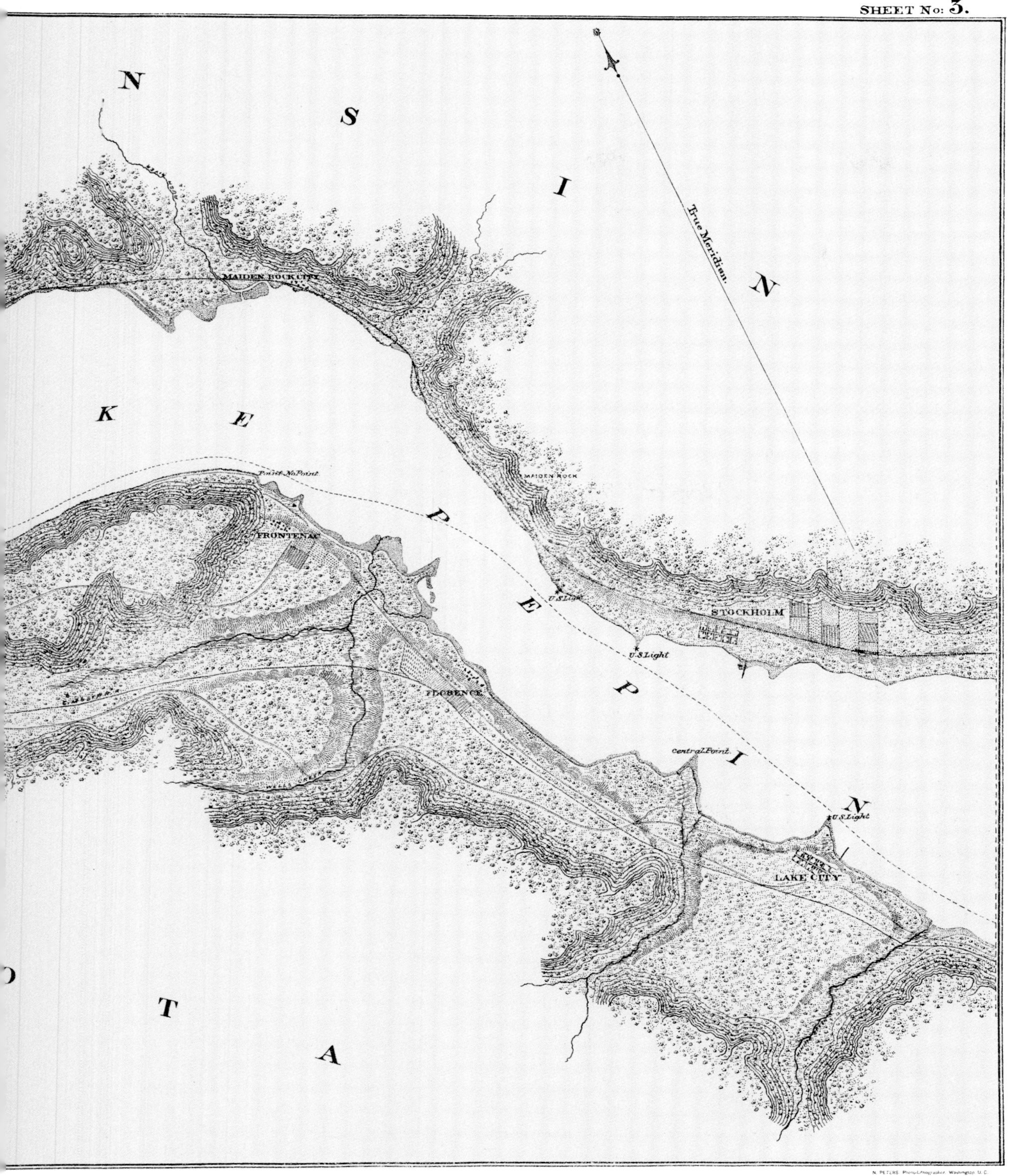
SHEET No: 3.
N
S
I
N
True Meridian
MAIDEN ROCK CITY
K
E
MAIDEN ROCK
Point No Point
FRONTENAC
P
E
U.S. Light
STOCKHOLM
U.S. Light
FLORENCE
P
Central Point
I
N
U.S. Light
LAKE CITY
O
T
A

MAP 4
LAKE PEPIN
NORTH PEPIN, WISCONSIN
CHIPPEWA RIVER
READ'S LANDING, MINNESOTA
WABASHA, MINNESOTA
BEEF SLOUGH
ALMA, WISCONSIN
WEST NEWTON CHUTE

Mouth of Chippewa River (PLATE 25)

From Quarry at Read's Landing, Minn. looking down stream (PLATE 26)

Boatyard at Wabasha, Minn. (PLATE 27)

From bluffs at Alma, Wis looking down stream (PLATE 28)

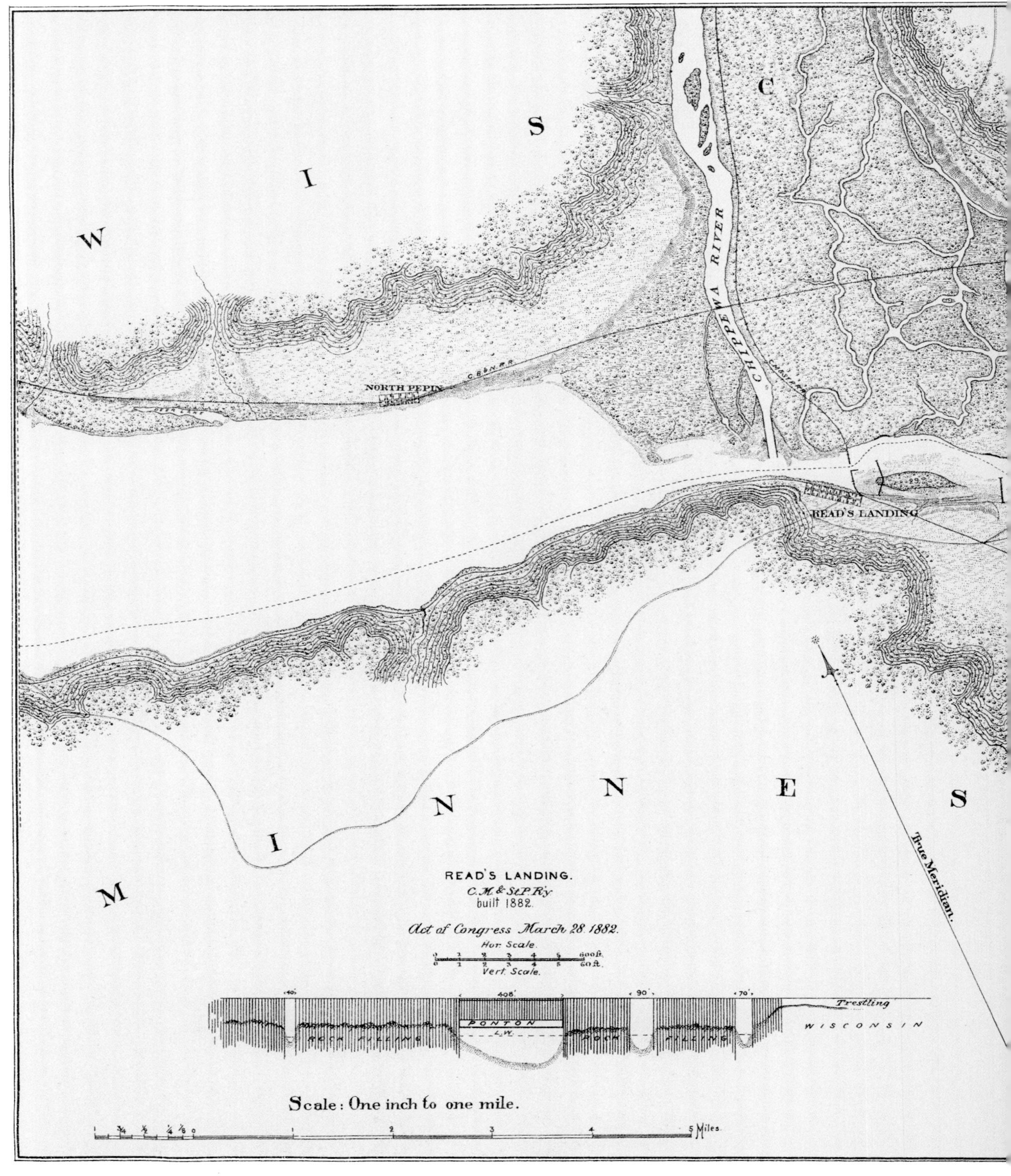

SHEET No: 4.

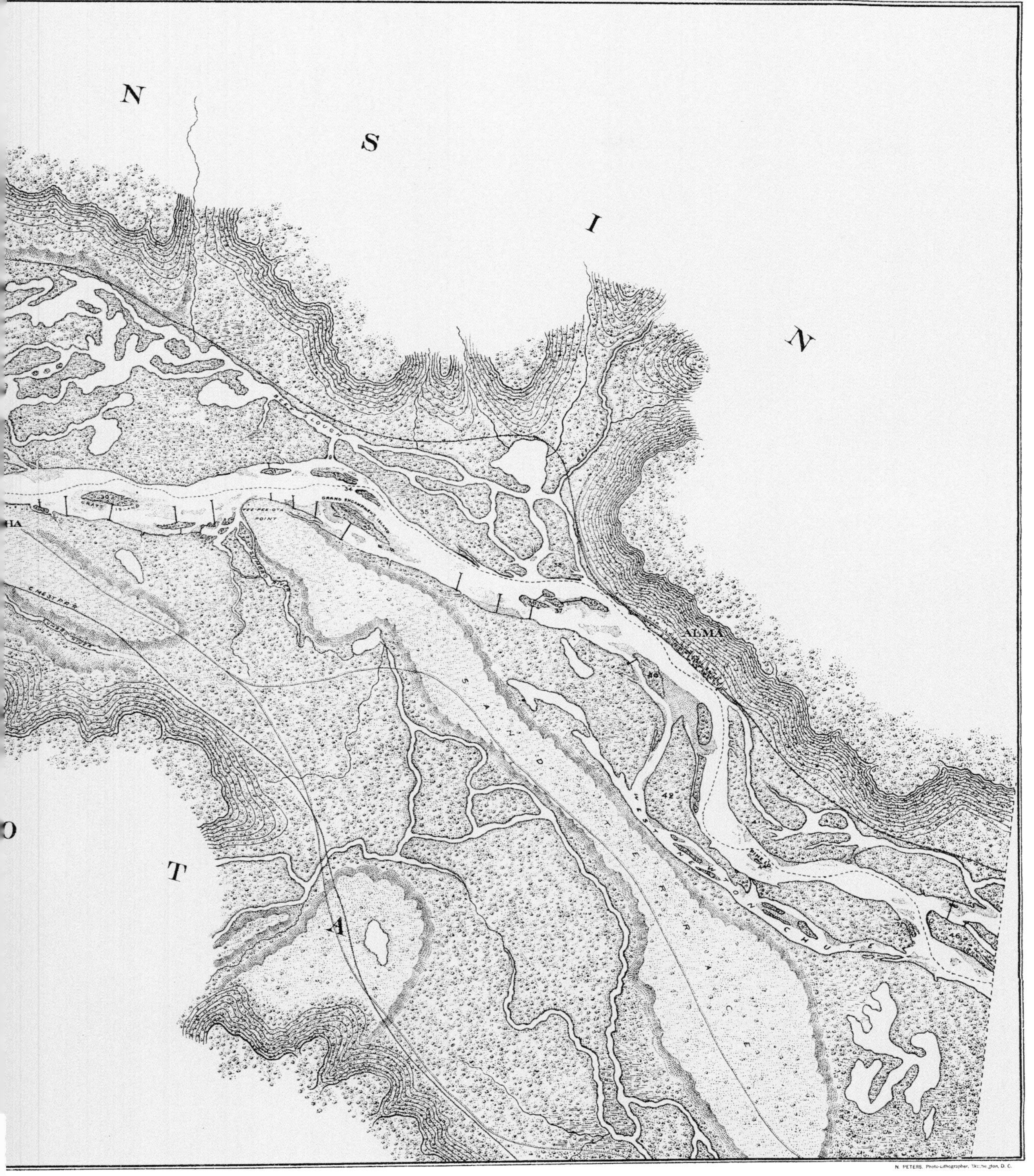
N
S
I
N
O
T
A
ALMA
GRAND ENCAMPMENT ISLAND
TEE-PEE-OTA POINT
ZUMBRO RIVER
WEST NEWTON CHUTE
42
46
N. PETERS, Photo-Lithographer, Washington, D.C.

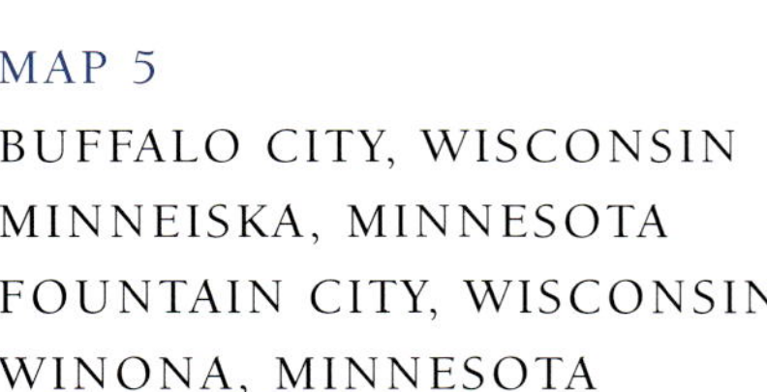

MAP 5

BUFFALO CITY, WISCONSIN
MINNEISKA, MINNESOTA
FOUNTAIN CITY, WISCONSIN
WINONA, MINNESOTA

Minneiska, Minn. (PLATE 29)

From bluffs at Fountain City looking upstream (PLATE 30)

Levee at Winona, Minn. (PLATE 31)

Wagon Bridge at Winona, Minn. (PLATE 32)

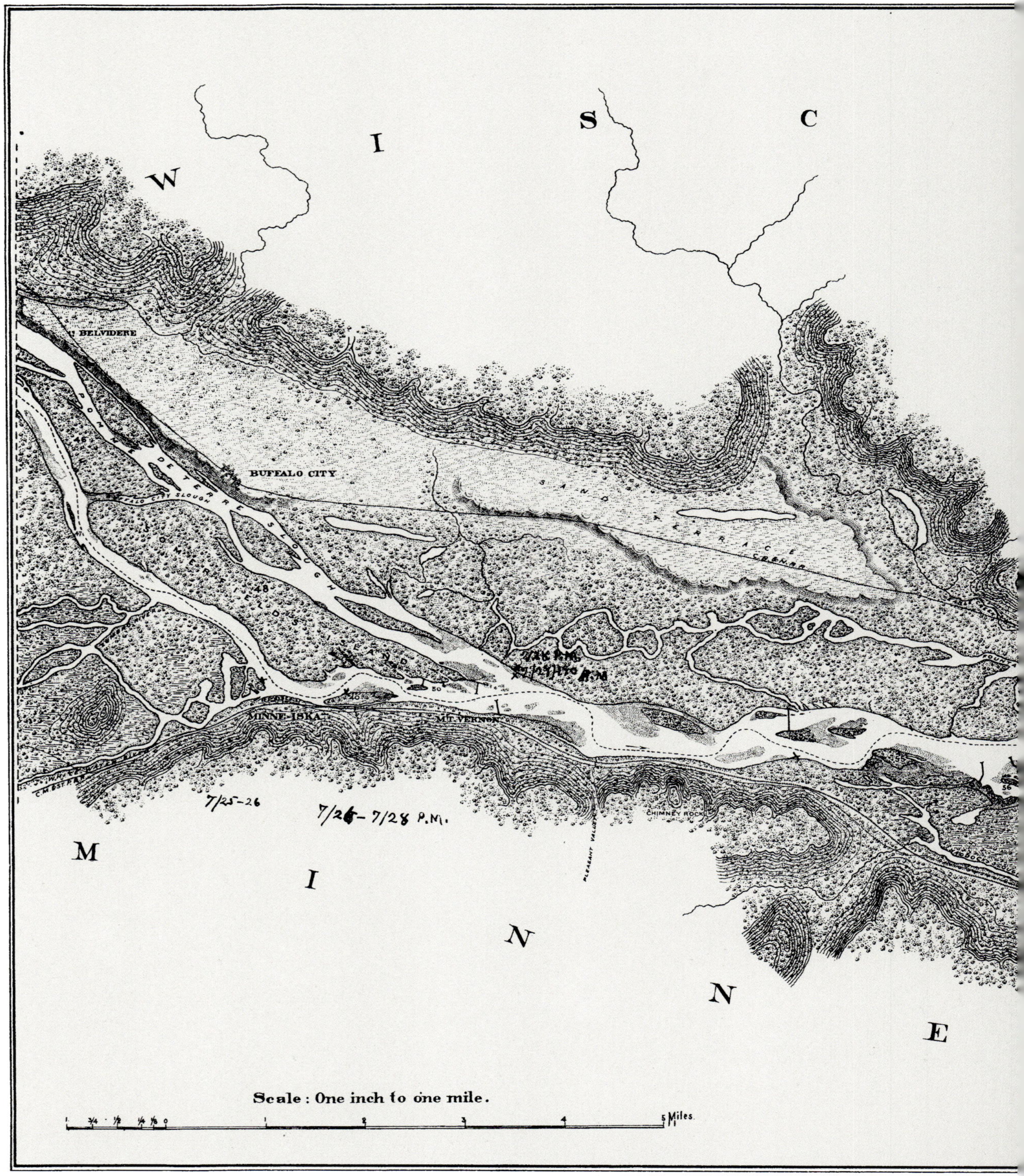

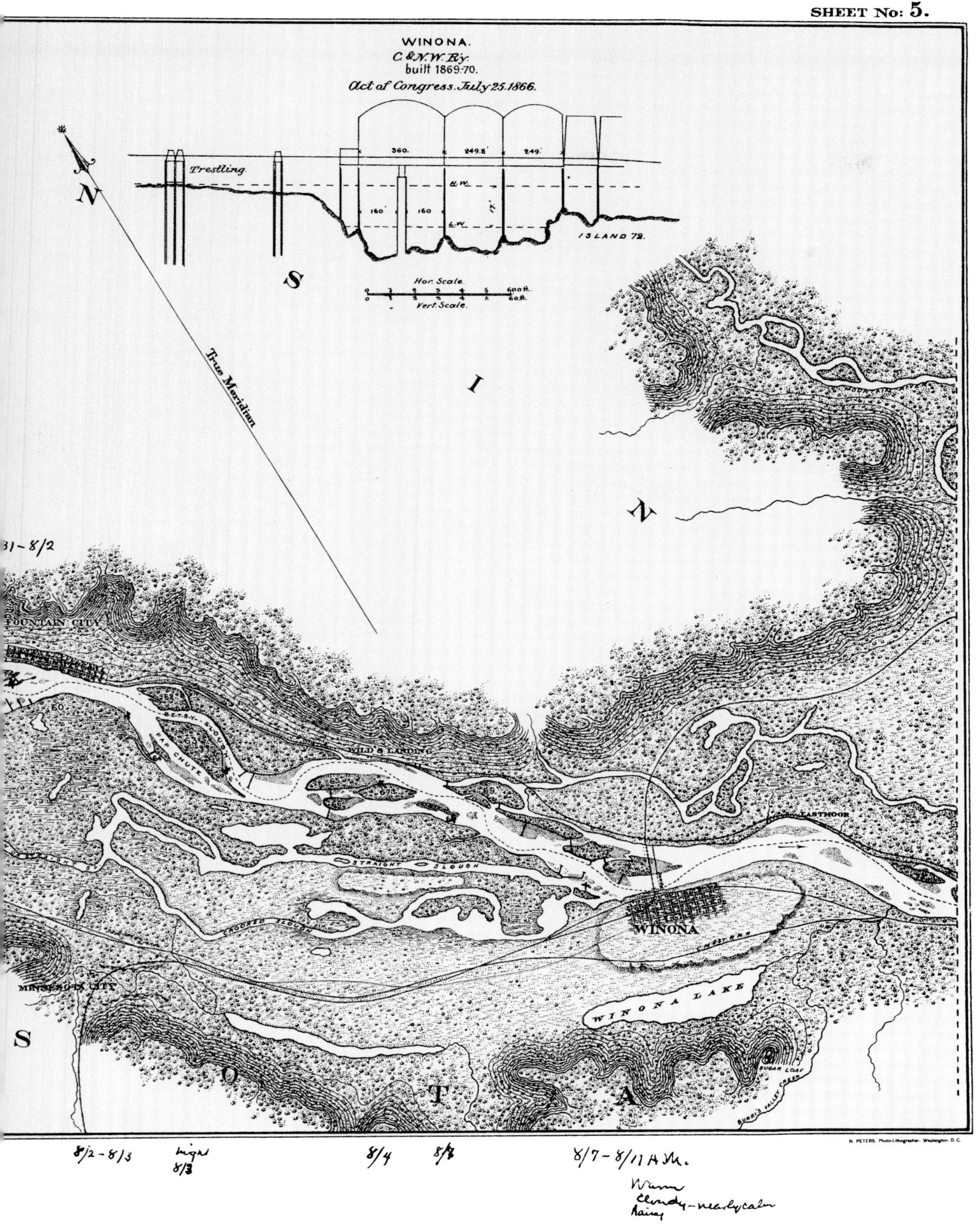
SHEET No: 5.
WINONA.
C.&N.W.Ry.
built 1869-70.
Act of Congress. July 25.1866.
360.
249.8'
249.'
Trestling
H.W.
L.W.
160'
160
ISLAND 72.
Hor. Scale.
600 ft.
60 ft.
Vert. Scale.
N
True Meridian
S
I
N
FOUNTAIN CITY
WILD'S LANDING
STRAIGHT SLOUGH
CROOKED SLOUGH
WINONA
WINONA LAKE
MINNESOTA CITY
S
O
T
A
SUGAR LOAF
N. PETERS, Photo-Lithographer, Washington, D.C.
31-8/2
8/2-8/3
8/4
8/7-8/11 A.M.

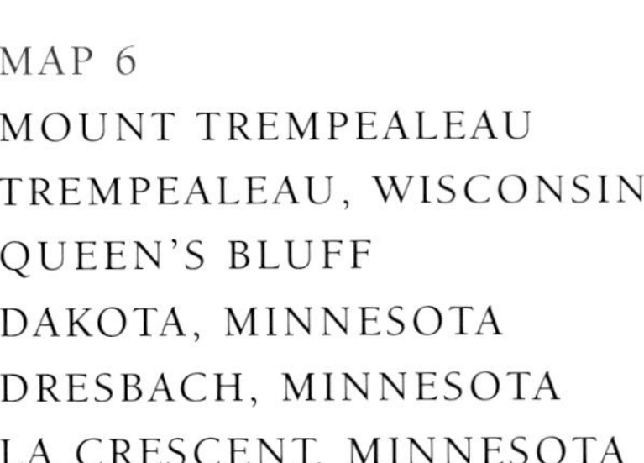

MAP 6

MOUNT TREMPEALEAU

TREMPEALEAU, WISCONSIN

QUEEN'S BLUFF

DAKOTA, MINNESOTA

DRESBACH, MINNESOTA

LA CRESCENT, MINNESOTA

From bluffs at Trempealeau, Wis. looking down stream (PLATE 33)

Queen's Bluff (PLATE 34)

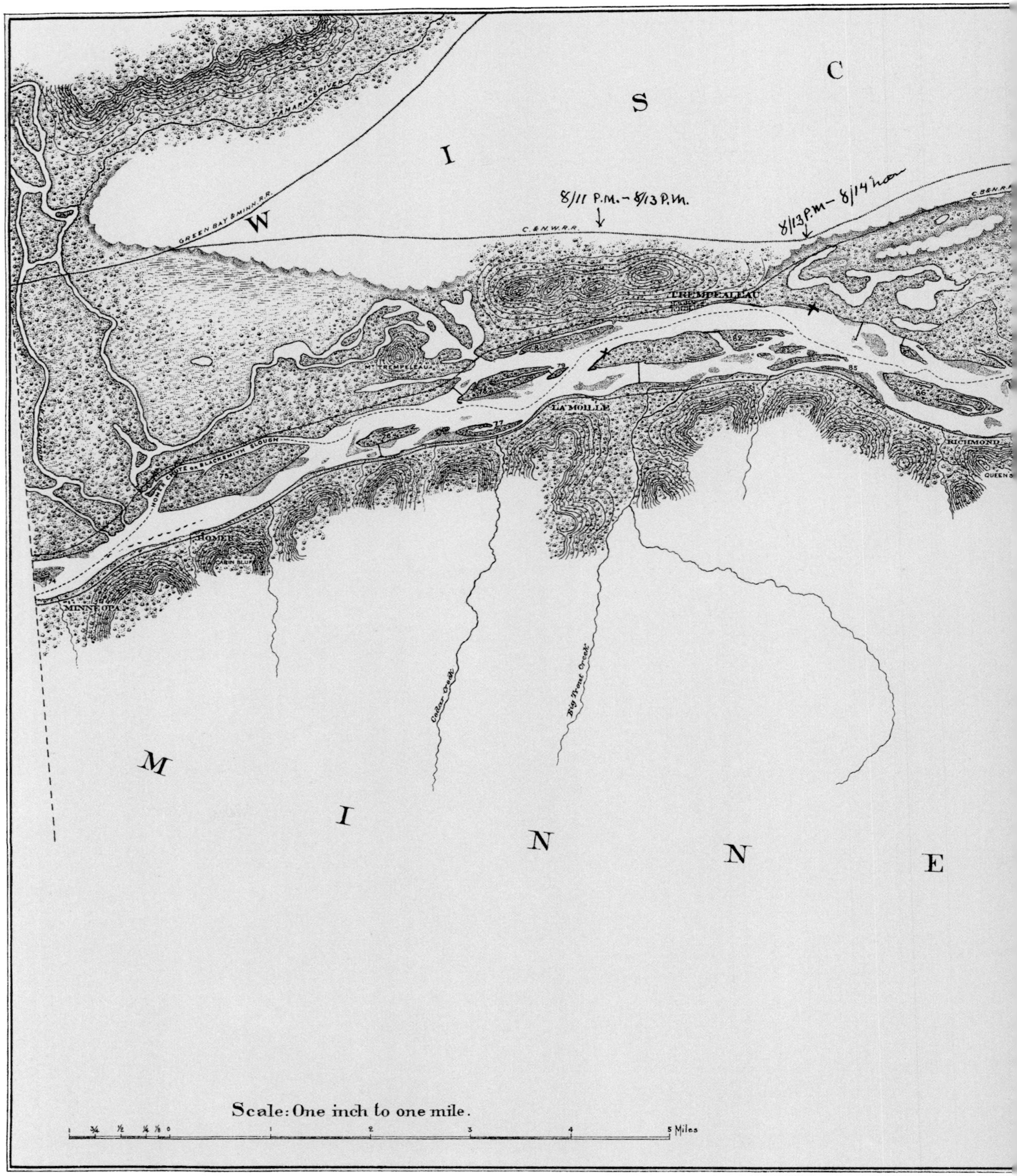

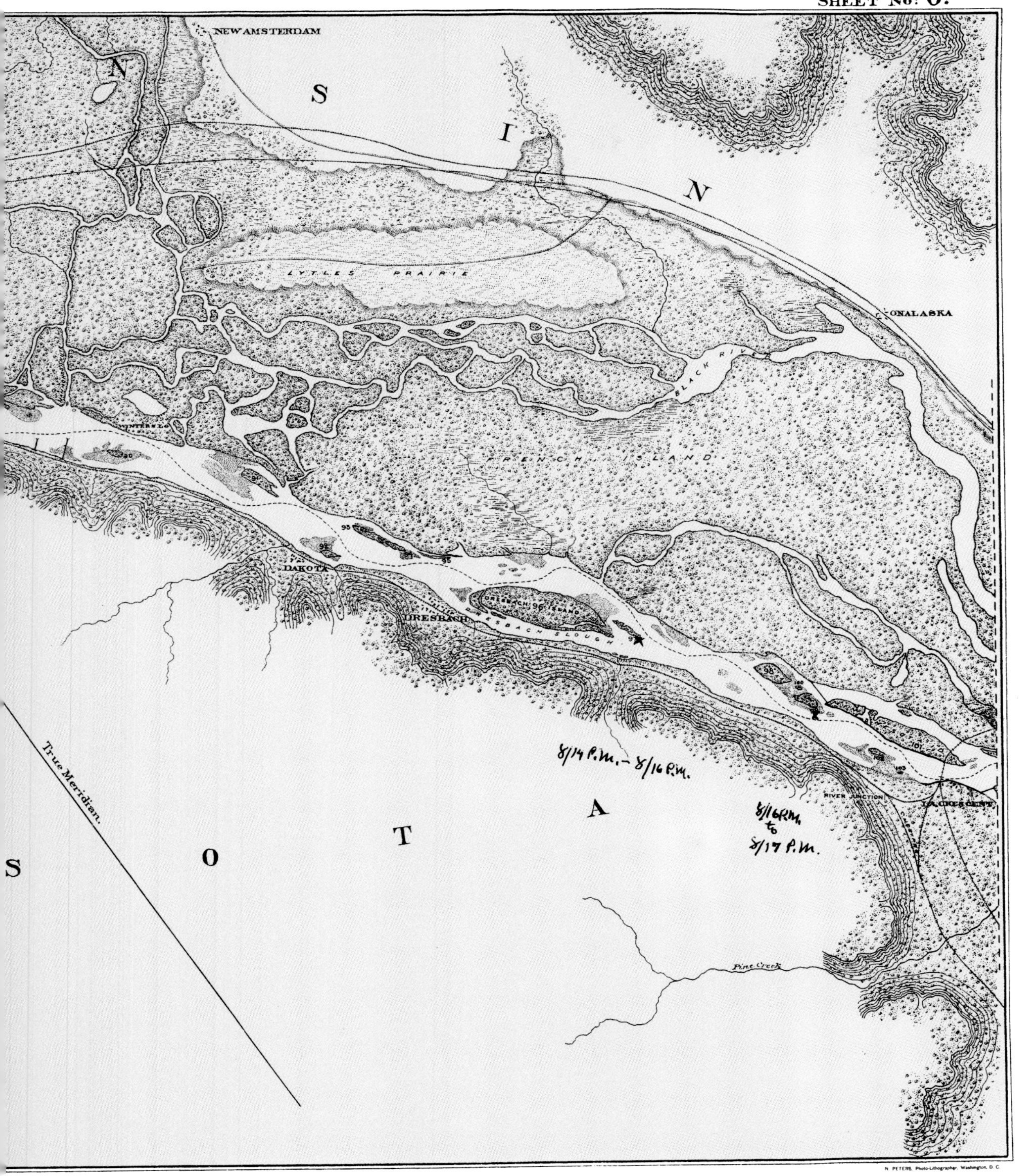
NEW AMSTERDAM
N
S
I
N
LYTLES PRAIRIE
ONALASKA
BLACK RIVER
FRENCH ISLAND
DAKOTA
DRESBACH
DRESBACH ISLAND
DRESBACH SLOUGH
8/14 P.M. – 8/16 P.M.
RIVER JUNCTION
8/16 P.M. to 8/17 P.M.
A
T
O
S
True Meridian.
Pine Creek
N. PETERS, Photo-Lithographer, Washington, D.C.

MAP 7
LA CROSSE, WISCONSIN
BROWNSVILLE, MINNESOTA
COON SLOUGH
GENOA, WISCONSIN
BAD AXE, WISCONSIN

Levee at La Crosse, Wis. (PLATE 35)

Wagon Bridge at La Crosse, Wis. (PLATE 36)

Bar in front of La Crosse, Wis. (PLATE 37)

Genoa, Wis. (PLATE 38)

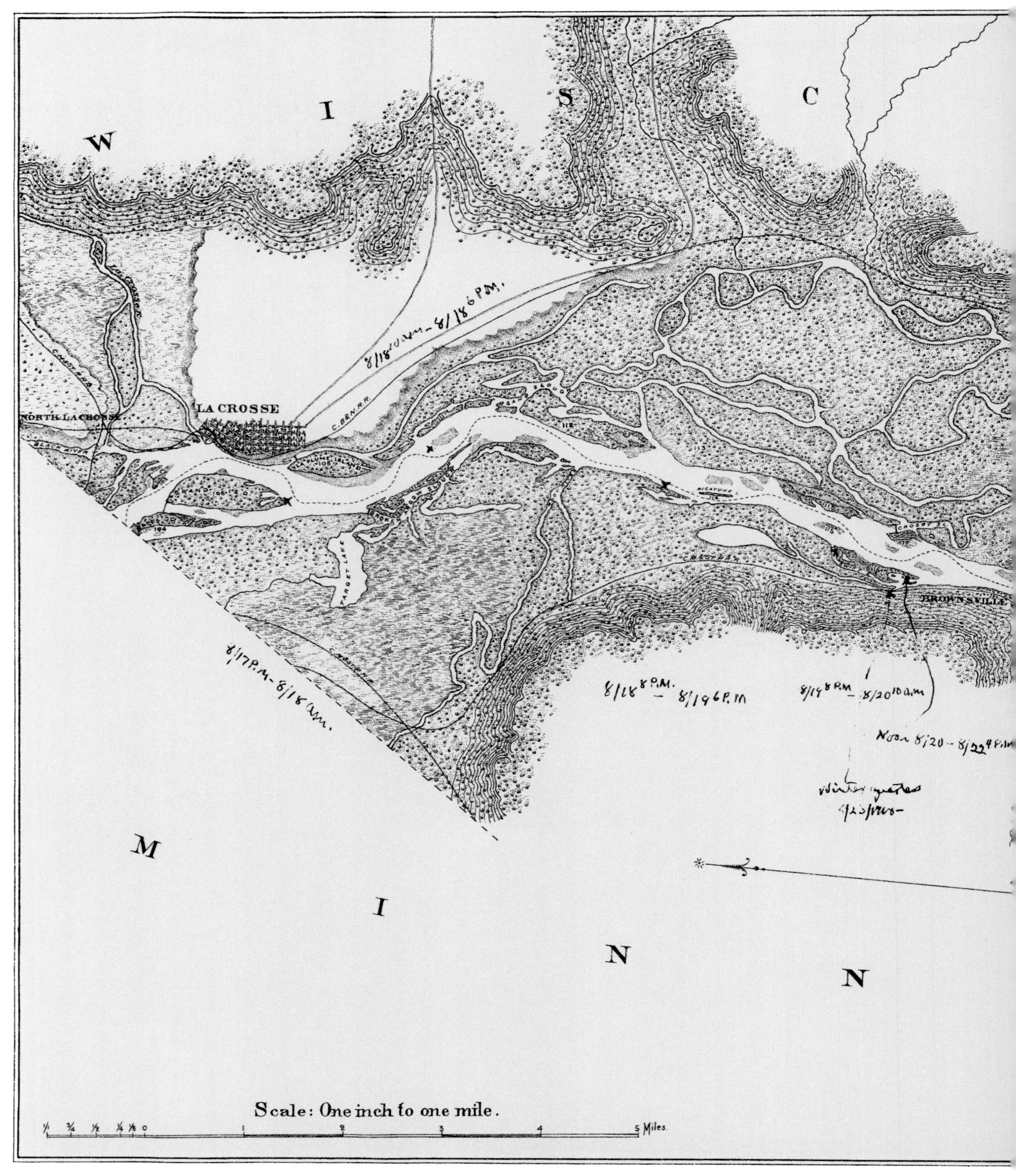

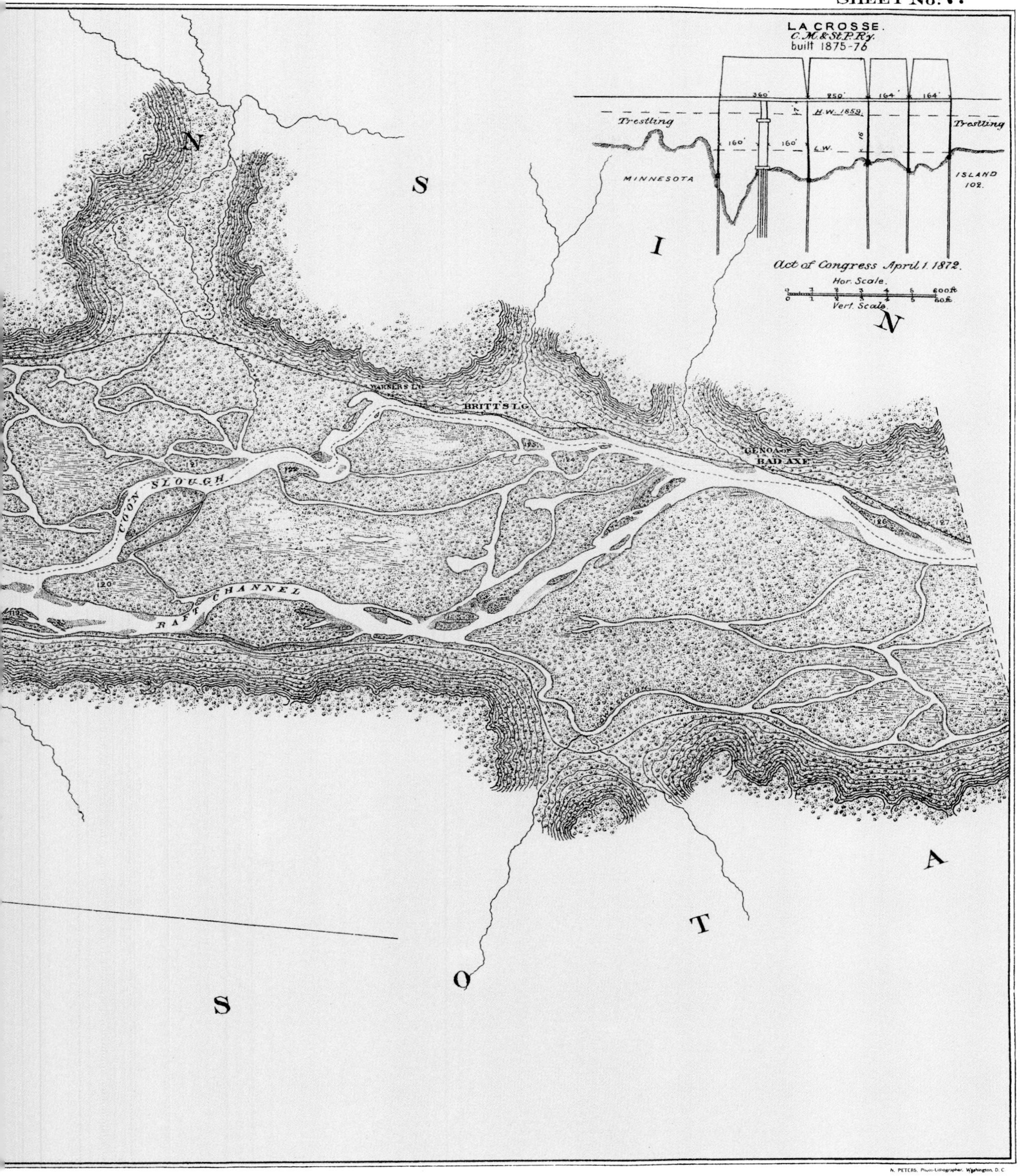

SHEET No: 7.

LA CROSSE.
C.M.&St.P.Ry.
built 1875-76

Trestling
H.W. 1859
L.W.
MINNESOTA
ISLAND 102.

Act of Congress April 1, 1872.
Hor. Scale.
Vert. Scale.

N
S
I
N

WARNERS LG.
BRITT'S LG.
GENOA or BAD AXE
COON SLOUGH
RAFT CHANNEL

A
T
O
S

N. PETERS, Photo-Lithographer, Washington, D.C.

MAP 8

DE SOTO, WISCONSIN

LANSING, IOWA

CROOKED SLOUGH

De Soto, Wis. (PLATE 39)

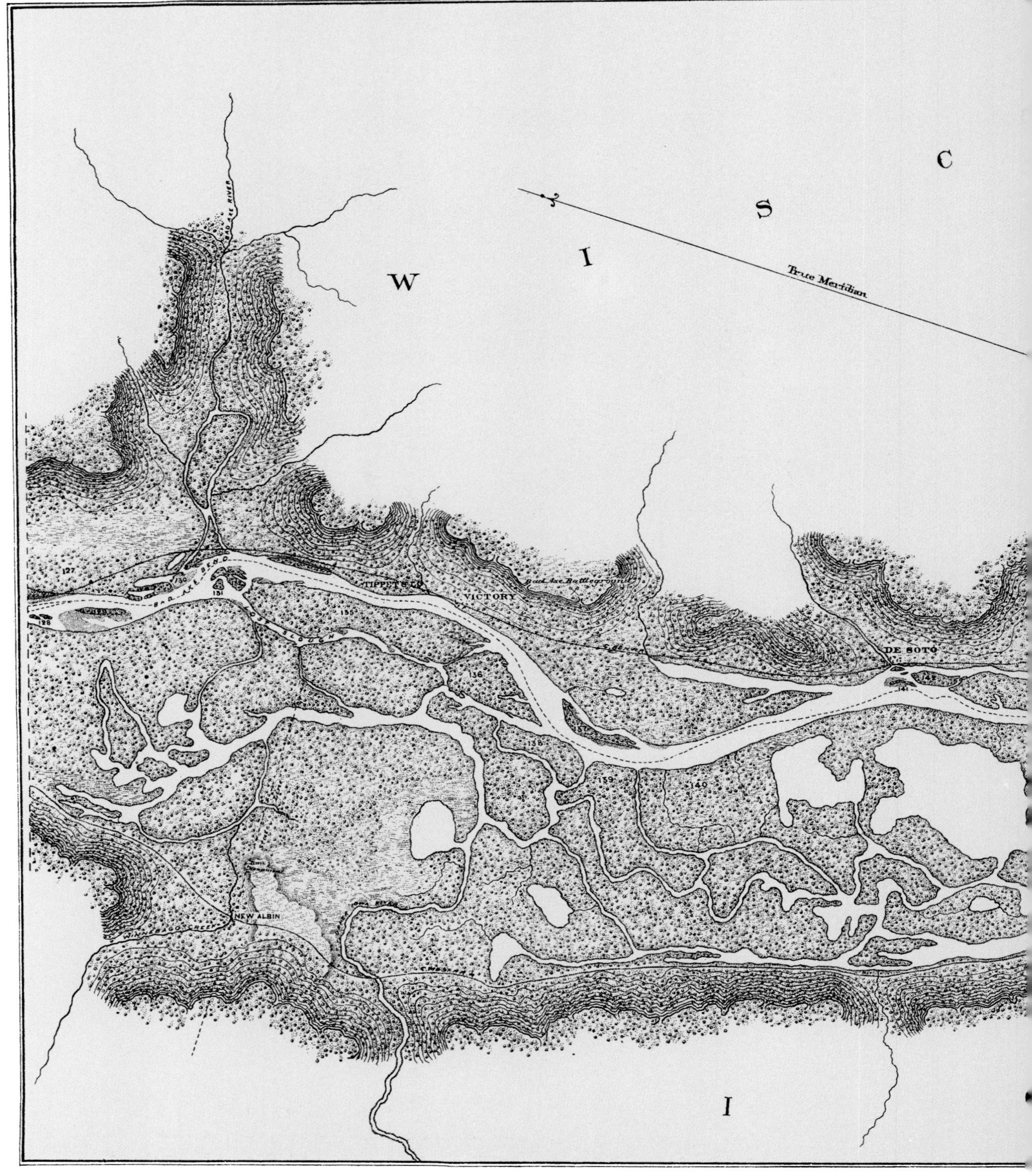

SHEET No: 8.

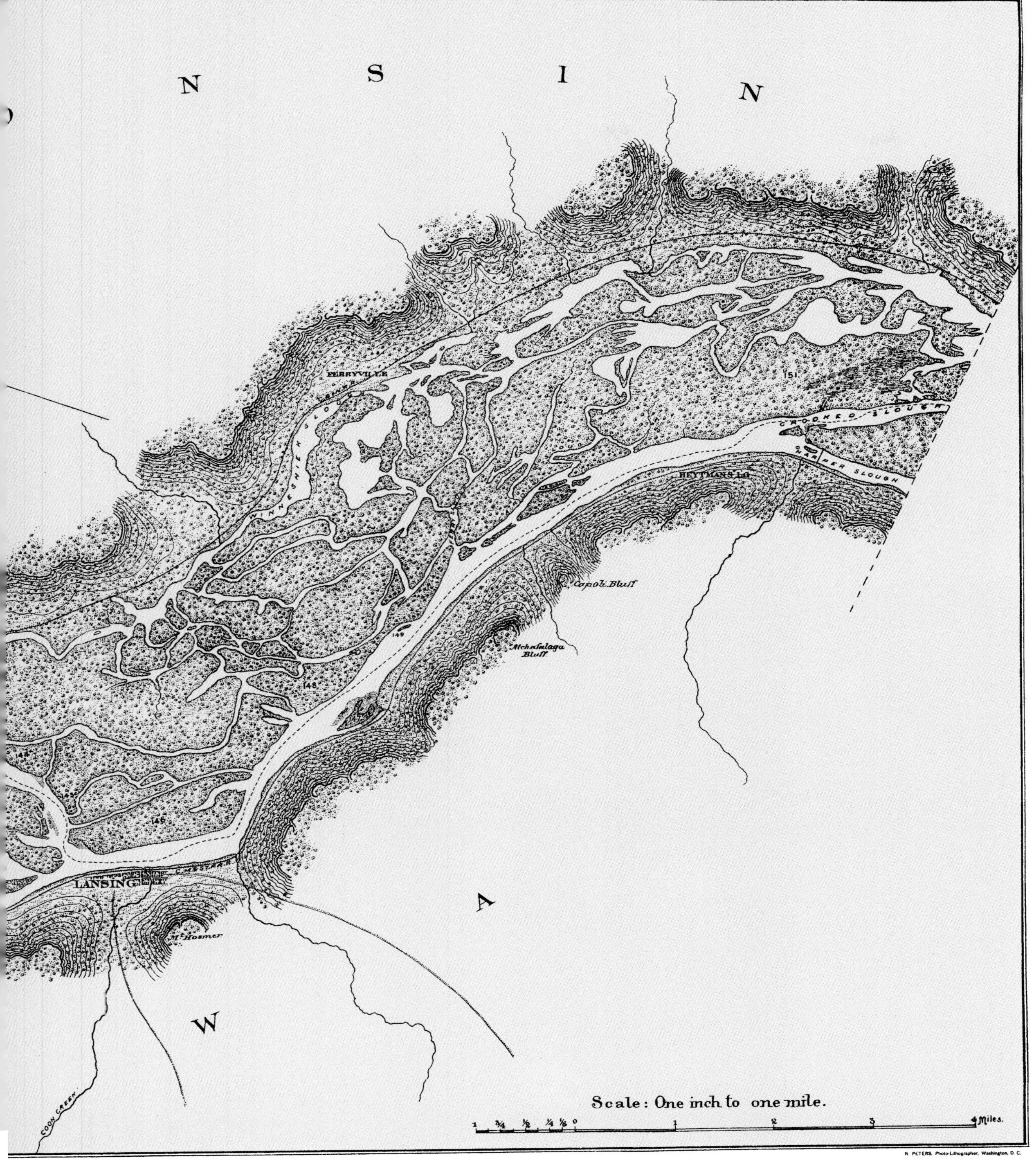

N S I N
PERRYVILLE
CROOKED SLOUGH
HEYTMANS LG.
Capoli Bluff
Atchafalaga Bluff
LANSING
Mt. Hosmer
A
W
Scale: One inch to one mile.
4 Miles.
N. PETERS, Photo-Lithographer, Washington, D.C.

MAP 9
HARPER'S FERRY, IOWA
PRAIRIE DU CHIEN, WISCONSIN
NORTH McGREGOR, IOWA
McGREGOR, IOWA
WISCONSIN RIVER

Old Ponton Bridge at N. McGregor, Ia. (PLATE 44)

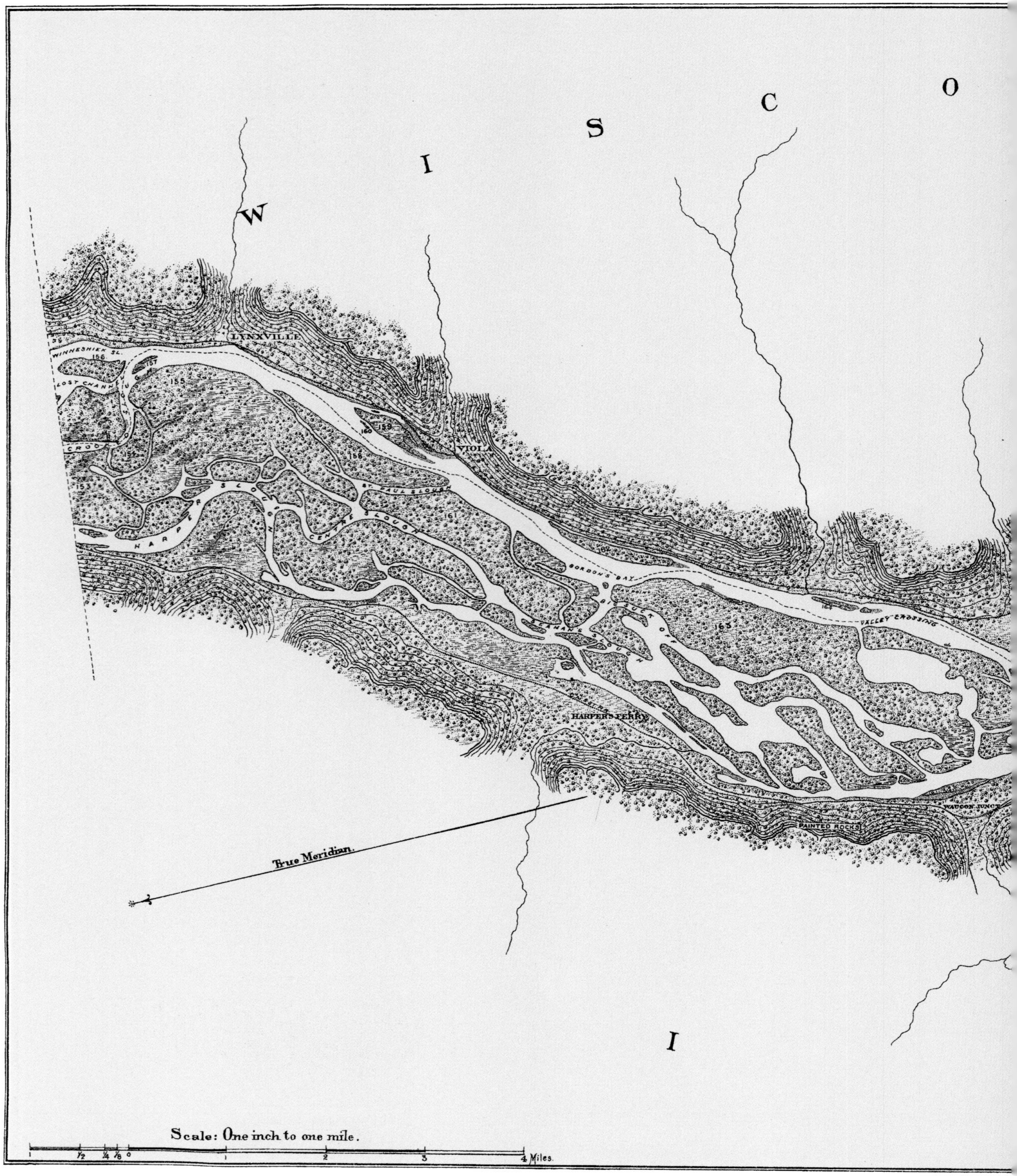

SHEET No: 9.

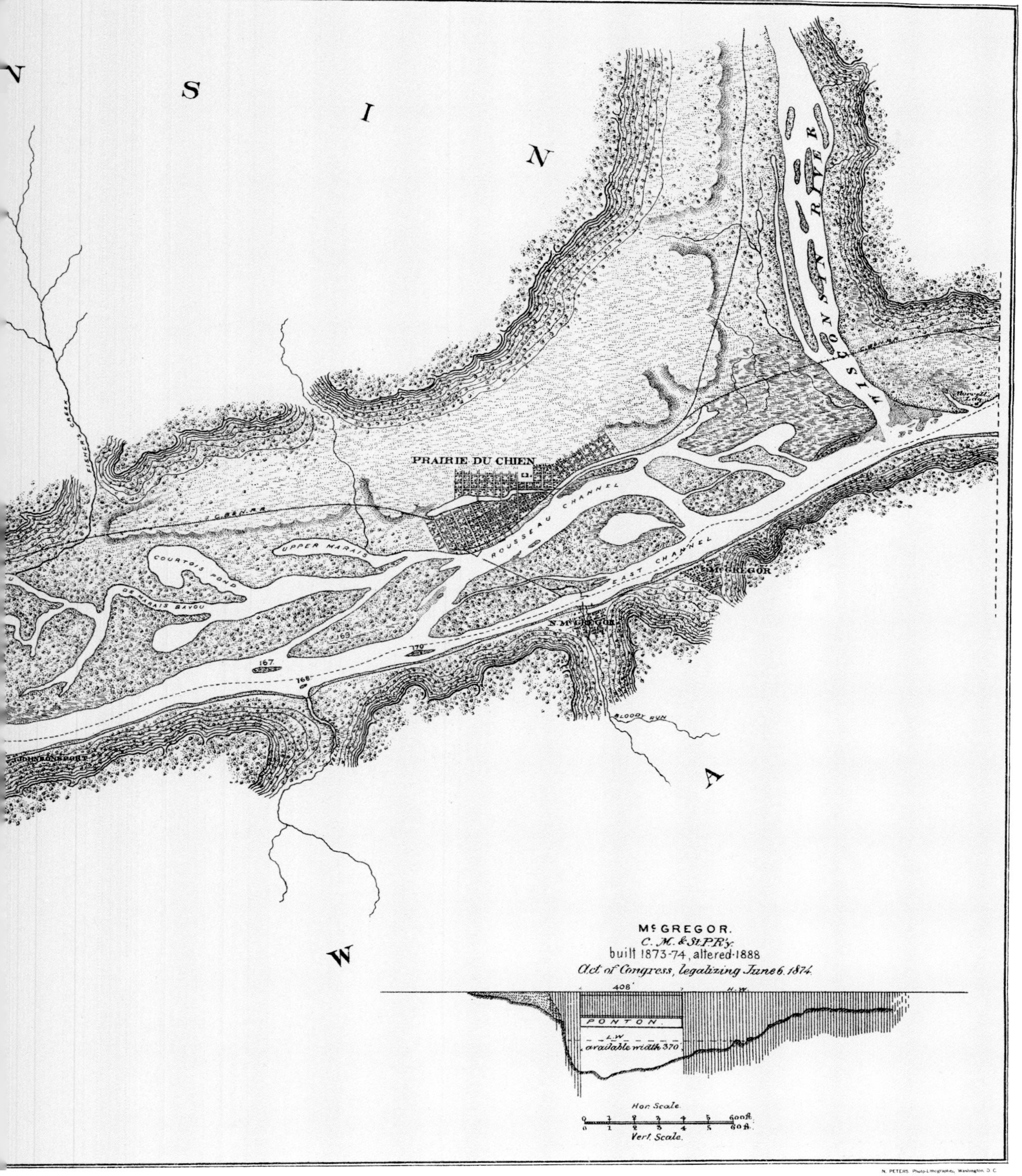

PRAIRIE DU CHIEN

ROUSSEAU CHANNEL

EAST CHANNEL

UPPER MARAIS

COURTOIS POND

WISCONSIN RIVER

McGREGOR

BLOODY RUN

W I S C O N S I N

I O W A

McGREGOR.
C. M. & St. P. R'y.
built 1873-74, altered 1888
Act of Congress, legalizing June 6, 1874.

408'

H. W.

PONTON.

L. W.

available width 370

Hor. Scale.

0 1 2 3 4 5 600 ft.

0 1 2 3 4 5 60 ft.

Vert. Scale.

N. PETERS, Photo-Lithographer, Washington, D. C.

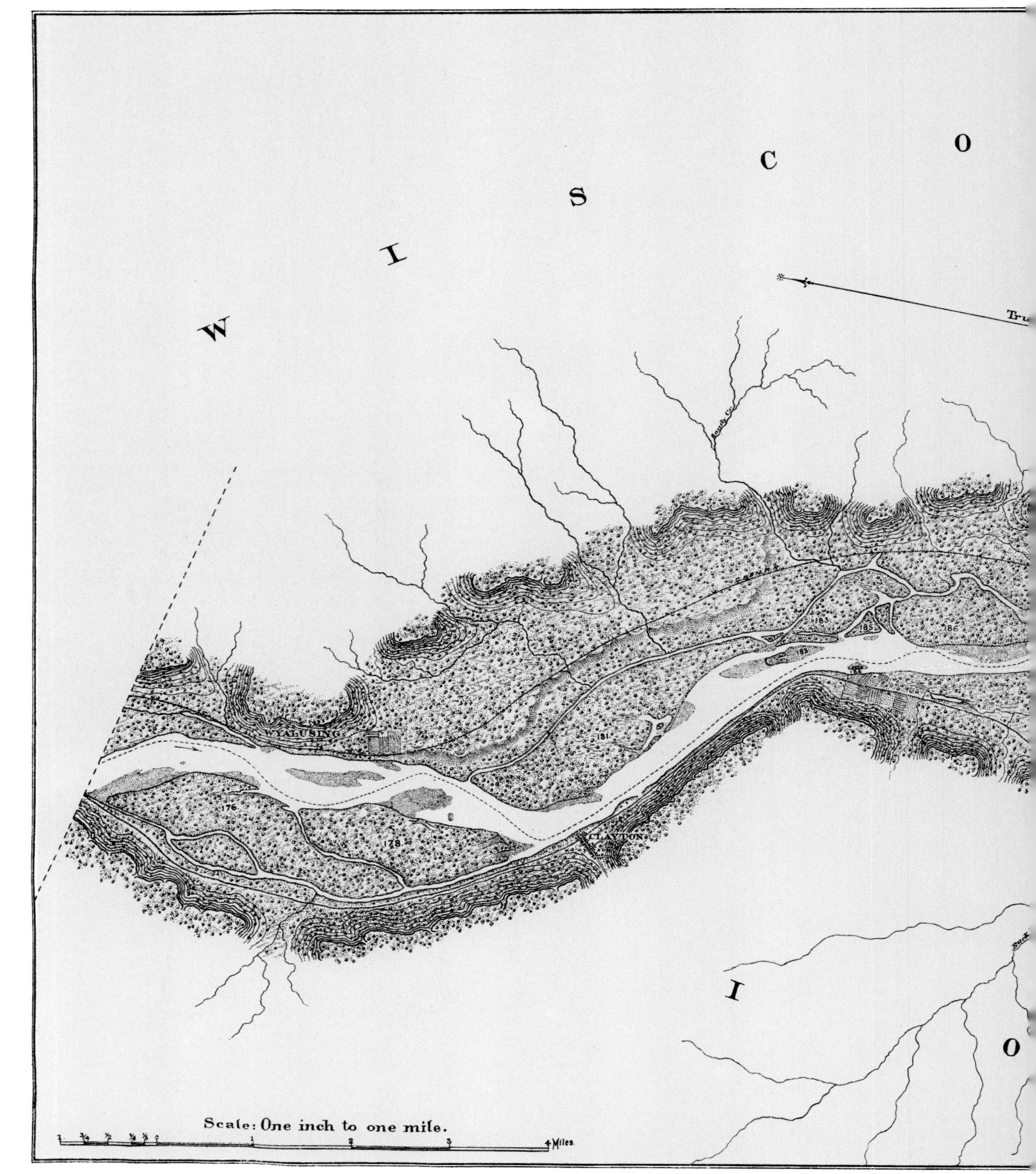

MAP 10
GLEN HAVEN, WISCONSIN
GUTTENBERG, IOWA
TURKEY RIVER
CASSVILLE, WISCONSIN

N
S
I
N
CASSVILLE
GLEN HAVEN
CASSVILLE SLOUGH
GUTTENBERG CHANNEL
TURKEY RIVER JUNCTION
GUTTENBERG
TURKEY RIVER
W
A

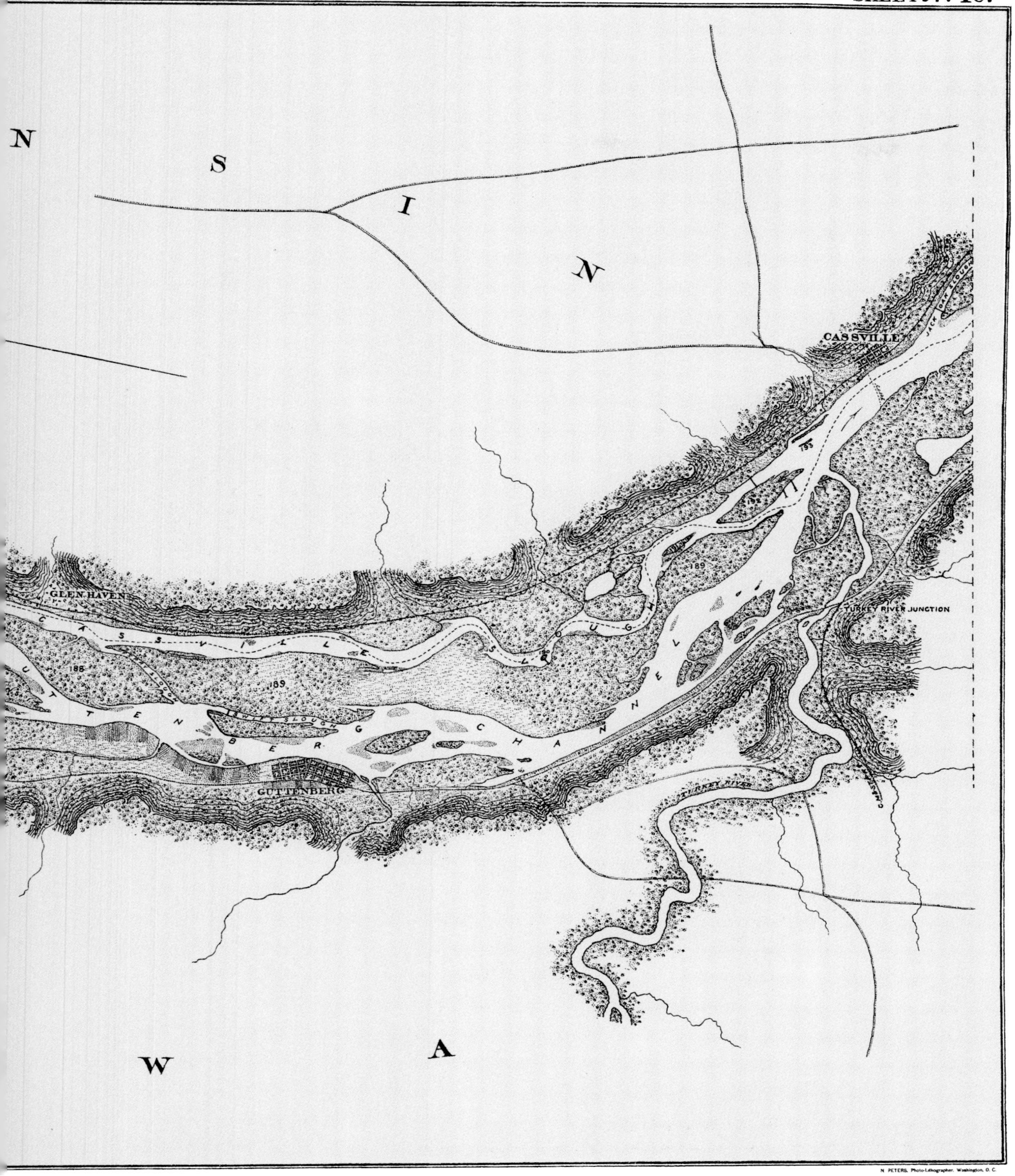

N. PETERS, Photo-Lithographer, Washington, D.C.

MAP 11
BUENA VISTA, IOWA
POTOSI, WISCONSIN
PLATTE RIVER
LITTLE MAQUOKETA RIVER

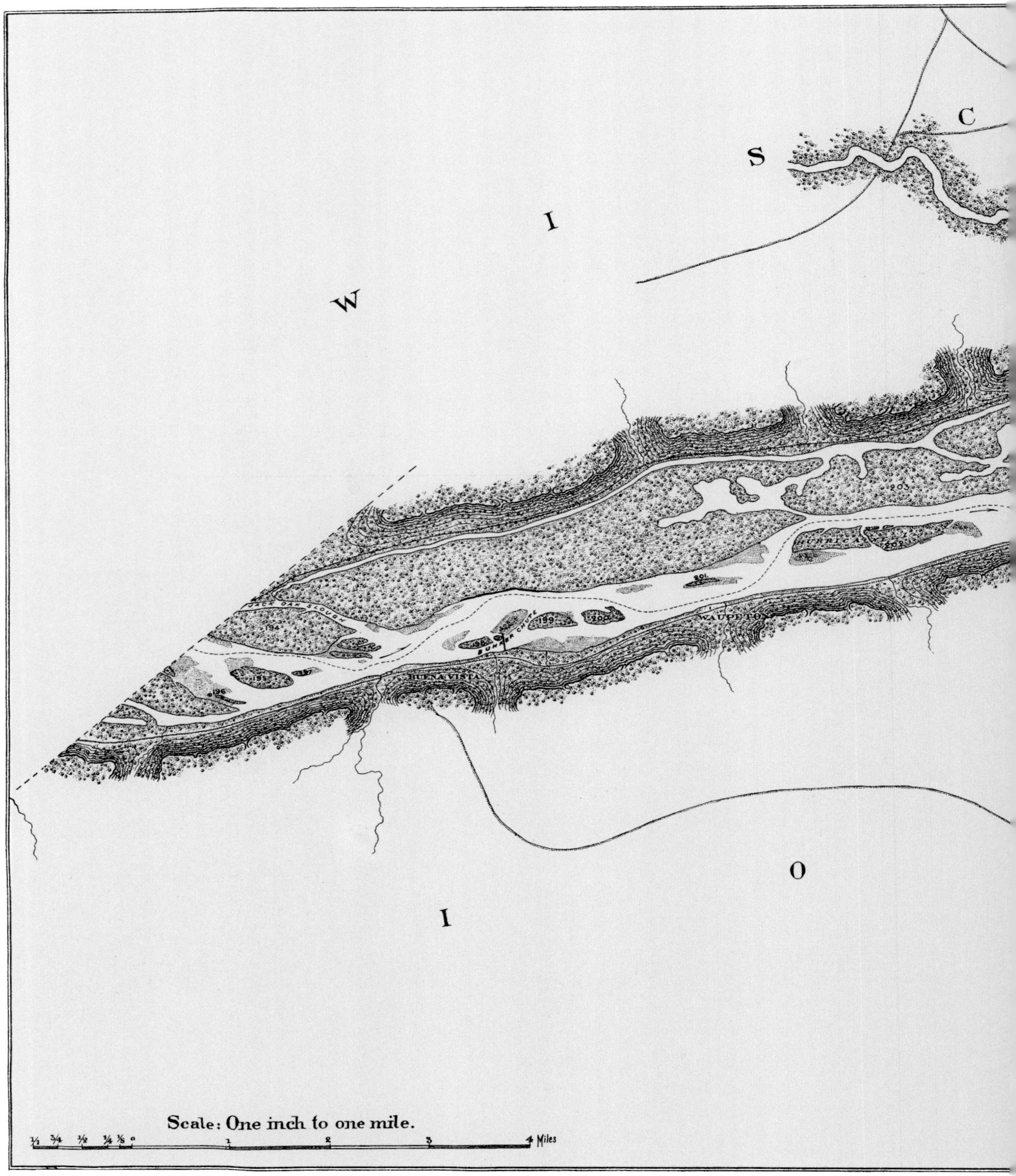

W I S C

I O

Scale: One inch to one mile.

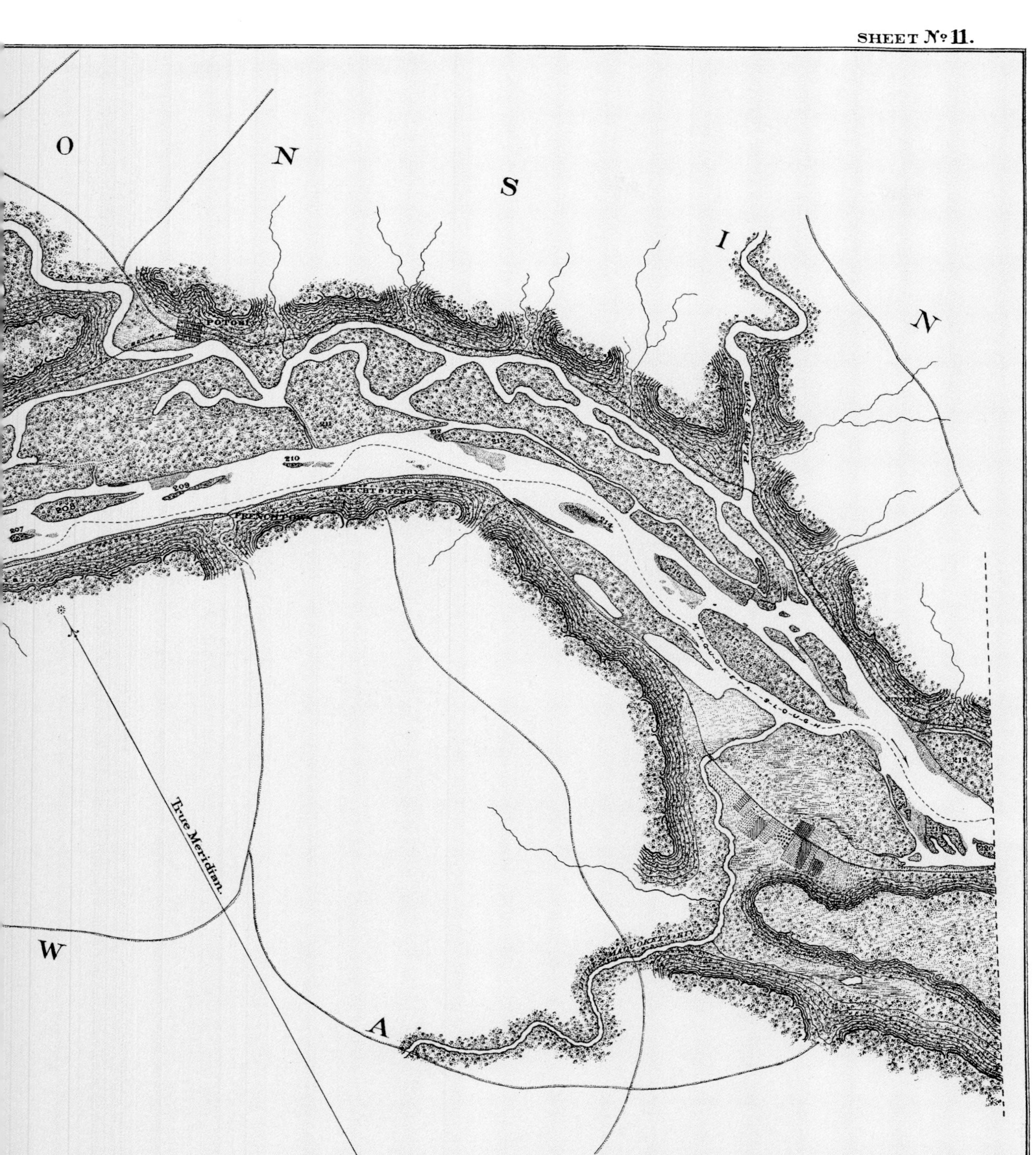
O
N
S
I
N
POTOSI
210
209
208
207
SPECHT'S FERRY
FRENCHTOWN
MAQUOKETA SLOUGH
LITTLE MAQUOKETA RIV.
True Meridian.
W
A
N. PETERS, Photo-Lithographer, Washington, D.C.

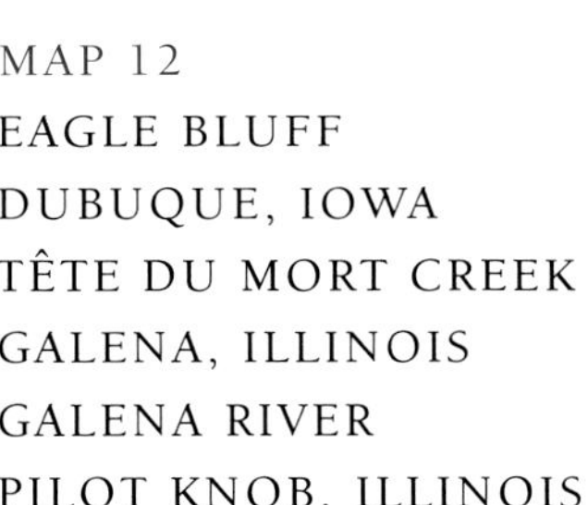

MAP 12

EAGLE BLUFF

DUBUQUE, IOWA

TÊTE DU MORT CREEK

GALENA, ILLINOIS

GALENA RIVER

PILOT KNOB, ILLINOIS

Eagle Point (PLATE 45)

Harbor at Dubuque, Ia., with hull of "Windom" (PLATE 46)

Locks, Galina River—Looking down stream (PLATE 47)

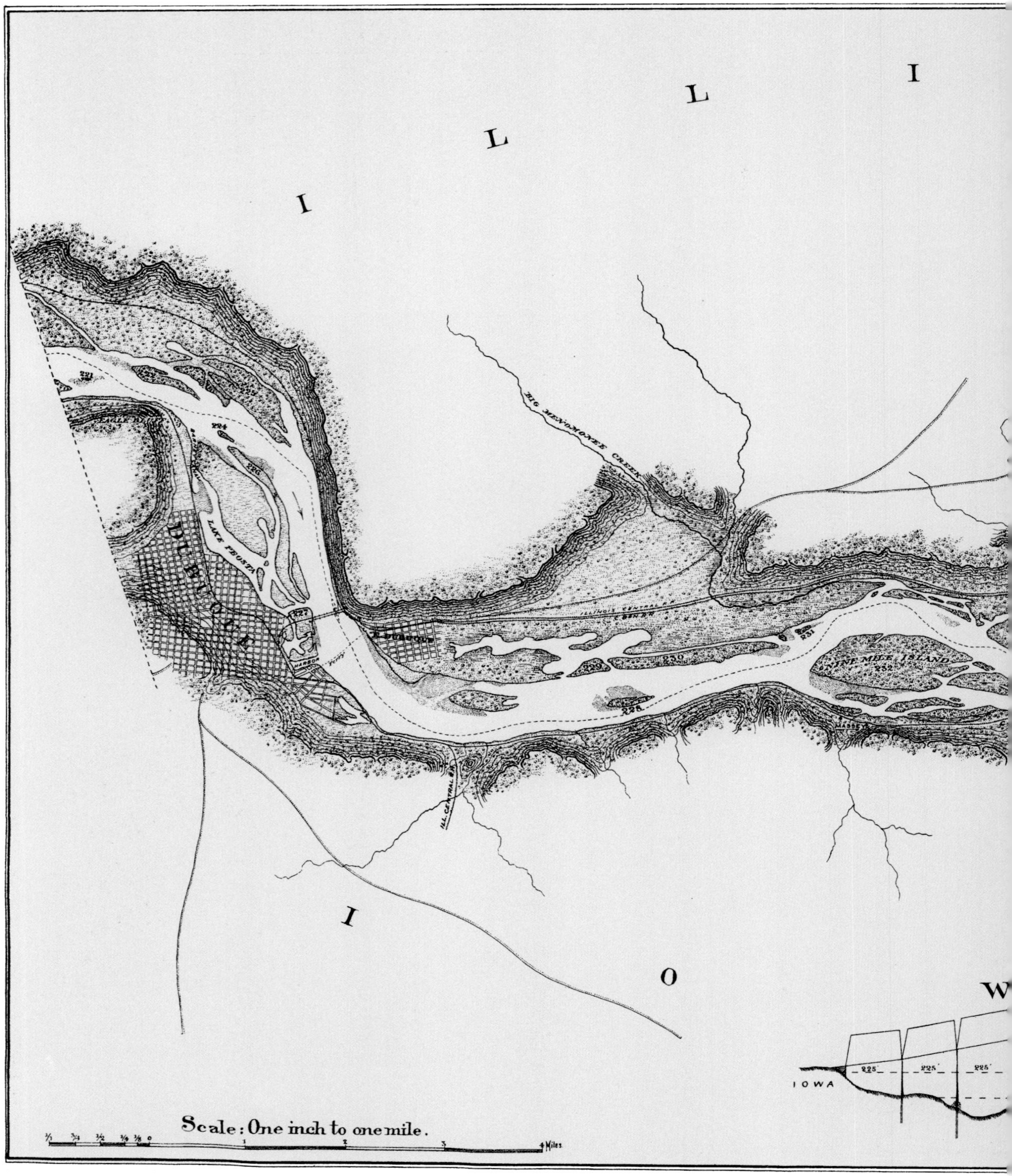

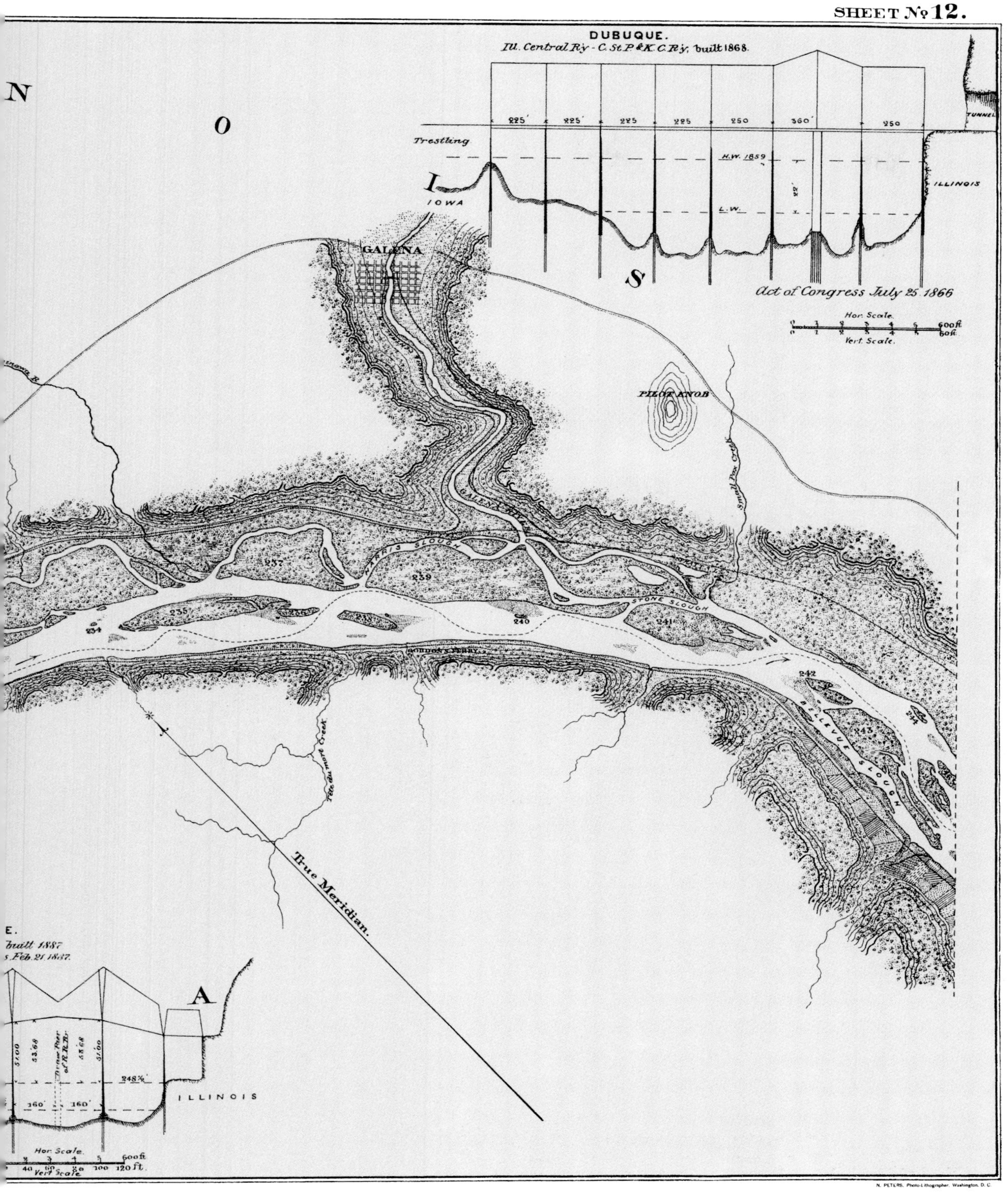
SHEET No 12.
DUBUQUE.
Ill. Central R'y - C. St. P. & K. C. R'y. built 1868.
225' 225' 225 225 250 360' 250
Trestling
TUNNEL
H.W. 1859
L.W.
IOWA
ILLINOIS
GALENA
Act of Congress July 25 1866
Hor. Scale.
Vert. Scale.
PILOT KNOB
Small Pox Creek
STONE SLOUGH
GORDON'S FERRY
BELLEVUE SLOUGH
True Meridian.
N
O
I
S
A
ILLINOIS
Hor. Scale.
Vert. Scale.
N. PETERS, Photo-Lithographer, Washington, D. C.

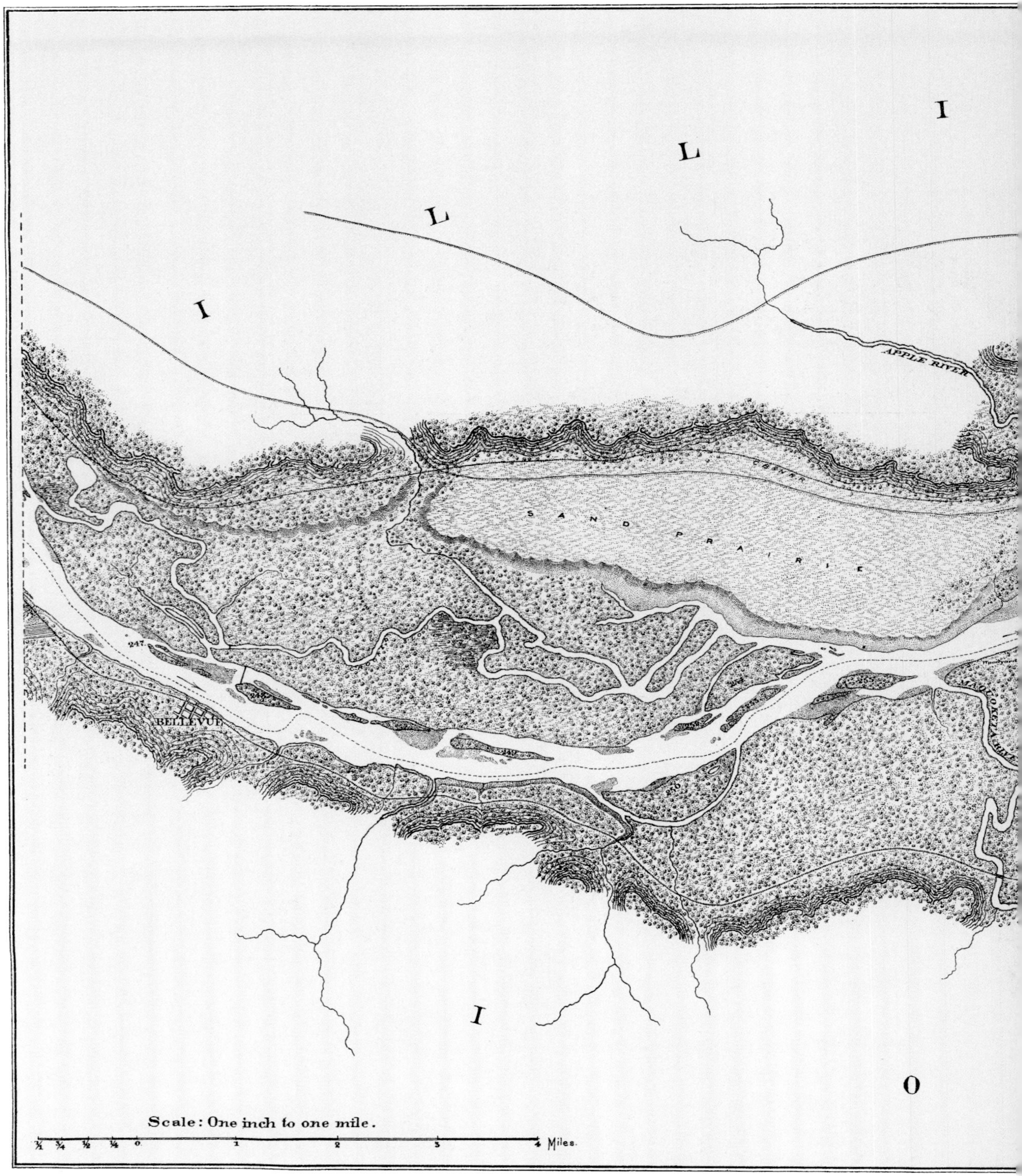

MAP 13
BELLEVUE, IOWA
MAQUOKETA RIVER
SAVANNA, ILLINOIS
SABULA, IOWA

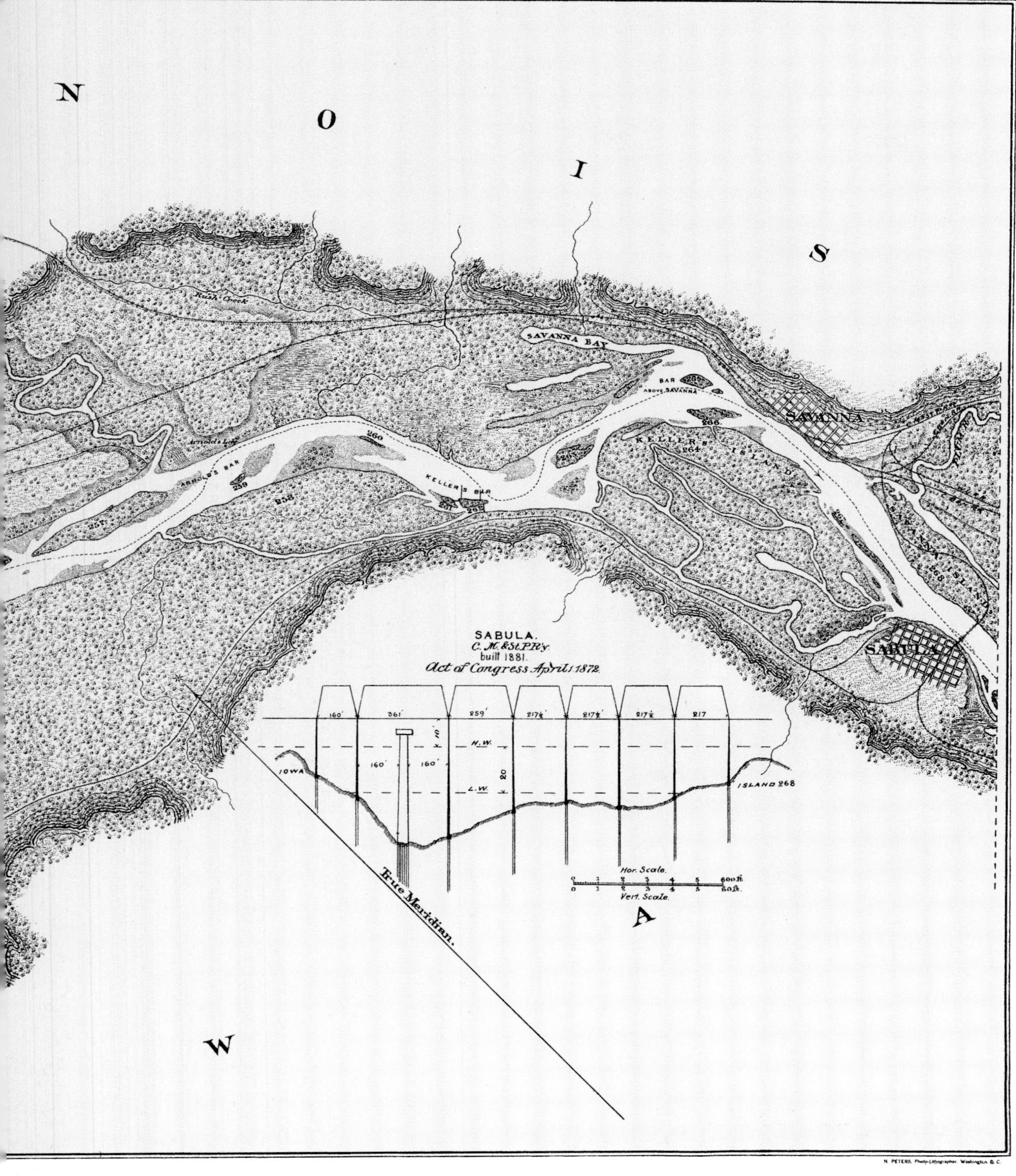
N
O
I
S
SAVANNA BAY
BAR ABOVE SAVANNA
SAVANNA
KELLER'S ISLAND
KELLER'S BAR
ARNOLD'S BAR
SAVANNA ISLAND
SABULA
SABULA.
C. M. & St. P. R'y.
built 1881.
Act of Congress April 1 1872.
160'
361'
259'
217½'
217½'
217½'
217
H. W.
L. W.
IOWA
ISLAND 268
Hor. Scale.
Vert. Scale.
True Meridian.
A
W
N. PETERS, Photo-Lithographer, Washington, D.C.

MAP 14
THOMPSON, ILLINOIS
FULTON, ILLINOIS
LYONS, IOWA
CLINTON, IOWA
ALBANY, ILLINOIS
CAMANCHE, IOWA

Lamb & Son's Saw Mill, Clinton, Iowa (PLATE 49)

Wagon Bridge at Fulton, Ill. (PLATE 50)

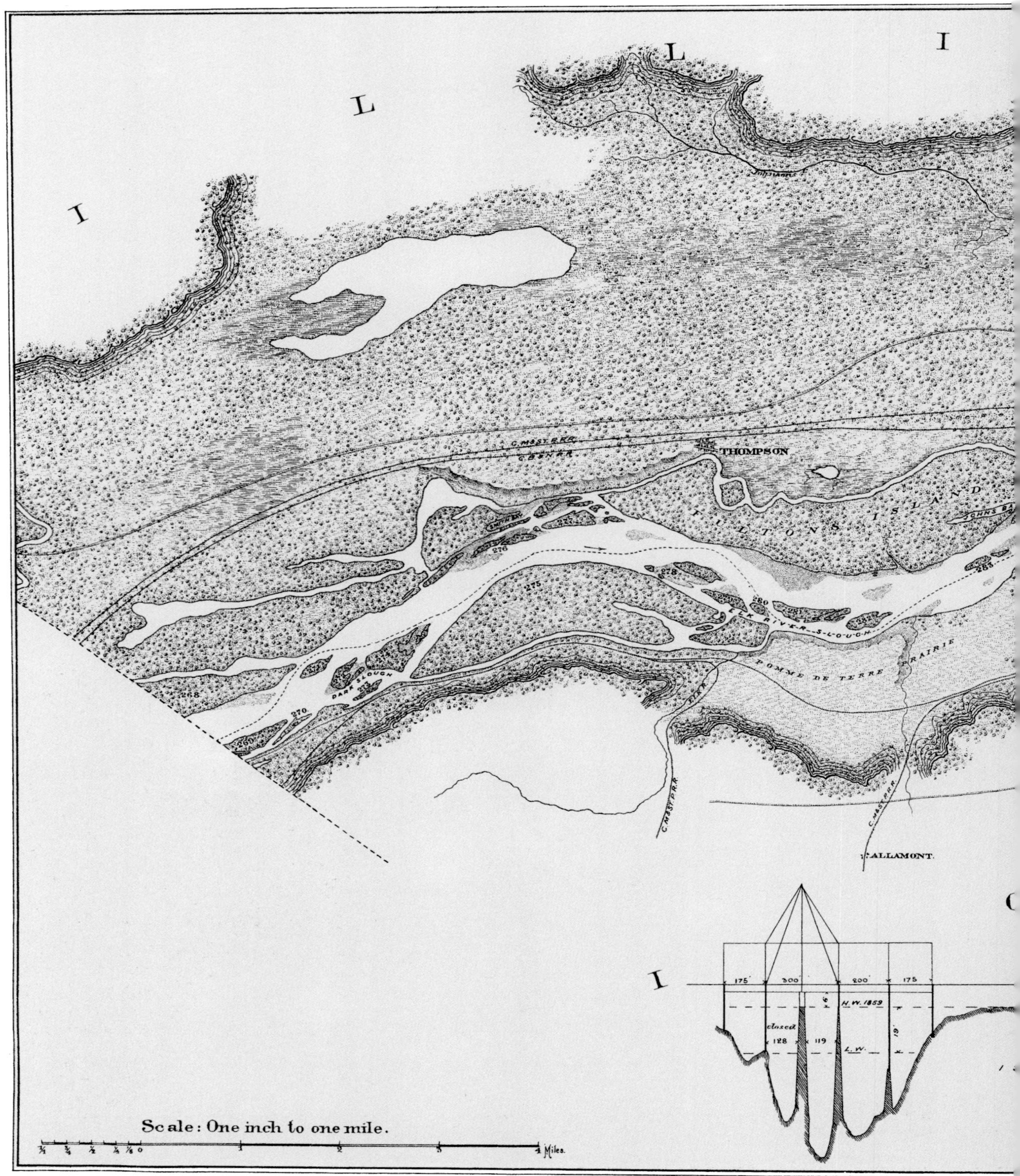

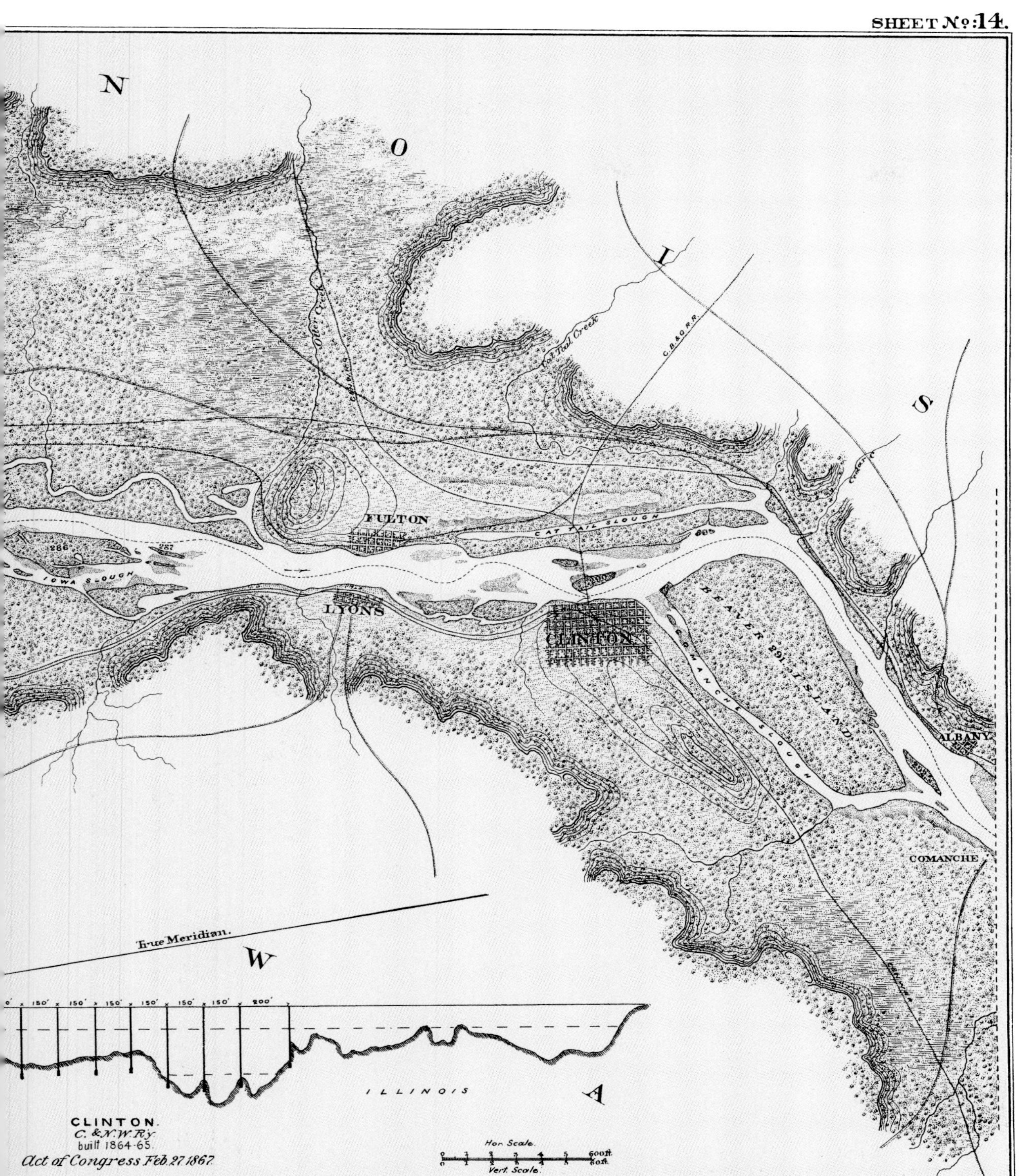
N
O
I
S
W
A
FULTON
LYONS
CLINTON
ALBANY
COMANCHE
CAT TAIL SLOUGH
IOWA SLOUGH
BEAVER ISLAND
COMANCHE SLOUGH
Cat Tail Creek
C.B.&Q.R.R.
True Meridian.
ILLINOIS
CLINTON.
C. & N. W. Ry.
built 1864-65.
Act of Congress Feb. 27. 1867.
Hor. Scale.
Vert. Scale.
N. PETERS, Photo-Lithographer, Washington, D. C.

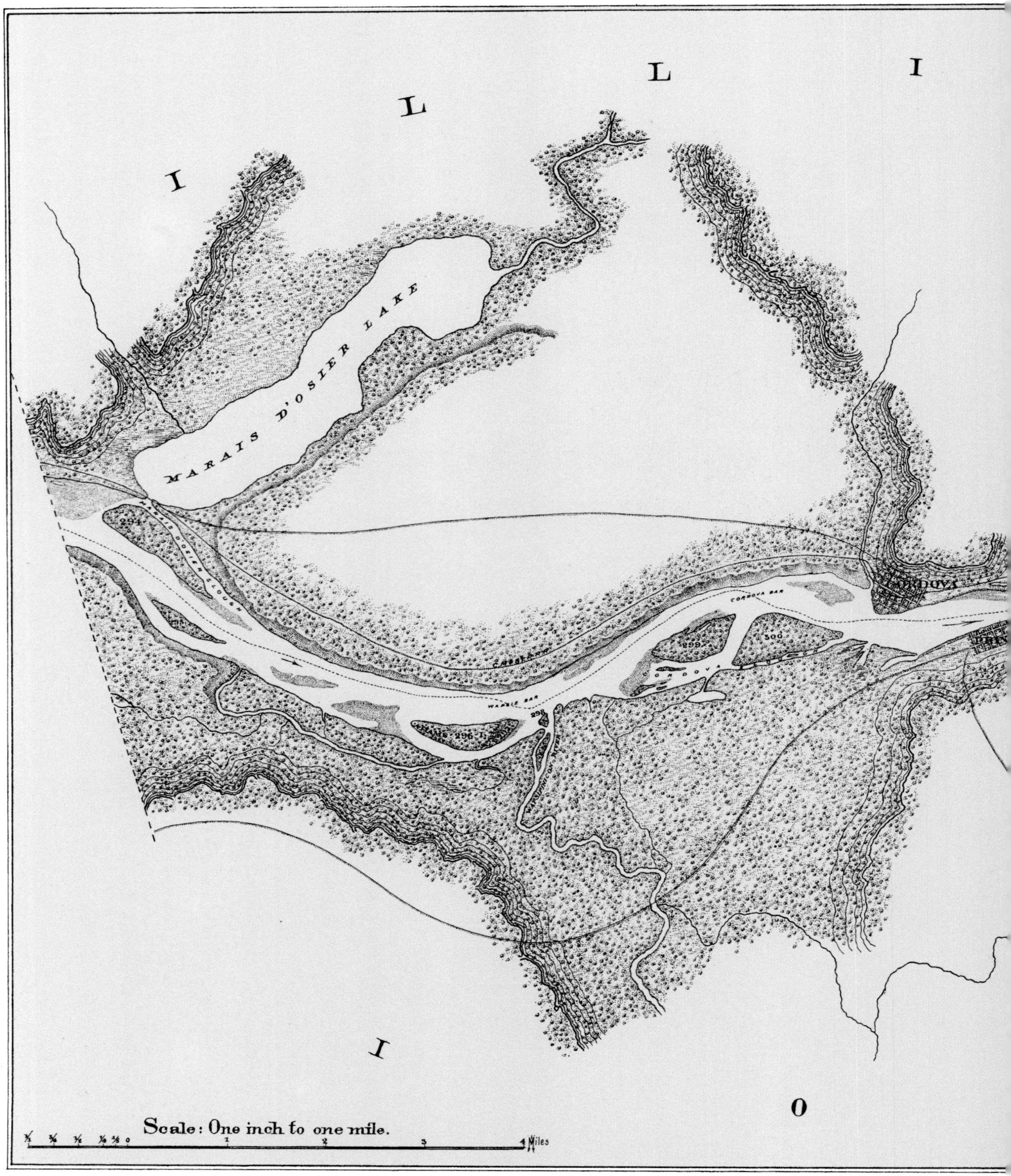

MAP 15
CORDOVA, ILLINOIS
PRINCETON, IOWA
PORT BYRON, ILLINOIS
LE CLAIRE, IOWA
HAMPTON, ILLINOIS
WATERTOWN, ILLINOIS
CAMPBELL'S ISLAND

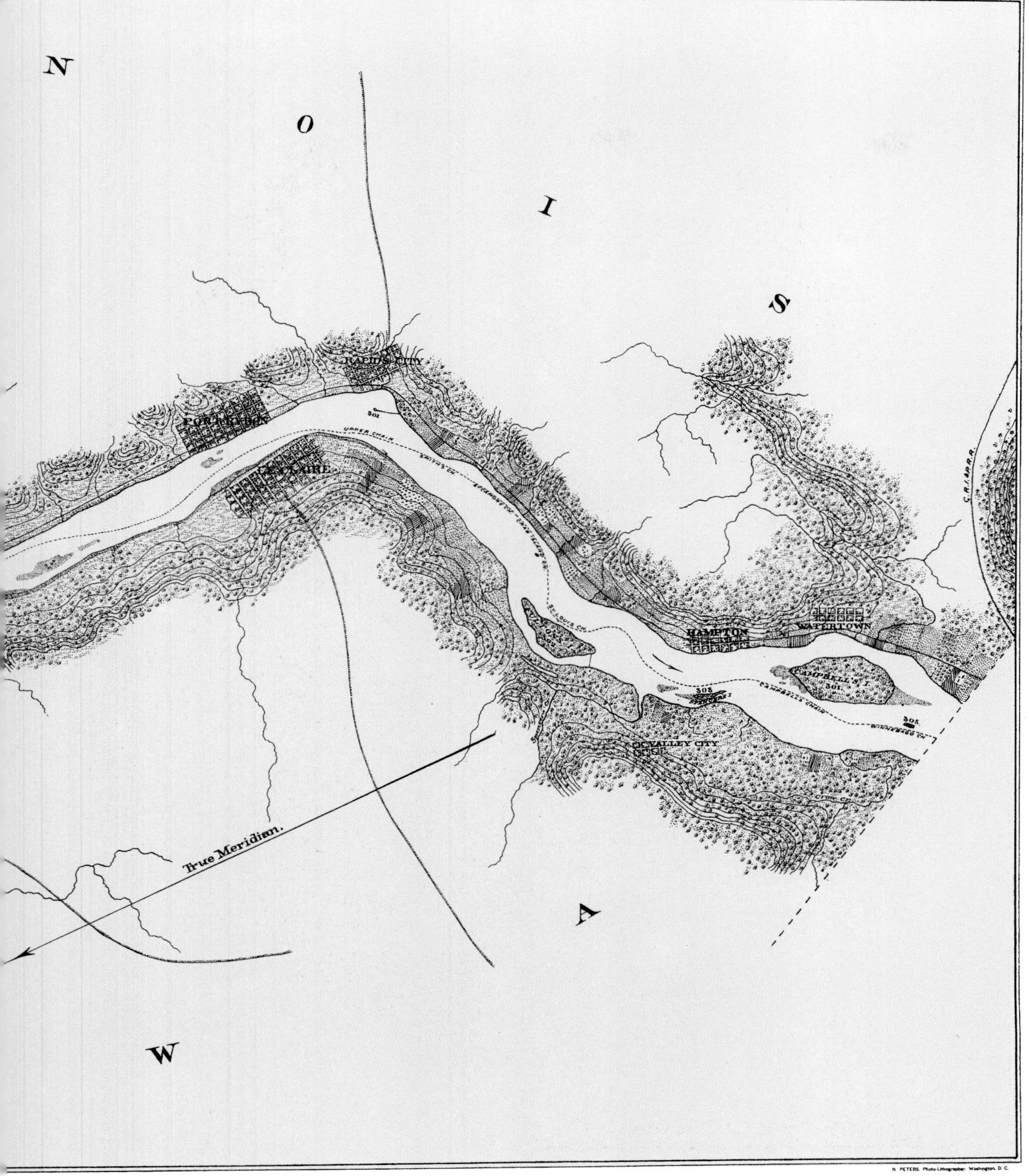
SHEET No: 15.
N
O
I
S
A
W
RAPIDS CITY
PORT BYRON
LE CLAIRE
301
UPPER CHAIN
SMITH'S CH.
HAMPTON
WATERTOWN
CAMPBELL'S I.
301.
303
CAMPBELL'S CHAIN
305
WINNEBAGO CH.
VALLEY CITY
C.R.I.&P.R.R.
True Meridian.
N. PETERS, Photo-Lithographer, Washington, D.C.

MAP 16

ROCK ISLAND RAPIDS
MOLINE, ILLINOIS
SYLVAN WATER
DAVENPORT, IOWA
ROCK ISLAND, ILLINOIS
MILAN, ILLINOIS
ROCK RIVER
ANDALUSIA SLOUGH
ANDALUSIA, ILLINOIS
BUFFALO, IOWA
MONTPELIER, IOWA

Ice Gorge at Rock Island, Ill. (PLATE 52)

U.S. Government Bridge at Rock Island, Ill. (PLATE 53)

Machine Shops of Rock Island Arsenal (PLATE 54)

Front St.—Davenport, Ia. during High water 1888 (PLATE 55)

Front St.—Davenport during High water 1888 (PLATE 56)

Second Ave.—Rock Island, Ill. during High water 1888 (PLATE 57)

Kahlke's Boatyard—Rock Island, Ill. (PLATE 58)

Raftboat in construction (Boatyard of Kahlke Bros, Rock Island, Ill.) (PLATE 59)

Boatyard of Kahlke Bros, Rock Island, Ill. (PLATE 60)

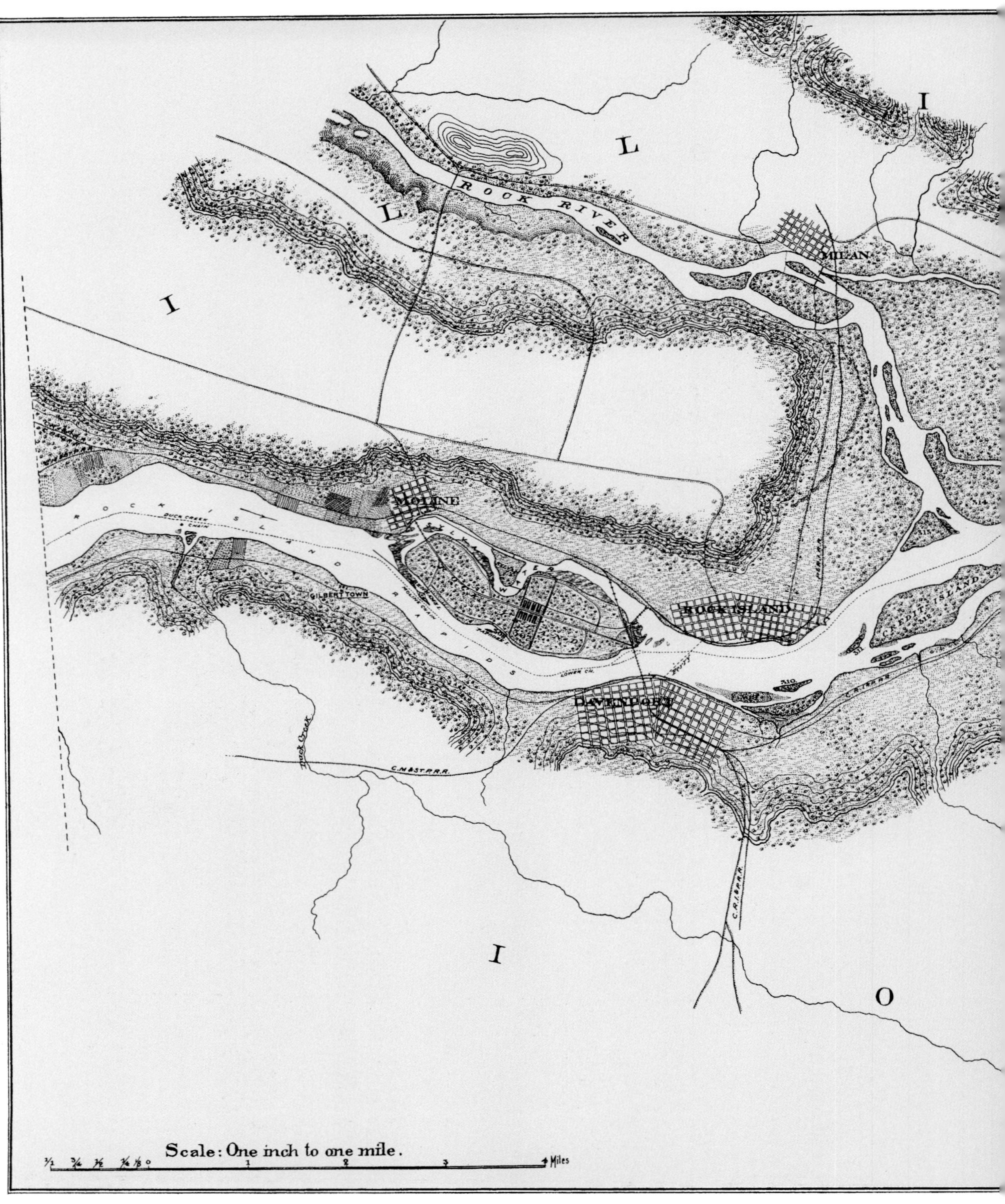

SHEET No:16.

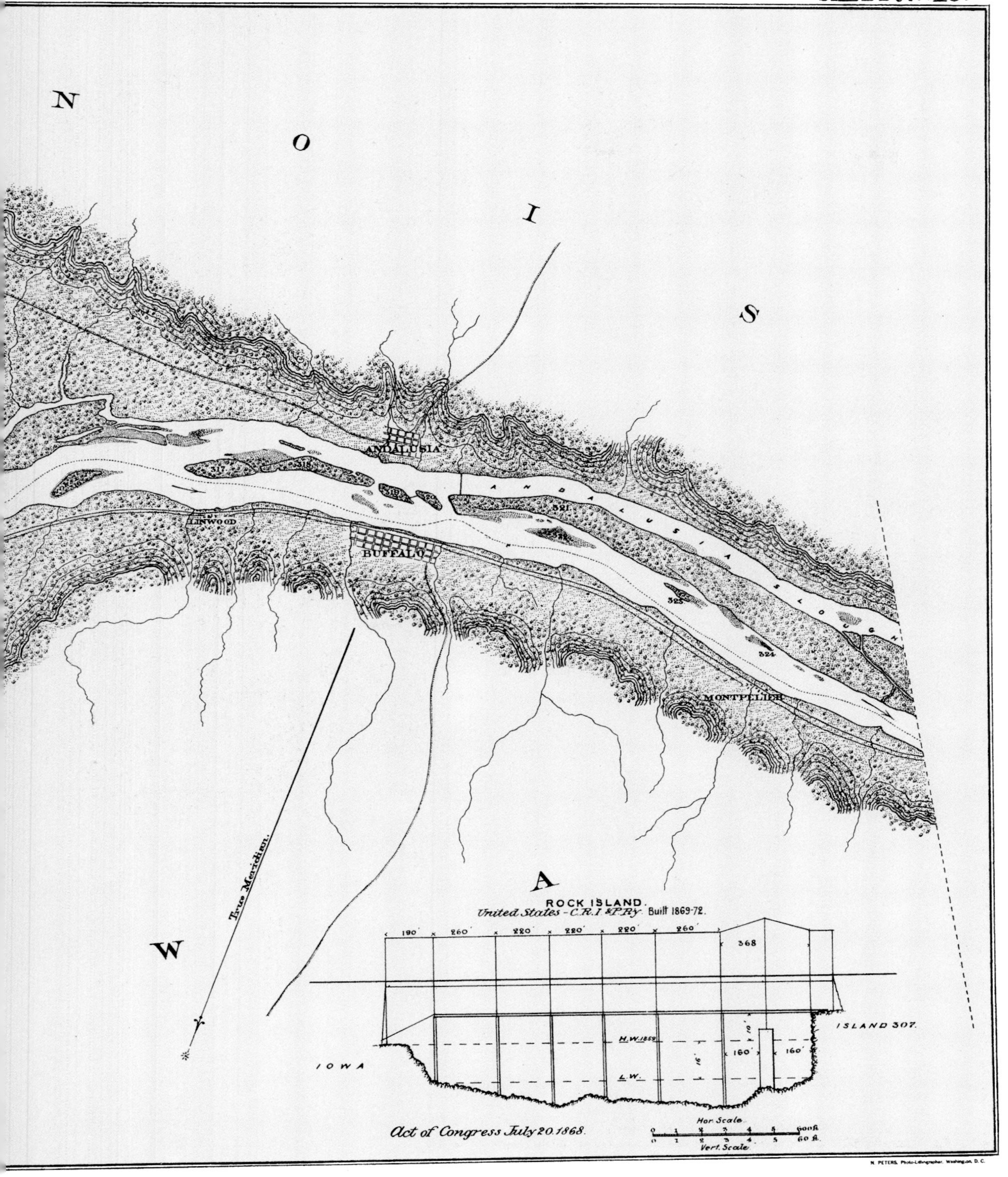
N
O
I
S
ANDALUSIA
ANDALUSIA SLOUGH
LINWOOD
BUFFALO
MONTPELIER
321
323
324
A
W
True Meridian
ROCK ISLAND.
United States - C.R.I. & P.Ry. Built 1869-72.
190'
260'
220'
220'
220'
260'
368
ISLAND 307.
H.W. 1859
L.W.
160'
160'
IOWA
Act of Congress July 20.1868.
Hor. Scale
Vert. Scale
N. PETERS, Photo-Lithographer, Washington, D.C.

MAP 17
FAIRPORT, IOWA
WYOMING SLOUGH
MUSCATINE, IOWA

Muscatine, Ia. (PLATE 61)

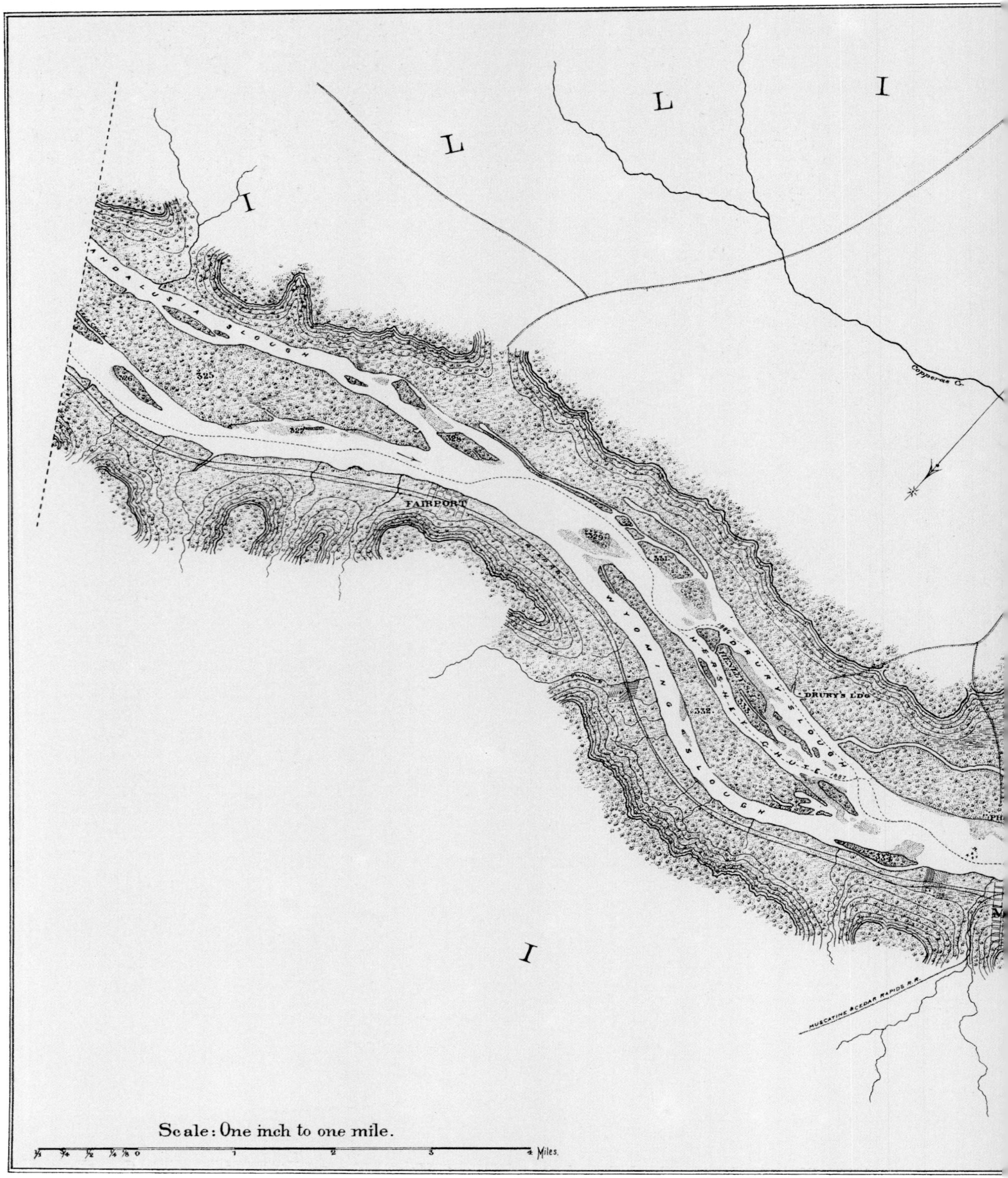

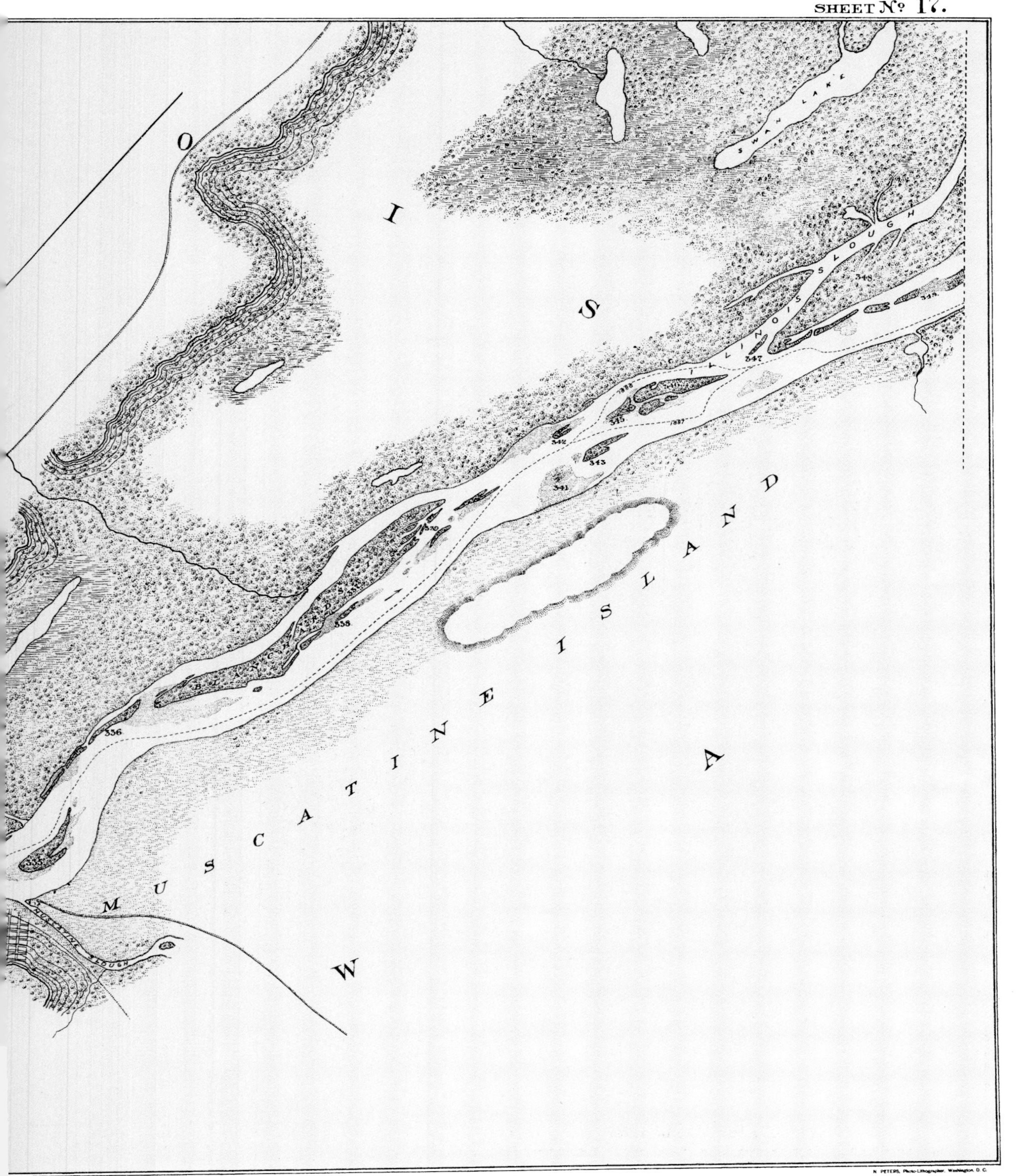
O
I
S
SWAN LAKE
ILLINOIS SLOUGH
MUSCATINE ISLAND
W
A
N. PETERS, Photo-Lithographer, Washington, D.C.

MAP 18

IOWA RIVER

NEW BOSTON, ILLINOIS

KEITHSBURG, ILLINOIS

Iowa Central R. R. Bridge at Keithsburg, Ill. (PLATE 62)

Closing Dam—Whisky Chute (PLATE 63)

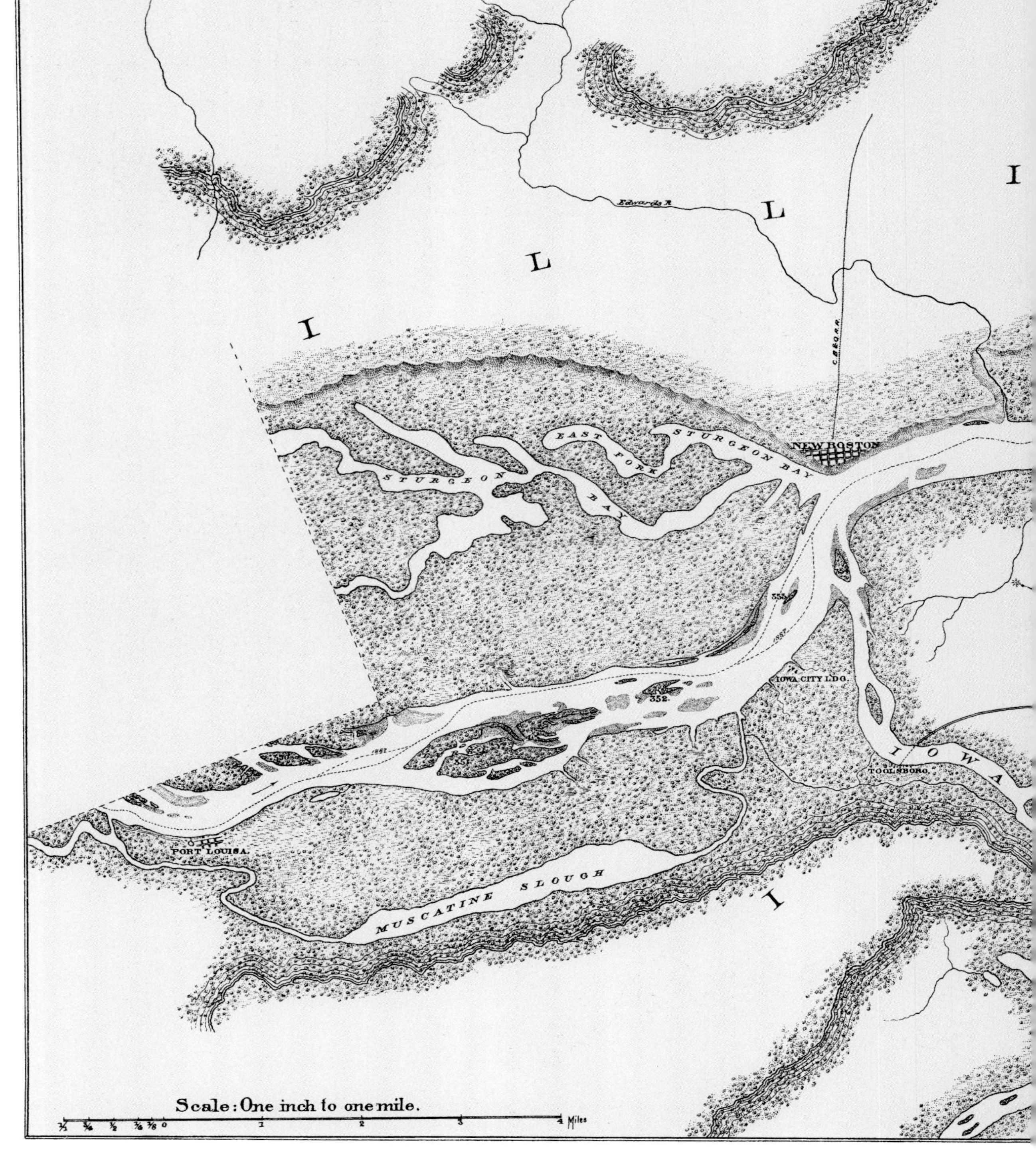

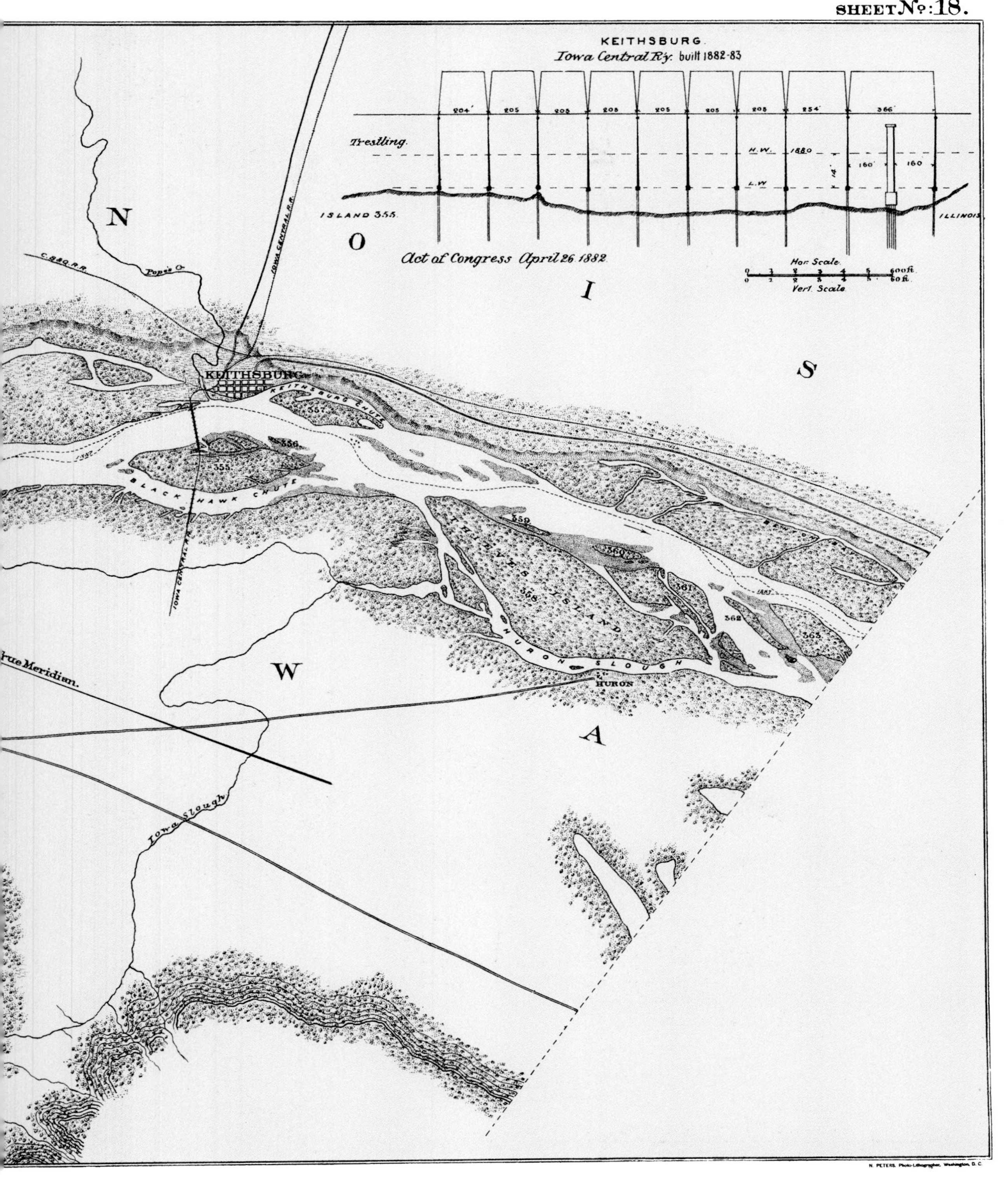
KEITHSBURG.
Iowa Central Ry. built 1882-83
Trestling.
H.W. 1880
L.W.
ISLAND 355.
ILLINOIS.
Act of Congress April 26 1882.
Hor. Scale.
Vert. Scale.
N
O
I
S
W
A
KEITHSBURG
KEITHSBURG CHUTE
BLACK HAWK CHUTE
HURON SLOUGH
HURON
Iowa Slough
True Meridian.
C.B.&Q.R.R.
IOWA CENTRAL R.R.
N. PETERS. Photo-Lithographer, Washington, D.C.

MAP 19
BENTON, ILLINOIS
OQUAWKA, ILLINOIS
OTTER SLOUGH
BURLINGTON, IOWA
SHOKOKON SLOUGH
SHOKOKON, ILLINOIS

Closing dam in Otter chute (PLATE 64)

C. B. & Q. Ry Bridge at Burlington, Ia. (after reconstruction) (PLATE 66)

River Front at Burlington, Ia. (PLATE 67)

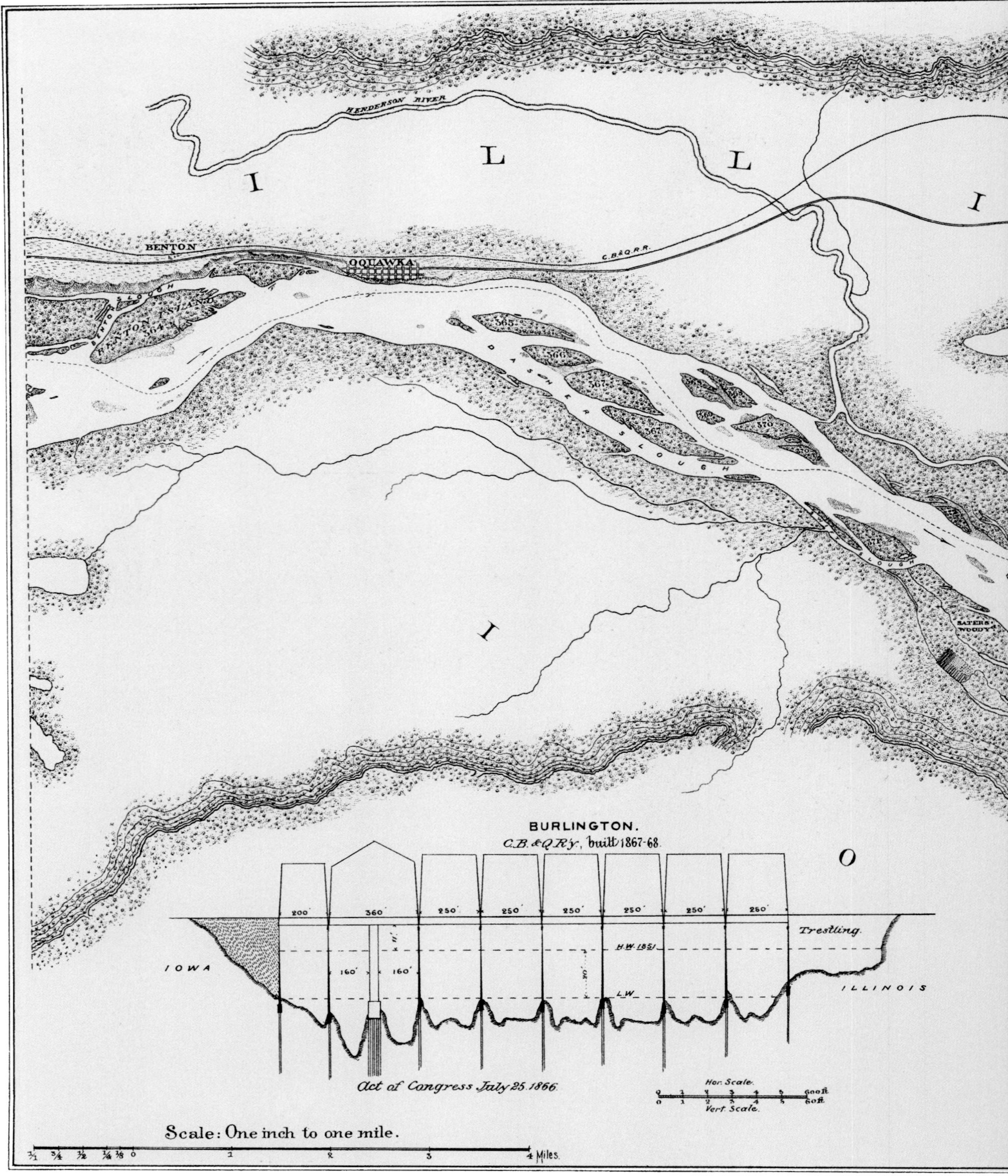

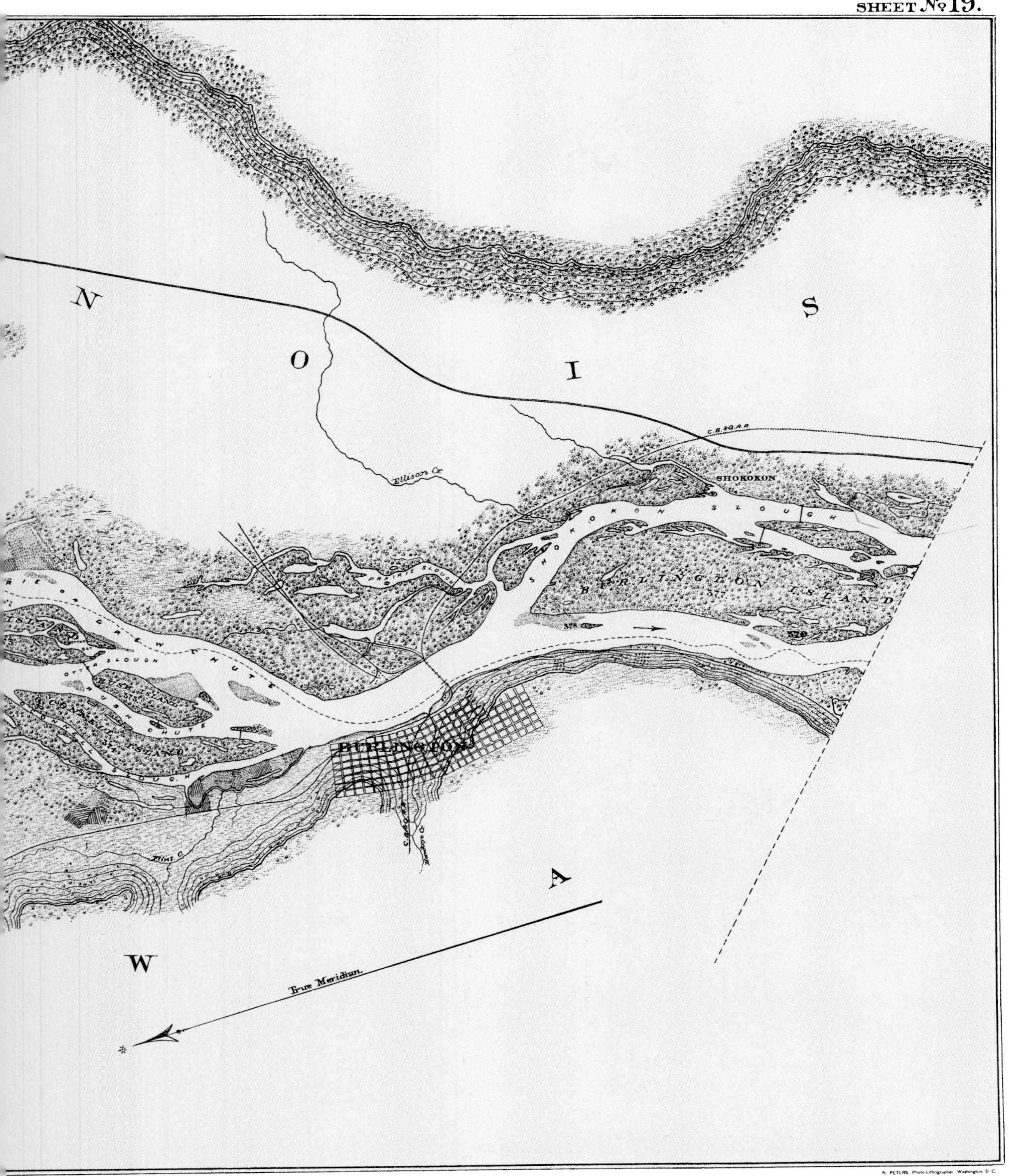
N
O
I
S
C.B.&Q.R.R.
SHOKOKON
Ellison Cr.
SHOKOKON SLOUGH
BURLINGTON ISLAND
BURLINGTON
A
W
True Meridian
N. PETERS, Photo-Lithographer, Washington, D.C.

MAP 20

SKUNK RIVER

DALLAS CITY, ILLINOIS

NIOTA, ILLINOIS

FORT MADISON, IOWA

NIOTA CHUTE

NAUVOO, ILLINOIS

MONTROSE, IOWA

UPPER CHAIN, DES MOINES RAPIDS

Fort Madison, Ia. (PLATE 68)

Iowa State Penitentiary—Fort Madison, Ia. (PLATE 69)

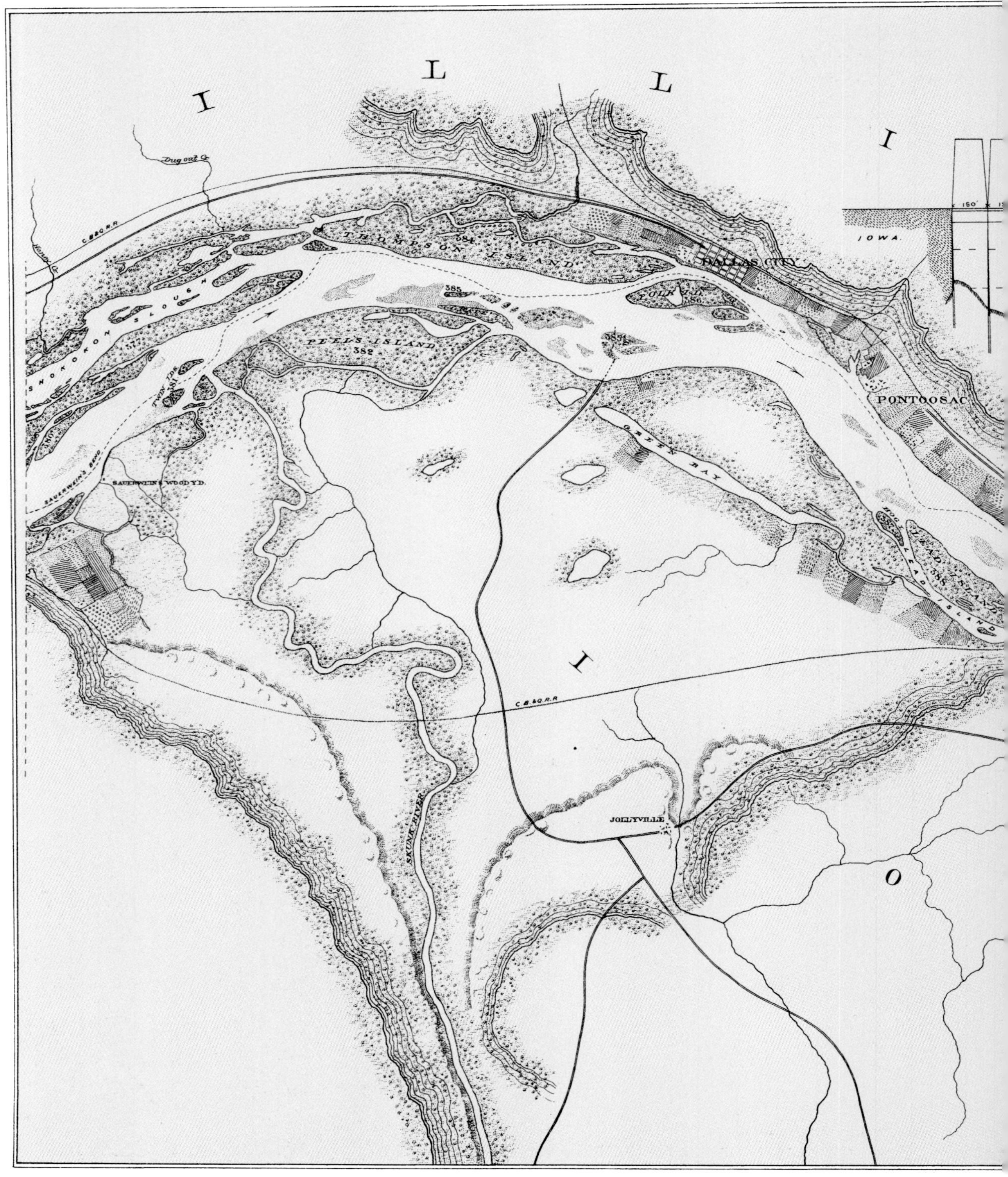

FORT MADISON.
C. S. F & C. Ry. built 1887-88.
Act of Congress May 25. 1872.

274.5 237.5 237.5 237.5 237.5

Trestling
ISLAND 391.

True Meridian.

Hor. Scale.
Vert. Scale.

O I S

APPANOOCE
NIOTA
NIOTA CHUTE
NIOTA ISLAND
FORT MADISON
NAUVOO
SOLFERINO
UPPER CHAIN
HEAD OF RAPIDS
MONTROSE
DEVILS I.
DOBSON SLOUGH

W A

Scale: One inch to one mile.
0 1 2 3 4 Miles

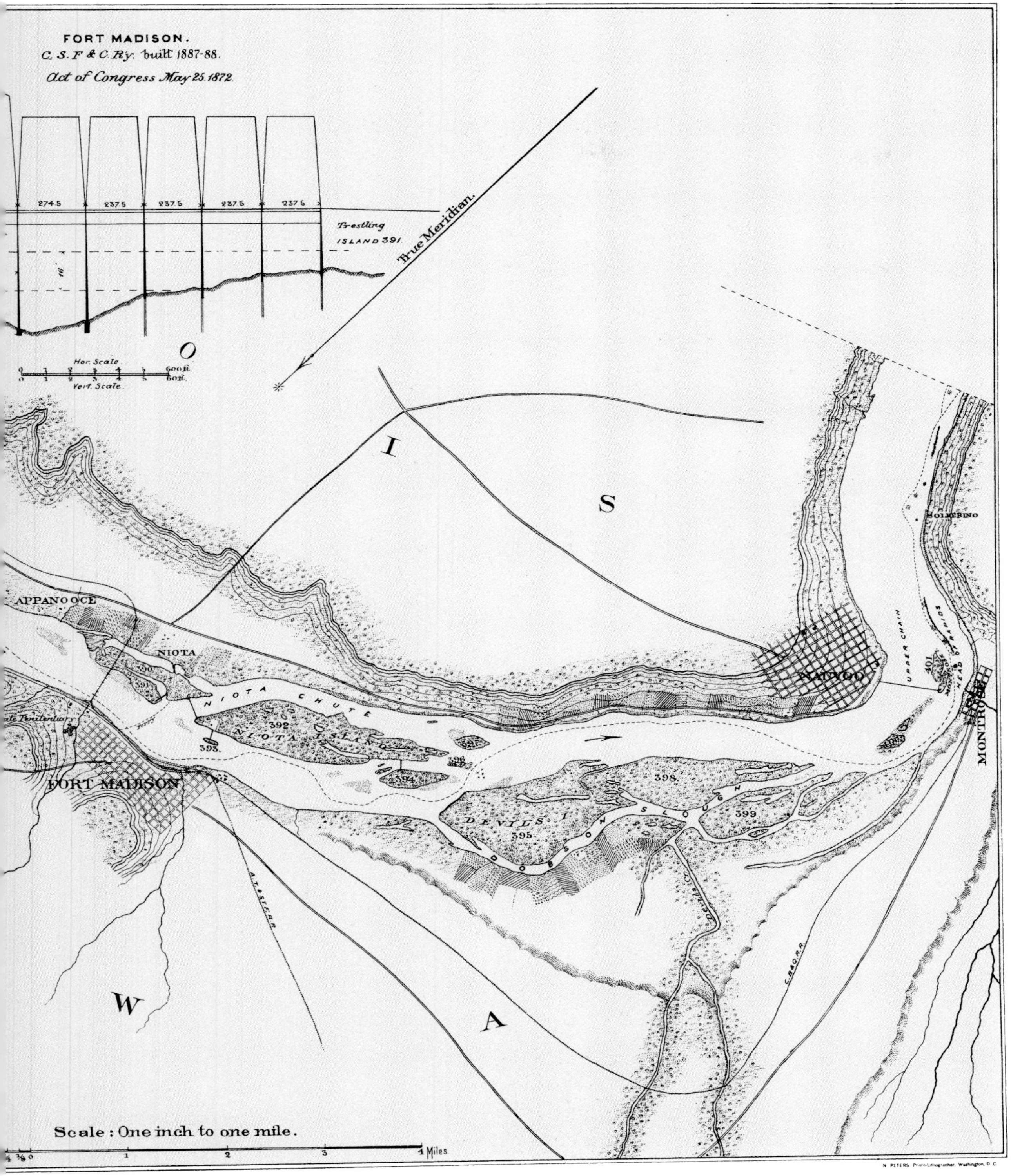

N. PETERS, Photo-Lithographer, Washington, D.C.

MAP 21
DES MOINES RAPIDS CANAL
KEOKUK, IOWA
HAMILTON, ILLINOIS
DES MOINES RIVER
WARSAW, ILLINOIS
ALEXANDRIA, MISSOURI

Mechanic's Rock (PLATE 70)

Entrance to Guard Lock (PLATE 73)

Middle Lock and Dry Dock (PLATE 74)

Lower Lock (PLATE 75)

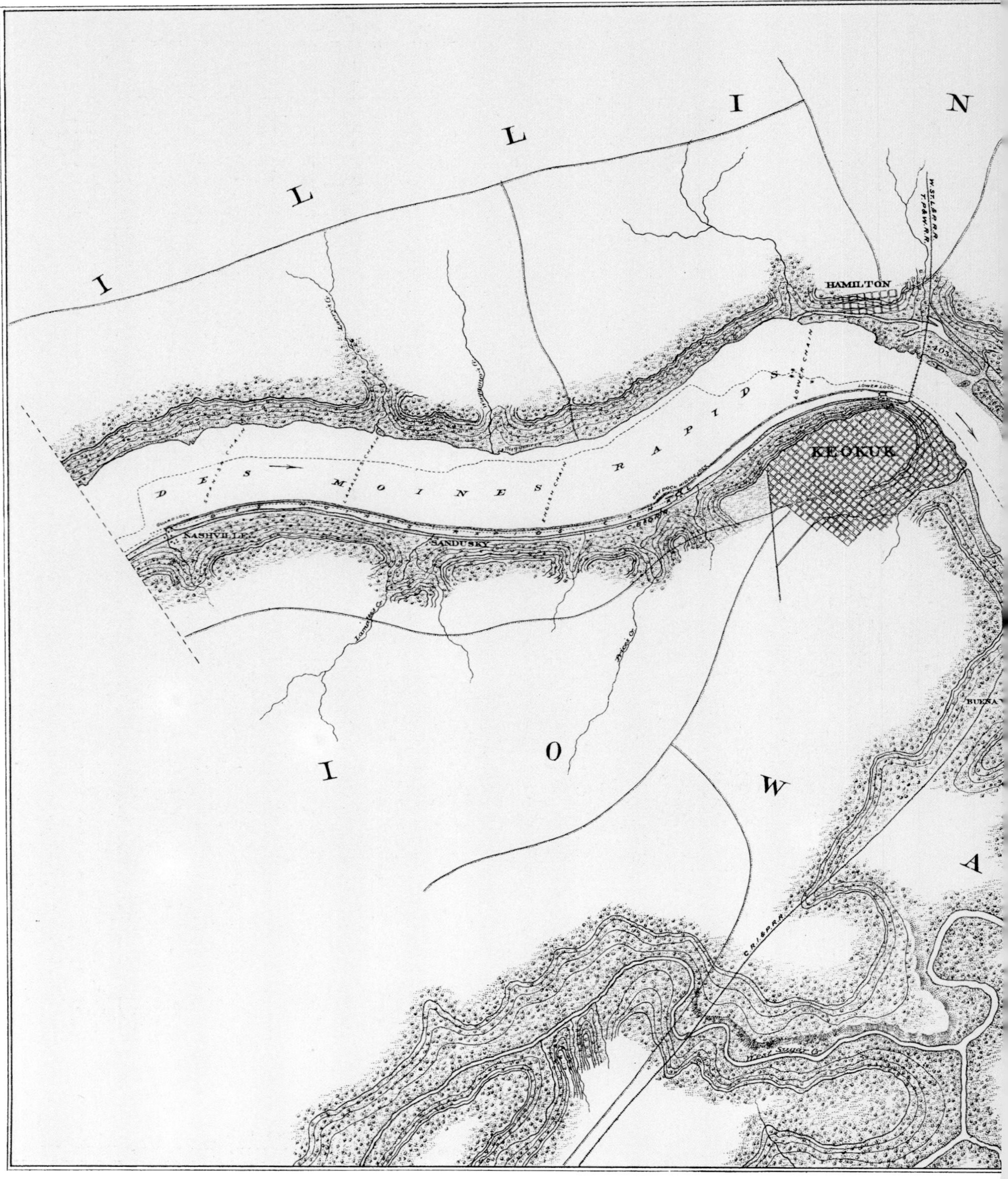

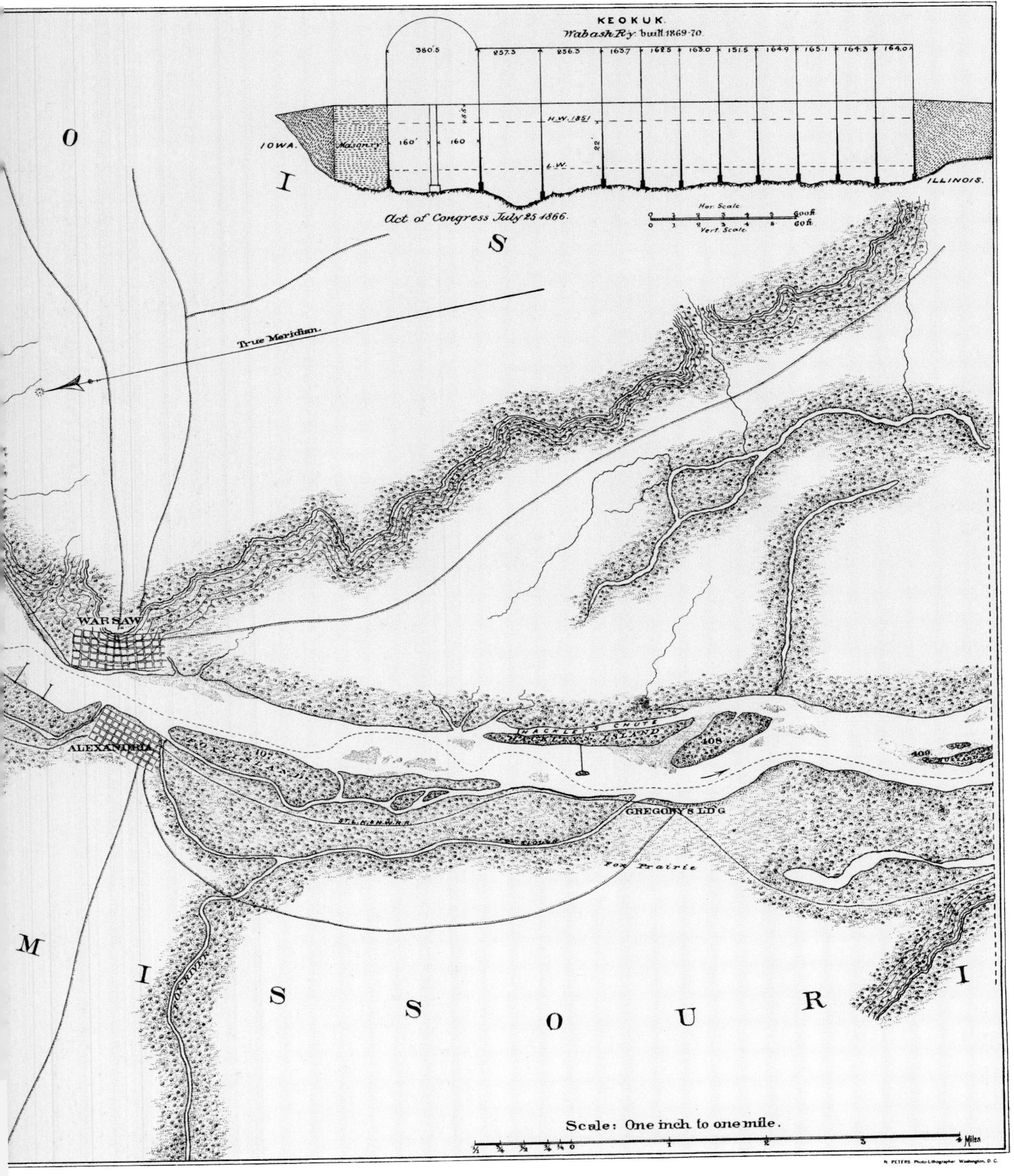
KEOKUK.
Wabash Ry. built 1869-70.
IOWA.
ILLINOIS.
Act of Congress July 25 1866.
True Meridian.
WARSAW
ALEXANDRIA
GREGORY'S LDG
Fox Prairie
Scale: One inch to one mile.
M I S S O U R I

MAP 22
CANTON, MISSOURI

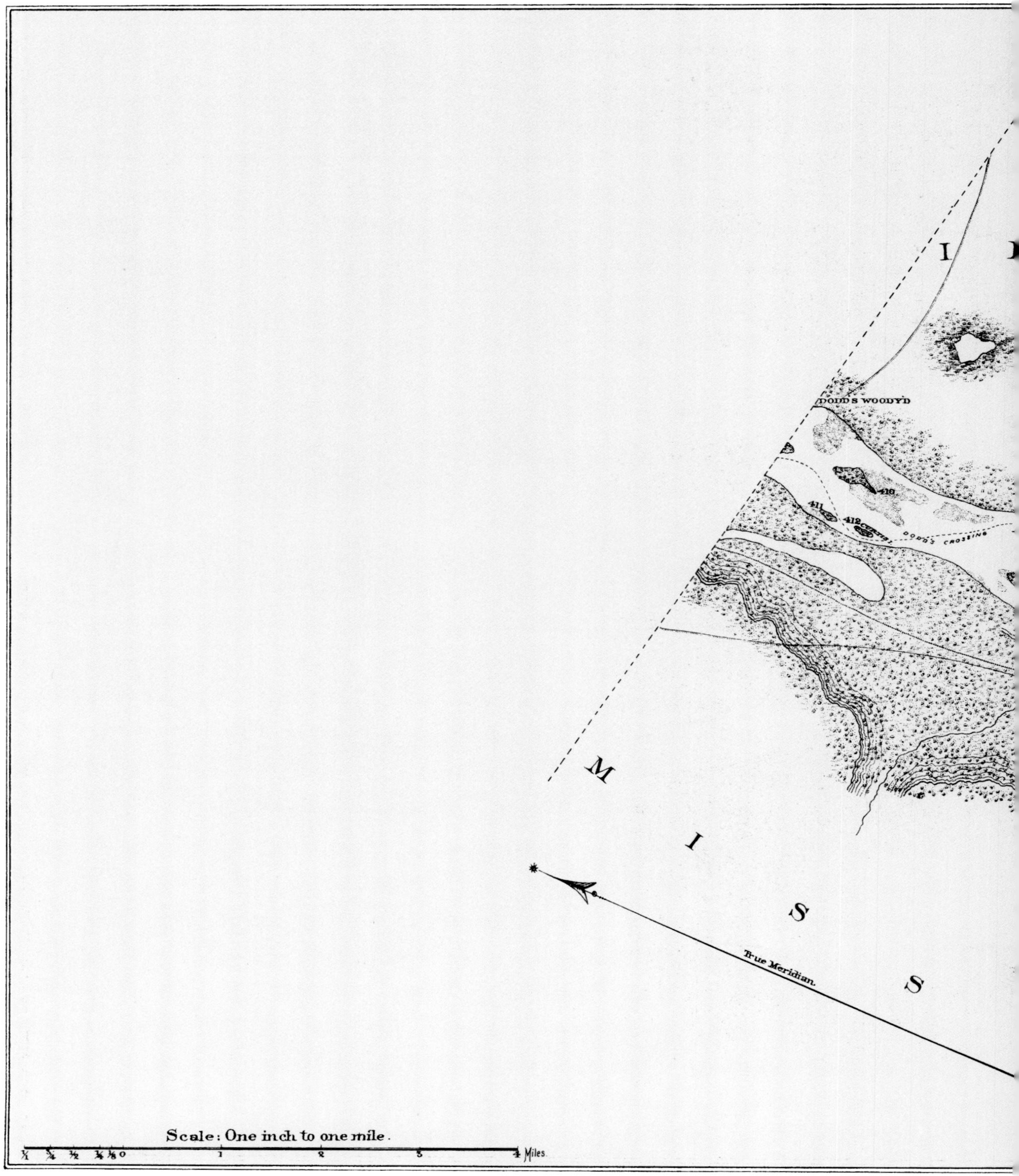

Scale: One inch to one mile.

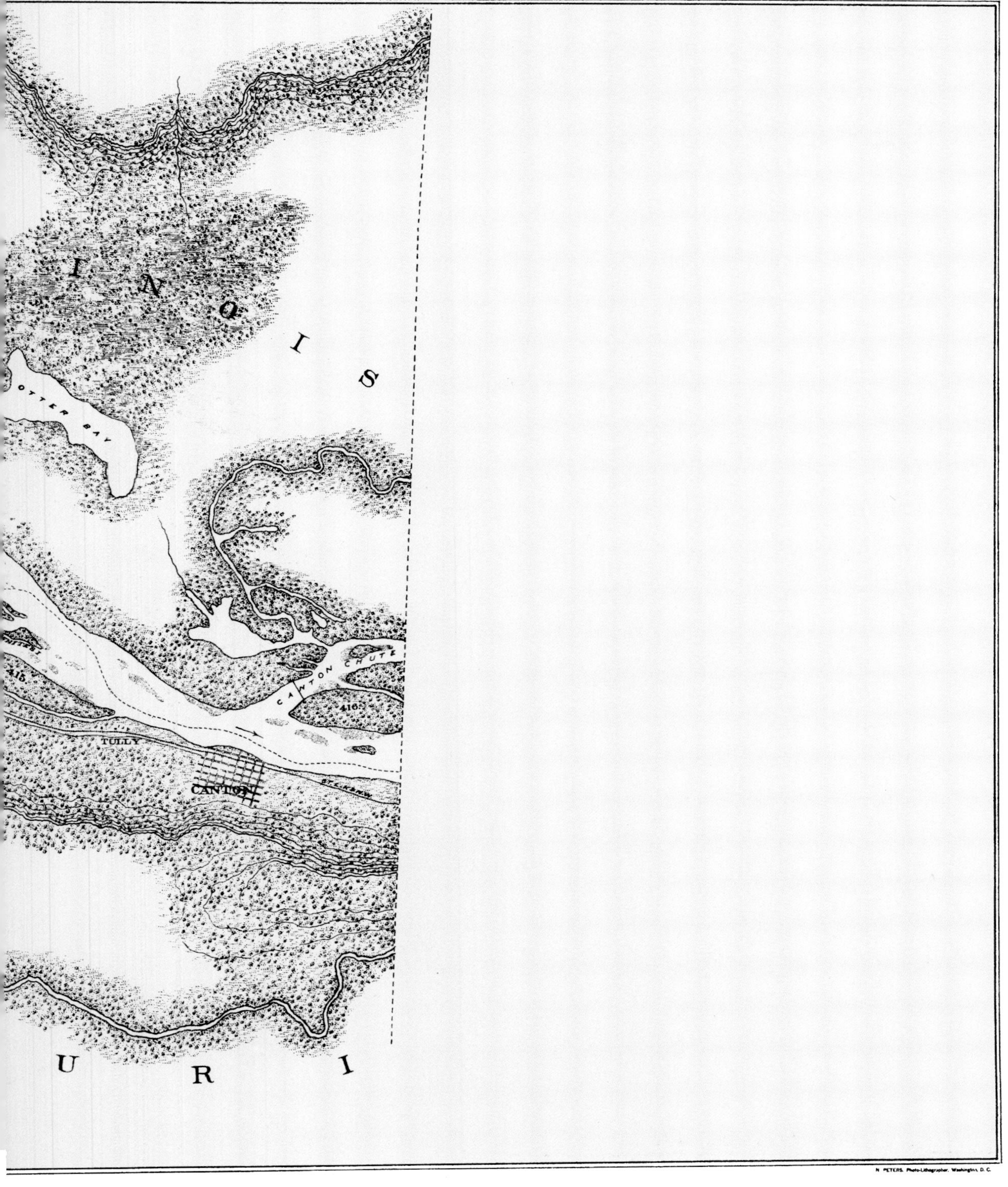

N. PETERS, Photo-Lithographer, Washington, D.C.

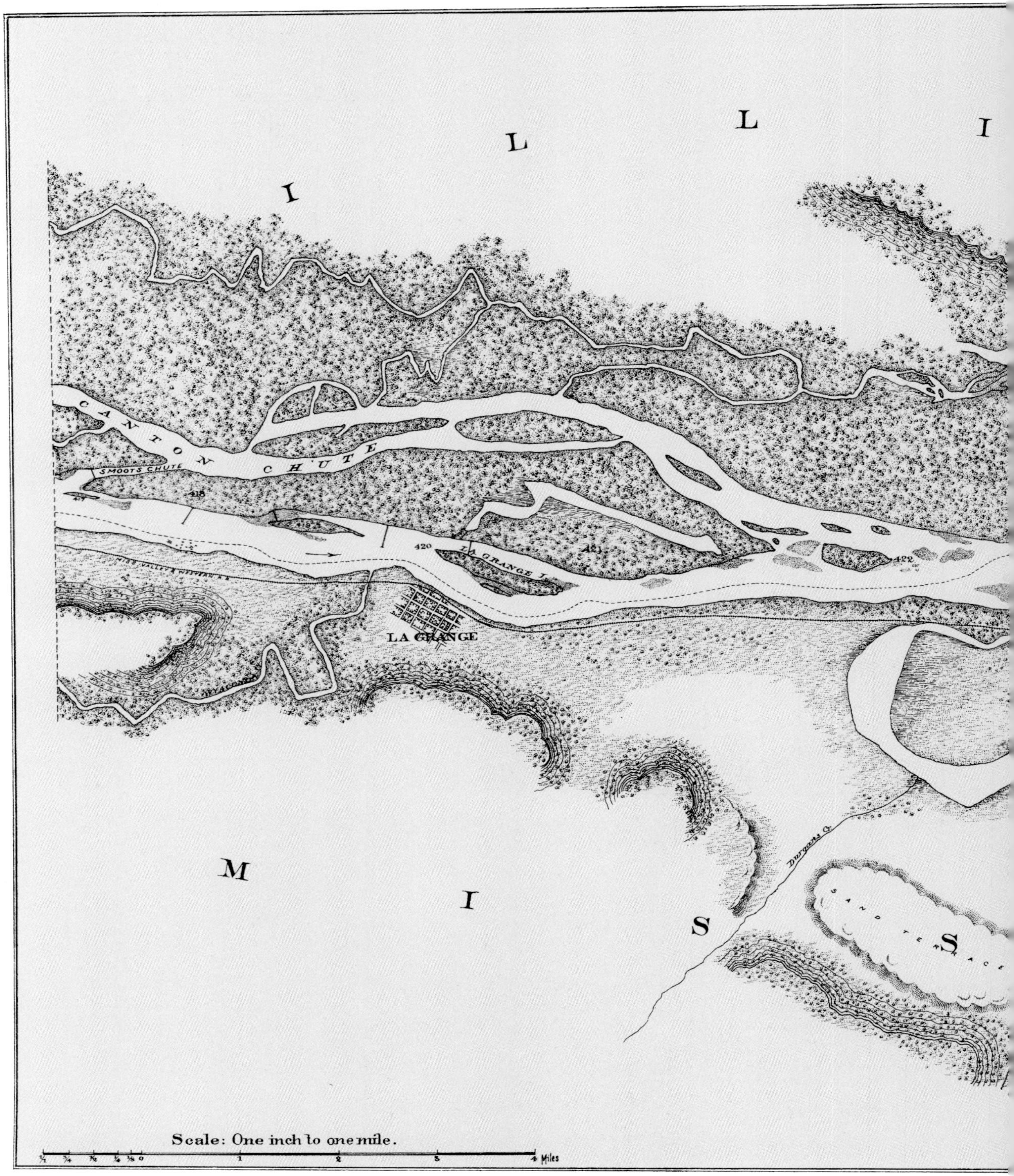

MAP 23
CANTON CHUTE
LA GRANGE, MISSOURI
QUINCY, ILLINOIS

C. B. & Q. R. R. Bridge at Quincy, Ill.
(PLATE 78)

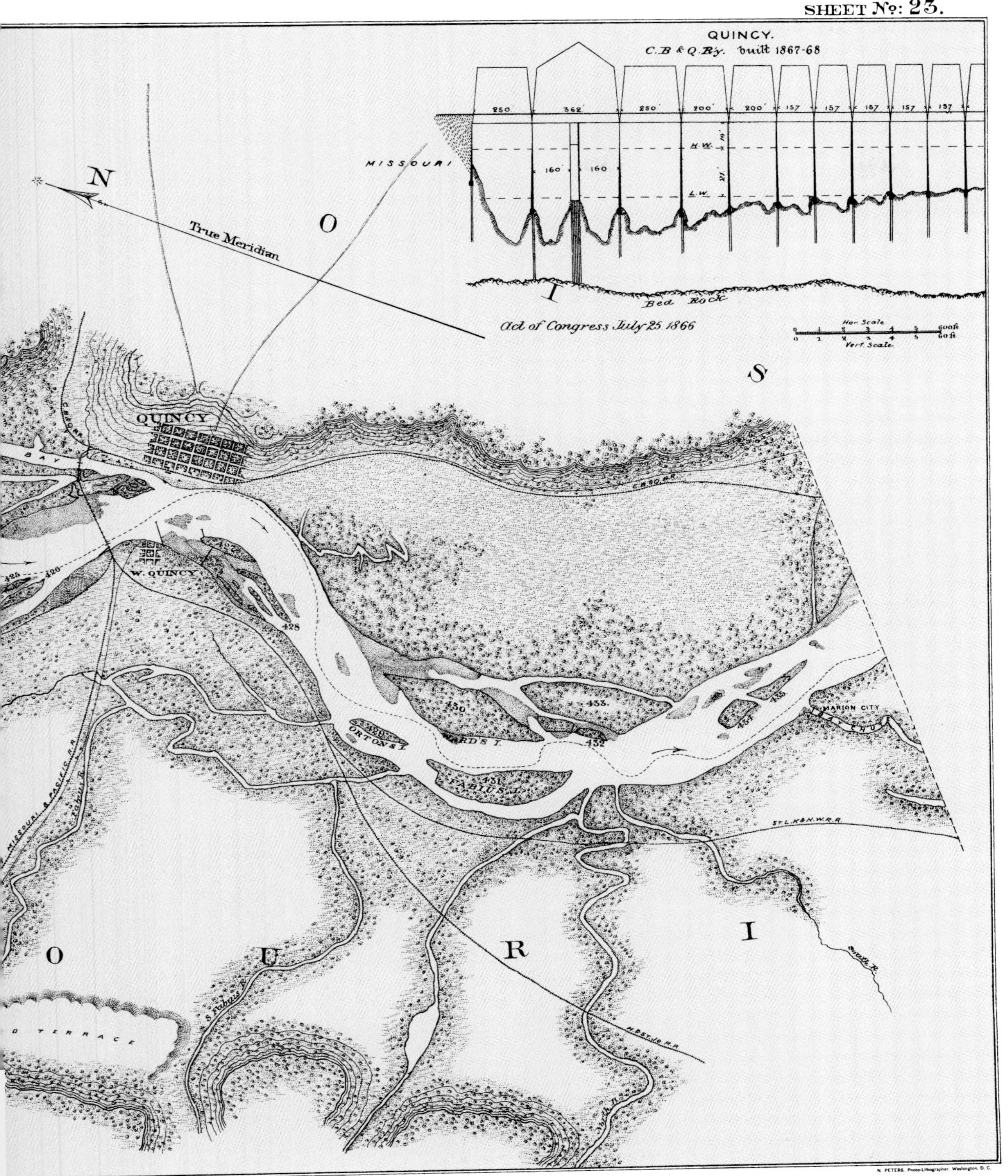
QUINCY.
C.B.&Q.Ry. built 1867-68
MISSOURI
Bed Rock
Act of Congress July 25 1866
Hor. Scale
Vert. Scale
True Meridian
N
O
I
S
QUINCY
W. QUINCY
MARION CITY
ST L.K.&N.W.R.R.
O
U
R
I
TERRACE
N. PETERS, Photo-Lithographer, Washington, D.C.

MAP 24
HANNIBAL, MISSOURI
SAVERTON, MISSOURI

Hannibal, Mo. (PLATE 79)

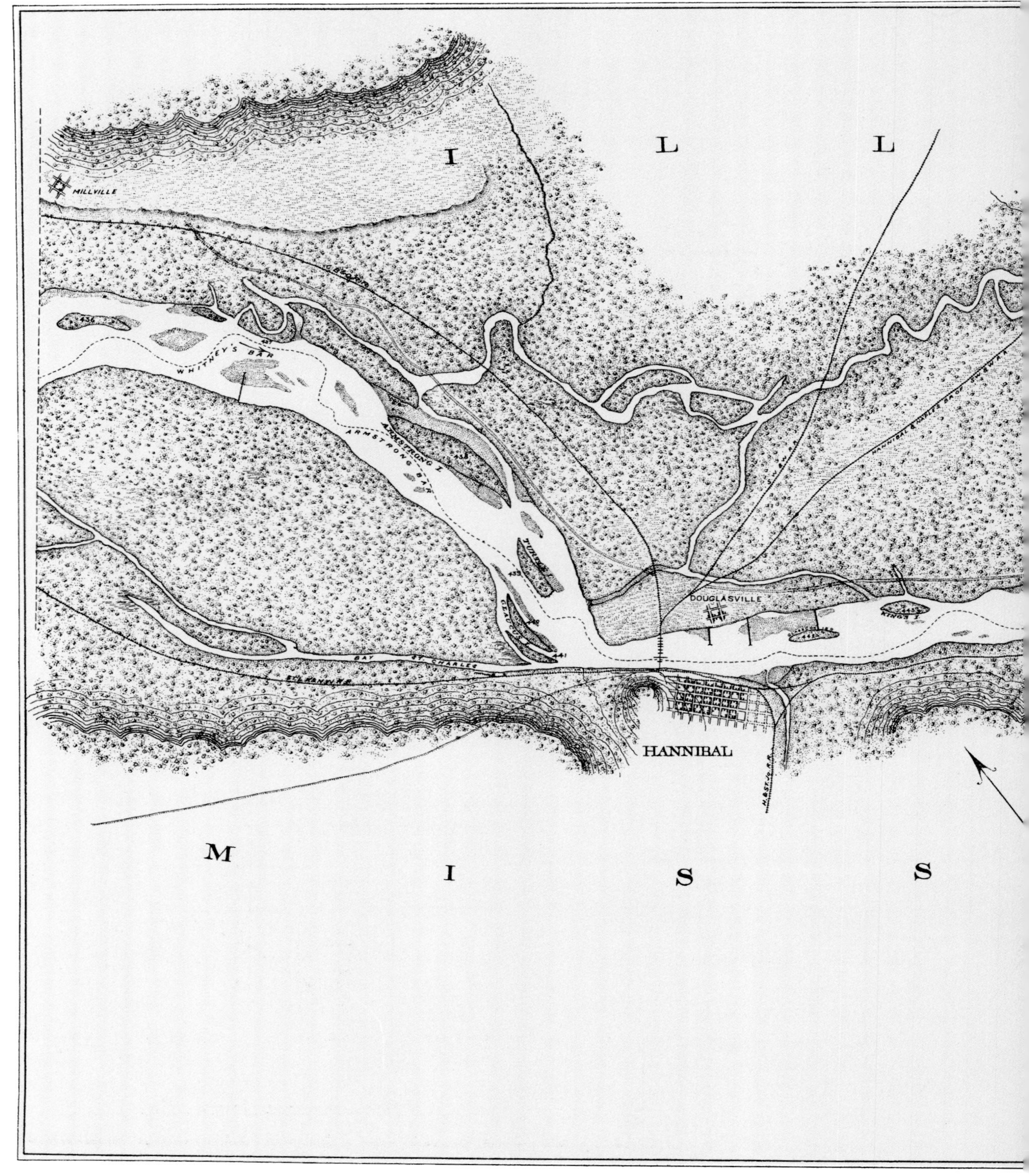

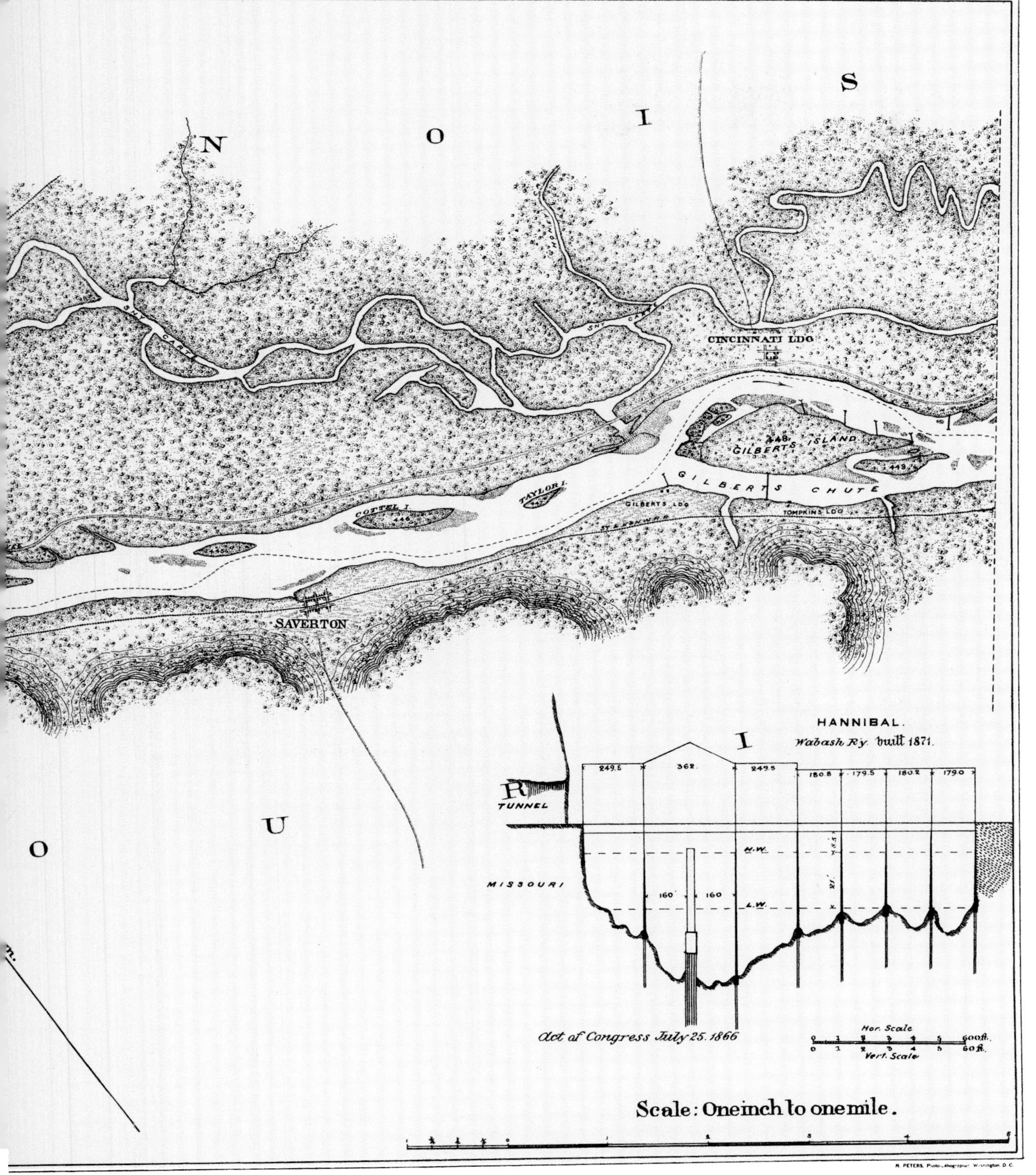
SHEET No: 24.
N
O
I
S
CINCINNATI LDG
GILBERTS ISLAND
GILBERTS CHUTE
GILBERTS LDG
TOMPKINS LDG
TAYLOR I.
COTTEL I.
SAVERTON
HANNIBAL.
Wabash Ry. built 1871.
I
R
TUNNEL
O
U
MISSOURI
H.W.
L.W.
Act of Congress July 25. 1866
Hor. Scale
Vert. Scale
Scale: One inch to one mile.

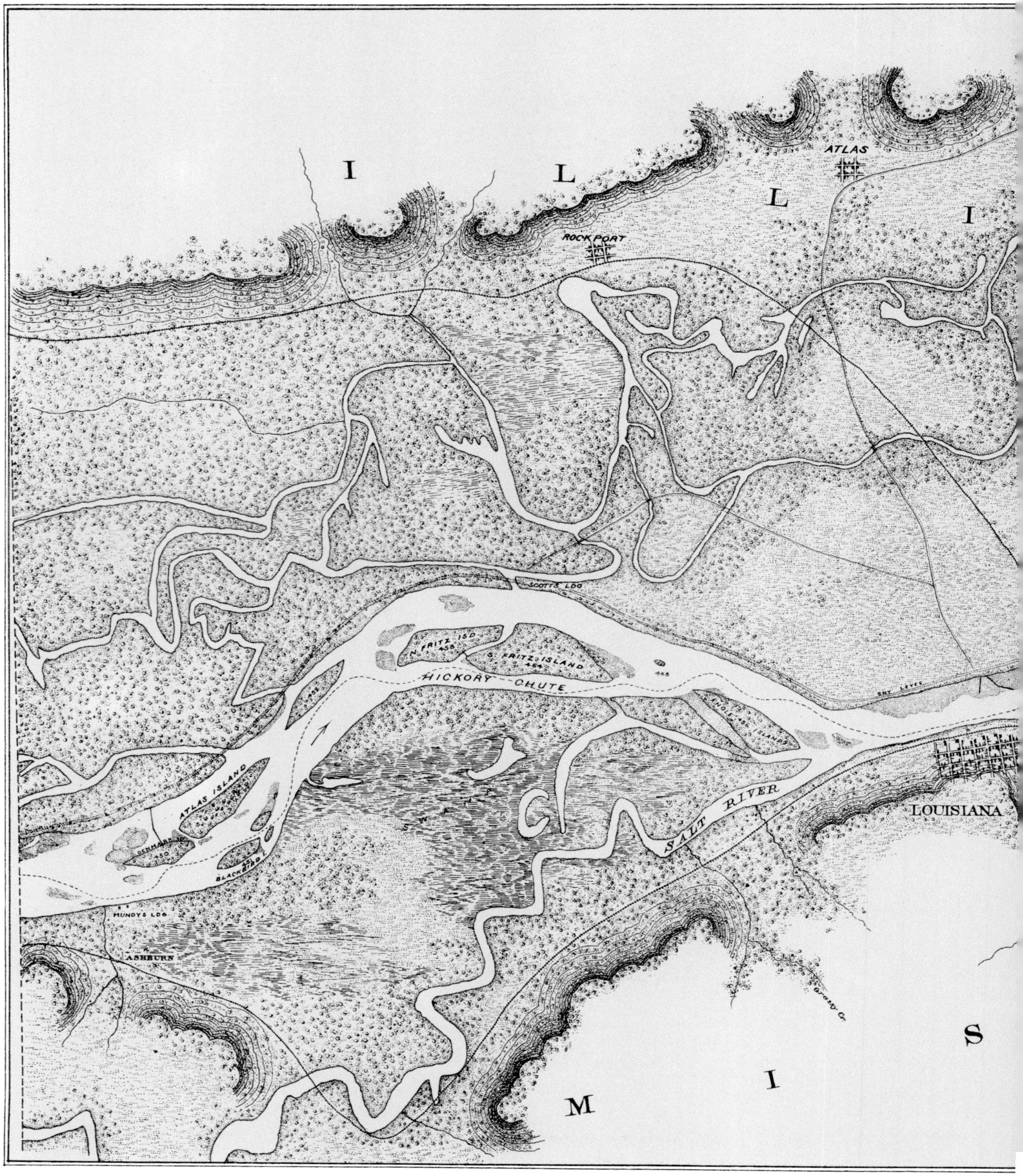

MAP 25
SALT RIVER
LOUISIANA, MISSOURI
CLARKSVILLE, MISSOURI

Louisiana, Mo. (PLATE 80)

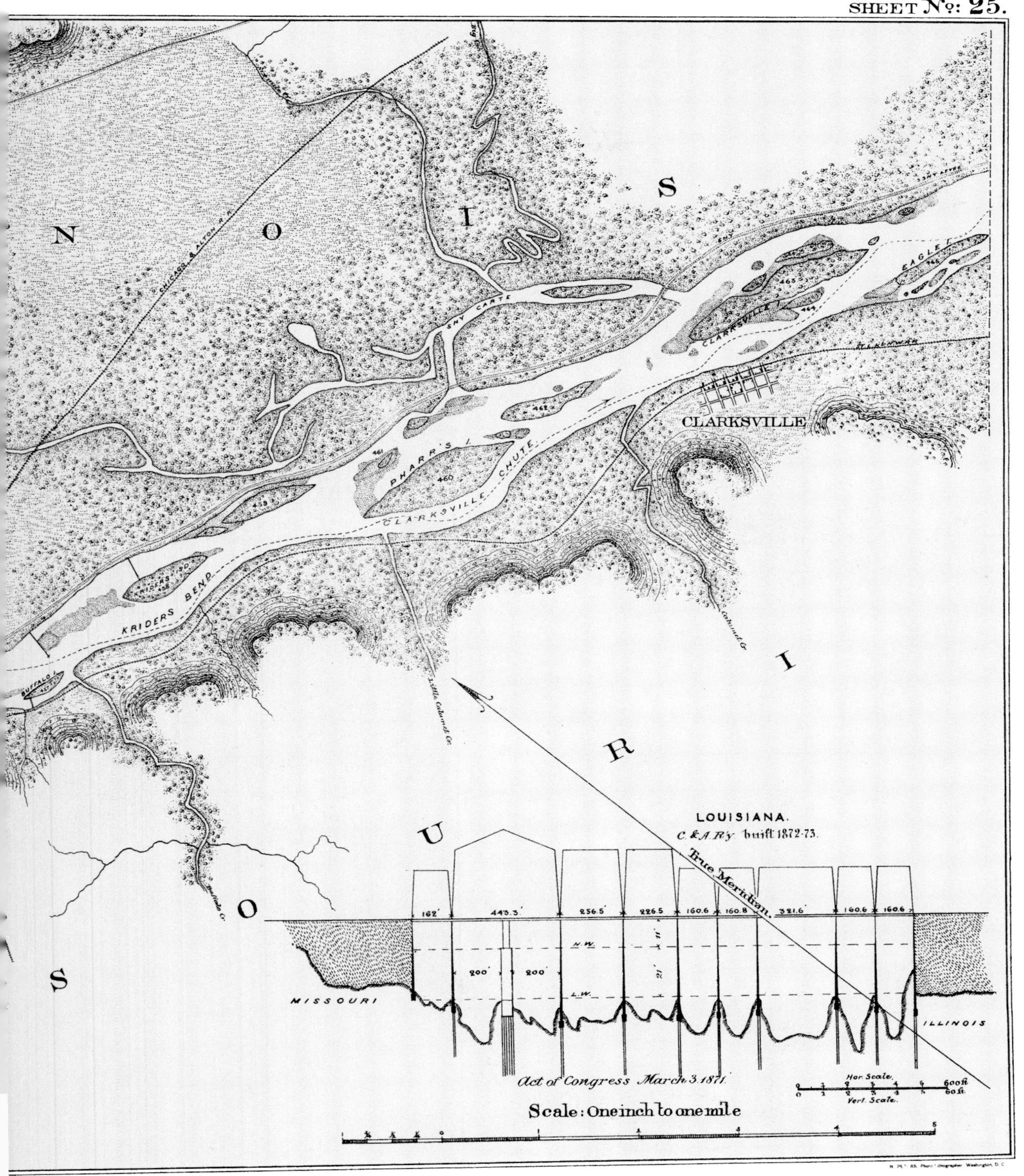
N
O
I
S
CHICAGO & ALTON R.R.
SNY CARTE
EAGLE I.
CLARKSVILLE I.
CLARKSVILLE
PHARR'S I.
CLARKSVILLE CHUTE
KRIDERS BEND
S
O
U
R
I
LOUISIANA.
C.&A.R'y built 1872-73.
True Meridian.
MISSOURI
ILLINOIS
Act of Congress March 3.1871.
Hor. Scale.
Vert. Scale.
Scale: One inch to one mile

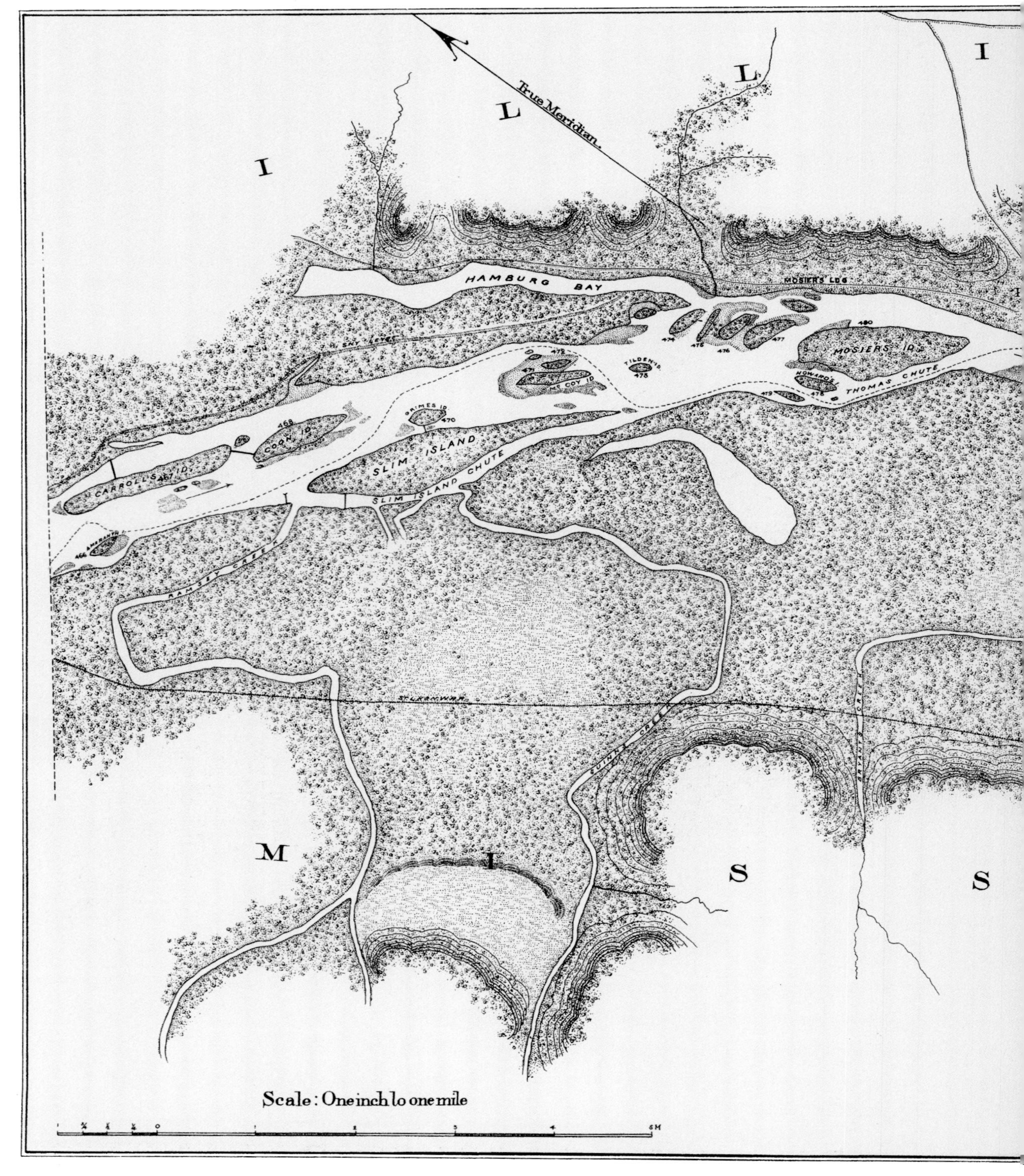

MAP 26
HAMBURG, ILLINOIS
WESTPORT, MISSOURI
STERLING, MISSOURI

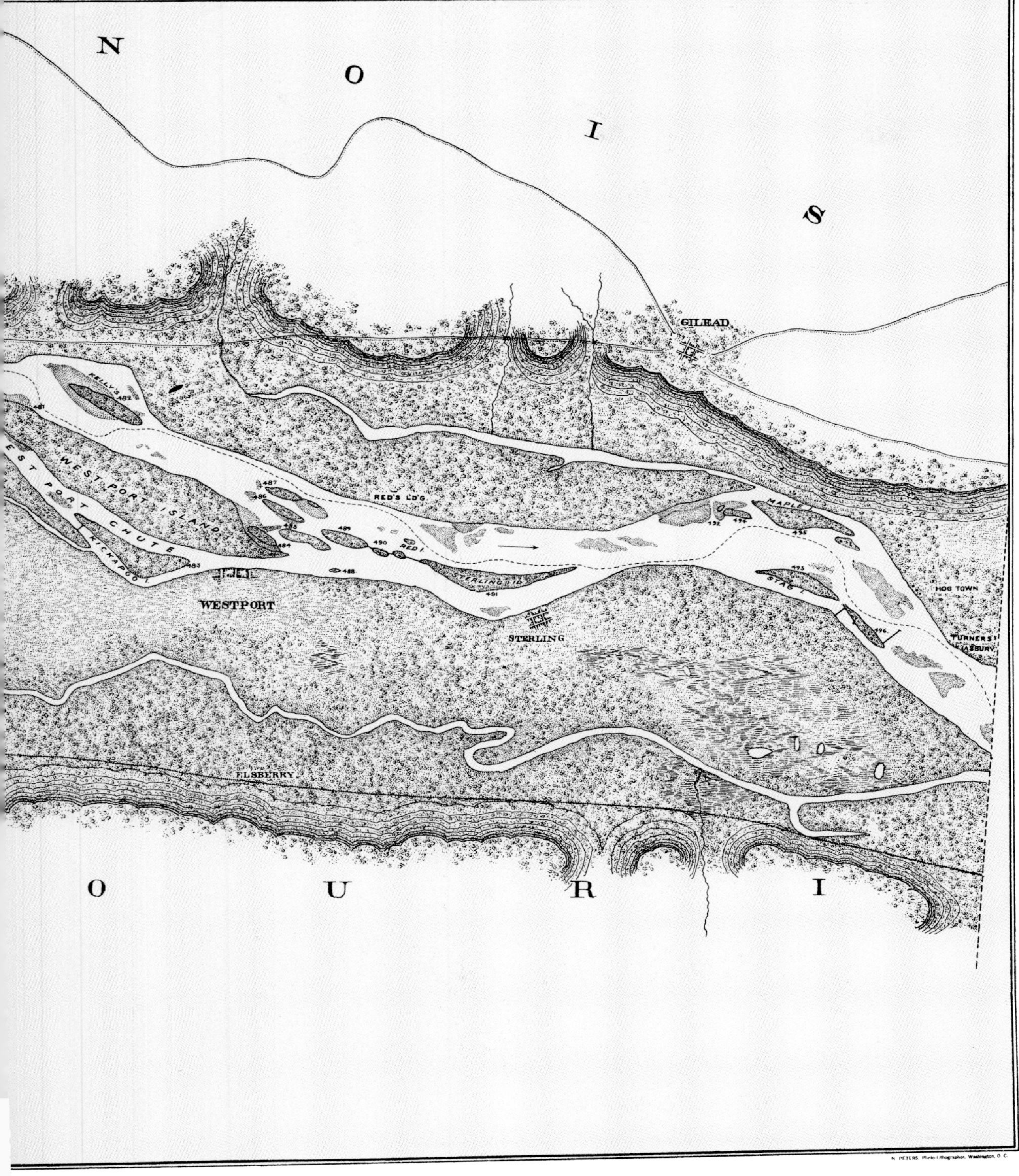
N
O
I
S
GILEAD
KELLY'S
482
481
WEST PORT ISLAND
EST PORT CHUTE
KICKAPOO I.
487
486
485
484
483
489
490
RED I.
488
RED'S LD'G
STERLING ID.
491
WESTPORT
STERLING
MAPLE I.
494
495
493
STAG I.
496.
HOG TOWN
TURNERS
ASBURY
ELSBERRY
O
U
R
I

MAP 27
CAP AU GRIS ROCK
MILAN, ILLINOIS
ILLINOIS RIVER
GRAFTON, ILLINOIS

Quarry at Grafton, Ill. (PLATE 81)

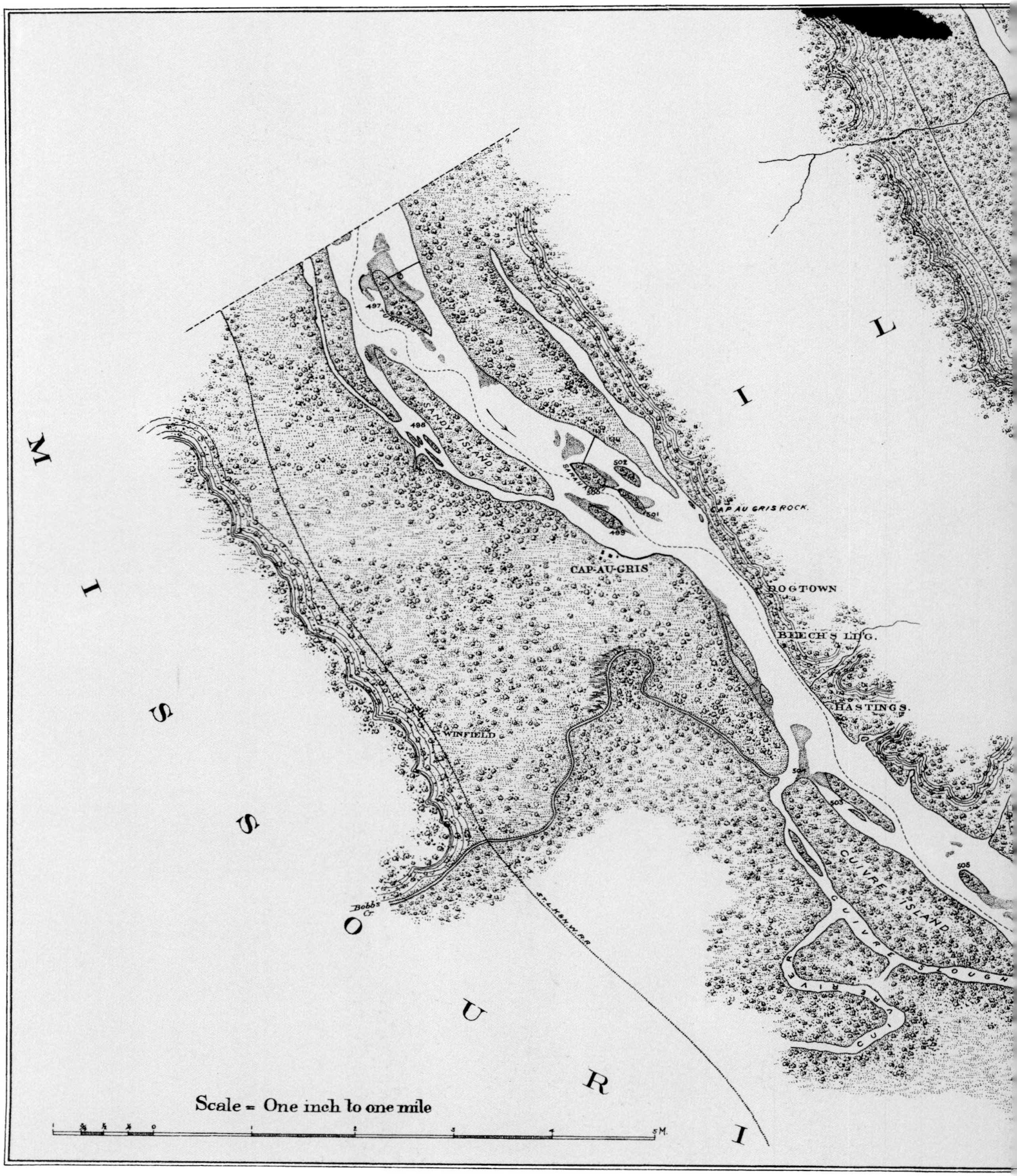

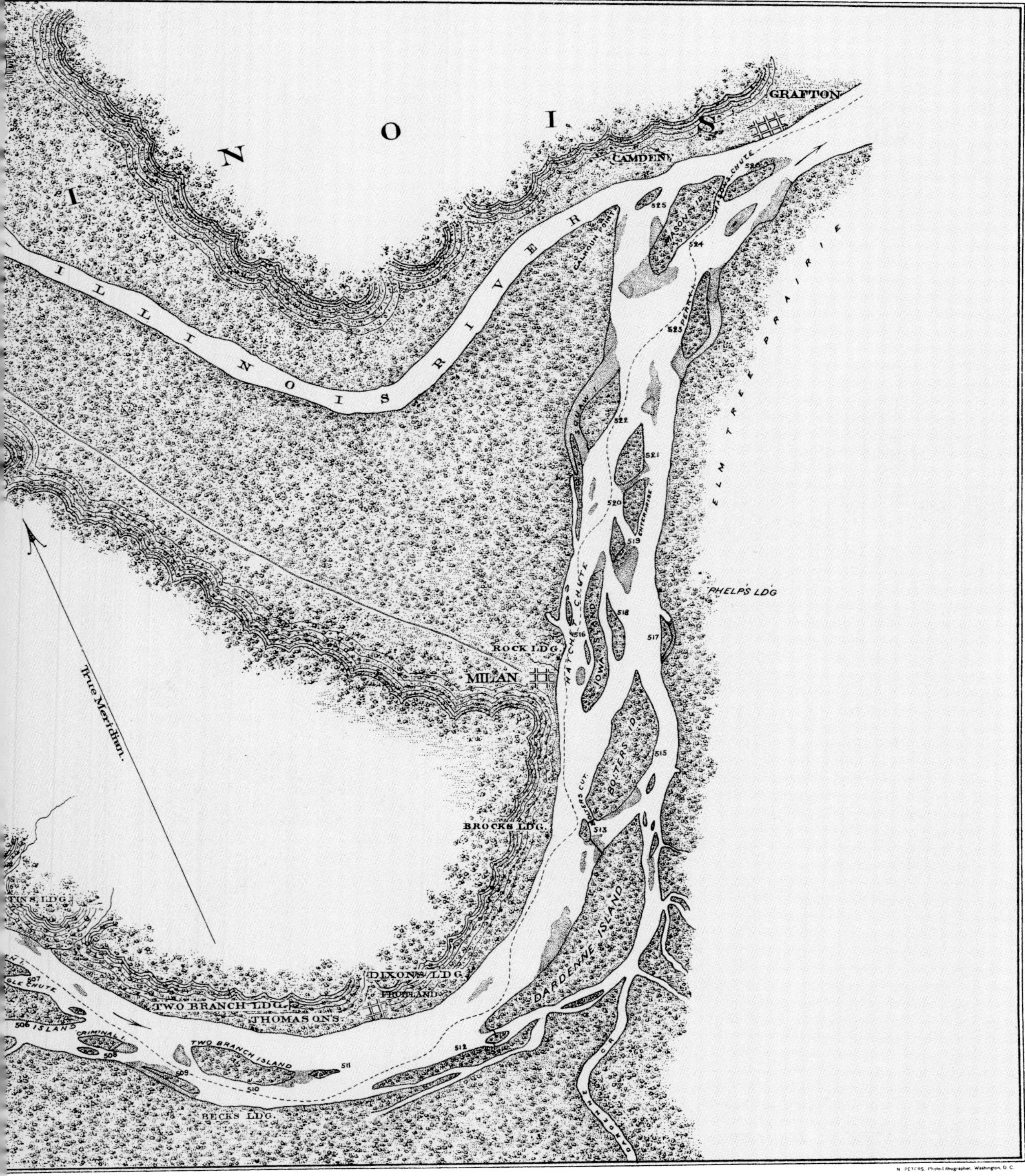
GRAFTON
CAMDEN
ILLINOIS
ILLINOIS RIVER
ELM TREE PRAIRIE
PHELP'S LDG
ROCK LDG.
MILAN
True Meridian.
BROCKS LDG.
DARDENNE ISLAND
DIXONS LDG.
FROTLAND
TWO BRANCH LDG.
THOMASONS
TWO BRANCH ISLAND
BECKS LDG.
N. PETERS, Photo-Lithographer, Washington, D.C.

MARK NEUZIL is associate professor of journalism and mass communication and a faculty member of the environmental studies program at the University of St. Thomas. He has worked as a reporter and editor for the Associated Press, the Minneapolis *Star Tribune,* and several other newspapers and magazines. He is the coauthor (with William Kovarik) of *Mass Media and Environmental Conflict: America's Green Crusades.* An avid outdoorsman, he has lived all his life on the Mississippi River and its tributaries.

MERRY A. FORESTA is senior curator of photography at the Smithsonian American Art Museum in Washington, D.C. She writes frequently about American art and photography and is most recently the author of *American Photographs: The First Century* and *Between Home and Heaven: Contemporary American Landscape Photography.*